On Faith, Rationality, and the Other in the Late Middle Ages

Princeton Theological Monograph Series

K. C. Hanson, Charles M. Collier, D. Christopher Spinks,
and Robin Parry, Series Editors

Recent volumes in the series:

William A. Tooman and Michael A. Lyons, editors
*Transforming Visions: Transformations of Text, Tradition,
and Theology in Ezekiel*

L. Paul Jensen
*Subversive Spirituality: Transforming Mission
through the Collapse of Space and Time*

Roger A. Johnson
*Peacemaking and Religious Violence: From Thomas Aquinas
to Thomas Jefferson*

Joel Burnell
*Poetry, Providence, and Patriotism: Polish Messianism
in Dialogue with Dietrich Bonhoeffer*

William J. Meyer
*Metaphysics and the Future of Theology: The Voice of Theology
in Public Life*

Christopher L. Fisher
Human Significance in Theology and the Natural Sciences: An Ecumenical Perspective with Reference to Pannenberg, Rahner, and Zizioulas

Randall W. Reed
*A Clash of Ideologies: Marxism, Liberation Theology,
and Apocalypticism in New Testament Studies*

Nikolaus Ludwig von Zinzendorf
Christian Life and Witness: Count Zinzendorf's 1738 Berlin Speeches

On Faith, Rationality, and the Other in the Late Middle Ages

A Study of Nicholas of Cusa's Manuductive Approach to Islam

GERGELY TIBOR BAKOS

With a foreword by Paul Richard Blum

◆PICKWICK Publications · Eugene, Oregon

ON FAITH, RATIONALITY, AND THE OTHER
IN THE LATE MIDDLE AGES
A Study of Nicholas of Cusa's Manuductive Approach to Islam

Princeton Theological Monograph Series 141

Copyright © 2011 Gergely Tibor Bakos. All rights reserved. Except for brief quotations in critical publications or reviews, no part of this book may be reproduced in any manner without prior written permission from the publisher. Write: Permissions, Wipf and Stock Publishers, 199 W. 8th Ave., Suite 3, Eugene, OR 97401.

Pickwick Publications
An Imprint of Wipf and Stock Publishers
199 W. 8th Ave., Suite 3
Eugene, OR 97401

www.wipfandstock.com

ISBN 13: 978-1-60608-342-0

Cataloging-in-Publication data:

Bakos, Gergely Tibor.

On faith, rationality, and the other in the late middle ages : a study of Nicholas of Cusa's manuductive approach to Islam / Gergely Tibor Bakos ; foreword by Paul Richard Blum

Princeton Theological Monograph Series 141

xviii + 342 p. ; 23 cm. Includes bibliographical references.

ISBN 13: 978-1-60608-342-0

1. Nicholas, of Cusa, Cardinal, 1401–1464. 2. Christianity and other religions—Islam. 3. Church history—Middle Ages, 600–1500. I. Blum, Paul Richard. II. Title. III. Series.

BP172 .B33 2011

Manufactured in the U.S.A.

Dedicated to the fond memory of
Jos Decorte,
Professor at the Catholic University of Leuven
killed in an accident,
October 2, 2001
R.I.P.

…here is my secret, a very simple secret: It is only with the heart that one can see rightly; what is essential is invisible to the eye.

—Antoine de Saint-Exupéry, *Le Petit Prince*

Contents

Foreword by Paul Richard Blum / ix

Preface / xi

Acknowledgments / xv

Abbreviations / xvii

Chronology / xviii

PART ONE: Prolegomena

On the Formal Aspect of Medieval Rationality / 3

PART TWO: Nicholas of Cusa's Manuductive Theology and Its Relation to Islam

1. Setting the Stage: Questions and Problems of the Time / 33
2. Two Medieval Approaches to Islam and Their Limitations / 87
3. On the Manuductive Strategy of Nicholas of Cusa's Mystical Theology / 142
4. *Manuductio* in the *De Pace Fidei* and the Beginnings of *Pia Interpretatio* / 205
5. *Manuductio* and *Pia Interpretatio* as a Way of Giving Glory to God / 241
6. Towards a Conclusion / 297

PART THREE: Questioning the Prolegomena

Resurrecting Wisdom or a Return to the Middle-Ages? / 313

Epilogue / 327

Appendix / 331

Bibliography / 333

Foreword

A BOOK ON NICOLAS OF CUSA DOES NOT NEED AN APOLOGY, NOR DOES a study of interreligious dialogue. What needs to be encouraged is raising awareness of the meaning of religion at the time when this book is being published, and beyond.

Plurality of religions is now a given. Religions do not just exist diversified over history and geography; they unavoidably co-exist because humanity has evolved to the extent that ideas of societies and peoples cannot but converge. Coexistence is rarely free of conflict. Not only do creeds coexist and converge, attitudes towards religion and theologies can also be at variance. Some religions have not yet ceased to exist, out of social inertia; others appear as a Machiavellian ruse. Some have ceased to preach their message, while others have limited themselves to preaching to the choir, or seem to be toying with the two swords (the word and the weapon). Purposefully ignoring the Other is frequently achieved by ignorance of oneself.

In all those attitudes it is transparent that the study of religion is eminently practical. Self-awareness and awareness of the believing Other can only go together. Speculation on the meaning of one's faith yields insight into the functioning of any creed. This is a Renaissance insight, I dare say. The pivotal insight came to Cusanus on his mission of *manuductio*, i.e., guiding the Byzantine delegation to the Council of Ferrara/Florence. His exposure to the Eastern Christian view excited both his critique of religious reasoning and his search for peace in faith. The same encounter triggered the revival of Platonism and paganism in the Florentine Renaissance.

Gergely Tibor Bakos is nevertheless right in locating Cusanus in the Middle Ages, as though he agreed with the first modern Cusanus scholar, Franz Jakob Clemens (1847): other than the neo-scholastic view, Bakos emphasizes the unity of perspectives—human and divine, anthropological and epistemological, sapiential and rational. And yet, all this does not go without saying. And Cusanus said it. This book dispels the default position that Cusanus would have forced the Christian agenda down upon everyone else. It turns out, rather, that the main subject of the *manuductio* is the pious believer himself. As long as religion faces the absolute, this absolute faces every human being.

Paul Richard Blum
Loyola University Maryland, Baltimore

Preface

MY INQUIRY THAT RESULTED IN THE COMPOSITION OF THIS STUDY HAD started under Jos Decorte's (1954–2001) guidance who was my first *Doktorvater* at the Institute of Philosophy. This study was presented and defended at the Catholic University of Leuven in September 2003 and later kindly accepted for publication by Wipf & Stock Publishers. The differences between that text and the present book are mainly of editorial nature, while the line of my thought remained essentially the same.

• • •

Here, allow me a somewhat longer personal note. At the beginning of the new millennium, in the autumn of 2001 the academic community of the Institute of Philosophy at the Catholic University of Leuven was struck by two disastrous events. One was recognized generally and world-wide. This first shock came with the terrible tragedy caused by the terrorist attacks in the United States on 11th September. The sudden and unexpected death of Professor Jos Decorte meant the other. To the Leuven community, this latter loss was rather personal and therefore more painful.

In the aftermath of such losses we want to understand and are trying to make sense. And this was too, certainly, what Professor Jos Decorte wanted to do. His desire to know was in the first place not a question of his academic duty or that of a university carrier. Quite simply, he desired knowledge in order to understand. There should be no doubt that he was a first class medievalist, yet his wide interest in and broad knowledge of many other areas of thought enabled him to see with a fresh look both the Middle Ages and our own world.

The last time I saw him in this life, he was giving a class on Nicholas of Cusa's *De pace fidei*. To be sure, Professor Jos Decorte was fascinated by Nicholas's thought and contributed personally to the ever-growing body of Cusanus studies with several papers, articles and translations. Indeed, his interest in Nicholas of Cusa can be seen as a link between the two tragedies we were trying to cope with. After 11th September Professor Jos Decorte himself compared Nicholas's time with our own age, and particularly the terrorist attacks with the fall of Constantinople in the year 1453. In his eyes, both events meant a cultural shock: they were perceived as shaking the very fundaments of Western civilization. Both events induced rage and retribution as reactions all-too self-evident.

My present study does not only want to show that in this respect Nicholas of Cusa was a rather exceptional intellectual, but it also aims at a deeper understanding of Nicholas from his and for our own time. I believe that it is a continuation of Jos Decorte's lively interest in the subject. It is only natural that some of his ideas will figure on the following pages, but the responsibility is mine. Jos Decorte has no means either to correct me or to share his precious comments any more. As I have to realize, I do not only miss him as a critic or as a reader, but first of all I miss him as a friend. The writing of this thesis became rather important for me. It can be seen as a way of making sense of the tragedies of life. While its inspiration is rather personal, in its realization academic objectivity was aimed at, as no doubt Jos Decorte would have liked it. I cherish the hope that he would be pleased with the outcome.

In times of destruction and desolation prophets are needed to show us the way. Usually we do not listen to them carefully enough. Yet whenever the fires have died away, emotions cooled down and flowers withered on the graves, we can turn to their memories and to the written records and try to understand and try to make sense of them. To the deeds and words of some such prophets I shall now turn.

• • •

As my title says, I set out to investigate Nicholas of Cusa's manuductive approach towards Islam. The term »manuductive« is a neologism crafted consciously to express what can be described as the practical, practice-bound or formal dimensions of Nicholas's thought. Both the semantics and the origins of this term in Nicholas's work will be analyzed in the main body of this study (chapters 2–6). At once, the dimension of knowledge I am hinting at with the term »manuductive« is intrinsically connected with my theoretical framework and methodology. Both this framework and my method will be explained in the first part (*Prolegomena*) and critically reconsidered in the third part

(*Questioning the Prolegomena*), while the investigation itself is carried out in detail in the main, i.e., second part of the present study.

Accordingly, after the exposition of what will be called a formal approach towards medieval thought (Part One), I will apply and test the same approach in practice (*Nicholas of Cusa's manuductive theology and its relation to Islam*). In this second and most extensive part of the study, first a sketch of the historical background of Nicholas's dialogue with Islam will be drawn and also some possibilities for a later comparison will be introduced (chapter 1). For sake of a clearer contrast, I also analyze two other medieval approaches to Islam in more depth (chapter 2). The subsequent three chapters (chapter 3–5) will discuss Nicholas of Cusa's project from a perspective offered by his mystical theology. In the last chapter, the former possibilities for comparisons will be realized and a judgment will be formed concerning the special strength and the lasting importance of Nicholas of Cusa's project. Finally, after its application, the framework of my study will be revisited and critically evaluated (Part Three).

In this way, my study has a double objective. On the one hand, I want to contribute to a better understanding of Nicholas of Cusa's thought, while on the other hand, I am also testing a particular methodology and interpretative framework for the understanding of medieval culture. Whether I achieve this double goal will be judged by my reader.

Acknowledgments

THIS ENTIRE STUDY AND ITS DEDICATION TESTIFY TO THE INTELLECtual debt I owe to the late Professor Jos Decorte from the Institute of Philosophy (HIW) at the Catholic University of Leuven (KUL), Belgium. After him, my thank is due to Professor Carlos Steel from the same Institute who had not only willingly taken over the guidance of my doctoral project, but he also helped me to carry this burden in many different ways. I am especially grateful that with Dr Guy Guldentops he made it possible that I could present and discuss with some enthusiast philosophy students in Leuven a first version of what later became the *"Prolegomena"* of the present study.

From this group of students I would like to mention my colleague, Mr. Cal Ledsham. His genuine criticism helped me to clarify several ideas that have found their way into what finally became the *"Questioning the Prolegomena."* Mr. Jason Booth and Mr. Jason McBride also helped me with their papers, interesting remarks, and valuable contributions. A fellow doctoral student, Matthew Kostolecky generously helped me with his knowledge of Spanish on John of Segovia. Furthermore, I should like to mention especially Dr. Michael Deckard. Without him my thesis could have never reached publication. During the last years of my studies, his friendship and enthusiasm for medieval thought have become a constant source of comfort and inspiration in my life. He edited with meticulous attention one of my papers on Nicholas of Cusa, and later kept urging me to do more work. He also willingly read and corrected the text of my thesis as a native speaker of English. It was he who put me into contact with Wipf & Stock Publisher who were very welcoming and cooperative in the whole process of making a book from across the Atlantic Ocean.

I am also grateful to Dr. Inigo Bocken (teaching at the Katholieke Universiteit van Nijmegen at that time) and to Monsieur Jean-Michel Counet from the Université Catholique de Louvain. After Jos Decorte's sudden death, both of them personally encouraged and invited me as a speaker to give presentations on Nicholas of Cusa, thereby helping the progressing of my research. My thanks also go to Professor Richard Blum. Many years ago in Hungary it was he who exposed me to Cusanus for the first time, and now he gladly wrote the foreword to this book.[1] During the last phase of my work I could also profit from Professor Maarten Hoenen's generous advice.

I have to express my gratitude also to the larger and smaller communities I am a member of. In the first place, I would like to thank the Hungarian Benedictine Congregation and its Archabbot Dr. Asztrik Várszegi—himself holding a honorary doctoral degree from the Université Catholique de Louvain—both for making possible my studies and research, and for helping me in this publication. I am similarly grateful to the Benedictine community of Keizersberg and its Abbot Dom Kris Op de Beeck OSB for supporting me during my studies. Not only did they accept me as a guest and a confrere but at the same time they granted me with all the liberty and independence of a student. During those long years, their famous library and its librarian, Dom Guibert Michiels OSB, have become a constant point of reference for my work. Besides its fine libraries, my *Alma Mater*, the Katholieke Universiteit van Leuven also offered the possibilities for participating in many discussions giving clues and shaping ideas, which have also found their way into this study.

Special mention should be made of the Research Council of the KUL for their generous financial help. Through the scholarship of Central and East-European Initiatives they considerably supported the completion of my thesis during the academic year 2002–2003.

Among all those who supported me during my studies—last but not least—I would like to mention my family: my father, my mother, my sister, and all those who granted me with their friendship in or out of Belgium.

There is no need to say that all the remaining mistakes on the following pages are mine.

U. I. O. G. D.

---

1. For his own assessment of Cusanus, see e.g., Blum, *Philosophy of Religion in the Renaissance*, especially the chapter "Nicholas of Cusa and Pythagorean Theology," 21–42 and his bibliography.

Abbreviations

Apologia	*Apologia Doctae Ignorantiae*
C	*De Coniecturis*
CC	*De Concordantia Catholica*
CA	*Cribratio Alcorani*
DA	*De Deo Abscondito*
DI	*De Docta Ignorantia*
Donatio	*Texto de la donacion*
DP	*De Possest*
DVD	*De Visione Dei*
NA	*De Non-Aliud*
PF	*De Pace Fidei*
RA	*Raak me niet aan*
RF	*De Rationibus Fidei*
ScG	*Summa contra Gentiles*
ST	*Summa Theologiae*
VS	*De Venatio Sapientiae*
WI	*Het waanzin van het intellect*
WW	*Waarheid als weg*

Chronology

410	Sack of Rome by Visigoths
622	*Hijra*: Muhammad enters Medina; beginning of the Islamic era
732	Charles Martel defeats Muslims at Poitiers, halting their advance into Western Europe
846	Arabs sack Rome
1054	Schism between Eastern and Western churches
1096–1099	First Crusade, sack of Jerusalem by the Crusaders
1099–1291	Christian kingdom of Jerusalem
1142–1143	Latin translation of the Koran by Robert Ketton
1187	Saladin recaptures Jerusalem without a sack
1201–1204	Fourth Crusade, sack of Constantinople by the Crusaders
1220s	Founding of Franciscan and Dominican orders
1291	Fall of Accon, the last Christian stronghold in Palestine
1311–1312	Council of Vienne
1338–1452	Hundred Years' War between England and France
1378–1417	Great Schism in the papacy
1414–1418	Council of Constance
1419–1436	Hussite movement
1431–1437	Council of Basle
1438–1445	Council at Ferrara/Florence
1453	Mehmed II captures Constantinople
1453–1922	Istanbul as capital city of the Ottoman Empire
1455–1485	the War of Roses in England
1459	up to the beginning of 19th century Serbia as part of the Ottoman Empire
1460	Mehmed conquers Greece
1463	Mehmed conquers Bosnia
1478	Mehmed conquers a large part of Albania
1492	the end of the Arab kingdom in Granada, Columbus discovers America

PART ONE

Prolegomena

On the Formal Aspect of Medieval Rationality

> Unless you are really trying to look through the lens you cannot discover whether it is good or bad.[1]
> —C. S. Lewis

Before starting an inquiry into medieval intellectual responses to Islam, it is appropriate to clarify my methodology. As my approach was inspired by Jos Decorte, the following *Prolegomena* is meant to expose and explain some key features of his work in relation to medieval thought.[2]

The Concept of Knowledge

(Post-)Modernity has a particular concept of knowledge, that is to say, there are special formal criteria for a (set of) proposition(s) according to which these deserve the title of knowledge. This contemporary ideal of knowledge is set by (post-)modern science.[3] Knowledge should be in the first place objective, impersonal, and more or less liable to (mathematical) formalization.

However, the concept of knowing cannot be exhausted or simply explained away in terms of propositions and their verifiable contents. The well-known distinction between *knowing-that* and *knowing-how* points precisely toward this problem.[4] "Knowing-that" refers to the content of knowledge. Hence, it is translatable into a proposition such as "I know that X is the case" where X is a description of a state of affairs.

---

1. Lewis, *Experiment in Criticism*, 32.

2. Beside the living memory of his courses, I made especial use of his *WI* and *WW* and relied even more heavily on the posthumous *RA*.

3. Cf. Burms, "Disenchantment," 145: "science became our paradigm of genuine knowledge."

4. For the difference between the two, see e.g., German "wissen" and "können," French "savoir" and "pouvoir" or Dutch "weten" and "kunnen"/"kennen." Cf. Polanyi, *Tacit Dimension*, 6–7. For a detailed discussion, see Ryle, *Concept of Mind*, 26–60, esp. 28–32.

At first sight, this notion of propositional knowledge seems to cover our (modern) concept of knowledge. "Knowing-how," on the other hand, refers to something a person can or is able to do. It implies the presence of a certain competence, cunning or acquired skill. Knowing-how refers to the right way things can and should be done, in other words, to the form or structure of knowledge.[5] Such a formal or structural aspect of knowing does not concern (mathematical) formalization. Rather, it is contrasted with the propositional aspect of knowing that concerns the content of knowledge in the form of objective, verifiable truth-claims. In short, knowing-how draws attention to the *practical* dimension of knowing.[6]

As Michael Polanyi points out, these two aspects of knowing "have a similar structure and neither is ever present without the other."[7] Yet, modernity's intellectualist inclination and the modern scientific paradigm often blind one toward the "formal" or—to use a Polanyian term—*tacit* dimension of knowing.[8] As a counterbalance to and correction of the modern way of approaching knowledge, the focus of the present study will be on the knowing-how or the *form* of knowledge.

It is easy to justify such an approach towards medieval knowledge negatively in terms of the formal aspect. The actual content of our present day knowledge clearly surpasses that of former times, so that we cannot possibly learn too much "content" from medieval knowledge, the only possibility left open for us is concentrating on its form. The question, however, whether this formal approach can be positively justified, can only be answered after its application. Nevertheless, when turning to the medievals, one can argue that they were very good at this kind of practical knowing-how. They "knew" very well how to use their rationality. They did not use it at random. They condemned rationality

---

5. E.g., how to ride a horse or a bicycle, how to dance, how to fix a car, how to read a text, how to solve a mathematical problem. It refers to the form of that particular knowledge in question. Ryle calls this knowing-how "a special procedure or manner." Cf. Ryle, *Concept of Mind*, 32: "What distinguishes sensible from silly operation is . . . their performances."

6. This emphasis on the practical aspect entails that the distinction between "form" and "content" should not be equated with the Scholastic distinction between form and matter.

7. Polanyi, *Tacit Dimension*, 7.

8. While Ryle fights what he calls "the intellectualist legend," Polanyi tries to show the shortcomings of the modern scientific paradigm.

for rationality's sake as a sin, as a fatal moral weakness.[9] There is a simple reason for this healthy attitude: not only do data count, information is not sufficient and even pure theory cannot help one very far.[10] As Ryle reminds one in another context:

> [I]n ordinary life . . . as well as in the special business of teaching, we are much more concerned with people's competences than with their cognitive repertoires, with the operations than with the truths that they learn.[11]

This observation implies that one always has to know *how* to use his data, information, and theory. It is useless to have mere theoretical knowledge of a methodology without being able to put it also into practice and knowledge itself can be practically employed in a more or less intelligent manner.[12] In short, it was precisely this practical dimension of application that medievals were concerned with the most.

The following pages of this *Prolegomena* offer a sketch of this *how*, i.e., the way, the general form or structure of medieval knowledge is sketched out. Such a sketch is all the more necessary since the primacy of the practical dimension of knowledge is often overshadowed both due to the intellectualist tone of most medieval writers and similar intellectualist inclinations of their modern reader. In this way, the practical aspect of knowing remains for the most part indeed "tacit" and is hardly noticed by the modern reader.[13] In this respect, medieval (philosophical) texts can be compared to recipes that would make full sense only when read within the context of their application. Accordingly, the overall emphasis on the *how*, the way, the general form or structure of medieval knowledge obliges me to look

---

9. I will return to the problem of epistemic failures in ethical or/and religious terms later on.

10. Cf. Ryle, *Concept of Mind*, 27: "Intelligent practice is not the step-child of theory. . . . theorizing is one practice amongst others and is itself intelligently or stupidly conducted."

11. Ibid., 28.

12. Cf. Ryle, *Concept of Mind*, ibid.: "stupidity is not the same thing, or the same sort of thing, as ignorance. There is no incompatibility between being well-informed and being silly, and a person who has a good nose for arguments or jokes may have a bad head for facts." See also 32: "A soldier does not become a shrewd general merely by endorsing the strategic principles of Clausewitz; he must also be able to apply them."

13. However, for a clear example, see Hugh of Saint Victor's *Didascalion*, *Liber primus*, c.xi. Cf. Ryle, *Concept of Mind*, 30–32 and 47.

at the medieval recipes and see how medievals worked with them. It is this task to which I will turn now.

The Tacit Dimension of Medieval Texts

As has been already indicated, the important question for my study is not so much what medieval sources say, but rather how they say what they actually say. When trying to find an answer to this question, the researcher is actually looking for the basic epistemological structures of medieval knowing. However, as the metaphor of the recipes indicates, these epistemological structures are not always explicit in the texts themselves. What a modern reader of medieval texts will most probably miss is precisely the expert's knowing-how. Consequently, such a formal approach is confronted with a serious methodological difficulty.

The problem can be indicated with the following questions: How can one recognize and identify the tacit, implicit dimensions that are not always explicit in the texts themselves? How can one know how medievals used their knowledge? How can one see what is not visible on the surface?

If anything, then only a certain familiarity or acquaintance with medieval texts, in particular, and with medieval culture, in general, can solve this methodological difficulty. It is evident that to acquire such a familiarity is far from being an easy task—it should be mediated through meticulous study of many long years. Hence, it is only probable that most persons starting their academic career cannot pride vainly themselves to have such an expertise, to possess this knowing-how. Nor would I dare to make such a claim. However, this fact of non-expertise justifies turning towards the intellectual heritage of Jos Decorte and relying on his works and methods.

My basic methodological question can also be phrased in the following way: Who can tell one how to see / to read / to interpret medieval texts? This question can be answered by referring to a particular person with the required competence. My conviction that Jos Decorte was such a person is both practical and highly personal. The personal dimension of such a conviction is naturally beyond (dis)proof and it cannot be fully rationalized. Nevertheless, its practical dimension can and must be demonstrated in the course of the present study. To employ—

mutatis mutandis—one of Jos Decorte's favorite images, one can try on his glasses and see what they can show.[14]

A Finalistic Understanding of Reality

First of all, medievals lived in a finalistic-teleological Aristotelian-Christian universe.[15] In such a world everything is what it is for, in other words, essence equals end.[16] Within the medieval world-view the ultimate sense or meaning of every limited end is related to God. For instance, according to his essence man is *imago Dei*, but he has yet to realize this end.[17] For medievals, human beings were created "in the image of God."[18] Man's "essence" is his "soul" (or identity) and is marked by two basic faculties: thinking/understanding and willing/desire. One can almost say: Tell me what a person thinks and what he wants, and you have said what kind of person he is. You have said something essentially about that person. You have said what his "essence" is.[19] More precisely, however, man's essence and his end properly speaking do not coincide, although there is an essential link between the two. That is to say, man still has the task to fully realize his being as a divine likeness. Consequently, the essence of human knowing and willing consists of becoming (more and more) a likeness of God.

Obviously, human beings cannot be simply united to God in this life.[20] Even the fullness of the beatifying divine vision is not usually

---

14. In Wittgensteinian language, my study can be called an exercise in *aspect recognition*. Wittgenstein's *Philosophical Investigation* and especially the concept of *aspect seeing* plays an important role in *RA*, 203–5.

15. For this point, see *RA*, 15–20.

16. Cf. *DI* I, 1, 2:3–11.

17. Cf. 1 John 3:2: "nunc filii Deus sumus; et nondum apparuit quid erimus. Scimus quoniam cum apparuerit, similes ei erimus, quoniam videbimus eum sicuti est."

18. Gen 1:27a–b: "Et creavit Deus hominem ad imaginem suam; ad imaginem Dei creavit illum." Cf. *PF* 3:2–5.

19. Soul in the Ancient and Medieval understanding means an animating, moving, driving force, a dynamism or force rather than a static substance.

See e.g., *CA* First Prologue 5:1–2: "Experimur in nobis appetitum quendam esse, qui ob motum, qui in eo est, spiritus dicitur, quodque ratio motus ipsius est bonum." or *CA* I, 18, 76:5–6: "Omnis enim motus a causa occulta spiritus dicitur etiam ventus . . ." Cf. *DVD* 19, 85:7–8: "Spiritus enim est ut motus procedens a movente et mobili."

20. This statement encapsulates the entire problem of mysticism—a topic to which Jos Decorte devoted much attention. See *RA*, 30–60 analyzing Bernard of Clairvaux, Richard of Saint Victor, Marguerite Porete, and Master Eckhart.

given in the here and now. Yet, medievals were convinced that God can be "seen" already in this life—partially, to some extent, in some moments.[21] Human happiness in this life consists precisely in this vision: *visio Dei*.[22] As this vision is the human goal par excellence, it should cause no wonder that every kind of human activity, thus even science can and must serve this purpose. Both human rationality and desire have to realize essentially the same teleology.[23]

God's activity and happiness consists of the fact that He knows and loves Himself (within the Trinity); and that He knows and loves Another than Himself (in the Creation). Since man's task is that of becoming similar to God, man has to arrive at knowledge of and love for God in something other than God. In this way, the difference between Creator and Creation is maintained for as a creature man can only know and love within the Creation outside the Trinity. This means that humans must strive for recognition of God in all of that which is not God. Through understanding and loving this Other, humans can understand and love God Himself (in this Other).

The difference between an infinite Creator and a finite creature referred to lays a basic constraint on the latter. According to medievals, humans can never reach the Divine Perfection—notably, not even in their knowledge. Human knowing and rationality is fundamentally limited. Ultimately, one cannot even know absolutely the essence of one single being—much less God Himself. However, this circumstance does not necessarily entail that one cannot have adequate knowledge, but it certainly means that one cannot have absolute knowledge. According to the medieval conviction, one can certainly know enough in order to lead a good life, in order to attain the goal of (his or her) human life, i.e., well-being, salvation, happiness. This fact already signals the practical dimension of medieval knowledge.

---

21. Cf. 1 Cor 13:9.12: "Ex parte enim cognoscimus, et ex parte prophetamus; cum autem venerit quod perfectum est, evacuabitur quod ex parte est. . . . Videmus nunc per speculum aenigmate; tunc autem facie ad faciem. Nunc cognosco ex parte . . ."

22. Cf. *CA* III, 20, 234:3–5: "Hereditas autem est regnum vitae aeternae, in quo videtur deus pater in gloria sua et Christus victor in gloria dei patris."

23. For a detailed analysis of human desire and knowledge, see *RA*, 22–72 and 73–96 respectively.

The Symbolic Structure

There is also a further important point that can be connected with the fundamental limitations of human knowing and concerns directly the *visio Dei*. To wit, as medieval knowledge is aiming at a vision of God, i.e., seeing the invisible / the absent / the transcendent within the visible / the present / the immanent, therefore all medieval knowledge shares a basic symbolic structure: for S (the subject) an X stands for Y.[24] Something present (X) designates / indicates / signals something absent (Y). Given the crucial importance of this symbolically structured vision for human life within medieval culture, it is no wonder that during the Middle-Ages, everything seems to have been structured symbolically. Not only theological knowledge, but natural science, art, politics, and even economy displayed a symbolic structure.[25] Within this culture, the wise could see that everything (visible) refers to something (invisible). Everything reveals the presence of an absence: medievals were living in a symbolic universe and they were very good at seeing things as signs or symbols.

The intrinsic relation between this symbolic structure and the *visio Dei* can be understood in the following way. Since God is invisible, He cannot be seen literally.[26] Consequently, if God can be seen at all, this could only happen according to a figurative meaning of "seeing" or metaphorically. That is to say, God cannot be present within the universe in any other way than symbolically. Theologically and philosophically speaking, God is not one of the creatures or finite beings as

---

24. Cf. Rom 1:19–20: "quia quod notum est Dei, manifestatum est in illis; Deus enim illis manifestavit. Invisibilia enim ipsius, a creatura mundi, per ea quae facta sunt, intellecta, conspiciuntur; sempiterna quoque virtus, et divinitas." Cf. Nicolaus de Cusa, *De Pace Fidei*, the editor's note to *PF* 3:6–12: "permulti Patres et medii aevi scriptores qui, hoc versu fulti, a cognitione sensibilis ad cognitionem Dei ascensum faciunt." Cf. also *DP* 72:6–7: "Quid igitur est mundus, nisi invisibilis Dei apparitio?" In his bilingual edition of the *CA* (Nicolaus de Cusa, *Cribratio Alkorani*, II, 87 n. 13) after quoting this passages and referring to Rom 1:20, Hagemann adds: "Diese Thematik durchzieht die mittelalterliche Theologie." See also *RA*, 84.

25. For a discussion of different areas of knowledge, see *RA*, 97–188. There, medieval historiography, natural philosophy, medicine, and economic thought are examined and contrasted with their modern and post-modern counterparts.

26. See 1 John 4:12: "Deum nemo vidit unquam." Characteristically, in John 1:18 the same sentence continues with the following "unigenitus Filius, qui est in sinu Patris, ipse enarravit." 1 Tim 5:16 refers to God as "quem nullus hominum vidit, sed nec videre potest..."

He surpasses them all. God is infinite, non-temporal, and non-spatial. This entails that God cannot be confined to any single objective mode of appearance. Characteristically, for medievals, every being can "communicate" God symbolically. This also meant that medievals were aware of the fact that God cannot be equated with any one of the creatures.[27]

A Fundamentally Religious Culture

If religion cannot work without symbols and the symbolic structure played a central part in medieval culture, one can conclude that this culture was deeply religious. When looking at the medieval world, one encounters the very same symbolic structure everywhere—as it has been said, every area of human life was symbolically structured. Everything revealed the presence of an absence and thereby everything drew the attention to an invisible dimension.[28]

Consequently, one rather important "cultural difference" between the Middle-Ages and our contemporary culture is that the latter is not a fundamentally religious culture anymore. This is not to deny that there are still living genuinely religious persons in the (post-)modern world. However, (post-)modern culture itself, with its society, politics, etc., is not necessarily and publicly religious any longer. All human practices of our society take place on a secular or non-religious scene and for the most part religion itself is confined to the private sphere of the individual. Many (post-)moderns are neither religious nor do they want to be religious any longer. This observation in itself is a factual statement and not yet an evaluative judgment. However, the other fact is that religion has to be taken very seriously into account if one ventures to understand the Middle-Ages.

Naturally enough, the objective of any kind of academic research— thus also that of the present study—cannot simply be merely apologetic. Hence, before looking at the structure of symbolic knowledge in more detail and seeing its application to the subject of this study, it is worth reflecting on the possible application of symbolic knowledge to

---

27. Cf. *PF* I, 5:9–10.

28. The issue of symbolic seeing raises complex epistemological and metaphysical questions. *RA*, 12 gives a list of these questions and the whole book is an attempt to find the answers to these questions.

other fields of human experience than what is today called "religion" in a rather narrow or specific sense of the word.

A Fundamental Human Structure

It can be argued that in spite of the fact that scientific knowledge made a great carrier in the Western world, there are still areas of human life where it can achieve little or nothing at all.[29] As Arnold Burms points out: "Science satisfies our curiosity and enormously increases our practical control, but has no answers to our quest for meaning."[30] The scientist aims at an objective, neutral, controllable truth and the symbolic dimension is systematically excluded from his inquiry. However, all of the most fundamental human experiences—the aesthetic, the ethical, the relationship of love and religion too—are symbolically structured.[31] For instance, if one looks at a picture and he can see nothing except lines and colors; he does not actually see the picture. In a similar way, if a person cannot see the injustice done to a poor, starving child, that person will miss a fundamental ethical dimension of human life.[32] Further, if one regards his partner as mere "flesh," then one is simply not capable of a normal (sexual) relationship. If one cannot interpret a look as 'tender,' then one cannot fall in love at all. Finally, if a person is not able to see the world as the expression of a great mystery (Creator), then he or she cannot become religious. Briefly, one can say that if someone is not able to see "more" in the visible than that which is strictly speaking empirically observable, that person is excluded from what would make him human: he or she will miss the aesthetical enchantment of the Sublime, the sensibility for the Good, the fascination with Love and the sense for the Mystery of Being.[33]

---

29. For this section, see especially *RA*, 11–13.

30. Burms, "Disenchantment," 145.

31. Note that in *love*, Jos Decorte explicitly includes the erotic-sexual dimension. Cf. *RA*, 13.

32. In order to see the injustice, one has to see more than just the starving child, namely, one must have a symbolic sensitivity. Cf. *RA*, ibid.

33. One can rightly wonder whether such a person—if he or she exists at all—can be still called human. See *RA*, ibid.

On Medieval Anthropology and the Practical Relevance of Knowledge

While the previous point was a reminder of the fundamental importance of the symbolic dimension, it also raised the question: What does it mean to be human? What is man (*homo*)? The medieval answer to this question has already been given earlier: man was created "in the image of God." This can be called their (religious) definition of man: homo = *Imago Dei*. It was also pointed out that what was really important for medievals was man's soul with its two basic faculties: thinking / understanding (*intelligere* or *intellectus*) and willing / desire (*voluntas*). The importance of these two respective faculties can be amply illustrated by the well-known medieval debate concerning the superiority of the intellect or the will. Among others, Thomas of Aquinas, Bonaventure, Meister Eckhart, Duns Scotus, and Henry of Ghent all contributed to this ongoing debate in the High Middle-Ages. Moreover, this question was as much a theoretical problem as it was a very practical issue of human life. The intellectual battle for or against the superiority of the intellect or will had a meaning that was understandably more obvious to the medieval observer than it is to a modern reader of the historical documents. Although the discussion took place within the institutional framework of the medieval university, it concerned different kinds of spiritualities. In the discussions, different ways of life were at stake. Accordingly, while Dominican Masters tended to prefer the primacy of the intellect, Franciscan Masters generally emphasized the priority of the will (or love).

It has also been also pointed out earlier that medievals always connected the idea of "essence" with the notion of "end" (*finis*). Consequently, both essential human faculties had necessarily a finality. Knowledge of something also had to include the knowledge of its end, the finality of that particular thing. In a similar way, desiring something meant also aiming at an end and happiness consisted in having realized or reached that end. According to the medievals, in attaining their respective goals, both understanding or knowing and desire or will realize themselves. They realize happiness. If man's "essence" is his "soul" (=identity) and it is marked by these two faculties, then man's happiness lies in attaining his own goal: the *visio Dei* through these respective faculties. Not only human desire but rationality too has to realize essentially the same end.

This entails that even theoretical understanding should be related to a practical goal. Thus, medieval science must also find its ultimate goal in a happily lived human life.

This practical relevance of knowledge and science still leaves open the question as to how the different branches of sciences should be ordered among themselves. As much is at least certain that every kind of knowledge must be subordinated to the highest end, thus the same is true even for scientific knowledge. The same holds true for (medieval) philosophy. The famous phrase referring to philosophy as "the handmaid of theology" (*ancilla theologiae*) captures well this truth, but, it is easy to misunderstand this medieval phrase.[34] One should remember that although philosophy can be called a handmaid and theology the queen of sciences, yet this subordination will not necessarily entail subjugation.[35] The reason for this is that in Christianity, agapeic service shown to the Other counts as the noblest and most precious—indeed Divine—activity. In this respect, it is worth remembering that for medievals, ultimately, even the sovereign was at least meant to serve his or her own subjects.[36]

Wisdom: Between Vanity and Pride[37]

The general teleological structure of medieval knowledge helps one also to identify the practical-existential dimension of medieval thought. It does so by making the modern reader conscious of the fact that a great distance exists between his culture and that of the Middle-Ages.

Seeing it from the contemporary perspective that is closely associated with the scientific outlook, objective knowledge is entirely different from views about how one might give meaning to one's life. As Arnold Burms points out, "This separation of knowledge and wisdom is in sharp contrast with a more traditional vision"; and one can only

---

34. For Nicholas of Cusa, philosophy is not subordinated in any sense to theology, rather he sees them as friends belonging together. See von Bredow, "Einleitung," xi.

35. I am grateful to Professor Miklós Maróth, my former teacher at the Pázmány Péter Catholic University in Hungary for this point.

36. Cf. Matt 20:20–28, Mark 10:35–45, Luke 22:24–27, and John 13:1–16. The word *minister* itself originally designated a servant; and Pope Gregory the Great (c. 540–604) called himself "servus servorum Dei."

37. *RA*, 73–90. For a more concise discussion, see Decorte, "Sapientia: Between Superbia and Vanitas."

add that in this respect medieval culture retained this traditional kind of vision.[38] As has been said earlier, for medievals, knowledge cannot be mere knowledge, but it also has to be related to human life. It has to help men to their salvation or happiness. Hence, the point of medieval knowledge was not so much to know as much as possible, but rather to know how to employ this knowledge or how to live with it.

This competence for knowing-how has been referred to several times on the foregoing pages and now it is appropriate to identify it by using a medieval concept, namely, that of wisdom or *sapientia*. This wisdom can be understood as wisely avoiding two extremes:

One extreme would be a sheer acquisition of data, a kind of encyclopedic knowledge. In the course of collecting these data, one can forget what is essential, namely, one can forget the end of this knowledge: one forgets its proper meaning for human life. Going on to study for study's sake only becomes a never-ending obsession. The same idea can also be expressed by Hegel's notion of a *bad infinity* that refers to an ongoing and hopeless process never coming to a peaceful end.[39] Coming to this extreme of human rationality, one does not see anymore the invisible, transcendent referent behind all that one knows. By virtue of this blindness knowledge becomes vain (*vana*) and futile (*ad frustra*).[40] Medievals referred to this figure of knowing by the name of "vain curiosity of the world" (*vana curiositas mundi*) and condemned it as a moral failure.

The other extreme form of human rationality commits the opposite mistake. While it is true that one can become completely immersed in

---

38. Burms, "Disenchantment," 145.

39. Cf. the entry "infinity" in Inwood, *Hegel Dictionary*, 139–42. On page 140, Inwood reminds the reader that both in Schelling's and Hegel's view "an infinite regress or an infinite progress(ion) is vicious intellectually and practically self-defeating." Both thinkers "objected to Kant's and Fichte's idea that humanity has a goal which it ought to strive for, but will not attain in a finite time." On page 141 it is stated that "[T]he bad infinite is represented by a straight line, infinitely extended at either end" and it is "an endless advance from one thing to another."

For a medieval example, cf. Colomer, *Raimund Lulls Stellung*, 223 and Hösle, "Einfürung," lvii–lix.

40. Cf. Thomas of Aquinas, *ScG* III, c, 44: "Vanum enim est, quod est ad finem, quem non potest consequi" (ed. Leon., XIV, 115a) and his *Quaestiones disputatae de malo*, q. 9, art. 1: "quandoque vero dicitur vanum, quod aliquid non consequitur finem debitum, sicut dicitur aliquis in vanum medicinam sumpsisse, qui non est consecutus sanitatem" (ed. Leon., XXIII, 210b, 105–8). Quotation taken from Decorte, "De man van het millenium," 393 n. 26.

collecting ever new and still irrelevant data, on the other hand, one can also think that he or she already knows and can understand everything that is important. Coming to this extreme, one will believe that one can have a perfect theory explaining everything. One thinks that one can see the "great design." Such a person would think that he can know God's own thoughts. This gesture would actually reduce the transcendent, invisible dimension of reality to the finite categories of human thought. Medievals called this figure pride (*superbia*) and denounced it in like manner as they condemned vain curiosity.[41] Since Latin "superbia" is stronger than English "pride," in relation to knowledge, this attitude can be better referred to as "intellectual arrogance."[42]

In short, this is what *sapientia* meant for the medievals: only in wisdom—i.e., in and through seeing the invisible within and beyond the visible—could human rationality reach its proper end and find rest. If the human subject is either concerned only with the visible or he thinks he can reduce the invisible to the visible dimension, one is simply wrong. While the former attitude is vain curiosity, the second is that of intellectual arrogance. Ultimately, both are in vain as both forfeit the proper teleology of human rationality.

However, even if one accepts the evaluative framework of *curiositas-sapientia-superbia*, the following practical question is still to be asked: How can one know that one is wrong? How can one see that in his inquiry one has made an epistemological (moral) mistake? The medieval answer is quite simple and rather practical. It says that by looking at the practical consequences of one's so-called knowledge, at the way

---

41. Cf. Thomas of Aquinas, *ST*, IIa IIae, q. 162, art. 1: "superbia nominatur ex hoc, quod aliquis per voluntatem tendit supra id quod est; unde dicit Isidorus in libro 10° Etymologiarum: 'Superbus dictus est, quia super vult videri quam est'; qui enim vult supergredi quod est, superbus est. Habet autem hoc ratio recta, ut voluntas uniusquisque feratur in id, quod est proportionatum sibi" (ed. Leon., X, 310a). See also ibid., Ia IIae, q. 84, art, 2; IIa IIae, q. 162, art. 2, 5, 6, 7. Quotation and references taken from Decorte, "De man van het millenium," 393 n. 27.

Cf. also Augustine, *De civitate Dei*, xix, 12, 86: "superbia peruerse imitatur Deum. Odit namque cum sociis aequalitatem sub illos, sed inponere uult sociis dominationem suam pro illo." I am grateful to my colleague, Jason Booth for this latter reference.

42. Cf. Blaise, *Dictionnaire latine-français des autuers du moyen-age* translating "superbiose" as "avec arrogance." In German, "Hochmut" could express a similar idea. For a very practical instance of superbia, see Tolkien, "Ofermod," 143–50. This essay is interesting since it shows the attitude of *superbia* and the same (medieval) condemnation of it working in a secular—actually military—context. ("Ofermod" is Old English for "an excess of high spirit.")

one is making use of it, at the actual manner one behaves and lives, one will see his or her shortcomings.[43] This point can be illustrated with a telling medieval example taken from Hugh of Saint Victor.[44] Suppose that a medieval reader has a wonderfully illuminated manuscript in front of him. As long as that person is only looking at the beautiful decorations of its pages he or she will miss the point of the text, that is to say, one misses the (spiritual) meaning of the text. In fact, such a person is properly speaking not a reader yet. By satisfying only one's own curiosity for decorative features of the text, one is looking at the book in vain. The same example can also be developed in the opposite direction, illustrating the other danger for human rationality. To wit, if one has read and examined the text (of the Bible) carefully and then afterwards one thinks that from its letter he can deduce, for instance, a precise prognosis of the future history of mankind or a detailed critique of church and society, one is also plainly wrong. By thinking that one understands God's exact plan with the world and presuming that on the basis of this understanding of this Divine plan, one can judge his own contemporaries, the clergy, the pope, the emperor, etc., in effect, one vindicates the role of a supreme judge to himself. With this gesture, one commits the sin of *superbia*.

Faith as an Epistemological Foundation

So far, in this *Prolegomena*, some important medieval ideas have been put forward. They were not only analyzed but also brought into relation with the religious framework of the Middle-Ages. Given the importance of this framework, it is no exaggeration to say that there was no sound rationality without sound faith in the Middle-Ages. For medievals, knowing and believing belonged together. Hence, in a study concerned with medieval knowing, something more should be said concerning the exact role faith played in medieval knowledge. In a sense, all of the aforesaid leads up to this very question by placing it within its proper

---

43. Cf. Ryle, *Concept of Mind*, 60: "I find out most of what I want to know about your capacities, interests, likes, dislikes, methods and convictions by observing *how you conduct your overt doings*." (Emphasis added.)

44. See *WI*, 21 and *RA*, 76–77. The reference is to the *Didascalion*, vii, c. 3 (PL 176, 814) and to the *In expositiones caelestiam hierarchiam magni Dionysii*, d. 1 (PL 175, 926).

context. Consequently, the next section will shed some light on the epistemological relevance of religious faith for medievals.

Rationality and the Act of Faith

The medieval attitude towards questions of faith and knowledge can be summed up by stating a fundamental theological premise of medieval knowledge: since true knowledge is the knowledge of God—human rationality should lead humans towards God—no one can attain this kind of knowledge without believing in God's revelation. Any attempt to come to Truth and Life will necessarily fail, if one is not using the proper Way thereto. Walking on this Way is nothing other than relying on revelation, on the Word of God, or in other words, adhering to Christ by faith. According to the Bible, Christ Himself said: "I am the way, the truth and the life."[45] In this biblical dictum, the practical (the way), the epistemological (the truth), and the existential (the life) dimensions of (medieval) knowledge meet.

Accordingly, religious faith (*fides*) has several dimensions. Epistemologically speaking, it lays clearly a constraint on the intellect and is tempting to interpret this fact as merely negative and perhaps even rationally unjustified. The question whether this critical attitude towards faith is justified will be briefly discussed at the end of the present chapter. Here, it is more important to recapture something of the medieval attitude itself. For medievals, namely, an intellect constrained by the act of faith certainly accepts Christian teaching, but this acceptance goes far beyond what would be relevant to modern epistemology. This is true because by the act of faith, the human subject does not only accept truth claims, but he also becomes a member of the Church and thus will share a form of human life. However, even if one concentrates on the issue of intellectual constraint, one has to acknowledge that on the medieval premises, this constraint cannot be seen as completely irrational, since it is ultimately related to the Word (*verbum*), in other words, to Divine Wisdom Itself.

---

45. John 14:6—a verse referred to several times by Jos Decorte. Cf. e.g., Decorte, "De man van het millenium," 393 n. 24; *WW*, 9. See also Decorte, "Middeleeuwse," 546–48.

The Biblical Principle

The idea of faith as a prerequisite for knowledge comes from a biblical source: "If you will not believe you cannot come to understanding," says the prophet Isaiah (7:9).[46] Almost all medieval philosophers referred explicitly to this biblical principle.[47] Concerning this principle, at least two things must be kept in mind.

First, within the medieval philosophical context, the teaching of the Bible was interpreted as an epistemological principle asserting the epistemic virtue of faith. As will be shown later, this does not necessarily entail that any serious effort to think was spared from the beginning as ultimately everything was already given by faith.[48] Secondly, for clarifying the point of the biblical principle, the traditional distinction between the content of the faith and the act of faith may be of some help here.[49] The point is that the epistemic value of faith resides at least as much in the former as in the latter. What is particularly important is that faith has an existential-practical dimension transcending the formal and neutral assertion of a (group of) proposition(s). The basic meaning of faith is that of an act of personal trust: 'to believe someone' (*fidere alicui*).[50] This act of faith can only be separated from its content by abstraction and it cannot be equated simply with mere intellectual assent. It is this dimension of faith that will be briefly examined in the following.

The Act of Faith

It can be argued that although the quotation from Isaiah can be rightly seen as a misreading of the Hebrew Bible, nevertheless the epistemological interpretation of this passage is congruent with the biblical text

---

46. "Nisi credideritis, non intelligetis," according to the Vulgate. Modern translations, such as e.g., The New American Bible, are based on the Hebrew text and read differently. ("Unless your faith is firm, you shall not be firm!") However, medievals were only acquainted with the Latin text of the Vulgate. Cf. footnote 51.

47. *WI*, 25.

48. *WI*, 24–27.

49. *Fides quae* and *fides qua* respectively. For a similar analysis of religious faith, see Kolakowski, *Religion*, 48–49 and 54.

50. Decorte, "Middeleeuwse," 548 and *RA*, 81.

with respect to the act of faith in terms of trust.[51] The biblical suggestion is that in the actually lived faith, i.e., within and through (Christian) religious practice itself the believer will come to knowledge in a way that is not open to the unbeliever.[52] Only by following the Way—i.e., living as Christ did—can the believer attain any knowledge about the way and its direction.[53] Having a merely neutral, objective or ontological knowledge about God would be of no practical use whatsoever to a human person. The kind of knowledge required for the believer must be existential; otherwise it would forfeit the teleology of human rationality.[54] Theologically speaking, the believer's knowledge of God is a question of salvation—and actually that of damnation as many medievals would be glad to add.

Faith as Obedience

If knowledge has a necessarily existential dimension, this fact reinforces the existential character of faith: religious faith appears here as an existential commitment having both an intellectual and a practical dimension. This faith has a Wittgensteinian aspect as belonging to a *Lebensform*. It concerns a respect for the right order of the universe and society (*ordo*), i.e., both recognizing and following this order in practice. Since the order of the medieval cosmos is hierarchical it should cause little surprise that this act of faith means a subordination, i.e. an obedience to a transcendent order.[55]

An Excursus on Faith and Concord

One can illustrate the same points about faith and its practical relevance with an example taken from Nicholas of Cusa's conciliar theology. Anticipating the discussion of the following chapter, one can say that

---

51. The Neo-Vulgate translates Isa 7:9 in the following way: "Si non credideritis, non permanebitis."

52. *RA*, 80–81.

53. On Christianity as a *way*, see especially Decorte, "Middeleeuwse," 546–48.

54. Cf. *RA*, 78–80. It is interesting to note that the English words *trust* and *truth* are etymologically related. Cf. Wyld, *Universal Dictionary of the English Language*.

55. Accordingly, it is a bit misleading to call the medieval world view anthropocentric.

the movement of conciliarism wanted to locate the highest authority in the official and regular assembly representing the entire church, i.e., in the general council. Naturally, within such a (political) movement, the practical part of the story also played a rather important role.

For Nicholas of Cusa, a council's distinctive characteristic was concord.[56] The ultimate basis for this consensus is Christ's union with the Church in terms of a spiritual marriage.[57]—Speaking about a "spiritual marriage" rings a bit exaggerated or even unrealistic to modern ears. However, an essential point of the (Catholic) marriage—rather important to a canon-lawyer such as Nicholas himself—is that marriage presupposes (mutual) consent (*consensus*) of the partners. Indeed, according to canon law, the "consensus" between husband and wife makes the very essence of a Christian marriage. In a similar way, the actualization of the concordance of the Church in the council is dependent on the consent of its participants.

Consent here has at least two meanings. First, it is an initial concord in the Catholic faith, and secondly, it refers also to the willingness to consent during the actual discussion. It is thus faith in the form of existential commitment that makes the actual consensus possible. The conciliar discussion not only arises with the simple formal goal of arriving at concordance in mind, but more importantly from a strong existential commitment common to all members of the council. Thus, it is clear that for Nicholas, conciliar decision-making was not merely procedural, but was rooted in a shared way of life. In his opinion, faith in terms of a common belief and willingness to consent is the concrete form of concordance within the life of the Church.[58]

Faith and Intellectual Life

The philosophically interesting question is what the consequences of such an understanding of faith are for intellectual life. What is the specific relationship between the content of faith and human knowledge?

---

56. Cf. *CC* II, 1 n. 4–6.

57. An important consequence of Divine Love is that gradation (of being and of the church) does not have to oppose concordance. The diversity of grades in the hierearhy is there in order to work to preserve the whole in a differentiated order. See also *CC* I, 1 5. n. and II, chapters 7 and 8.

58. *CC* I, 5, 29 n. 9–10.

From the aforesaid, it should have become clear that the "Truth" of faith or revelation is to be taken in the first place as a practical-existential truth: as understandable in the context of a way of life, i.c., within the true praxis of Christian existence. In an important sense, this truth cannot be properly tested by any outsider: only one who is actually walking along the way can truly "know" the way. This way starts in this life and aims at God, or more exactly at the beatifying vision (*visio Dei*). "Truth" also has a more theoretical dimension, but the point is that this cannot be separated from the lived praxis. However, even if this understanding of knowing and believing is granted, the issue of their mutual relationship can be rephrased in the following way: What can human rationality add to this theoretical-practical truth?

This question can be answered negatively and positively. Negatively speaking, the task of human knowledge cannot be to evaluate critically the truths of faith, as the genuineness of these can only be tested by and in the practice itself (i.e., in a happy life). So, this first task seems rather superfluous. Another possibility for human rationality would be laying a theoretical fundament or producing speculative proofs for faith. This latter task appears not only sacrilegious but even ridiculous since after all the truth in question is Divine Truth. To put it into medieval language, if finite creatures with their finite intellect think that they can theoretically prove, for instance, the existence of God, they are actually launching a hopeless, vain project and commit the sin of *superbia*.[59]

Such an evaluation, however, does not positively say how human rationality and faith can work together. Thus, the question what role human rationality can have within such an understanding of faith is still open. The medieval answer would be saying that human rationality can only work if it is embedded within a transcendent truth, i.e., if it is related to the lived praxis (of the Church). But saying that rationality must help one to lead a happy life (=salvation), does not clarify what role the "content" of faith could play within an intellectual enterprise. Therefore, to this question I will now turn.

---

59. On the problem of the proofs for God's existence, cf. *RA*, 214 and also Kolakowski, *Religion*, 67–68 and 75.

The Bible as Truth

For medievals the "content" of faith was Divine Truth as it had been revealed to humans in two different ways, namely, in the Book of Nature and in the Books of the Bible.[60] As mentioned earlier, within the medieval cosmos, practically everything could function as a sign or symbol of God.[61] Unfortunately, since the Fall men cannot read and understand the cosmos (the Book of Nature) in the right way. In this respect humans suffer from a kind of dyslexia. Yet, there still shines forth a light of hope for them since God in His mercy and love published a second book: the Bible. Fortunately, this latter book can be more easily deciphered. It is thus in the Bible that humans would find revealed Divine Truth. Thus, by virtue of its being the revelation of Divine Truth, the Bible enjoyed unrestricted authority during the Middle-Ages. However, concerning its priority the following must be kept in mind:

A Threefold Priority

The Bible was thought to be superior to the Book of Nature in at least three important respects:

Word and Truth

The Bible was thought to contain God's own Word (*Verbum*). It was thus Truth (*Veritas*): God would not cheat, so it was absolutely certain what the Bible says. The sciences on the other hand (in reading the Book of Nature) can only speak in human (finite, non-absolute) language. In the last analysis, human beings speak of what another (=God) created and hence, they cannot know this creation in an absolute sense. They speak in disturbed languages.[62] What is more, it can be even argued that the book of Nature died as it were for humanity and its text was tragically effaced (*deletus*).

---

60. For this section, see *WI*, 20–26. See also *WW*, 108–9 and Rosemann, *Understanding Scholastic Thought*, 93–96.

61. See e.g., Alan of Lille's (1125/1130–1203) famous verse, *De miseria mundi* (rhytmus alter): "Omnis mundi creatura / quasi liber et pictura / nobis est et speculum."

62. Concerning this point Jos Decorte referred to the story of Babel and the general medieval notion of degeneration of languages.

DIRECT SPEECH

The Bible is "direct speech" (from the Creator), while sciences are only an "indirect speech" (via creatures). As Rosemann writes:

> ... the book of the world and the book of Scripture contain the same basic text, the only difference between them being that the *liber Scripturae* is easier to read for humanity after the Fall. This point is of the highest importance; not only is reality itself a text, but there can never be any contradiction between it and the text of the Scripture.... it is by attempting to understand Scripture ... that we have the best chances to decipher the meaning of reality correctly.[63]

SPIRITUAL MEANING AND ULTIMATE PURPOSE

Finally, Sacred Scripture contains the "final truth" about the world, or, in other words, the Bible has a view on the totality of it since it explains the ultimate purpose and spiritual meaning of reality. The Bible is literally "A and Ω," starting with Genesis (Creation, the Beginning) and culminating in the Apocalypse (Consummation, the End). Without this Book, humans cannot know something essential about the world.[64] The sciences, on the other hand, deliver only purely descriptive information, partial, and fragmentary. They cannot reveal the (real) meaning of being(s).

The Task of Interpretation

Here, the same question returns in a more concrete form: If the project of medieval knowledge necessarily starts with the Bible prescribing the content of Christian faith and containing absolute, Divine Truth, what is the concrete task set before the interpreter of the biblical text? If one has access to God's absolute language, then why think at all?

The interesting thing is, that in reality, the special epistemic status of the Bible and the fundamentally religious attitude of the Middle-Ages did not at all forbid reflection. It can be argued that the contrary was rather true: medievals and their patristic predecessors understood

---

63. Rosemann, *Understanding Scholastic Thought*, 94–95.
64. Cf. the discussion of the essence in terms of finality earlier.

all too well that the Bible is in need of interpretation. Christian thinkers from antiquity onwards have been also well aware of the fact that interpreting Scripture is not an easy task. Medievals were rather sure that what was written in Holy Writ was God's revelation, yet they were far from being confident about its proper meaning. There was an awful lot to do: clearing up apparent paradoxes, explaining obscure words, reconciling differing authorities, harmonizing with present day culture, etc. Hence, the abundance of the genre of biblical (and other) commentary during the Middle-Ages.

Somewhat paradoxically, what was given as the content of faith in the text of the Bible was not so much what kind of answers should be given to certain questions, but rather what kind of answers must not be given. In this connection, it is worth remembering that Christian doctrine itself and even its dogmas were often phrased negatively—with the necessary concluding phrase of an anathema. In fact, throughout the history of Christianity, there are very few dogmas that have been positively defined.[65] So, it can be argued that what the Bible gave to medieval culture was not so much rational truth but rather the mere "facts." Intellectual inquiry can start with these "facts" and human rationality has to interpret them. It is not that if something were rational then it is also true or vice versa. Knowledge of the "facts" is indeed necessary and medievals found these facts in the text of the Bible. Medieval intellectual discussion did not properly concern the "hard facts" themselves: they were beyond dispute. What was interesting was their interpretations.

The same point can be expressed also by saying that the "content" of faith could never be absolutely clear within medieval culture. This is obviously not to say that it cannot be explicated to some extent. Yet, faith cannot be reduced to (an) explicit knowledge—of or about facts—either. Faith is essentially a commitment towards God and His people. As Nicholas of Cusa reminds us, within the shared context of one faith "occasional differences of opinion" may arise but such an occasional difference of opinions is no heresy in itself.[66] It only becomes heresy if someone becomes obstinate concerning his own opinion and will not

---

65. A thorough reading of Denzinger's *Enchiridion* would reveal that less than 10 percent of the biblical texts are fixed as to their strict dogmatic meaning. I am indebted to this point to my confrere, Dr. László Simon OSB teaching at the San' Anselmo University in Rome.

66. *CC* I, 5, 27 n. 5–6.

respect the right order and the right praxis (of church and society).⁶⁷ This example illustrates well the practical concern of medieval knowing.

Existential Engagement as a Condition of Possibility for Knowledge

This discussion of the content of faith brings the possibility for a proper reconsideration of the exact role of the other dimension of faith. The foregoing analysis makes it clear that far from being an absolute hindrance to intellectual life, faith (*fides* or *credulitas*) functioned within medieval culture—to use a Kantian term—as a "condition of possibility" for all kinds of knowledge.⁶⁸ Since the present study is a philosophical investigation, it is appropriate to ask what this entails for philosophy.

As shown earlier, medieval philosophy was subordinated to theology because even the former had to serve a practical purpose within medieval culture. Thus medieval philosophy was influenced and to some extent even determined by clearly extra-philosophical factors. However, this fact alone should not be in itself surprising since a pre-philosophical context has always determined and will necessarily determine the starting point of every kind of thought. Within the culture of Antiquity, the saying "primum vivere deinde philosophare" already testified the recognition of this necessity. As far as the Middle-Ages are concerned, one cannot deny the obvious, namely, that this pre-philosophical field was then a fundamentally religious one. The foregoing discussion has presented a brief survey of this practical field and of its interactions with (more) theoretical thinking. One aim of this survey was to highlight both the theoretical relevance and practical meaning of (medieval) religious commitment. In short, it has been shown that, for the medieval thinker, engagement or commitment comes first and for him this starting-point cannot be completely rationalized.

Such a starting-point beyond rationalization appears suspect to the modern mind since an *a priori* form of faith seems to escape rational criticism right from the outset.⁶⁹ To this problem the aforesaid already

---

67. Therefore heresy can be seen as fundamentally a practical question since it has to do with the (religious) praxis. Cf. the discussion of the Hussite heresy in the following chapter.

68. For this point, see *WW*, 319–21; *WI*, 24–25, and *RA*, 85–90.

69. Cf. Kolakoswki, *Religion*, 48: "trust is not shaken precisely because it is not based on empirical evidence but given a priori."

suggests a very strong answer. Nevertheless, in order to gain a better understanding of the medieval attitude, it is worthwhile to reconsider another aspect of medieval knowing. It can be pointed out that if the existence of something like the evaluative scheme in terms of wisdom, vanity and pride is accepted as operative throughout medieval knowing, then the intellectual practice of relying on such a scheme can be taken as an indication of the fact that medievals themselves were aware of their own commitment and of its proper nature.

If this is true then—to say it in Wittgensteinian language—medievals were conscious of their own "background practices" as "background practices." The conciliar example also indicates that without this background practice, existential engagement and intellectual-practical commitment to a way of life and idea(l) of human community there cannot exist any true rationality for medievals.[70] According to the *sapiential* evaluative scheme, anything else was to be judged either as vanity or pride: a cynical-snobbish intellectual amusement or vain curiosity of the world. This is evidently not to deny that within medieval culture, some intellectuals did commit the epistemic-moral mistakes condemned by the scheme. The contrary would be true: precisely because such failures actually took place, they had to be pointed out with an eye to a possible correction. This explanation sounds realistic, since it takes seriously the practical relevance of the scheme.

However, precisely this practical viewpoint confronts the researcher with a seemingly insurmountable difficulty. The problem is basically nothing else than the apparent absence of this scheme from many if not all medieval texts. This difficulty is an issue already encountered at the beginning of this *Prolegomena*: the general difficulty of recognizing a tacit dimension of medieval texts returns now in a concrete form.

This point will cease to disturb the reader as soon as he recognizes that what the *sapiential* scheme tries to (re-)capture is not a theory but a practical knowing-how. Properly speaking, this scheme is not a system but a systematization—actually a reconstruction of a certain practice. In this sense, it can be paralleled by the reconstruction of other kinds of (intellectual) practices, for instance the reconstruction of an archaic and for the most part dead language. No one with a sober mind would claim that such a reconstruction can achieve absolute precision. Yet, neither can its possibility be excluded right from the outset. Just as a

---

70. For another example, see the debate the on the intellect mentioned earlier.

reconstruction, say of Old English grammar, is to be evaluated in terms of its practical utility, so it is with this reconstruction of a medieval intellectual practice. If such a reconstruction makes one understand more of the already known historical—or in the case of a grammar, linguistic—facts and their mutual connections, then its epistemic value could hardly be contested. In a similar way as a reconstructed grammar can help one read ancient texts better, it is possible that the *sapiential* reconstruction can help one towards a better understanding of medieval thought.

The application of this scheme and the following of this kind of practice, as exercised by the medievals themselves, presuppose both a clear awareness of a personal commitment and a critical moment of distanciation therefrom. These two sides should never be completely separated from one another. What the medieval thinker tried to do was investigate, interpret and eventually even critique this or that particular aspect of his own commitment without, however, putting this commitment as a whole into question. Hence, a medieval thinker or scientist was in the first place always a non-philosopher or non-scientist. Philosophy or science or knowledge became first possible for him only after having been unconditionally—that is not to say uncritically—committed to a cause.[71]

It is not accidental that this discussion can be summarized with the help of an authentic medieval phrase, the famous "fides quaerens intellectum." This phrase—faith looking for insight—points towards a search for meaning within and from an engagement.[72] Thus, for the medieval intellectual, the humble acceptance (of facts) came first and without this move, no rational project was possible.[73]

Perhaps this medieval attitude can best be understood if one contrasts it with (post-)modern thinking but in a non-conventional way. Usually, one is used to judge medieval culture from a contemporary, (post-)modern perspective. Seen in this way, medieval knowing shows

71. For a contemporary example of recognising the fundamental role of commitment see Part Three of the present study.

72. For a brief discussion of the "fides quaerens intellectum" in relation to Anselm of Canterbury, see *WW*, 108–11.

73. Cf. Kolakowski, *Religion*, 54: "Philosophical investigation is forever unable to produce, to replace or even to encourage the act of faith, and probably nobody has ever been converted to faith by philosophical discussion except perhaps when the latter has served as an 'occasional,' rather than an 'efficient' cause."

many defects—defects that for the most part cannot be easily cured. However, one can also venture an opposite move, that is to say, one can try to see (post-)modernity with medieval eyes. It was precisely this that Jos Decorte wanted to do and the present study is aiming at a similar change of perspectives. Not surprisingly, such an exercise would make (post-)modernity appear in a different light. Thereby, not only its cultural distance from the Middle-Ages will be better revealed but somewhat paradoxically—through one's own empathy for the medieval world—one can also gain a better understanding both of his own position and that of the medievals.[74]

I hope that by now the reader has already a general impression of what kind of picture such a (medieval) perspective would show to the (modern) spectator. To the medieval eye, (post-)modern thinking would appear rather as an "intellectus quaerens fidem," i.e., understanding seeking faith: relying on intellectual insights and looking for an engagement—without or outside of any engagement. It is only a truism that many (post-)modern intellectuals cherish independence as a more or less absolute value. In this sense, their first "engagement" is "not to be engaged anyhow."[75] Accordingly, just as acceptance and trust are *a priori* and a-critical starting points that appear to the modern mind as irrational, the medieval intellectual would have a similar judgment on the alleged neutrality of the moderns. It has been argued earlier that such neutrality cannot exist. Indeed, it can never be fully realized in practice. In this respect, it appears that after all the medieval does have a point over against the modern party.[76]

What is especially important here, at the end of this *Prolegomena*, is that the medieval perspective offers this advantage characteristically not by giving more (accurate) data, i.e., by possessing more objective, scientific knowledge. On the contrary, the usefulness of the medieval perspective lies in the fact that it shows something that no objective, data-oriented modern inquiry can disclose. So far, an effort has been made to present a general outline of this medieval outlook and to indi-

---

74. See also my discussion on empathy in the third part of the present study.

75. Descartes' universal doubt is almost a philosophical common place for illustrating such an attitude.

76. The hermeneutical movement offers a similar correction to the modern attitude. As H-G. Gadamer pointed out no interpreter can completely abandon his own prejudices, instead, he or she must become conscious of these.

cate the possible advantage of a Decortian approach to medieval thinking. Since its focus is primarily the practical knowing-how or what has been called the "formal" aspect of knowledge, such a reading of medieval texts can be itself best appreciated as a practice. It has yet to be shown in detail how this approach would actually work and how it could improve upon more traditional kinds of research. What has been given so far is a scheme that has to be put into practice and tested through and by the practice itself. This is the reason why this first part must be taken as a *prolegomena* to what follows in the subsequent pages.

PART TWO

Nicholas of Cusa's Manuductive Theology and Its Relation to Islam

1

Setting the Stage

Questions and Problems of the Time

> Logically, in terms of verbal communication the only alternative to dialogue is either a monologue or a total silence, and it is hard to see how dialogue could be completely set aside ...[1]
>
> —Hugh Goddard

> One should acquire some wisdom when communicating with others.[2]
>
> —Thomas of Aquinas

On the Eve of the Middle-Ages

WHEN LOOKING BACK TO THE FIFTEENTH CENTURY, BOTH THE HIStorical distance and the continuity between that age and the contemporary world becomes perceivable. Viewed from such a modern perspective, the fifteenth century can be regarded as the eve of the Middle-Ages. In many respects, this century was the last hour before the nightfall of a whole civilization. The crisis of the Holy Roman Empire and of the papacy, the troubles of the Hussite movement, the new cultural ideal of renaissance humanism, and the Ottoman-Turk advance on the Balkans, when taken together, signal the coming of a new age—or at least the end of the medieval feudal society and its Catholic culture. The old reflexes, inherited patterns of interpretation, traditional rhetoric strategies were still alive and operative, but the unity—once real or at least dreamt of—

---

1. Goddard, *History of Christian-Muslim Relations*, 186.

2. "Debet homo acquirere sapientiam cum allis communicando," in his Sermon *Puer Jesus proficiebat* as quoted in Hoping, *Weisheit*, 1.

was being shattered. When looking back to this century, the modern observer can perceive what was not so evident to the contemporaries—we can see Modernity approaching.

Naturally enough, if we want to understand thinkers from the distant fifteenth century and to evaluate their contribution to a possible dialogue with Islam, we need some information both concerning that century in general and about the medieval responses to Islam in particular. It is the task of the present chapter to offer such an introduction especially to the first of these problems, but it will also briefly consider some medieval responses to Islam. While the subsequent chapters will give a more detailed analysis of some medieval approaches to Islam, here I am mainly concerned with the historical background. Naturally, only some important historical factors can be identified and explained in the following brief historical introduction.

On Conciliarism

Fortunately, several factors important for understanding the late Middle-Ages can be conveniently treated under the label of "Conciliarism." This can easily be seen from the example of the Basle controversy that itself was the last important event of medieval Conciliarism. The council of Basle (1431–1437) was convoked in order to settle the problems of the Hussite heresy, to effect a union with the Greeks, and to solve problems of the papal monarchy.[3] Conciliarism formed the general background against which Nicholas of Cusa's and many of his contemporaries' lives and their intellectual achievements can be understood.

Conciliarism itself is a many-sided notion, but, generally speaking, it signifies a theological-political movement within the late medieval church.[4] This movement tried to reduce the power of the papal monarchy and wanted to locate the highest authority—and thereby also the highest jurisdiction—in the official and regular assembly representing the entire church, i.e. in the general council.[5] Conciliarism reached its

---

3. As will become clear from the following, this ecclesiastical assembly was not unrelated to the Ottoman-Turk military advance.

4. Bäumer, "Vorwort," vii: "Der Konziliarismus ist ein vielsichtiger Begriff." See also Bäumer, "Die Erforschung des Konziliarismus," 3: "Der Konziliarismus ist kein einheitlicher Begriff."

5. Cf. ibid.: "Als „Konziliarismus" bezeichnet man gewöhnlich die Lehre, die

highest peak during the councils of Constance (1414–1418) and Basle.⁶ These councils both can be understood as reactions against the disasters of the Great Schism (1378). This Schism had rendered the Western Church lame and seemed to petrify and almost sanction political-national oppositions. Thus, the Council of Constance met in order to resolve what was perhaps the greatest disaster to medieval Christendom.⁷ Later, the Basle assembly adopted the goals of Constance and formulated the suppression of heresy, the maintenance of peace and reform of the Church "in capite et membris" as its chief concerns.⁸

The conciliar idea of debates of a parliamentary kind has a certain appeal to our modern mind. Perhaps, it is even tempting to see a possible encouragement therein for an inter-religious dialogue. Indeed, it will be made clear in the following that there was at least one medieval intellectual who apparently cherished a similar conviction.⁹ What is important now, however, is that precisely because Conciliarism as a political-ecclesiastical movement ultimately failed; those contemporaries who witnessed this failure could hardly find inspiration for any dialogue in this movement. Therefore, to speak about a growing sensitivity for the acknowledgement of the Other and a fundamental trust in rational discussion as a result of the conciliar discussions in the 15th century, would be, for the most part, simply untrue. With respect to the question of the unity with the Greeks and the problem of papacy and council, Basle could achieve little: Its history was rather that of a continuous confusion and ongoing desperate debates. During these debates, both sides—papalists and conciliarists alike—made mistakes. Thus, the moral of Basle meant little or no encouragement for a rational discussion. For many contemporaries Basle was not a source of inspiration but rather of despair.

---

das allgemeine Konzil als die höchste Instanz in der Kirche betrachtet, der auch die Päpste—entweder in Ausnahmesitutationen oder grundsätzlich—unterworfen sind."

6. Bäumer, *Vorwort*, vii: "Der Konziliarismus erlebte seinen Höhepunkt auf den Konzilien von Konstanz und besonders Basel."

7. Cf. Christianson, *Cesarini*, 2.

8. Cf. ibid., 30.

9. See the discussion on John of Segovia in the third section of the present chapter.

On Hussitism

The Hussite movement, however, complicates the picture. Before the council of Basle, both Church and Empire failed to overcome the Hussites. John Hus (c. 1371–1415) himself was invited to defend his cause at Constance, but in spite of the protection promised by the German king Sigismund, finally he was burned at the stake. Nor could the different crusades that were launched against the Hussites solve the problem. Moreover, military victory was not the only weapon that the Hussites yielded. They also began a campaign of psychological warfare, spreading their doctrines across Catholic Europe by means of countless pamphlets. As Nicholas of Cusa's teacher, the Cardinal Cesarini (1398–1444) noted, this potentially catastrophic combination of armed force and religious propaganda was especially destructive.[10] The fact that the Hussites were not only invited to come to the Basle assembly but were also allowed to defend their case there was beyond doubt an improvement on everything that had gone before.

In some important respects Islam could be seen as similar to Hussitism. From a medieval perspective it was justified to identify both movements as popular (Christian) heresies achieving exceptional military success. Hussites shared, however, much more with medieval Western Christianity than Moslems did. The very fact that Hussites could be invited to conciliar discussions shows the common social-intellectual framework within which Hussites and Catholics operated. The least one can say is that the step from a conciliar discussion with a(n alleged) heretic to a similarly peaceful discussion with a Moslem was neither a logical nor a social necessity in the late Middle-Ages.

On the Fall of the Imperial City

Apparently, when they had to face the Islamic challenge, very few late medievals were actually thinking of a peaceful solution. So, when Mehmed II took Constantinople on May 29, 1453, Europe was astonished. Generally speaking, the astonishment resulted in one practical answer—that of a possible crusade.[11] In 1453, pope Nicolas V had al-

---

10. Christianson, *Cesarini*, 17.

11. For a detailed discussion of the immediate effect of this tragic event on the European consciousness, see Meuthen, "Der Fall von Konstantinopel und der lateinische Westen."

ready started the organization of a campaign and subsequent pontiffs labored in vain for the same purpose. The princes of the West had their own troubles and conflicts among each other. Thus it was hardly possible to produce a military alliance against the Ottoman Turks.

After this very brief look at the immediate historical background of Nicholas of Cusa's approach to Islam, it is appropriate to give a general introduction to the state of the Islamic question in the Middle-Ages.[12]

On the State of the Islamic Question

Western thinkers had been confronted long before the fifteenth century with Islam. Indeed, from the end of the 11th century onwards, Islam appeared both as a military and intellectual challenge to Western Christendom. Such towering figures as Anselm of Canterbury (1033–1109), Peter Abaelard (1079–1142), Peter the Venerable (1092/1094–1156), Alan of Lille (1114/20–1202) all hesitated to define the strange phenomenon of Islam. It was not clear whether Moslems were Pagan idolaters, adepts of pure reason or perhaps some kind of Christian heretics.[13] This confusion may explain the need for the huge amount of apologetical, anti-Moslem literature that had been produced during the Middle-Ages.[14] The general quality of this literature was primarily determined more by the polemic intention of its writers than by a genuine dialogical interest, and for the most part, its apologetics was based on misinformation and misunderstanding. Hence, the few exceptions to this rule deserve special mentioning.

Later, Pius II (1548–1464) composed a letter to Mehmed promising him the acknowledgement of the Christian world in exchange for his conversion to Christianity. According to Meuthen (1982), this letter was never actually sent.

12. My main sources are Goddard, *History of Christian-Muslim Relations*, 79–108; Hagemann, *Christentum contra Islam*, 1–96, and Southern, *Western Views of Islam*, 86–92. Cf. also Kritzek, *Peter the Venerable*, and Fromherz, *Johannes von Segovia*.

13. The Canonist tradition usually classed Jews and Saracens together. Cf. Gauthier, *Introduction*, 109–10 and 119–21.

14. The confrontation between Europe and Islam started in Spain where the Moslem invasion caused the downfall of the Visigothic Empire in 711. Their expansion was halted only by Charles Martell in 732 near Tours. A year earlier, Bede the Venerable (c. 673/674–735), in his *History of the English Church and People*, interpreted a comet as signalling the Moslems as the descendants of Ishmael. Cf. Hagemann, *Christentum contra Islam*, 16 and Goddard, *History of Christian-Muslim Relations*, 80. On Bede, see also Southern, *Western Views of Islam*, 16–19.

Question of Translations: Peter the Venerable and Robert of Ketton

In the years 1142-1143, on the initiative of Peter the Venerable, the Abbot of Cluny (1122-1156), the Englishman, Robert of Ketton (c. 1110-c. 1160) produced the first Latin translation of the Koran.[15] Peter, during his visit to Spain, recognized that in relation to the Islamic challenge, "there was no one who could answer for there was no one who knew."[16] As to many other medieval Europeans, Peter had also no doubts concerning Muhammad's diabolical inspiration. Nevertheless, he intended to confront Moslems "not, as our people often do, with arms, but with words, not by force but with rational argument, not with hate but with love." His work would become a main source for later polemical and apologetical anti-Moslem literature written in the Medieval West.[17]

His *Summa totius haeresis Saracenorum* summarised Moslem doctrine and identified the crucial differences with Christianity, while the *Liber contra sectam sive heresim Saracenorum* offered a refutation of Moslem doctrine. Thus, Peter showed the Moslems' difficulties with the respective doctrines of the Trinity, Incarnation, Redemption (the Cross), Resurrection, and Eschathology.[18] Notably, he gave a quite accurate chronology of Muhhamad's life.[19] After a very unsympathetic treatment of Muhhamad's person (reiterating many clichés concerning the Prophet's immoralty) Peter announced a double judgement. On the

---

15. This text became known as part of the "Toledan Collection," which also contained other related works. For the history and evaluation of Peter's project, see Kritzek, *Peter the Venerable*, or the more concise account in Hagemann, *Der Kur'an in Verständnis und Kritik*, 17–54 and also Hagemann, *Christentum contra Islam*, 29–36.

16. "Nam non erat qui responderet quia non erat qui agnosceret," in the prologue of his *Summa*. For the Latin text of the Prologue, see Kritzek, *Peter the Venerable*, 228–29.

17. Ibid, 231: "non ut nostri saepe faciunt armis sed verbis, non vi sed ratione, non odio sed amore . . . " Cf. Goddard, *History of Christian-Muslim Relations*, 93: "Out of loyalty he [i.e., Peter] did not oppose the Crusades, but he did propose an alternative, namely to study the religion of Islam comprehensively and from its own sources."

18. Note the first difficulty: "primus et maximus ipsorum exercendu est error, quod trinitatem in unitate deitatis negant," Kritzek, *Peter the Venerable*, 204.

19. Mohammed lived 570/71–632 and Peter describes him as a contemporary of the Emperor Heraclius (610–641) and pope Gregory the Great (590–604). Cf. Hagemann, *Der Kur'an in Verständnis und Kritik*, 21.

one hand, he regarded Islam as the sum of all previous heresies—hence the title "Summa totius haeresis Saracenorum"—while, on the other hand, he saw it as the work of the devil. To put it plainly: in Peter's perception, Muhammad's place was somewhere between Arius and the Antichrist.[20] In the final analyis, the Abbot of Cluny rejected the Koran, but his writings at least demonstrate a fundamental good will. Notably, Peter was ready to disagree with his fellow Christians, he was willing to apply Islamic terminology and recognised the similarities between Christianity and Islam.[21]

Peter had to rely on Robert's knowledge of Arabic. He asked the Englishmen for an exact and precise translation of the original text.[22] In fact, Robert's translation was the first one that rendered the original in a foreign language.[23] Traditionally, Islam forbade the translation of its Sacred Scripture, because, according to the Moslems, God chose Arabic as a vehicle for His definite revelation.[24] Besides the literary reasons of keeping the style and rhythm of the original, the prohibition also served well the expansionist politics of the Arab empire. As a consequence, exclusively paraphrases, commentaries, and interlinear explanations in foreign languages were permitted by religious authorities.

Some six years after Robert's work, Mark of Toledo (fl. 1193–1216) also rendered the Koran into Latin. His text was more true to the letter of the original but became less known than Robert's version.[25] Practically

---

20. In connection with this point, both Hagemann's and Kritzek's judgement are worth quoting. Hagemann, *Der Kur'an in Verständnis und Kritik*, 24: "Bertrachtet man . . . die von Abt von Cluny in seiner "Summa totius haeresis Saracenorum" dargestellte kur'anische Lehre, so kann man nicht umhin, ihm zu bescheinigen, bei aller unsachlichen und verleudmerischen Polemik in wesentlichen Punkten die ku'ranische Auffassung authentisch wiedergeben zu haben." Kritzek, *Peter the Venerable*, 116: "one cannot expect him [i.e., Peter] to have written as a Moslem. A completely sympathetic presentation of Islam's case to Christians was never a principal aim of his, or any aim at all."

21. Goddard, *History of Christian-Muslim Relations*, 95.

22. Robert worked on translating astronomical and geometrical works in Spain. On his person, see Kritzek, *Peter the Venerable*, 62–65.

23. I will return to the problem of correct translation when discussing John of Segovia's criticism of Robert's work.

24. Cf. *Surahs* 12:2; 20:113; 42:7; 43:3.

25. When turning to the problem of the Koran's translation at the middle of the fifteenth century, John of Segovia—himself Spanish by birth—did not even mention Mark's version. See Decorte, "Ter inleiding," 19–20.

speaking, Robert's translation remained the standard Koranic text available in Europe up to the end of the seventeenth century.[26] Nevertheless, by the fifteenth century the copies of this translation became extraordinarily difficult to find.[27]

Confrontation: Military or Intellectual?

Already before Peter's time one characteristic negative Western answer to Islam was signaled by the Crusading movement.[28] Since November 27, 1095, when Urbane II (1088–1099) first called for the liberation of the Holy Sepulcher, several different Crusades were preached. Later even military campaigns of a lesser scope or not directly related to the Holy Lands were seen in the light of the Crusading ideal.[29] The fact that after the Fall of Constantinople several popes called out for a Crusade shows that the same idea was still available in the fifteenth century, while, the fact that few were ready to follow the subsequent calls shows that for the most part the ideal had lost its force.

Generally speaking, the Crusades brought little success to the West even in military terms. The moral damage that was caused by them could hardly be repaired even today.[30] As one of the greatest modern historians of the Crusades, Ruciman writes:

26. Kritzeck, *Peter the Venerable*, 109: "Much of the Toledan Collection, as one would expect, was doomed to become mere jetsam, scraps of truth and legend never to be cited by any writers and never to appear in any other form."
It is a curious fact that in 1543, when Theodor Buchmann and Johann Herbst wanted to publish Robert's Latin translation at Basle, this Koranic text was confiscated by the city council because it contained "fables and heresies." Due to a letter from Martin Luther, the publication was approved next year. Cf. Kritzek, *Peter the Venerable, Preface*, vii.
Alongside the Latin Koran, Buchmann published other works, most notably Nicholas of Cusa's *Cribratio Alkorani* and this edition even saw a second printing at Zürich in 1550. Cf. Hagemann, "Einleitung," xvii–xviii.

27. Cf. Klibansky and Bascour, "Praefatio," xlviii and also the discussion on John of Segovia in the present chapter.

28. On the Crusades, see Hagemann, *Christentum contra Islam*, 19–28 and Goddard, *A History of Christian-Muslim Relations*, 84–92.

29. Cf. Schragl's judgement quoted in Hagemann, *Christentum contra Islam*, 26: "Die Kreuzzugsidee hatte Europa derartig gezündet, daß bald auch andere Kriegszüge als Kreuzzüge deklariert wurden."

30. Cf. Hagemann, *Christentum contra Islam*, 25–26: "Das Verhältnis zwischen Christen und Muslimen wurde aufs stärkste belastet. Eine neue islamitische Solidarität

> The triumphs of the Crusade were the triumphs of faith. But faith without wisdom is a dangerous thing. . . . the Crusades were a tragic and destructive episode . . . There was so much courage and so little honor, so much devotion and so little understanding. High ideals were besmirched by cruelty and greed, enterprise and endurance by a blind and narrow self-righteousness; and the Holy War itself was nothing more than a long act of intolerance in the name of God, which is the sin against the Holy Ghost.[31]

The lasting negative effects of the Crusades notwithstanding, they brought about and sustained four Latin states in the Middle East and thereby made it in principle possible that Christians could learn more about Islam. With the arrival of the Mendicant orders of the Franciscans and the Dominicans, this possibility was soon to be realized, since their missionary activity was also aimed at the Moslems. Saint Francis of Assisi (1181/1182–1226) himself exemplified a radical alternative to the crusading paradigm. He realized that military victory might be good for Christendom, but it did not promote Moslem knowledge of Christ, since it is better to create Christians than to destroy Moslems.[32] The Dominicans, on the other hand, were founded with the explicit aim of fighting heresy intellectually. Thus they too became involved with the Moslem world. Most importantly, their greater emphasis on learning inspired them to pursue serious studies of the Arabic, but Franciscans also realized the importance of languages for the missions.[33] The growing awareness of the importance of study gained official acknowledgement at the council of Vienne (1311–1312) where a plan was conceived to advance the study of Eastern languages (Arabic, Hebrew, and Syrian) at European universities. It is rather unfortunate that neither money nor men were available for this task. As a consequence, some hundred years

---

gegen die Christen war die Folge. Die östliche Kirche war verbitterter als zuvor"; and Goddard, *A History of Christian-Muslim Relations*, 91: "The Crusades have . . . left a powerful legacy of mistrust in the Arab world and throughout the Muslim world, and the crusading era is not forgotten."

31. Quoted in Goddard, *History of Christian-Muslim Relations*, 90.

32. On Francis of Assisi, see Goddard, *History of Christian-Muslim Relations*, 114 and Hagemann, *Christentum contra Islam*, 39–41. On the missionaries, see Goddard, *History of Christian-Muslim Relations*, 113–23 and Hagemann, *Christentum contra Islam*, 37–67.

33. I will come back on the question of languages when discussing Ramón Lull in my next chapter.

later, it was hardly even possible to find a single Koranic text in Europe or one Western Christian scholar who could read and understand the Arabic original.[34]

However, by the fifteenth century, the urgency of the Islamic question was evident to many.[35] Later historical developments show that the fall of Constantinople signaled a real and present danger to Western Christianity. Ottoman armies would not stop at the Bosporus. In the following hundred years or so, their advance was continuous. Soon, they were to arrive on the coast of the Adriatic sea, thereby facing Italy. They would also reach the Hungarian borders. To make a long story short: by the year 1460, their threat to Western Europe meant an emergency situation.[36]

It has been said that during the crisis of the fifteenth century, the European political powers were unable to react properly to the Moslem threat. Nor could the former intellectual efforts at understanding Islam exert any lasting, positive effect by that time. Face to face with such a painful predicament of practical and intellectual incompetence, new answers were necessary to meet the Islamic challenge. To these answers I will now turn.

• • •

John of Segovia

> Public disputations on theological truths are necessary . . . because in them there appear more clearly many signs of sound doctrine and of its opposite . . .[37]
>
> —John of Segovia

There was no hardness in him.[38]

—a contemporary on John of Segovia

---

34. See page 46 of the present chapter.
35. Southern, *Western Views of Islam*, 83–84.
36. Ibid., 84.
37. Quotation from Black, *Council and Commune*, 125.
38. Ibid.

Within the historical setting of the fifteenth century, John of Segovia (1393-1458) emerges as a rather exceptional intellectual.[39] As it will be shown what John of Segovia intended was probably just as surprising and unexpected to his contemporaries as it appears to the modern mind. He was not thinking of organizing another crusade against the Turks as, for instance, pope Nicholas V and the cardinal John of Torquemada were doing.

As we have seen, by the middle of the fifteenth century, the discussions at Basle created an atmosphere of 'concliliar disappointment' that on the whole did not encourage rational discussions between differing parties. John of Segovia himself, however, did not feel this demoralizing effect. Although John himself left the Basle assembly as a member of the defeated party, he still held on to the ideal of rational discussion. The long and tiresome debates taught him to value this as a proper means for solving vexing and burning questions. In his perception, the council brought about the unity of the papacy, resolved the Hussite problem, and created a union with the Greeks—albeit these solutions proved to be all too transitory.[40]

In 1453, John was no more active in (church-)politics. When the terrible news from Constantinople reached him, John started to reflect deeply on the issue. From that day onwards, he would dedicate his life to finding a solution to the Islamic question.

John's Basic Perception of the Islamic Problem

John tried to work out a concrete plan both for a real *theological peace-conference* and a *peaceful coexistence* between Islam and Christianity. His conviction according to which Western Christianity should not answer the Islamic challenge with a military campaign, but with a peace treaty and theological discussion (*contraferentia*) was based on a particular theological argument of his: *"the first reason for the wars between the Saracens and Christians is the difference in their law* (lex)."[41]

---

39. For the following, see especially Fromherz, *Johannes von Segovia*, 42-59; Southern, *Western Views of Islam*, 67-109, and Black, *Council and Commune*, 124.

40. Most Orthodox priests regarded the union at Florence as a betrayal; and from 1448 onwards the Russian Church did not acknowledge the jurisdiction of the Patriarch of Constantinople anymore.

41. Cf. the *Summaria capitulorum*: "prima radix bellorum inter Sarracenos et Christianos est legum differentia." This text is attached to one of the copies of John's let-

Thus, John recognized very well the sharp contrast between the two respective cultures and religious worlds of Christianity and Islam. He thought that the basis of this difference was to be sought in the two respective "laws" (*lex*)—i.e., in the two different religions and their respective sacred scriptures. If this was true, then there was no hope for solving the Moslem-Christian conflict as long as these different religious-theological foundations were not considered properly. John realized that a successful dialogue is not possible when one does not understand the basic convictions of one's opponent. So, Christians had to learn about Islam, but Moslems too had to be properly informed about Christian doctrine.

Since no dialogue was possible as long as the opponents were waging wars on one another, peace was also a necessary condition for such an exchange. Both his Christian faith and common sense suggested to John that peace is preferable to war. His basic perception of the Islamic problem can be summarized by stating that the *epistemological-theological* condition of the dialogue was the study of the Koran, and this condition could only be made possible by a *practical-political* step of making a peace treaty with the Turks.

The Treatise De gladio Spiritus in corda mittendo Sarracenorum

On hearing the news regarding Constantinople's fall, John of Segovia started to compose a letter to his old friend, cardinal Cervantes. In the course of its actual composition, this text gradually grew into a lengthy treatise.[42] Finally, it became twice as long as the Koran itself.

---

ter to Nicholas of Cusa. It summarises his work on the Islamic question. See Cabanelas' edition: "Sumarios del opusculo «De mittendo gladio»," 265–72.

For a collection of transcripts from Segovia's related manuscripts see also Cabanelas, "Apéndices," 263–349. I am grateful to Matthew Kostolecky, then my fellow docotoral student at Leuven, for his help with Cabanelas' Spanish text.

Note also that Segovia used the term "lex" just as Torquemada and Nicholas of Cusa would. Black, *Council and Commune*, 124 also gives the translation of the same sentence. See also Southern, *Western Views of Islam*, 90–91.

42. See Fromherz, *Johannes von Segovia*, 42 and following. The title of John's work and the special meaning of the terms "gladius spiritus" I will discuss later.

This work consists of two parts: the framework (thirteen and twenty-five "considerationes") and the central part ("intelligentiae" + "questiones"). The text is structured in the following way:

a. Prologue;

b. thirteen "considerationes," i.e., methodological principles with a report on a dispute between John and a Moslem at Medina el Campo;

c. twelve "intelligentiae" on the Trinity;

d. seven "questiones"/ "animadvertiones" on the Incarnation;

e. twenty-five "considerationes" returning to the theme of the second point.

While the framework treats the fatal relationship between Christianity and Islam with respect to the past and the present, the central part shows how Christians should relate themselves to Islam. The latter part both discusses Christian doctrine, i.e., the Trinity and the Incarnation, but also develops strategies in order to convince the Moslems in a debate.[43] Later, on October 9, 1457, John donated the whole collection of his library to the university of Salamanca. The document of this donation list two other copies of the work *De gladio Spiritus in corda mittendo Sarracenorum* (*De gladio* in the following) and the recurring phrase of "per Johannem nouiter edictus" (i.e., "newly edited by John") in the respective titles testifies Segovia's continuous efforts to complete this work.[44]

Accordingly, the process of actual compositions of the treatise is very difficult to reconstruct. The details of this troubled textual history raise the question as to why the additions and the continuous rewriting was necessary.[45] Although it is true that John had a special predilection

43. There also exists a sort of index or summary of the same work by John's hand showing a slightly different structure: 1) Prologue; 2) 7 points (≈ *considerationes*, but more general); 3) a (second) Prologue; 4) report in the discussion at Medina with some excursions on Trinity and Incarnation; 5) extract from the 38 *considerationes* (the same as the other version, but not diveded into two parts).

44. For this document, see Segovia, "Texto de la donacion," 77–115 (for the two titles ibid., 89–90).

45. Fromherz, *Johannes von Segovia*, 44 offers the following probable account: In 1453 John set out to write a letter to cardinal Cervantes. He sent this long text to Sevilla

for spelling out his ideas with too many words, this circumstance in itself does not explain the laborious reworking of his treatise.[46] Rather the actual difficulties his entire project had to face should be taken into considerations. Only thereafter can the reason for John's delay be properly understood.

The Textual Difficulty: The Koran

John was aware of the existence of Robert of Ketton's Latin translation of the Koran and even received one copy of it from Nicolas of Cusa.[47] Further, John also got hold of a copy of another text from a German library and managed to obtain an Arabic version.[48] Although he knew that other Latin and Castilian translations existed in Spain, he was not able to access these Moslem-made texts.[49] Nevertheless, John contacted and hired a Moslem translator. Later, when this Arab scholar left him, John would search in vain for a Christian replacement.[50]

John saw the new translation as an absolute must as he was dissatisfied with Robert's Latin text.[51] John's criticism can be easily summarized: Robert sought to translate the Arabic text by using Latin concepts. Thereby, Robert read Christian ideas into the Koran and could hardly convey the original meaning.[52] In Robert's defense one must remem-

---

around the end of the same year. Later, John expanded the work with more additions. In this way the two volumes mentioned in the letter of donation came into existence. Finally, John intended another revision based on his new translation of the Koran, but he died before he could actually write that.

46. On John's verbosity, cf. Black, *Council and Commune*, 124.

47. Cf. Klibansky and Bascour, "Praefatio," li and *CA First Prologue*, 2:2–3.9–10.

48. Cf. Klibansky and Bascour, "Praefatio," xlviii and Cabanelas, *Juan de Segovia*, 288.

49. Cf. Klibansky and Bascour, "Praefatio," xlviii.

50. Although he found two candidates in the Franciscan order, he was not able to come to an agreement with the one, while the other was not able to understand the Koran's (ancient) language. Cf. Fromherz, *Johannes von Segovia*, 55. For Segovia's relationship with an Arab scholar see also Alfaquí, "Carte del alfaquí de Segovia al maestro salamantino."

51. On the question of translation, see Southern, *Western Views of Islam*, 87–88.

52. Cf. Kritzek, *Peter the Venerable*, 62–65, 97–100, and 110–12. Cf. also Hopkins, "Introduction," 15: "Scholars today agree that the translation is too paraphrastic, though many of them also share Ludwig Hagemann's verdict: »Trotz der vielen Unzulänglichkeiten, Fehler und Mängel, die die erste lateinische Kur'anübersetzung

ber the special difficulties posed by the language of the Koran. It has already been pointed out that the Islamic tradition did not encourage translations; and this may well explain the reason why there was so little lexicographical information available to a translator.

In his letter to Peter the Venerable, Robert of Ketton made the following confession: "I did not give special accent to anything and did not make it more sensible—altering only for the sake of (a better) understanding."[53] However, Robert's text tends to be florid, wordy, and often even obscure. He clearly appears to have had a weakness for rhetorical bombast in his Latin.[54] Furthermore, his text contains both internal and external imperfections. The latter concerns Robert's misunderstanding and disrespect for the original division of chapters and verses, while the former includes, for instance, translating superlatives instead of positives. It can be added that occasionally Robert committed mistakes in rendering Arabic terms.[55]

Generally speaking, modern scholarship justifies John of Segovia's criticism. With respect to the question of translation, John recognized a sound hermeneutical principle but as Southern reminds one, this principle can hardly be executed practically; there cannot be such a thing as the perfect translation.[56]

Nevertheless, it is important that John recognized the problem and he tried very hard to resolve it. Most importantly of all, he did not want to misunderstand or misrepresent the Moslems' sacred book. John intended to start the dialogue with the basics. The most important question for him was whether the Koran was God's word or not. John thought that if its text was full of inconsistencies, contradictions and clearly not written by one hand, then the answer to his basic question would be a negative one. This understanding explains well the importance of a

---

zweifellos in sich birgt, gilt es doch festzuhalten, daß in ihr die wesentliche Glaubensinhalte des Ku'rans authentisch interpretiert und wiedergegeben sind.«" For Hagemann's assessment of Peter's project and Robert's translation, see Hagemann, *Der Kur'an in Verständnis und Kritik*, 17–29 and Hagemann, *Christentum contra Islam*, 29–36.

53. Quoted by Kritzek, *Peter the Venerable*, 72 "nil excerpens, nil sensibiliter nisi propter intelligentiam tantum alterans."

54. Kritzek, *Peter the Venerable*, 110.

55. Cf. ibid., 110–12.

56. Cf. Southern, *Western Views of Islam*, 87–88. Kritzek, *Peter the Venerable*, 110–12 states that the question of accuracy (of Robert's translation) is central but still open.

faithful translation: otherwise—relying only on a faulty version of the text—nothing can be said concerning the original.

It can be argued that similar textual problems present themselves with respect to the Bible. Both Renaissance and modern textual criticism would be quick to point them out. Naturally, no such attitude can be detected in medieval intellectuals towards their own Sacred Scripture. Yet, it is equally important to keep in mind that the Bible was never really claimed to be God's direct word in the same sense as the Koran was.[57] Even to a naive reader, the Bible presents itself as written during a very much extended period of time, by several distinct authors who sometimes criticize or even contradict each other. In contrast, the Koran was traditionally seen by Moslems as coming directly from God's mouth and communicated to Muhammad through the archangel Gabriel.

The Difficulty with Publication: The Crusading Politics

In John's enterprise a certain Renaissance character can be recognized since first of all, he wanted clarity about the facts and these facts were broadly speaking of a philological nature.[58] However, while trying to solve these problems, John realized that without proper publicity, his plan for a peaceful solution would necessarily remain in vain. Political support was an imperative. Hence, it is small wonder that when pope Nicholas V called for a crusade in the year 1453, John became disappointed and perhaps even despaired. His work on the Islamic question had been already in progress and he intended to dedicate it to the pope. The news of the new crusade seemed to shatter his hopes. At that moment, all of his precious work done so far on Islam came to a sudden halt.[59]

Both material and historical conditions were extremely hostile to John's enterprise. It is not surprising that his treatise, the *De gladio*, though huge in scope remained a work existing in a fragment-like condition.

---

57. Cf. the *Prolegomena*. A consciously literal reading of the Bible is a typically modern phenomenon and it is often connected to fundamentalism.

58. For this point, see Southern, *Western Views of Islam*, 89.

59. In 1458, he made a last effort to exert some influence on the political events by sending some of his writings to Rome into the hands of the Cardinal Enea Silvio Piccolomini. Cf. Fromherz, *Johannes von Segovia*, 44.

An Urgent Question to an Old Friend

This hostile political situation also prompted John to compose several letters addressed to his influential friends. This correspondence shows John of Segovia trying rather desperately to convince those friends and win their support. Most importantly, the longest one of these letters was addressed to Nicholas of Cusa. Since the current political situation had made John uncertain, he was asking for practical advice and help and—if need be—even for corrections from his old friend, Nicholas. This letter offers a good summary of John's enterprise.[60]

At Basle, on March 20, 1437, as their different church-political allegiances became clear, John's and Nicholas's ways had parted.[61] The fact that sixteen years later John could still count on Nicholas's understanding is not only an expression of Segovia's conciliar optimism and does not only show the importance of the issue being at stake, but it also testifies both to the lasting friendship between these two men and the common interest in the Islamic question they shared with each other.[62]

John's letter is structured in the following way:

a. Chapter 1 addresses words and poses the basic question as to "whether the Saracens' sect should not be destroyed or reduced rather with peaceful means than by way of war."

b. Chapter 2 relates John's discussion (*collatio*) with a Moslem on the Holy Trinity.[63]

c. Chapters 3 and 4 are dedicated to different aspects of the mystery of Redemption and of the Moslem concept of God and faith. In their course, the theme of the Trinity constantly recurs.[64]

---

60. For an abbreviated text, see Cabanelas, "Apéndices," 303–10. For a theological treatment thereof, see Haubst, "Die Wege der christologische manuductio."

61. E.g., on the *Reichstag* of March 1441 John's defense of the conciliar case was countered by Nicholas's stronger arguments. Cf. Haubst, "Die Wege der christologische manuductio," 115.

62. Ibid., 116: "Er [i.e., John] tut es mit einer vorsichtigen Erinnerung an ihre früheren freundschaftlichen Begegnungen in Basel ... und in dem besonderen Vertrauen, daß dessen [i.e., Nicholas's] überragend großer Geist, wie er ihn selbst aus eigener Erfahrung kennen lernte, gerade an den schwierigen, von ihm aufgerollten Fragen, lebhaftes Interesse finden werde." On John's "conciliar optimism," see ibid. 118.

63. To this point I will return to later on.

64. Haubst, "Die Wege der christologische manuductio," 117.

d. Chapters starting with number 5 up to number 20 set out John's ideas concerning a peaceful confrontation and argue for its theological and practical usefulness in detail.

e. Chapter 21 John asks for Nicholas's advice and possibly corrections. After 21 chapters a summary of the work is placed.[65]

This letter shows John's conviction according to which Christians should strive for "the destruction or reduction of the Saracens' sect" with peaceful means. Segovia's theological reason for this peaceful attitude was that while the Moslems' law prescribes fighting, the law of the Christians especially commands peace (*pax*). There was also a practical reason for preferring peace to armed conflict. John realized that even if Christians could recover the territories controlled by the Moslems, it was hardly possible for them to maintain what they could thus gain. More importantly, war could only discredit Christianity as not only past experience had taught, but also due to the simple fact that no one is ready believe his enemy.

Besides the crusades, John considered three further possibilities for converting the Saracens in Divine intervention, missions, and a peace-treaty. Of these three, the first two could be easily ruled out, since both waiting for a miracle or sending preachers to the Moslems would be in vain. John argued that no idle Christian can expect Divine help and he also pointed out the evident failure of Christian missions to Moslems.[66] Moreover, even within Christian Europe no one was allowed to preach publicly without the consent of the local authorities. How could one dare do so in the enemy's land?[67] Consequently, there remained one possibility—that of a peaceful rapprochement. In John's opinion, this fourth way is the genuine Christian answer as peace is nothing else than Christ's special dowry to his Church.[68]

---

65. For this summary, see Haubst, "Die Wege der christologische manuductio," 116–18 and Cabanelas, "Apéndices," 303–10.

66. Cf. Hagemann, *Christentum contra Islam*, 37–67.

67. Cf. the discussion of Ramón Lull's case in my next chapter.

68. John argued that once even the apostles had made peace with the heresy of the Pharisees. It is not clear to which biblical event John refers here. Cf. Cabanelas, "Apéndices," 306.

Cf. Cabanelas, "Apéndices," 305–6: "quia pax propria Ecclesie dos est a Christo relicta, et cum satis illi sit gladiis duobus, qui divini verbi permaxime exercendus est, a quo incepit Ecclesia, incrementa suscipiens. . . . Mahumeti secta gladio materiali

Should the Sword of the Spirit Be Driven into the Saracens' Hearts?

While realizing John's sincere peaceful intention, my reader may wonder concerning the phrase "the sword of the Spirit" (*gladius spiritus*) as it appears in the title of John's *Hauptwerk* on the Islamic question. The full title translates "as whether the sword of the Spirit should be driven into the hearts of the Saracens?" The right understanding of this question is all the more important, since John himself gave an affirmative answer to it. Hence, it is necessary to tackle the exact role and meaning of this combative metaphor in Segovia's otherwise surprisingly irenic enterprise.

The phrase "the sword of the Spirit" is connected with the well-known medieval theory of the "two swords." The metaphor was inspired ultimately by biblical imagery.[69] Of these two swords, "the sword of the Spirit" designated God's word, i.e., Christian teaching. In John's perception, God's Word establishes the Church and makes it grow. Consequently, the Church must employ "the sword of the Spirit" and drive or send (*mittendo*) this sword into the hearts of the Saracens. Thus, the Church must properly teach the Moslems Christian doctrine.[70] Carrying the same metaphor further, John pointed out in his letter that although Islam as a militant religion is based on employing an all-too real sword, it nevertheless prescribes peace to its believers. Moslems

---

defenditur et incrementum suscipit prolis multiplicatione . . ." Fromherz, *Johannes von Segovia*, 50, contrasts John's and Nicholas's respective approaches with respect to the question of war and peace. As will be made evident later, Nicholas's stance was not far from his friend's attitude.

69. Cf. Matt 26:51–56, Mark 14:44–48, Luke 22:36–38, 49–52, John 18:10–12. See also Eph 6:17, Heb 4:12–13, Rev 1:16, 2:12, and Ps 149:6–7.

70. Cabanelas, "Apéndices," 306: "Quam merito Ecclesiam decet pro sui defensione contra impugnationes sarracenorum intendere ad verbi divini predicationem, per quam originem accepit et robur, sicut Mahumeti secta materiali gladio et multiplicatione prolis se extendit."

themselves would like to be just persons. Therefore their law warns them to keep peace or to strive for it.

John also recognized the difficulties of a peaceful rapprochement to Islam. He carefully considered the necessary preparations. His call for a peace-treaty aiming at a public discussion instead of a crusade was not born out of naiveté. It was as much inspired by his Christian faith as it was supported by an ethically critical reading of the history of Western Christianity and his own personal experience. Segovia recognized that in spite of all the rhetorical decor, the Crusading movement had not brought either much honor or success to Europe. Peace was both a practical necessity and a Christian religious-moral duty. John argued that even if the Saracens do not accept a peaceful rapprochement, Christians must still walk this way.

There cannot be any doubt that in his concern for peace, John of Segovia's was very consequent and sincere. Historical experience had taught him the clear lesson that conversions to Christianity can only be effected in a peaceful way. In this respect, the sad story of the Hussites can also be recalled since in relation to this militant movement, the Church achieved more by peaceful means than with all the tragic crusades.[71]

The Practical Plan

Before considering John's rational discourse more closely, the practical dimension of his project deserves our attention. His plan appears to be detailed and realistic and can be summarized in the following way:

a. First by peace-treaties (*tractatoribus pacis*), the war between Christian and Moslems must be ended.

b. The second step is to develop commercial and cultural connections between the two worlds. In this way, Christians and Moslems will be in mutual contact with one another. Through the exchange they could come to a better knowledge of each other in peaceful coexistence (*conviventia humana*).

---

71. See earlier.

c. Only thereafter will come the proper time for a theological exchange in the form of a conference (*contraferentia*) between the two parties.[72]

For John, the ultimate goal of this dialogue was to convince the Moslems to have a better judgment on Christianity. He wanted them to join the Christian faith. This was also the meaning of the phrase "reducing or dissolving the sects of the Saracens."[73] Ultimately, at least this reduction or dissolution was not an aggressive one. John realized that without a peaceful milieu of mutual trust, all attempts, however pious or zealous they may be, are necessarily doomed to fail.[74]

There cannot be any doubts concerning John of Segovia's own medieval Christian convictions. He was just as much a child of his own age as any other of his contemporaries. He regarded Islam as a religion animated by a satanic inspiration.[75] Interestingly, John did not see in this diabolic label a justification for military aggression against this (religious) Other. John's attitude was much more positive than merely demonizing this Other. Being confident in his—and Christianity's—own intellectual inventory, Segovia wanted a genuine discussion. His intention was to argue with and for the sake of this Other within the framework of an open, public, and rational debate.

Coming from the shared Christian-Moslem context of Spain, Segovia's plan aimed at a "conviventia humana." He reproached the Church for not taking seriously enough the Moslem challenge and he

---

72. Cf. Fromherz, *Johannes von Segovia*, 47. The term "contraferentia" (possibly John's own invention) would designate an exchange between opposing parties. See Southern, *Western Views of Islam*, 91 and the more detailed analysis with a philosophical interpretation in Decorte, "Ter inleiding," 29–32.
   John himself referred to his own theological debate with a Muslim as a "collatio." Cf. Cabanelas, "Apéndices," 265 and 287.

73. For the motive "reduccio Bohemorum" in Segovia's *Gesta concilii Baseliensis*, see Fromherz, *Johannes von Segovia*, 75–76 and footnote 350. Fromherz quotes Martin V's summoning bull where the Basle assembly's aims—among others—are defined as follows: "augmentum religionis fidei christiane, . . . reductionem orientalis ecclesiae at quorumlibet oberrancium populorum . . . salutem, quietem et pacem regnorum et quorumlibet fidelium populorum."

74. Hence, the translation "dissolution" as being more neutral than "destroying."

75. In his letter, John says that "the author of this law is Belzebub." Cf. Cabanelas, "Apéndices," 304.

tried to mobilize it for a peaceful rapprochement.[76] Ultimately, since Moslems did not know the truth of Christianity or at least were misinformed about it, taking up the trouble of the labors for a peaceful encounter and carrying the burden of teaching them properly was the concrete form of Christian *caritas* for John.[77]

The Discussion at Medina del Campo

John's confidence in a rational discussion has already been referred to and the personal and somewhat unusual connection of this idea with his conciliar experience was also pointed out. However, the context of Christian-Moslem inter-religious dialogue and that of the conciliar discussions were different. Therefore a transition from the latter to the former required a more specific reason than mere "conciliar optimism." One such reason can be identified with a real discussion John once had with a Moslem in 1431 at Medina del Campo, in Granada. Much later, in his letter to Nicholas, John recalled that debate.[78]

One of the traditional Moslem arguments against Christians was the accusation of their alleged polytheism. Moslems attacked the doctrine of the Trinity as they understood it as Christians worshipping three gods. This misunderstanding is already attested to by the Koran.[79] The conversation at Medina del Campo focused precisely on this topic. If we can believe John's report, he succeeded in convincing his dialogue partner that the Moslem accusation was unwarranted.[80] Moreover, John did so without making use of the Bible, only employing rational argu-

---

76. Cf. Fromherz, *Johannes von Segovia*, 50–51.

77. For this interpretation see Decorte, "Ter inleiding," 7–17 and 27–32. Cf. Cabanelas, "Apéndices," 308–9.

78. Ibid., 302–4, 309. See Fromherz, *Johannes von Segovia*, 21–23.

79. Cf. *Surah* 5:72–73 and Goddard, *History of Christian-Muslim Relations*, 26–28. Goddard argues that there polytheism or idolatry (Arabic "shirk") and unbelief (Arabic "kufr") are only suggested and not clearly stated of the Christians. He reminds also that these Koranic verses "are difficult to interpret, not least because the accusations which are made, saying that God is Jesus or that God is the third of the three are not statements which would usually be made by most Christians." Indeed, it could be the case that Muhammad's knowledge of Christian doctrine came from mixed or heterodox sources.

80. For more details, see Fromherz, *Johannes von Segovia*, 21–23 and Haubst, "Die Wege der christologische manuductio," 116–17.

ments. He showed to the Moslem that the Trinity is grounded by the same necessity that also grounds God's Oneness.

Similar arguments can also be found in other Christian theologians such as Richard of Saint-Victor (†1173), William of Auvergne (c.1180–1249), and Ramón Lull (1232/1233–c.1316). According to Haubst, these theologians can still be understood as offering rational presentations of the reasonableness of those dogmas that transcend human reason. In contrast to them, John's rational argument runs the risk of transcending the limits of human rationality. Later, I will come back to the last of these thinkers, i.e., Ramón Lull, and will examine him in more detail in my next chapter. Here what I should only like to point out is that in the course of the long discussion with John of Segovia, the Moslem was getting more and more surprised. To this amazement, John replied by claiming that he was not the only Christian scholar in that area being able to counter Moslem criticism. The story of this encounter with the Other as told by John reaffirms Segovia's confidence in rational discussion.

On the Limitations of John of Segovia's Approach

The forgoing discussion has identified some positive features of John's approach, but it has also clearly shown the material and political difficulties of his project. Finally, a few words must be said on his theoretical shortcomings.

John of Segovia was in the first place a theologian. Already, as a young student, he was initiated in the Scotist school.[81] Later at Basle (in the course of the discussions concerning Immaculate Conception) he proved to be a Scotist. When tackling the problem of the Trinity within the context of the Islamic challenge, he also employed the same logical-metaphysical inventory. In some important respects, however, Segovia consciously distanced himself from Duns Scotus (c. 1266–1308). In contrast to the *Doctor Subtilis*, John of Segovia ventured to offer pressing proofs of the Trinity.[82]

---

81. For this section, see Haubst, "Die Wege der christologische manuductio," especially 120–22 and 128–29. Haubst points out several Scotist points in John's Trintarian discourse. Cf. his note 17 on page 121 and note 28 on page 123.

82. See Haubst, "Die Wege der christologische manuductio," 128. Segovia also differed from Scotus with respect to the problem of the procession of the Holy Spirit.

After the debate at Medina del Campo, John could claim with some justification that in a discussion with Moslems, no one has to recur to the Bible or to the scholastic doctors. This fact was all the more important, because Moslems did not demand mere opinions, but regarded only the clear knowledge of truth as the highest authority.[83] From his own part, John himself was convinced that everything that is acknowledged on the basis of authority should also be made more solid by undeniable arguments. Only in this way could the Moslems' mockery be turned away.

In his rational theological discourse, John went very far: by more or less equating logical and ontic truth—thereby ultimately equating the order of Divine and human knowledge.[84] The trust in his conceptual inventory combined with his zeal for highlighting the Trinitarian Mystery to Moslems drove him to make further and more subtle distinctions with respect to God. Thereby his discussion became more and more complicated. His project came dangerously close to a form of vanity. As Haubst writes:

> It seems that John sensed ... the "abyss" of the Divine the most, when finally he realized how all rational deduction will always only lead to a more difficult deduction.... He ... had the feeling that in spite of all his intellectual sharpness and experience, in spite and precisely because of his too subtle dialectics, he had fallen prey to the danger of losing any sense of direction and drifting away within his discursive thinking—without measure and "without orientation."[85]

In his answer to John of Segovia, Nicholas addressed his friend as "learned and with a very penetrating intellect" (*doctum, peracutum*)—as someone more learned than himself and not needing further instruc-

---

83. As will be discussed in the next chapter, Ramón Lull held a similar view.

84. Haubst, "Die Wege der christologische manuductio," 120 speaks of an "öfters wiederholten fatalen Sprung."

85. Haubst, "Die Wege der christologische manuductio," 129: "[A]m meisten hat anscheinend noch Johannes von ...„Abgrund" des Göttlichen geahnt, als er es schließlich merkte, wie alle rationale Deduktion noch immer nur in schwierigere Deduktion führt.... Johannes ... hatte das Gefühl, daß er mit aller Schärfung und Routine seiner rationalen Fähigkeiten, mit aller, und gerade wegen seiner überspitzen Dialektik der Gefahr verfallen sei, in seinem diskursiven Denken ungemäßigt und „richtungslos" daherzustürmen und die Orientierung zu verlieren."

For John's "confession" of his uncertainty in is letter to Jean Germain, see Haubst's note 58. On Germain, see also Southern, Southern, *Western Views of Islam*, 94–98.

tions (*doctior et prudentior non eget instructore*).⁸⁶ As Haubst reminds the reader, Nicholas knew well that the realm of sensual experience cannot be properly measured by human reason and that the same is true concerning the historically conditioned entire complexity of philosophical and theological ideas.⁸⁷ One can also recall Nicholas's painful conciliar experiences that made him often employ the term *praesumptio* in his letters and sermons around the year 1440. For him, this term referred, among others, to the Baselians whose champion Segovia once had been. The title of Nicholas's *Docta Ignorantia* can also be read as an indication of Nicholas's recoil from the conciliar or other kinds of rational presumptions.⁸⁸

Naturally, Nicholas's stance towards his friend, John, and to the latter's rational enterprise can only be fully understood after the examination of Nicholas's own position in relation to the Islamic question. So, I will return to the question of Nicholas's possible criticism of John's project later on. Since my concern in the present chapter is the examination of Nicholas of Cusa's closer social and intellectual background, at least one more representative of fifteenth century Western thought must be considered. Such an examination of another figure is necessary for the following reason. Taking into account their environment, both John of Segovia and Nicholas of Cusa seem atypical or even exceptional medieval figures to the modern mind. However, atypical and exceptional are necessarily *relative* terms of evaluation, i.e., they can only be applied with a reference to what is typical and regular. Otherwise, these terms lose any clear meaning whatsoever.⁸⁹ Therefore it is necessary to examine a more "typical" representative of the late medieval world and contrast him to Nicholas and John. In this way, the latter thinkers and their respective views on the Otherness of Islam will appear in a clearer light—precisely by virtue of the contrast with a more "typical" thinker.

• • •

---

86. See Haubst, "Die Wege der christologische manuductio," 129. For Nicholas's text, see Nicolaus de Cusa, *De Pace Fidei*, 93, line 19 and 96, lines 18–19.

87. Haubst, "Die Wege der christologische manuductio," 129.

88. Ibid., footnote 60. For "praesumptio," cf. also my discussion of Ramón Lull in the next chapter.

89. It is also true that no absolute judgement is possible concerning excellence vs. regularity.

John of Torquemada

> I propose as first Cardinal Torquemada whom the pope granted with this honorary title so that he be called protector of the faith.[90]
>
> —Ambrosius Catharinus Politus OP[91]
>
> The most reverend lord and cardinal of Saint Sixtus in Rome who with cogent reasons refutes the heresies and errors of Muhammad.[92]
>
> —Nicholas of Cusa on John of Torquemada

John of Torquemada (1388–1468), the Cardinal of Saint Sixtus could serve as a good "contrast figure" for two reasons. He was both of equal intellectual excellence and political importance as the two other thinkers.[93] Moreover, there is also a more specific reason for examining John of Torquemada's approach to Islam. John of Torquemada and Nicholas of Cusa personally knew each other since Basle, where they became associated in their joint defense of the papacy. Nicholas of Cusa was even aware of the John's work concerning Islam. In the prologue to his *Cribratio Alkorani*, Nicholas explicitly referred to John as "the most reverend lord and cardinal of St. Sixtus who with cogent reasons [*vivis rationibus*] refutes the heresies and the errors of Muhammad." These cogent reasons, or vivid and lively arguments are referred to in the very title of John's treatise.[94]

---

90. Quotation from Izbicki, *Protector of the Faith*, xiv: "Et primum offero Cardinalem Turrecremata, quem pontifex hoc epitheto honoravit, ut protector fidei diceretur . . ." Cf. ibid., ix.

91. A Thomist (1484–1553), papal theologian at the Synod of Trente.

92. Cf. *CA* First Prologue, 4:5.7–8: "Vidi et aliorum fratrum de ea materia [i.e., on the Islamic question] scripturas Catholicas, . . . et ultimo reverendissimi domini cardinalis sancti Sixti haereses et errores Mahumeti vivis rationibus confutantis."

93. In their respective evaluations of Nicholas's project both Hopkins and Decorte compare it to Torquemada's approach. I follow their analysis with attempting to add some new considerations. See Hopkins, "John of Torquemada's *Evidentes Rationes*," 99–118. Decorte, "Ter inleiding," 19–23. For John's general theological outlook, see Izbicki, *Protector of the Faith* and Cantarino, "John of Torquemada." Cf. Hagemann, *Der Kur'an in Verständnis und Kritik*, 67–68.

94. Hagemann translates the Latin phrase as "in lebhafter Argumentation." Cf. his bilingual edition of the *CA* (Nicolaus de Cusa, *Cribratio Alkorani*, I) First Prologue, 4:8.

Since my main concern is not a detailed philological investigation, I am not so much interested in the question of influence between Nicholas and John of Torquemada, but rather the intellectual contrast between their respective positions. Fortunately, with respect to Islam, John's influence on Nicholas can mainly be seen in negative terms.

The Evidentes Rationes

It was no wonder that within its own historical context, Segovia's plan for a peaceful rapprochement was not really successful. It is somewhat ironic, that neither could the subsequent papal calls for a crusade achieve much against the Turks.[95] During the struggles of organizing a military operation, in the winter of 1458–1459, another great theologian of the fifteenth century, John of Torquemada composed his *Tractatus contra principales errores perfidi Machometi et Turcorum sive Sarracenorum* (*Treatise against the principle errors of the perfidious Muhammad's and the Turks or Saracens*, *Tractatus* in the following).[96]

John was as an active supporter of the papal anti-Turkish policy. In his work, he pilloried Moslem errors and he very much saw these errors as they were commonly understood in his own time. He laid out the age-old charges against Muhammad's false doctrine, the prophet's immorality and the influence of Nestorian heresy. The *Tractatus* had also a clear practical orientation since Torquemada wanted to rouse the fervor of Christians for a war against the infidels with his treatise.[97] He explicitly called upon the Christian princes for a crusade against the Turks.[98]

---

95. Cf. Izbicki, *Protector of the Faith*, 20–21.

96. Since Izbicki, *Protector of the Faith*; Cantarino and Hopkins refer to different manuscripts and printed editions of the *Tractatus*, further research is needed to shed light on the details of its textual history.

97. Izbicki, *Protector of the Faith*, 23 writes that: "Pius II, interested in arousing such sentiments, preferred Turrecremata's repetition of old charges to the more enlightened views of John of Segovia and Nicholas of Cusa, who advocated dialogue with Islam." See also page 24, where Segovia is called a more enlightened author. Cantarino, "John of Torquemada," 247–50, interprets John's work predominantly in terms of political-religious propaganda.

98. Hopkins, "John of Torquemada's *Evidentes Rationes*," 116.

Sources and Thomist Influence

Torquemada was a respected theologian and spiritual writer of his own time.[99] When writing against Islam, his most important influence came from the Dominican Richard of Montecroce (c. 1243–1340), more precisely from his work *Contra Legem Sarracenorum*.[100] For instance, the following part of his treatise comes from the opening words of Richard's first chapter: "The first thing to know is what are the basic errors posited in the Saracens' law in which errors God's law is very much opposed."[101] In its more doctrinal dimensions, however, the *Tractatus* was based on Thomas of Aquinas's *Summa Theologiae* and it is only natural that being a Dominican friar himself, John likewise quoted Thomas's *Summa contra Gentiles*.[102] In contrast to Thomas Aquinas, when Torquemada was defending Christianity, he both made use of the Bible and his own rational considerations.[103]

---

99. Izbicki, *Protector of the Faith*, 31 calls John's *Summa de ecclesia*—composed between 1449–1453—"his masterpiece" and page 99 adds that: "[T]hough his chief scholarly work was his *Summa* . . . , he was also known for his *Meditationes*." Cf. ibid. 122: "Though not a brilliant thinker like Cusa, Turrecremata was an able polemicist and well versed in theology and law, with a reputation for probity and a zeal for orthodoxy." Cantarino, "John of Torquemada," 238 classifies John as "a prolific writer and . . . an important canon law scholar, one of the greatest theologians of his time."

100. On Richard of Montecroce, see Hopkins, "Islam and the West," 57–97, Hagemann, *Der Kur'an in Verständnis und Kritik*, 55–67, and Hagemann, *Christentum contra Islam*, 55–63. One can also read John's *Tractatus* as a late answer to Peter the Venerable's call. Cf. Hopkins, "John of Torquemada's *Evidentes Rationes*," note 2. For John's sources, cf. Cantarino, "John of Torquemada," 243.

101. Hopkins, "John of Torquemada's *Evidentes Rationes*," 99: "Primo igitur oporetet scire qui sunt *principales errores* quos lex Sarracenorum ponit, in quibus maxime legi dei contrariatur."

102. Cantarino, "John of Torquemada," 243. Cf. also Hopkins, "John of Torquemada's *Evidentes Rationes*," 100 and 104. Izbicki several times refers to John as a "Thomist," see e.g., Izbicki, *Protector of the Faith*, 73 and 83. Thomas's exact position and his own intellectual approach towards Islam will be examined in my next chapter.

103. According to Cantarino, "John of Torquemada," 245, John of Torquemada's discourse "although Thomistic in doctrine, no longer follows a Thomistic line of polemical inquiry" as he departs from Thomas's position according to which "disputing and contending parties must agree in some basic principles." Cf. *ScG* I, c. 2.

Content and the Author's Intention

The title of John's treatise makes clear the author's intention: his objective was only to examine and dissolve Muhammad's main errors.[104] The *Tractatus* has the following structure:

a. *Introduction*;

b. *the central polemical part* consisting of fifteen chapters;

c. the final, *concluding section*.[105]

Forty of Muhammad's main errors are listed and discussed.[106] Hopkins observes that the discussed material "is presented in a rather magisterial way, where the audience is Christian, and Moslems and their faith only the subject of the argument."[107] He also points out that John's treatise is "super-organized . . . with the result that its explicit itemizing of every point of argument becomes an irritant."[108] This is so because John either repeated Richard of Montecroce's words or restated the latter's polemical points. However, John went even further by amplifying Richard's points and strengthening the arguments.[109] Notwithstanding John's literary dependence on Richard, their respective emphases were different. On the one hand, Richard's goal was to refute the faulty beliefs of the Moslems rather than defending Christian doctrine positively, as he recognized the first task being much easier.[110] Hence, Richard set out to expose the inconsistencies, historical errors, and moral turpitude found in the Koran. John, on the other hand, made an additional effort: "though not seeking to prove the truth of Christian faith, he does nonetheless take pains . . . to fortify Christianity by clarifying its teachings in

---

104. I.e. "destruere . . . errores Damnatissimi Machometis," for the full quotation see Cantarino, "John of Torquemada," 245.

105. Cantarino, "John of Torquemada," 243.

106. Cf. Hopkins, "John of Torquemada's *Evidentes Rationes*," 99. Cantarino, "John of Torquemada," 246 gives a list of 38 controversial doctrinal and moral points.

107. Cantarino, "John of Torquemada," 243.

108. Hopkins, "John of Torquemada's *Evidentes Rationes*," 99–100.

109. Ibid., 100. Cf. Izbicki, *Protector of the Faith*, 122 where the author calls John "very thorough."

110. Hopkins, "John of Torquemada's *Evidentes Rationes*," 100: "facilius ostendere fidem illorum esse frivolam quam probare nostram esse veram."

the light of »rational« considerations."¹¹¹ His project came much closer to a rational defense of Christianity. The *Tractatus* was as much an apology as polemic.

John of Torquemada's Twofold Strategy

What is more interesting philosophically is that John made his own strategy, his presuppositions, and arguments-patterns more clear. One can have a closer look at how John made use of the kind of rationality he employed, precisely because he consciously displayed this rationality. In this sense, John's approach to Islam can be called more rational than Richard's was.

The metaphor of a double-edged sword captures well an important feature of John's approach. On the one hand, since Muhammad himself "commended" the Bible, John felt himself justified arguing from Biblical texts. He pointed out both that Scripture would show what is right and the fact that Muhammad was wrong. But John's Scriptural arguments were strengthened by his "practical" considerations verging on absurdities.[112] As it will be shown later, in his interpretation of biblical texts, John tended to assign a well defined meaning to Scriptural passages.[113] However, John did not only employ Holy Scripture but he also argued from what he called "rationes convenientes" or "evidentes rationes."[114] It is important to properly understand the nature of these necessary or cogent reasons before having a closer look at John's approach to Scripture.

The concept of these "*rationes*" was construed broadly to include philosophical principles as well as theological axioms along with common wisdom concerning practical matters. John was keen on using any means available in the defense of Christianity. Thus, biblical arguments and rational considerations make up the respective edges of John's intellectual sword.

---

111. Ibid., 101.

112. It is important to note that John agrees with Richard that the Koran's description of Paradise is not intended symbolically.

113. Hopkins, "John of Torquemada's *Evidentes Rationes*," 108–9 observes that: "John prefers to interpret the Old Testament in ways that render it directly in agreement with the New Testament." On the interpretation of the Bible, see also my *Prolegomena*.

114. In the second chapter of his work, Islam is contradicted by him with "apertissimis rationibus." Cf. Cantarino, "John of Torquemada," 244.

On John of Torquemada's Presuppositions

John stated many of his presuppositions explicitly, but not all of them. Naturally, in some cases, such an explicit statement was not necessary within his own cultural context. His presuppositions included various Aristotelian doctrines from the *Metaphysics*, which John saw either as self-evident (*per-se*) or else established as correct by Aristotle himself.[115] John also accepted natural law as a basis for ethics. Hopkins points out that

> [T]hough his assumptions are rightly subject to question by others, they are not unusual ones within the medieval Christian tradition; they are simply more explicit in Torquemada than they were in Richard.[116]

For instance, together with many other medievals, John also thought that celestial happiness will consist in the exercise of the higher intellect and this *visio divinitatis* will be nothing else than *visio facialis ipsius dei*.[117] For John, this vision would be of an intellectual and not of a sensible kind. The medieval ideas of *order* and *finality* were also present in John's thought. In his view, no feature of the created universe could be in vain. Thus, for instance, man is created as "erect" (*homo erectus*) in order that he may look up to Heaven.[118] Further, John assumed that the future blessed life will not be less orderly than the present life. He seemed to believe that "less orderly" means "less in accord with nature and reason."[119]

On Argument Patterns

It is important to note that taken in themselves, John's starting points do not only fit well with the medieval intellectual framework in principle,

---

115. See e.g., the Thomistic view according to which "omnis cognitio a sensu initium habet"; quoted in Hopkins, "John of Torquemada's *Evidentes Rationes*," 104.

116. Ibid. On the same page, Hopkins writes the following: "Similarly, his assumption that Paradise ... and every other spatial region has finite dimensions coheres with the Christian tradition and with medieval »common sense« as influenced by Aristotle."

117. Hopkins, "John of Torquemada's *Evidentes Rationes*," 112.

118. Hopkins, "John of Torquemada's *Evidentes Rationes*," note 29 to page 104. This is an old Christian idea originating in the ancient Greek world.

119. Ibid., 104. For the full quotation, see ibid., note 25.

but are compatible with various argument patterns.[120] It remains to be seen exactly what kind of argument-patterns John of Torquemada developed and employed.

Similar to his confrere Richard, John also made use of the *reductio ad absurdum*.[121] In this, John found a useful means since it is understandably easier to counter contradictions and faulty conceptions (of the Koran) than to prove the truth (of Christian faith) positively.[122] Another move John used was anticipating Moslem defenses of Muhammad's views. First, these defenses had to be posited (or projected), and thereafter John could refute them. For instance, John gave a rational argument concerning concubinage in the Old Testament. He stated that at that time, God allowed the practice of polygamy in order to produce more children, because of the scarcity of believers. He was even able to find some scriptural basis for this statement.[123] In view of other passages of the Old Testament, however, John's argument sounds absurd.[124] Although it can be argued that such an explanation of biblical polygamy was common in the Middle-Ages, it will be all the more interesting to see that Nicholas of Cusa made no recourse to them.

John, from his own part, carefully examined Muhammad's beliefs and motives, and also tried to complement Muhammad's thought. Concerning the Paradise, John added certain tacit considerations, and once again sought to reduce them to the absurd. Hopkins gives the following general observation on the way John argued:

> What strikes one foremostly about John's argument-patterns is not their innovativeness, for there is nothing new about his techniques or his argumentative style. What strikes one is, rather, the determination with which he pursues, in great detail and with elaborate analysis, points that others might be inclined

---

120. Ibid., 104. As will be shown, many of these points are shared also by Nicholas of Cusa.

121. Hopkins, "John of Torquemada's *Evidentes Rationes*," 104–5.

122. Cf. Decorte, "Ter inleiding," 22 and Hopkins, "John of Torquemada's *Evidentes Rationes*," 105–7.

123. Cf. Gen chapter 16 and 30. See further Gen 1:18, 9:1, Deut 21:15, and Ps 127:3–5.

124. E.g., he tried to convince his readership that even David's and Solomon's concubines—the number of the latter given as many as 300—served the same *procreative* purpose. Cf. Hopkins, "John of Torquemada's *Evidentes Rationes*," 105; 2 Sam 5:13, 1 Kgs 11:1–3, and especially Deut 17:17.

to deal with only summarily.... secondly, in his argumentation, Torquemada moves clearly from technique to technique, explicitly, making things clear—making even clear when he is hypothesizing and conjecturing.... there is no subtlety in his reasoning: all of his points tend to be made overtly and deliberately.... In all these respects, John shows more leisureliness than did Richard, who was more concise in elaborating Muhammad's principales errores.[125]

The Positive Dimensions of Christianity versus the Negative Features of Islam

It is worthwhile remembering that John's approach *"discloses important features of the late medieval Christian perspective."*[126] For instance, he gives a very positive picture of Christian marriage in terms of two equal's friendship. He regards marriage as a kind of community that meets the human need for companionship and friendship, and thinks that this friendship should be *aequalis* or *liberalis*.[127] He also speaks of the parents' common responsibility for their children and regards divorce as unnatural because of the universal moral code of natural law. His comment on the indissolubility of marriage shows that John was not blind toward practical factors either. As he himself wrote: "if both partners regard the marital bond as indissoluble, each will be more motivated to be faithful to the other."[128] Being a medieval Christian thinker, John also regarded paternity as important.

When coming to discuss the question of Moslem Paradise, John took Muhammad's description literally. John contrasted the Koranic description of a sensual Paradise with the spiritual pleasures of Christian Heaven. There, spiritual pleasure will be beyond any measure and the whole human person (*totus homo*) will be transformed and enjoying the Lord. Since a sensual Paradise can hardly be seen in agreement either with Christ's description thereof or with the principles of reason,

---

125. Hopkins, "John of Torquemada's *Evidentes Rationes*," 106–7.

126. For this section, see ibid., 107–14.

127. An "amicitia liberalis" is always more valuable than an "amicitia servilis." Cf. Hopkins, "John of Torquemada's *Evidentes Rationes*," 104.

128. Ibid., 108.

John rejected it without hesitation. Yet again, even concerning this point John drove his own "reason" *ad absurdum*.[129]

On John's Use of Scripture and his General Theological Outlook

It is not surprising that in his defense of Christianity, John contrasted the metaphorical language of the Bible with the Koran's literal meaning. In relation to Paradise, he pointed out that when the Bible speaks of feasting in Heaven, it does so only figuratively.[130] As John himself wrote "[F]or divine Scripture sets forth intelligible things under a likeness of sensible things so that from the [sensible things] with which we are familiar we may learn to love things unknown."[131] However, John was not only trying to fix the Koran's meaning but he also had a similar approach to the Bible. Hopkins reminds the reader that when John employs Scriptural proof-texts, he "does so in a manner that he believes to be straightforward and uncontrived."[132]

During the confrontation with the Hussites a key issue at stake was the theological status of Catholic priesthood. One particular exegetical problem concerned the so-called "power of the keys."[133] While tackling this problem, John reduced all the relevant biblical passages to Christ's promise of priestly ordination, i.e., to one fixed meaning. When discussing the "burning issue" of medieval theology, the relationship of Church and Scripture, John believed that in defending the Scripture, he was defending a body of uniform truths, unfailing and universally valid principles whose acceptance by the faithful was necessary for their salvation.[134] It can be safely stated that this would remain John's basis for approaching Scripture throughout his career. According to his con-

---

129. For John's view on sexual intercourse in Heaven, see Hopkins, "John of Torquemada's *Evidentes Rationes*," 110–11. Cf. also John's discussion of the risen Christ's eating and drinking, ibid., 112.

Decorte, "Ter inleiding," 22 calls the reductio ad absurdum "one of Torquemada's favorite procedures."

130. E.g., both Luke 22:30a and Isa 25:6 are to be taken metaphorically.

131. Hopkins, "John of Torquemada's *Evidentes Rationes*," 103.

132. Ibid., 102. Hopkins himself seems to judge this approach as something positive.

133. For this whole point, see Izbicki, *Protector of the Faith*, 53–60 and 63–66.

134. See ibid., 63–64.

viction God's Spirit had established an evident meaning in the biblical texts and only the heretics could ignore this. Thus, Scripture contains everything necessary for the salvation of mankind—at least implicitly.

It is not difficult to see the dangers of this approach. First of all, any evident meaning will necessarily be evident only to some. More importantly, once the concept of implicit meaning has been invoked, it can be argued that even passages with an "evident" meaning have yet another or perhaps more than one implicit meaning. Then the question poses itself as how to decide about the correct assignment and distribution of these—implicit and explicit—meanings. The troubles of the Basle assembly show that it was not at all clear on what grounds such a decision procedure should be conducted. Declaring that only a heretic may raise this kind of problem and only he may argue in like manner does not help the issue any further either. John was even aware of this difficulty. He saw clearly the importance of the related problem of the Scripture's relationship with its interpretative tradition.[135] Nevertheless, in his hierarchy of authorities, Scripture, and the truths derived from it by necessary reasoning remained the most important ones.[136]

John agreed with the medieval understanding that reads the Bible as employing intelligible similitudes so that from the sensible things humans may learn to love things unknown. However, in his approach to theology in general and to Sacred Scripture in particular, John displayed what can be called an "univocalizing" tendency. As was shown, John was looking for evident and well-defined meanings that would enable him to build up necessary arguments. The problem with this kind of approach is that it can lead to a neglect of symbolism. There are indications that John did not avoid this mistake. It seems that John was able to tolerate symbolism only if it leads him to a well-defined meaning.[137]

---

135. See ibid., 63–67. Traditionally, there existed a hierarchy of such authoritative texts, including the Bible and other materials of Christian origin. There were alternative lists of these authorities at that time. In composing his own hierarchy of authorities, John listed dogmatic definitions of councils, those of the popes and officially approved definitions prepared by learned doctors. In the first list, however, he emphasised the sufficiency of Scripture.

136. John also granted that valuable materials could be found even in learned pagans. See Izbicki, *Protector of the Faith*, 67.

137. Thus, e.g., John does not care much about Peter's martyrdom in Rome. Although he does cite the famous *Quo vadis* story, he rejects the term "vicarius Christi." Cf. Izbicki, *Protector of the Faith*, 77 and 84. See also ibid., 50, where the author points out that apart from the image of the keys, John "dismissed all other patristic metaphors for the power

All in all, John's practical concerns, his ideal of human finality and order show him as a typical medieval intellectual, but he was less sensitive to an invisible presence and less capable of properly respecting and appreciating the symbolic dimension of his own culture and religion.

However, to such an evaluation of the *form* of John's thought a note of caution should be added. Nothing of what has been said so far entails the absence of a belief in an invisible, transcendent dimension from John's thought. On the contrary, John's theological reflections arose from his own religious commitment. But it is equally true that he tried to elucidate this invisible dimension with the help of Thomistic terms and with his tendency towards a univocal meaning.

A Rational Defense of Christianity

As was said earlier, in the anti-Islamic polemic literature of the Middle-Ages a number of Moslem errors had been reiterated time and again. It is something of a truism that there was scarcely another option for a fifteenth century European intellectual than regarding such "errors" as errors.[138] Even the otherwise remarkably peaceful John of Segovia shared this perception to some extent. John of Torquemada, from his own part, did not simply restate the classical anti-Moslem reproaches, but he ordered them in 40 categories and argued against them as a proper scholastic theologian should do. He tried to show the moral and intellectual superiority of Christianity of which he was deeply convinced.[139] To say it simply: Christianity, as seen and interpreted by John, is or possesses absolute truth. No wonder that John saw Christianity as more rational than the Moslems' errors. Consequently, by employing any kind of argumentation that was available, he never became tired of showing his readership that the Moslems were wrong. With rigorous logic, he drove every point home. In effect, he was driving them to the extreme.[140]

---

of the Church" since he thought that "these metaphors lacked any real significance for a proper papalist doctrine on the nature and government of the Church."

138. For this section, cf. Decorte, "Ter inleiding," 21–23.

139. His *Tractatus* ends with twelve reasons explaining why Christianity is superior to Islam.

140. Hopkins, "John of Torquemada's *Evidentes Rationes*," 114–15, says that John took over many of Richard's objections and "developed them *ad extremum*."

In connection with this unbending logic, some scholars note that the merciless rigor of John's rationalism is already mirrored in his monarchical ecclesiology.[141] Perhaps it is still possible to form a more subtle judgment of John's enterprise. Because the connection between these two dimensions of his thought seems to be more complicated, I will question the interpretative force of a simple parallelism between John's ecclesiology and anti-Islamic polemics.[142]

The calamities of the conciliar struggles made John's defense of the papacy appear as a kind of absolute theorizing.[143] He worked hard to balance between papal power and a very real concern for the welfare of the Church. His most important motivation was to avoid chaos.[144] John's reaction to Islam accords well with his defensive interest. Secondly, John's defense of the papacy must be read as directed against the conciliar pretensions. These pretensions themselves were perhaps no less absolute and merciless than the austerity of the papalist side.[145] Although John, himself a cardinal, exalted their college, he did reject the cardinals' more extreme oligarchic pretensions.[146] Furthermore, John's own employment of the so-called hierarchical principle taken from Pseudo-Dionysius should not mislead the reader either, since in his theology, Torquemada certainly utilized as much Aristotle and Aquinas as Pseudo-Dionysius.[147] The thought of Pseudo-Dionysius was employed and interpreted by many different medieval thinkers in many different ways.[148]

---

141. On page 23 in Decorte, "Ter inleiding." While referring to Biechler, 202, Decorte also connects these two points with each other.

142. Cf. Izbicki, *Protector of the Faith*, ix: "papalist historians have produced a distorted picture of Turrecremeta's carrier, dissolving outlines of his personality and intellect into the image of a single-minded champion of papal absolutism."

Thus in the following I somewhat depart from the letter of Jos Decorte's analyis, at the same time developing my interpretation with the help of his *WI*.

143. Cf. Izbicki, *Protector of the Faith*, 87.

144. Ibid., On page 51, Izbicki writes that John's "chief interest was the visible Church, the sacramental and juridical body dedicated to the salvation of souls. This Church had to be defended from its heretical detractators; its internal foes, the conciliarists, had to be prevented from causing disorder and dissension." Cf. ibid., 106.

145. Cf. Izbicki, *Protector of the Faith*, 90 and 106.

146. Ibid., 91.

147. Cf. ibid., 73 where Izbicki criticises Black's assessment of John's thought. For the latter, see Black, *Monarchy and Community*, 56–60.

148. E.g., by Nicholas of Cusa himself in his *CC*. Cf. Izbicki, *Protector of the Faith*,

In the last analysis, one has to agree with Izbicki's judgment that John, when conceiving his ecclesiology, "was a Thomist more interested in the Church's mission than in political theory."[149] In other words, Torquemada and his contemporaries were not blind ideologues. John was a good Thomist theologian with a clear practical concern for order, unity, and the salvation of souls. His aim was to reunite and reform the Church rather than to build up a perfect theoretical system. He attempted to solve practical problems of Christianity. Notably, his ideas concerning the possible "solutions" were in fact shared by many of his contemporaries. Contextualizing thus John's enterprise makes it appear in a somewhat different, more realistic, and perhaps even sympathetic light.[150]

It is also important to realize that during the fifteenth century, there was a clear difference between writing on Christendom and writing against Islam. In contrast to Segovia, Torquemada lacked any direct contact with the Moslems. Realistically speaking, even the Hussites were much closer to him than Moslems: the former were Europeans, some of them communicating in Latin, and even coming to the discussions held at Basle. As was indicated earlier, for John of Torquemada and for his contemporaries, Islam could appear as extremely Other—much more than any conciliarist or even Hussite did who were in fact erring fellow-Christians.

All this being said, the point remains that just as in his opposition to the hardening conciliarist camp and the quarrelling Hussites, as well as in his *Tractatus*, John was basically on the defensive.[151] Ultimately, his rational defense of Christianity over against Islam should be thus contextualized: the *Tractatus* was answering the challenge of an extreme situation.

73–74.

149. Ibid., 73.

150. On page 94, Izbicki states that John "did not try to stand firmly in any one narrow, ideological camp." He considers John's theory of papal power as "coherent and balanced, if complex"; and he finds no "uncompromising purism" in his works. Cf. also Izbicki, *Protector of the Faith*, 74 and 106.

151. He also wrote the *Defensorium Fidei contra Iudeos, Hereticos et Sarracenos*. Cf. Hopkins, "Introduction," 228, note 11.

On Rationality, Extremities, and Madness

The observation that extreme situations could evoke extreme reactions from people sounds as a commonplace. However, as Leszek Kolakowski notes in another context, banality is "important, as the banal is no less than what is known and experienced by all."[152] This remark suggests that in spite of its banality, the extreme quality of Torquemada's answer is worth of a brief consideration.[153]

John's reaction to the Islamic challenge resulted in composing a work wherein he was striving to drive any possible point home. In so doing, however, he neither realized nor cared much that he was pushing these points to the extreme.[154] Most of his medieval readers would have accepted John's starting-points. They would also have been favorable both to his argument-patterns and strategy. John did not have to be bothered about a sympathetic readership. However, even a medieval readership could be sensitive to the extreme character of the work when his merciless rigor led him to discuss absurdities. To point this out is not to condemn John's work for its plain irrational character. On the contrary: it is the clear, very consequent performance of its inherent rational character that makes this work appear so extreme.

Generally speaking, there cannot exist any kind of rational discourse without making abstractions from reality. Rationality is dependent on making generalizations. But all generalizations are necessarily imperfect, falling short of the actual reality. Thus, at least in principle, every concept and every system of thought is open to further corrections. Once this possibility is forgotten, rationality will lose its own context. By losing sight of the actual reality and praxis, reason runs the danger of becoming *"ir-rational."* By the term *"ir-rational,"* I do not mean a complete absence of reason—such as a lack of distinct concepts, clear cut definitions, logical coherence etc. would be.[155] The term should rather indicate the exaggerated form a rational system.

---

152. Kolakowski, *Religion*, 36.

153. For the following analysis, see *WI*, especially 9–17.

154. This is not to say that the *Tractatus* was only a piece of religious-political propaganda. For the latter view, see Cantarino, "John of Torquemada," especially 243 and 247–50.

155. While Cantarino, "John of Torquemada," 245 refers to John's concern for "polemical methodology and logical argumentation"; page 247 calls his logic "impeccable." The same author page also speaks of a "deliberate misapplication of logic and exegesis"

In its exclusive adherence to such an overdriven form of rationality, reason can become *totalitarian*. On the one hand, it will produce a system of (seemingly) perfectly fitting propositions and concepts. On the other hand, it must pay a high price for this feat, in as much as totalitarian reason is impoverished by losing contact with actual reality. In this way it cannot fulfill its proper task anymore.

By making itself absolutely certain of its own truth, reason ceases to be receptive. It cannot but refuse foreign arguments or strange concepts. Reason is not able to recognize the Other. Instead it is both constantly restating its own claim on truth and reaffirming the inherent irrationality of the Other. Therefore, totalitarian reason is constantly reproducing its own image during this self-defense.[156] During this process also emerges an image of '*ir-rationality*' that is parallel to the self-image of totalitarian rationality. This mirror image shows the other as opposite of what reason is. In this way, the Other's own rationality becomes easily equated with irrationality *simpliciter*.

I hope to have made clear that John's project against Islam can be interpreted as an example of such a totalitarian rationality. John's reason had been closed down on itself and was not able to account for reality anymore. He was not able to really encounter the Other. For instance, John's desire for clarity—for it is an honorable desire, truly an intellectual virtue—allowed him to make tacit considerations explicit, while he scarcely wondered whether these would be accepted by the Moslems. After all John was on the defensive. His tendency for univocalizing Scripture's meaning became stronger. Analogous to this tendency John produced a similarly univocalizing, but overtly hostile analysis of the Koranic texts.[157] Finally and probably most characteristically, John made use of his favorite tool, the *reductio ad absurdum* to an absurd extreme.

from John's part. Hence, Cantarino is contrasted with the difficulty of explaining the latter "in a theological treatise . . . by a man of Torquemada's intellectual importance and stature."

156. Cf. Cantarino, "John of Torquemada," 245 where the author identifies "two dialectical errors very common in polemical writings" in John's *Tractatus* in "assuming understanding of what the adversary means and that he [i.e., John] is able to demonstrate with absolute validity on his own principles the adversary's error."

157. Cf. Cantarino, "John of Torquemada," 247: "the strictly theological argumentation exploits a literal interpretation of the Koran and even more often the eschatological legends in popular Islam that with their anthropomorphic description of God and of the angels provide an easy way to demonstrate the alleged materialistic quality of the Muslim religion."

In the last analysis, John of Torquemada's intellectual answer to the Islamic challenge shows him as a rational defender of Christian faith. In writing the well-ordered, scholastic defense of the *Tractatus*, it mattered little to him what kind of weapons he employed, provided he saw that one as effective in attacking his enemies. From a merely speculative point of view, his univocalizing tendency, his emphasis on the derivation of necessary arguments and the *reductio ad absurdum* served him well. However, the same rational inventory also made him blind to some other dimensions of the issue. While cardinal Torquemada's and the pope's subsequent cries for a crusade were lost in an apathetic silence, the *Tractatus* left a wide territory of possible intellectual discoveries untouched.

• • •

Nicholas of Cusa

> ... there is no hope for a campaign ... it is possible to come to dialogues, and from them fury will be mitigated and truth will manifest itself for the benefit of our faith.[158]
>
> —Nicholas of Cusa

It was said earlier that sometimes it is an easier job to attack than to defend. Yet, in intellectual inquiries the most difficult thing lies beyond simply defending one's own position or attacking the Other. My objective in the present study is to show that in this respect Nicholas of Cusa's intellectual project, more particularly his approach to Islam is worth a of a closer examination. The material discussed so far gives some insight into the historical background of Nicholas of Cusa's approach to Islam. It also serves for a theoretical contrast—a question that could be treated only later after a detailed examination of Nicholas's own project has been given. Since my concern in this chapter is the historical setting, its remaining pages will focus on the immediate background of Nicholas's work on the Islamic question.

The question of peace, harmony, and concordance had been Nicholas's central concern from the beginning of his intellectual career.

---

158. Nicholas's letter to John of Segovia, in Nicolaus de Cusa, *De Pace Fidei*, 96, 15 and 97, 13–15: "de passagio spes nulla ... ad colloquia posse perveniri, et ex illis furor mitigabitur et veritas se ipsam ostendet cum profectu fidei nostrae."

These themes had already played an important role in his theological-legal *Hauptwerk*, the *De Concordantia Catholica* written in 1432–1433.[159] There, Nicholas depicted a conciliar model of the Christian world (*Respublica Christiana*) in which peace and harmony (*pax, harmonia*) rules within the Roman Church and the Empire and also between the two.[160] Even though his experiences with the Basle assembly had taught Nicholas some bitter lessons, his concern for peace and reconciliation had remained a constant factor in his life. His works answering the challenge of Islam can be easily identified: the dialogue *De Pace Fidei*, Nicholas's letter to John of Segovia and the extended and somewhat tiresome tract of the *Cribratio Alkorani*. In the following I will situate these three works in Nicholas's own time. Their relation to other Cusanian works and their more theoretical dimensions will be discussed later.

The De Pace Fidei

The fall of Constantinople into the hands of the Ottoman Turks in 1453 caused Nicholas of Cusa a terrible shock and led him to further and deeper reflections. The opening passage of his *PF* expresses very well both this concern and his state of mind:

> There was a certain man, who having formerly seen the sites in the regions of Constantinople, was inflamed with zeal for God as a result of those deeds that were reported to have been perpetrated at Constantinople most recently and most cruelly by the King of the Turks. Consequently, with many groanings he beseeched the Creator of all, because of His kindness, to restrain the persecution that was raging more fiercely than usual on account of the difference of rite between the religions. It came to pass that after a number of days—perhaps because of his prolonged, incessant meditation—a vision was shown to this same zealous man. There from he educed the following: the few wise

---

159. For the English translation, see Sigmund.

160. The term "concordance" in the title already refers to this harmonious ecclesiastical-political *cooperation*. Some codices of the *PF* refer also to this work as a "concordance." E.g., as "de concordia religionum," "de pace seu concordantia fidei" or even "concordia nationum." In the work itself, the term "concordia" appears 8 times. Different forms of the verb "concordare" appear 6 times, while the text applies both "concordantia" and "concoditer" once. Cf. Nicolaus de Cusa, *De Pace Fidei*, the critical apparatus to page 3, and page 63 and Biechler—Bond's *Concordance* in their *Nicholas of Cusa on Interreligious Harmony*.

men who are rich in the experimental knowledge of all such differences as are observed throughout the world in the religions can find a single, readily-available harmony (*concordantia*), and through this harmony there can be constituted, by suitable and true means, perpetual peace within religion.[161]

If one could believe these words—and indeed, Nicholas had once visited the Imperial City,[162] held Greek philosophy in high esteem and was befriended with a Greek, the Cardinal Bessarion; thus the terrible news surely must have disturbed him deeply—his prayers were heard and as a result the dialogue *De Pace Fidei* was written.[163]

Answer to an Urgent Question: Nicholas's Letter to John of Segovia

Somewhat later, in December 1454, Nicholas received John of Segovia's letter.[164] While in his letter John had apologized several times for his lengthy discourse, Nicholas's answer is characterized by its concise nature.[165] He replied to John with friendly affection and thanked him

---

161. *PF* I, 1, 3-14. Throughout this study I refer to the paragraphs (and lines) of the *PF* as arranged by Biechler—Bond (*Nicholas of Cusa on Interreligious Harmony*) so that my reader could easily identify both Nicholas's original and its modern translation. However, I quote the English text according to Hopkins (*Nicholas of Cusa's De Pace Fidei and Cribratio Alkorani*) with some modifcations for my purpose.

162. Cf. Nicolaus de Cusa, *De Pace Fidei*, 66 *Adnotationes*. See also *Nicholas of Cusa on Interreligious Harmony*, 221 where Biechler and Bond remind the reader that Nicholas had already recieved a "vision from above" at sea upon his return from Constantinople in 1437. (Cf. *Epistola auctoris* in *DI* III, 263:3-9). They also add the following perceptive note on Nicholas: "How "zealous" and "inflamed" he was may be seen from the speed with which he produced *De Pace Fidei*."

Nicholas set out on ship from Venice in May 1437 To Constantinople and returned from there on February 4, 1438 with the Greek Emperor, the Patriarch, and other Orthodox churchmen. The ensuing council at Florence proclaimed the union between the Roman and the Greek Churches in July 1439. Cf. Duclow, "Life and Work," 32-33.

163. For the textual history, see also the discussion of the *DVD* in my next chapter. It is not my aim to reconstruct the actual composition of the *PF* or to solve all questions of textual criticism. For further details, the reader is kindly referred to Klibansky and Bascour, "Praefatio" and their critical apparatus.

164. John's letter dates from December 2, 1454, Nicholas's answer is from the 29th of the same month.

165. Nicholas's letter is published by Klibansky and Bascour as an the appendix to Nicolaus de Cusa, *De Pace Fidei*, on 93-102. If not noted otherwise, all English quotations from it are my translations.

for his trust. As the *PF* also shows, Nicholas too saw the importance of the Islamic question. In his answer to John's letter, he recalled their Basle days and assured his friend that his work would not need any correction.[166]

Following this *captatio benevolentiae*—whose earnestness there is no reason to doubt—Nicholas summarized his answer in three points:

a. first, he reported on the crusade recently called forth;

b. then he offered his reflection on John's ideas;

c. and finally he gave practical advice.[167]

Since the first and third parts of Nicholas's letter are related to the immediate historical context of the two friends' confrontation with Islam, it is these that will be considered here in more detail. The more theoretical discussion of the letter I will examine later.

Historical-Political Report

Nicholas had been laboring in vain on the preparations for the crusading campaign. The two *Reichstage* assembled in the meantime at Regensburg and Frankfort produced only one practical result: the latter granted Ladislaus V's, the king of Hungary, demand for military help. Thus, Ladislaus was promised to be given 30,000 footmen and 10,000 horse soldiers, but the task of realizing this project was assigned to the next imperial assembly to be held at Vienna. Additionally, pope Nicholas V was asked to produce a maritime force and look for new financial resources.

In spite of these spare but seemingly positive results, Nicholas of Cusa had his own personal doubts concerning the success of the campaign. Although he hoped that with the aid of the Italian city-states a proper fleet could be produced, because of their internal quarrels and the Venetian-Ottoman peace-treaty from April 1545 even this he found doubtful.[168] Concerning the help coming from Germany, Nicholas, himself a German, was even more skeptical. Finally, he reported to John

---

166. Cf. Nicolaus de Cusa, *De Pace Fidei*, 100, 10–13.

167. Ibid., 94–102.

168. Venice made her own peace-treaty with the Sultan and promised not to aid any of the Turks' enemies.

of the Turks' further victories and attacks, and of the great losses suffered by the Christians—e.g., by the Hungarians and the Serbs. "Hence, there is no hope for a campaign, and for the defense only what I have related," he wrote.[169]

Shared Perspectives

Their correspondence makes it clear that Nicholas and John were aware of the fact that the doctrines of Incarnation and Trinity were central to a Christian-Moslem inter-religious dialogue. Not only do they make up the "essence" of Christianity but precisely these two doctrines are notoriously misunderstood and attacked by Moslems. Nicholas started the second part of his letter with confessing that both he and John had the same understanding of the Islamic problem. He also mentioned the *PF* as a work already written and his intention of sending it to John.[170] Just as his friend did, Nicholas also recognized that Christ's teaching does not permit military aggression (*invasionis gladio agressio*) and the only possibility left open to Christians remains self-defense (*defensio*).[171]

Further, Nicholas saw a real possibility for John's theological conference as a way to peace and truth. He thought that Christian faith would profit from such an encounter. He also reminded John that it would be worth bringing into the discussion some Christians living under Moslem control—such as people from Cairo, Alexandria, and Caffa since they were familiar with Moslem customs and their fundamental beliefs and had some experience to counter them.[172] He also noted that it would be worthwhile consulting Christian monks of Armenia and Greece for their mature advice in this issue.[173]

---

169. Nicolaus de Cusa, *De Pace Fidei*, 96, 14–15: "Unde de passagio spes nulla, sed de resistendo illa quae praenarratur."

170. Ibid., 97, 1–4: "de hoc scripsi libellum parvulum quem nominavi *De pace fidei*. Utinam ad manum haberem quia mitterem, licet nihil in eo tale contineatur quod reverendissimae paternitati vestrae sit novum." Later Nicholas did send the *PF* and John received it. When donating his books to his *alma mater*, the university of Salamanca, John explicitly mentioned Nicholas's work as a "[T]ractatus de pace fidei compositus per cardinalem sancti Petri ad uincula, Nicolaum de Cusa." See Segovia, "Texto de la donacion," 93–94.

171. Nicolaus de Cusa, *De Pace Fidei*, 97, 6–11. Cf. Matt 26:52.

172. Nicolaus de Cusa, *De Pace Fidei*, 97, 16–18: "qui et mores atque fundamenta eorum optime sciunt et semper student ipsis obviare."

173. Ibid., 19–21. Nicholas points out the Turks' preference for secular princes over

Nicholas especially emphasized his preference for a peaceful approach towards Islam over against military action. He was convinced that one of Christianity's essential feature was to grow amidst difficulties and persecution.[174] However, with a realistic note, he also reminded John of the imminent danger. Nicholas remembered that once, in the year 846, Saracens had already reached Rome and sacked Saint Peter's church. In the light of historical experience, the Islamic threat was to be taken seriously.[175] It required immediate action. Otherwise, Christianity would be discredited by its being half-hearted and lukewarm.[176]

For Nicholas, taking the Moslem challenge seriously, strictly speaking, did not exclude a military response in terms of self-defense. Since he had already discussed this possibility in the first part of his letter, he felt no need to return to it later. However, Nicholas wanted to take seriously the "Moslem persecution" in a very special sense. He thought, namely, that the pope and the Church had to ask themselves the question of what God's plan was when He permitted this deplorable situation.[177] Thereby, Nicholas placed the whole issue into a critical-theological perspective. This suggests that a genuine answer to the question why such a thing as the Ottoman military success could happen would necessarily have to transcend mere military or political considerations and lead to the heart of Christian faith.[178] His letter to John shows that Nicholas's reflections on Islam did not completely lack practical relevance. Both as

---

against priests. Clerics would not be the ideal dialogue partners, but their advice may prove useful nevertheless.

Note also that in the *PF* while the dialogue partners are said to have expertise in the question of religious difference, none of them are explicitly referred to as priests.

174. Nicolaus de Cusa, *De Pace Fidei*, 100, 23–25: "Ego firmissime credo non ad mortem sed vitam, non ad supressionem sed exaltationem fidei persecutionem permitti. Ecclesia enim hoc proprium habet quod sub persecutione splendescit."

175. After capturing Constantinople, Sultan Mehmed II himself was boasting about his plan of going to Rome and making an end to Christianity. Klibansky and Bascour, "Praefatio," ix–xii show how well this fear is documented in contemporary letters.

176. Nicolaus de Cusa, *De Pace Fidei*, 16–17.20: "Nam pluries tepiditate Ecclesiam subintrante excitata sunt flagella. . . . Odit Deus tepiditatem, quia Deus zelotes." The fall of Rome was regarded as divine punishment for the Church's tepidity. Cf. the note to line 18 in the ciritcal apparatus.

177. Nicolaus de Cusa, *De Pace Fidei*, 100, 14–16.

178. Cf. ibid., 19–20: "excitata dormiens Ecclesia ad Dominum habuit refugium." See also 23–25 where Nicholas confesses his faith that even the present persecution had a meaning in God's plan.

a man of politics and a man of faith and intellectual reflection, Nicholas tried hard to take Islam's challenge seriously. There is no sound reason for doubting the sincerity of his answer to John.[179]

Further Practical Advice

The previous observation is important since it answers the question that troubled John of Segovia's mind: How could he address pope Nicholas V with his proposition after the latter's call to a crusade?

The third part of Nicholas's letter makes it especially clear that Nicholas genuinely appreciated John's personal dedication to the Islamic question. This is borne out well from the practical advice Nicholas gave to his friend. For instance, Nicholas listed those European libraries where Koran-texts could be found. He was ready to do an inquiry (in a letter) whether the text in one of these was a different version than the one John knew of. Remembering John's difficulties in finding a decent Koranic text in Europe, one can appreciate the importance of this offer. Characteristically, Nicholas also made mention of a contemporary work treating Moslem religion and he hastened to add that it was much more modest in volume than John's.[180]

To John it was probably even more important that Nicholas encouraged his friend to complete his work as soon as possible and make it known to the pope and subsequently to Nicholas himself and to others as well. One reason for this haste was clearly the pope's illness.[181] Another one—not specified here, but already discussed in the second part of the letter—was the imminent danger of the Turks' attack. Finally, Nicholas ensured his friend—an old conciliarist, now understandably somewhat estranged from the curia—of papal grace. All this clearly answered Segovia's question: Nicholas did recognize the practical relevance and actuality of John's project.

---

179. Cf. Nicolaus de Cusa, *De Pace Fidei*, lii.

180. Cf. ibid., 101, 12–14: "sed non est comparatio ad volumen illud gloriosum vestrae compilationis." The work in question is from the hands of Denys the Carthusian, monk of the monastery at Roermond, in the diocese of Liège. Nicholas had stimulated Denys to compose his work (*Contra legem Mahumeti* or *Contra Perfidiam Mahumeti*) that he sent to Nicholas. The library of Denys's monastery possessed also a copy of the Koran. (See ibid., 10–15.) Cf. Nicholas's *CA* First Prologue, 4:1–3.

181. Nicholas wrote this in December 1554. Since the summer of the previous year pope Nicholas V had been seriously struggling with his gout and in March of the following year he died.

The Birth of the Cribratio Alkorani

During the following years nothing happened that could disprove Nicholas's doubts about a successful crusade against the Turks. Neither could Segovia's project gain much public attention or appreciation. After a serious illness, John of Segovia died on May 24, 1458. Even though Nicholas lost a friend, he did not lose his interest in the Islamic question; rather the opposite would be true: after much study and reflection, in the winter of 1460–1461, Nicholas composed a long and tiresome tract, the *Cribratio Alkorani*.[182] The three books of this treatise not only make up one of Nicholas's last mature theological-philosophical works, but they can be understood as a continuation of and a response to John's project.[183]

Dedication to the Pope

Nicholas dedicated this work to his former friend the cardinal Julian Piccolomini—at that time (1458–1464) pope under the name of Pius II.[184] By drawing a parallel between Pius and pope Leo the Great (440–461), Nicholas expressed his hope that just as under Leo the Nestorian heresy was condemned the same would happen with the Islamic doctrine. The *CA* expresses the hope that pope Pius would eliminate the erroneous teaching of the Moslems. To a medieval reader, Nicholas's understanding according to which Islam originated in Nestorian Christianity and thus it was *tout courts* a form of Christian heresy made this parallel realistic enough.[185] The dedication already suggests that in the *CA*, Nicholas

---

182. Cf. Hagmemann, "Einleitung," vii. For an English text see Hopkins's translation in *Nicholas of Cusa's De Pace Fidei and Cribratio Alkorani*.

183. See my discussion of the *CA* in the fifth chapter of the present study.

184. Nicholas could expect to inspire the pope with his project and influence him towards a peaceful confrontation with Islam. However, strictly speaking, such an intention on Nicholas's part can hardly be proved or disproved, albeit it does not contradict the existing historical records. Cf. Segovia's intention and the earlier discussion.

Later, Pius II himself wrote a letter to Mehmed II, which was apparently never delivered. Therein he promised to make the Sultan a true emperor if he would become Catholic. However, Pius's understanding of Muslim errors, which he asked the sultan to renounce, were derived not from Nicholas's work but from John of Torquemada's *Tractatus*.

185. For the heretical and especially Nestorian influence on the Koran, see *CA* Second Prologue, 11–15; 1, 23; 4, 30, and also II, 18, 226; 21, 235. Hagemann, *Christentum*

employed a more polemical tone than he had done before in the *PF* or in his letter to John.

On the Sources

The First Prologue of the *CA* lists the sources—the primary one being a text Nicholas had once obtained at Basle, i.e., Robert Ketton's translation of the Koran.[186]

The secondary sources were understandably more numerous—including also other works of the Toledan collection. Nicholas apparently studied the work of an Arab Christian author, Al-Kindi under the title *Rescriptum Christiani*—this being the second part of the so-called *Disputatio Christiani*.[187] Other minor works from the same collection include the *Liber generationis Mahumet*,[188] the *Fabulae Sarracenorum*,[189] the *Doctrina Mahumet*.[190]

More importantly, Nicholas found an Arabic Koran in Constantinople and there others could explain some of its passages to him.[191] At the Dominican convent, in the neighboring Pera, he also found another copy of Ketton's Latin translation.[192] Denys the Carthusian's huge polemical treatise has been referred to earlier in connection to

---

contra Islam, 70–71 gives a brief and balanced evaluation of the role of Nestorianism in Nicholas's project.

186. Cf. *CA* First Prologue, 2:2–4: "Feci quam potui diligentiam intelligendi librum legis Arabum quem iuxta translationem per Petrum abbetem Cluniacensem nobis procuratam Basileae habui..."

187. Cf. *CA* First Prologue, 2:3–7. On Nicholas's sources, see Hagemann, "Einleitung," xiv–xvi and Hopkins, "Introduction," 20.

188. *CA* First Prologue, 2:7–8.

189. Ibid., 8–9.

190. Ibid. Although they are not referred to explicitly in the *CA*, Nicholas's example of the Toledan collection included Robert's *Preface* to the translation and Peter the Venerable's *Summa Totius Haeresis*. Nicholas, according to *CA* First Prologue, 2:9–10 "left this book with Master John of Segovia," presumably at Basle, before he journeyed to Constantinople.

191. *CA* First Prologue, 2:11–13. Nicholas stayed at the convent of the Friar Minors. There he found both this text and some Franciscans who understood Arabic.

192. *CA* First Prologue, 2:13–14. At Pera Nicholas also learned of the works of Saint John of Damascus (c. 675–c. 750), the first anti-Moslem polemicist of (Eastern) Christianity. Some of John's works—"pauca valde scripsisse, quae habentur"—may have been shown to Nicholas. Cf. ibid., 2:15–17.

Nicholas's letter to Segovia.[193] Nicholas was also familiar with Richard of Montecroce's work and found it "more gratifying than the others."[194] Especially important is that Nicholas both read Thomas Aquinas's *De Rationibus Fidei ad Cantorem Antiochenum* and John of Torquemada's *Tractatus*.[195] Interestingly in the *CA*, Nicholas makes no explicit mention of his friend's, John of Segovia's writing. One reason for his silence mus have been that John's works on Islam had not yet been published.

This list of the sources in the *CA* is impressive. It helps the reader to understand much of the work's medieval intellectual background, but it also makes one realize the extent to which Nicholas was misinformed concerning Islam.

On Faults and Defects: Is Islam a Christian Heresy?

Rather unsurprisingly, Nicholas's *CA* shares several faults and defects common to medieval Christian authors writing on and—for the most part—against Islam. As Hopkins comments on Muhammad's portrayal in the *CA*, there Nicholas "reproduced the image of Muhammad that had become virtually official within European and Byzantine Christianity."[196] Nicholas's reliance on Robert Ketton's translation can be identified as the main source for his misunderstandings on a number of places.[197] Hopkins adds that further errors arose "from ignorance of historical fact, from special pleading, and from inattentiveness to details."[198]

A brief examination of Nicholas's second prologue (*alius prologus*) may suffice to demonstrate these shortcomings.[199] There, a story taken from the *Rescriptum Christiani* is quoted.[200] This is the story of Sergius,

---

193. Ibid., 4:1–3. As Hopkins comments, there are few common points shared by Nicholas and Denys such as, among others, the idea of the "lex evangelica" and the conciliatory attitude. On the question of a possible influence, see Hopkins, *A Miscellany*, 278–79, note 92.

194. *CA* First Prologue, 4:3–5. For its evaluation, see Hagemann 55–63 and Hopkins, "Islam and the West," 57–97.

195. *CA* First Prologue, 4:5–8.

196. However, he adds: "[I]t would not have been possible for Nicholas . . . to paint a favourable picture of the prophet Muhammad." Cf. Hopkins, "Introduction," 20.

197. Cf. ibid., 15–16.

198. Ibid., 16.

199. *CA* Second Prologue, 11–17.

200. *CA* Second Prologue, 11:2–14.

the Nestorian monk, and Muhammad—a famous story having a long-standing tradition in Christian polemics against Moslems. According to this story, Muhammad had been first an idolater and afterwards became a convert to Nestorian Christianity. Later, he was perverted by three clever Jews and the same Jews managed to manipulate the text of the Koran.[201]

Relying on this story, Nicholas thought to recognize a Nestorian influence in Muhammad's religious development. Accordingly, he made an excursus on Nestorius (428–431 archbishop of Constantinople, † 451 in exile) and noted that Nestorius had accepted the Gospel but erred regarding the manner of the union between God and man in the person of Jesus Christ.[202] Nestorius considered Christ as fully human and also acknowledged his special relation to God though his view differed from what later became established as orthodox doctrine. He did believe in the Holy Trinity, but did not consider Mary as *theotokos*. Hence, it was no wonder in Nicholas's eyes that the Koran both confirms Christ's human nature and denies His full divinity.[203] As Nicholas saw it, Muhammad condemned explicitly only the idolatrous worshipping itself, in other words the Prophet opposed what he perceived as a form of polytheism (=a plurality of gods). In a sense, he remained a Nestorian Christian to his last day and his attack on the Trinity was conditioned by his disapproval of polytheism. Since Nicholas had taken seriously Muhammad's alleged Christian—albeit heretical—origins, he was convinced that

> there will be no difficulty in finding, in the Koran, the truth of the Gospel, although Muhammad himself was very far removed from a true understanding of the Gospels.[204]

Every modern reader familiar with the results of modern scholarship finds these words absurd if not paradoxical, since they very much contradict the known historical facts. However, a Nestorian influence on Muhammad and his ignorance of Christianity is even granted by modern historical scholarship. Nevertheless, Muhammad cannot be

---

201. While the story as a whole has no historical value, it goes back to ancient Islamic traditions. Cf. Hagemann, *Einleitung*, xi–xiii.

202. *CA* Second Prologue, 14:1–3.

203. Ibid., 15:1–2.

204. Ibid., 16:1–2: "Non igitur erit difficile in Alkorano reperiri evangelii veritatem, licet ipse Mahumetus remotissimus fuit a vero evangelii intellectu."

regarded as a former Nestorian Christian and strictly speaking neither can Islam be seen as a form of Christian heresy.

Having seen this example, it is tempting to dismiss the entire project of the *CA* right from the beginning. Modern Cusanus-scholarship has identified many of Nicholas's references and pointed out his mistakes.[205] Therefore there is no reason to restate either all of the individual mistakes of the *CA* (and of other works) or to excuse them by arguing from Nicholas's own ignorance of the (historical or linguistic) facts. Instead, my inquiry finds another focus in the formal aspect of Nicholas's thought. Especially from this perspective, it is important to look at a further historical detail recounted in the *CA*.

An Incident at Constantinople

The prologue of the *CA* relates an interesting incident during Nicholas's visit to Constantinople. Namely, Nicholas heard news about some Moslems who wanted to be instructed to the Gospel.[206] The passage is worth quoting in full:

> a merchant, Balthasar de Luparis,[207] who, seeing that I was concerned about the aforesaid matters, told me the following: that one of the most learned and most eminent (*doctior et maior*) of the Turks, having been secretly instructed at Pera in the Gospel of Saint John, proposed going to the Pope—together with twelve other eminent men—and becoming fully instructed if I would secretly provide them with transportation. That these things were true I confirmed by word of the brothers; and I arranged transportation, just as requested.[208]

Unfortunately, nothing became of the transport and the well-planned conversion. The "eminent Turk," mentioned in the text was carried away by the plague. As if to Nicholas's consolation, later he was

---

205. In this respect, my study is especially indebted to Hamegann's and Hopkins's works.

206. *CA* First Prologue, 3.

207. Luparis was a learned man. At the time of the writing of the *CA* he was stationed as a soldier at Bologna. He and Nicholas had been in contact after the latter's journey to Constantinople. Cf. *CA* First Prologue, 3:10–12.

208. Ibid., 3:1–7.

assured several times that "all their [i.e., of the Turks] learned men loved the Gospel exceedingly and preferred it to their book of law."[209]

No matter what one might think of this incident on thing is clear: Nicholas did take it seriously. The CA testifies to the fact that Nicholas took the related incident as an encouragement for his own interpretation of the Koran. He was convinced that if there really existed learned and eminent Turks who preferred the Gospel to the Koran, then it was not difficult to win them over. After their conversion, perhaps both their "eminence" and "learning" may help to convince the less learned too.

A Temporary Conclusion

As was shown in the foregoing, several different medieval intellectuals busied themselves mainly with exposing what they perceived as the Koran's faults and errors. In comparison to such figures, John of Segovia emerges as someone with an undoubtedly clearer and more realistic perception of the problem. Yet, he was no less critical concerning the Koran and its Prophet. Although he was writing under the spell of the medieval image of the Islam, the influence of this negative image did not prevent him from attempting to understand genuinely the Other. In this respect, his attempt to produce a correct translation of the Koran appears especially pleasing to the modern mind.

Nicholas of Cusa shared many ideas with Segovia and John may have inspired his friend to further reflections on the Islamic problem. On a more theoretical level, however, the question is still open whether any additional steps could be taken towards the religious Other of Islam. If the answer to this is affirmative, then the further question can be posed as to what kind of steps these will be. In this respect, even Segovia's attempt at understanding the Other failed. This failure was partly conditioned by John's desire for leading the Muslims back (*reducere*) to Christianity and partly by his rational self-assurance discussed earlier.

It is understandable that the negative influence of anti-Islamic apologetics can be equally felt in John and in Nicholas—not to mention other medieval thinkers such as John of Torquemada. However, what is important from the perspective of the present study is not so much that Nicholas shared with others the negative image of Islam. Different

---

209. Ibid., 10–12.

approaches can be developed on the basis of a shared set of common medieval principles, as has been seen in relation to Torquemada. The task is to examine Nicholas's own efforts and to evaluate them in contrast to these contemporaries. The question whether his project could serve as a more genuine attempt at understanding the Other can be answered only after this examination.

Before doing so, however, it will be beneficiary to take closer look at some other medieval approaches to Islam. The fact that this other task is not superfluous can be seen from the following. The list of sources in the *CA* had shown that besides John of Segovia and John of Torquemada, Nicholas of Cusa was also familiar with other medieval thinkers' works on Islam. From a theoretical point of view, it is advisable that at least Thomas of Aquinas and his approach to Islam be considered in more detail. The theoretical importance of Thomas cannot be underestimated and it will be interesting to see what a thinker of his prominence would say on Islam. Nicholas of Cusa himself did not only read Thomas's short treatise concerning the Moslems' objections against Christian faith, but he was also familiar with Thomas's *Summa contra Gentiles* and *Summa Theologiae*, both of which help to situate Thomas's anti-Islamic polemic in the latter's overall approach to theology. Further, there is at least one other name on the list of medieval thinkers that cannot be excluded, due to the fact that he was important to Nicholas, and, in particular, to his approach to other religions. Namely, the extravagant Catalan thinker Ramón Lull heavily influenced Nicholas and the former's entire work was intrinsically related to the Islamic question. Both the respective intellectual achievements of Thomas and Ramón *and* Nicholas's knowledge of them suggest that an examination of these two highly original medieval thinkers can contribute to a better understanding of Nicholas's own approach to Islam. This is true even if one is not primarily concerned with a *Quellenkritik*. Accordingly, the next chapter will examine Thomas's and Ramón's respective approaches towards Islam.

2

Two Medieval Approaches to Islam and Their Limitations

The "Doctor Angelicus" on Islam[1]

> Thomas of Aquinas composed a certain book against the Gentiles who ask for reasons not to give up one belief for the sake of another but only for the sake of understanding.[2]
>
> —Ramón Lull

> I also looked at the Catholic writings of other brothers on this same subject—especially in Saint Thomas's *On the Arguments Supporting Faith written to the Cantor from Antioch*.[3]
>
> —Nicholas of Cusa

---

1. My discussion of Thomas had been published earlier under the title "The doctor angelicus on Islam. Reading Thomas Aquinas's *De Rationibus Fidei*," in the volume edited by Losonczi Péter and Xeravits Géza, *Reflecting Diversity. Historical and Thematical Perspectives in the Jewish and Christian Tradition* (Reihe: Schnittpunkte—Intersections, Bd. 1, LIT Verlag, 2007). Here it is reprinted in a slightly altered form by courtesy of the publisher.

2. Ramón Lull, *Liber de convenientia fidei et intellectus in obiecto*: "Thomas de Aquino fecit unum librum contra gentiles, qui requirunt rationes, quia nolunt dimittere credere pro credere, sed credere pro intelligere" as quoted in Hösle, "Einführung," xxxvii, footnote 83. There, Hösle notes that "[Ramón's] sich-Berufen auf Thomas ist ... äußerst fragwürdig ... allerdings handelt es sich möglicherweise um eine spätere Ergänzung."

3. *CA* First Prologue, 4:5–6: "Vidi et aliorum fratrum de ea materia scripturas Catholicas, maxime sancti Thomae de rationibus fidei ad cantorem Antiochenum."

On Thomas's Life and Setting

It is true beyond any argument that Thomas of Aquinas (1224/1226–1274) was as one of the greatest theologians of the High Middle-Ages. Since he was a member of the Dominican order that had been established with the explicit aim of fighting heretics intellectually, it is no wonder that his studies were motivated by a search for truth and to find means of countering error.[4] Although it is likely that Thomas never saw a heretic during his life, one of his confrere, a Dominican missionary, a certain "Cantor" from Antioch prompted him to compose a work whose most important targets were the Moslems' errors.[5] While Thomas's *Summa contra Gentiles* (*ScG*) was written as a detailed general exposition of Christian wisdom, he used the *Rationibus Fidei* (*RF*) to tackle more specific issues concerning Islam.[6]

In the following I will first make some remarks concerning the *Summa*, before turning to the *RF* itself and offering a relatively close reading of Thomas's shorter treatise. However, my main concern here is not a thoroughgoing analysis or criticism of the *RF*, but rather its methodological dimension, especially the extent to which Thomas's work can be useful to an inter-religious dialogue.

Thomas's Approach to the Truths of Faith in the ScG

The first thing that must be understood in relation with the *ScG* is that this *Summa* is not a manual for missionaries. Apart from one special paragraph, the *ScG* does not address Muhammad and does not discuss

---

4. Cf. Gauthier, *Introduction*, 109–10, 130–42, and Kerr, *After Aquinas*, 4–5.

5. As my colleague, Dr. Hedvig Deák OP kindly informed me there is no certainty either concerning the title or the identity of this man.

6. According to Gauthier Islam receives less than 30 mentioning in Thomas's works. See Gauthier, *Introduction*, 109–10 and 130–42. See also Hagemann, *Christentum contra Islam*, 46–47: "Thomas selbst bekennt sich offen zu seiner unzureichenden Kenntnis, und es gibt keinen Grund anzunehmen, daß er je den Koran gelesen hat, obwohl doch lateinische Übersetzungen vorlagen. . . . Was sich bei Thomas über Muhammad und seine Lehre findet, sind die damals in intellektuellen Kreisen des Westens allenthalben bekannten Überlieferungen." Cf. Gauthier, *Introduction*, 119–22. This lack of interest from Thomas's part is somewhat curious, given the fact that he had access to some written sources and he could even receive information from his own confreres working in the missions.

Islam directly.[7] In the first place, this *Summa* confronts the philosophical wisdom of Greco-Arabic rationality with Thomas's own exposition of Christian wisdom.[8] The structure of the entire work is accordingly determined by the difference between philosophy and theology.[9]

It is true that throughout the *ScG*—as well as in many other works—Thomas made extensive use of Arab thinkers.[10] However, the idea of a philosopher writing originally in Arabic should not necessarily be equated with that of a Moslem believer. It is also true that at least some Dominicans must have regarded Moslems as for the most part philosophically unsophisticated. Historically speaking, this perception was largely justified, for even thinkers such as Avicenna (980–1037) or Averroes (1126–1198) exerted only a limited influence in their own countries.[11] In a work so intrinsically concerned with the thoughts of Arabic philosophers as the *ScG*, Thomas could not consequently convert or refute the Moslems.

What he intended to do was rather to provide a philosophical justification of his own Aristotelian position.[12] Thus, the infidels' errors play only a subsidiary role within the *ScG*. They form as it were the necessary background against which Christian truth can appear in a clearer light. Besides Thomas's loyalty to the Christian faith, this approach also reveals his own acceptance of the Aristotelian conception of wisdom.

---

7. This is not to deny that the *ScG* could be related to the situation of the Dominican missions of the thirteenth century and to an intellectual encounter with the Islamic world. See Hoping, *Weisheit*, 62–63. Gauthier, *Introduction*, 127, emphasises that although the passage on Muhammad and Islam in the *ScG* is a good summary of traditional Christian apologetics, it is very short: only 204 words out of a total of 325.820 for the entire work. Gauthier also notes that Muhammad's followers get some mention there. Cf. *ScG* I, 2, 3; III, 65, 10; III, 69, 11, and III, chapter deleted after 112.

8. Hoping, *Weisheit*, 70. Cf. also Goddard, *History of Christian-Muslim Relations*, 102–3: "Aquinas ... demonstrates both the extent and the limitations of Islamic influence on European Christian thinking in the thirteenth century."

9. Hoping, *Weisheit*, 70: "der Aufbau der ScG [ist] durch die Differenz zwischen Philosophie und Theologie bestimmt."

10. Just to name the most familiar ones, Thomas cites Avicenna 21 times, Averroes 26 times, and Algazel 2 times. See Gauthier, *Introduction*, 128.

11. Ibid. Gauthier recalls the Dominican William of Tripoli's testimony according to which Moslems were generally simple people not needing philosophical arguments.

12. Gauthier, *Introduction*, 130.

According to this Aristotelian idea, the task (*officium*) of the wise man (*sapiens*) included both meditation on truth and refutation of error.[13]

There existed many different kinds of error in need of refutation. Thomas recognized two basic difficulties in connection with them. First, there was a lack of information concerning the erroneous doctrines and their teachers. Secondly, and more specifically, some of those in error such as for example the Moslems themselves, did not accept Biblical authority. As a consequence, in discussions with these people, Christians must recur to the authority of human reason. Thomas is, however, conscious in his theological discussions of the weakness of human reason.[14] Given this weakness, the question can be raised in what way it is possible for human beings to know God. This leads to the problem of establishing a theological epistemology.

On Thomas's Theological Epistemology

The phrase "theological epistemology" here denotes only the theologian's own account of human knowledge about the Divine. The attribution to Thomas of an independent, merely philosophical epistemology would amount to a misinterpretation of his thought.[15] Within Thomas's Aristotelian framework, knowing something means knowing what that thing is (*quod quid est*), since real knowledge of a being concerns knowing the definition of its particular substance or essence. Viewed from an Aristotelian perspective, proper knowledge of a thing necessarily presupposes its definition and this definition must be tested against the accidental qualities of the thing. Just as the essence is an ontological principle for every kind of being, the definition of the essence functions as an epistemological principle (*principium*) for knowledge of anything whatsoever.

In this Aristotelian epistemology, every kind of human knowledge necessarily starts with and refers back to sensible reality.[16] Thomas him-

---

13. See *ScG* I, c.1 and c. 2.

14. *ScG* I, c. 2: "Quae [i.e., ratio naturalis] tamen in rebus divinis deficiens est."

15. On the question of philosophical epistemology and Thomas, see Kerr, *After Aquinas*, 17–34.

16. *ScG* I, c. 3: "cum intellectus nostri, secundum modum praesentis vitae, cognitio a sensu incipiat et ideo ea quae in sensu non cadunt, non possunt humano intellectus capi, nisi quatenus ex sensibilibus eorum cognitio colligitur." Cf. *ST* I, q. 1 a. 9 in the responsum: "omnis nostra cognitio a sensu initium habet."

self thinks that in some cases of this sensible reality human reason is deficient, but nevertheless that it is still possible by using human reason to elicit from sensible beings some kind of knowledge concerning God. However, the knowledge attained in this way concerns the Divine Substance Itself only in a weak sense. Thomas never thought that anyone could produce a full-fledged definition of God's substance. What can be known of God is only that He exists (*quia est*) but not what He is (*quid sit*). However, this does not entail that human reason cannot know anything at all about God.

The special status of human knowledge concerning God can be better understood from Thomas's discussion of the question whether acceptance of those things that surpass human reason can be expected from humans.[17] This is so because, even if one agrees—as Thomas does—that otherwise rationally attainable truths must be accepted by humans, he would not be inconsistent in claming that no one should be expected to believe more than what is accessible to (his) reason. It seems that, since even otherwise reasonable things can be actually understood only after the long period of time and labor required by reflection, Divine Wisdom ought to respect these limitations of human thought. This seems to entail that acceptance of things beyond their reason cannot be expected from humans.[18]

Thomas answers this objection by pointing out that both desire and zeal (*desiderium et studium*) presuppose a kind of foreknowledge (*praecognitio*). Not surprisingly, Thomas as a medieval thinker is convinced of the existence of a transcendent good, namely God. But, if God transcends all limited earthly goods and ends, then every human person has to "attend with zeal to something that entirely surpasses the state of present life."[19] Christian religion concerns precisely this transcendent reality, since "it specially promises spiritual and eternal goods, and hence many things are proposed in it that surpass human senses."[20]

---

17. See *ScG* I, c. 5.

18. For a comparison between the Divine and the human intellect, see the *RF* 3:19–129.

19. *ScG* I, c. 5: "studio tendere in aliquid quod totum statum praesentis vitae excedit."

20. Ibid., "singulariter bona spiritualia et aeterna promittit: unde et in ea plurima humanum sensum excedentia proponuntur." Chapter 5 of the *ScG* characteristically contrasts this feature of Christianity with the Old Testament, while chapter 6 makes a similar contrast with Islam.

Given this understanding, it is hardly surprising that Thomas refers sympathetically to some (non-Christian) philosophers who took care "that people should be led from the sensible delights to moral integrity and they tried to show that there exist other things preferable to the sensible ones."[21] Attending to this non-sensible and preferable dimension could serve as a preparation for the beatific vision. This learning process can be strongly aided by the revelation of those truths that cannot be properly understood by relying on human reason alone.

All this functions as a preliminary to Thomas's following statement on the knowledge of God: "we only," he says, "come to know God really when we believe that He Himself is beyond everything that which can be thought of God."[22] Against this, it can be objected that this statement is confusing, since it is not clear whether this "more" about which the statement speaks can or cannot ultimately be thought of God. A possible answer to this objection would be to point out that Thomas's statement cannot be understood as a simple judgment with God as its direct object. Notably, it does not say exactly what (*quid*) one should think about God. It only speaks of what cannot be thought of Him. Neither does this statement make explicit that which cannot be thought about God. Moreover, if taken in isolation, the statement would even be self-contradictory. This can be demonstrated by the following argument:

1. I know that God is more than what I can think of Him.
2. But, I am able to think that He is more than I can think of Him.
3. Thus, I do think that He is more than I can think of Him.
4. In this way, I seem to think "more" that I cannot think of Him.

The distinction between first and second order of predication can be of some help in resolving this apparent paradox. The first order of predication refers to the set of statements that directly concern objects. Such, for instance, is the classical proposition "Socrates is white" with Socrates and his "whiteness" as its objects. The second order, on the other hand, refers to another set of propositions that are predicated about the members of the first set. The proposition "The sentence 'Socrates is white.'

---

21. *ScG* I, c. 5: "ad hoc ut homines a sensibilium delectationibus ad honestatem perducerent, ostendere esse alia bona his sensibilibus potiora."

22. "Tunc enim solum Deum vere cognoscimus quando ipsum esse credimus supra omne id quod de Deo cogitari ab homine possibile est," ibid.

belongs to the first order." itself belongs to the second order. Its direct object is the simple proposition "Socrates is white."[23]

Consequently, in the sentence "I think$_2$ that God is more than I can think$_1$ of Him." the verb "think" has two different meanings. (These two meanings are indexed here as think$_1$ and think$_2$ respectively.) These two instances of the verb "think" belong to different orders of predication. While the direct object of think$_1$ is God, think$_2$ does not concern God directly. Its immediate object is what I or Thomas can think—i.e, think$_1$—of God. While think$_1$ belongs to the object-language, think$_2$ pertains to a *meta*-level where judgments can be formed about judgments—in this case about judgment(s) concerning God. An important consequence is that understood as a judgment of the second order, Thomas's statement does not entail both thinking and not thinking the same "thing" of God in an unqualified sense.[24] As was noted earlier, Thomas's statement does even not specify the content of "what can be thought of God" any further but leaves it open. This is not problematic in itself, the point being that God cannot be thought of as a simple object of first order predication.

This short analysis—Thomistic in content, although not in form—sheds light on an important dimension of Thomas's thought: namely that he realized that no judgment concerning God—nothing that can be thought of Him—can be seen as the final result of human thinking. Everything that can be thought or known of God can and must be transcended. This helps us grasp that one fundamental reason why Divine Revelation proposes things otherwise rationally unattainable. As Thomas himself puts it, in this way "the human opinion is strengthened that God is something that surpasses anything that can be thought of Him."[25] Thereby, God's transcendence is affirmed and saved.

---

23. Hence, a second order judgement cannot say anything directly about the object of a first order judgement. E.g., calling the sentence "Socrates is white." a first order judgement is itself a second order judgement. Being such, it does not tell whether Socrates is actually white or not, or whether he (or whiteness) exists at all. The second order judgement assumes only that Socrates—along with whiteness—is a possible object of (first order) predication.

24. The deception involved in the argument resides in the proposition "I seem to think the very "more" that I cannot think of Him." Both this sentence and the question "Can I or can I not think of this 'more'?" are based on a confusion of the two different meanings of the verb "think": namely of the first oder (think$_1$) and second order (think$_2$) judgements.

25. *ScG* I, c. 5: "firmatur in homine opinio quod Deus sit aliquid supra id quod cogitare potest."

This observation leads to a point made by Thomas himself. In his opinion, another advantage of revealing things unattainable through reason was that in this way the presumption (*praesumptio*) of human rationality can be held in proper control. Indeed, in Thomas's eyes, presumption was "the mother of errors" (*mater erroris*). He noted that

> there are certain people who presume so much concerning their own intellectual capacity that they think themselves to be able to measure the whole nature of things: i.e. they think completely true what seems to be true to them and false what does not seem to them so.[26]

In contrast to these people, Thomas intends to advance only a modest inquiry into truth with his *ScG*.[27]

Reason and Faith

After discussing the limitations of human rationality, it is appropriate to turn to a basic distinction Thomas made with respect to the truths of Catholic faith. This distinction is important, because it is fundamentally connected to and determined by the relation between reason and faith.[28]

Thomas simultaneously affirmed and limited reason's capacity for attaining knowledge of God. He insisted that while some truths, such as the oneness of God, can be reached through the light of natural reasoning, some others, such as, for instance, the doctrine of the Trinity, surpass human reason. This distinction between the two kinds of theological truth determines the whole structure of the *ScG*.[29]

---

26. Ibid., "Sunt enim quidam tantum de suo ingenio praesumentes ut totam rerum naturam se reputent suo intellectu posse metiri, aestimantes scilicet totum esse verum quod eis videtur, et falsum quod eis non videtur."

27. Cf. his warning at the end of chapter 9. Note also the difference between "capere" and "fide tenere" in the last section of chapter 5.

28. *ScG* I, c. 3.

29. For Thomas the existence of intelligible divine things that "humanae rationis penitus excedunt ingenium" is evident. However, this entails no "double truth" in God. To quote Thomas again: "Dico autem duplicem veritatem divinorum, non ex parte ipsius Dei, qui est una et simplex veritas; sed ex parte cognotionis nostrae, quae ad divina cognoscenda diversimode se habet." See *ScG* I, c. 3 and c. 9 respectively.

Hagemann, *Christentum contra Islam*, 54 gives an interesting comment that can be related to this point: "Wie für Thomas ist auch für den Islam die Wahrheit unteilbar, eine doppelte Wahrheit kann es nicht geben."

Truths belonging to the first class can be investigated by reason alone. For them rational demonstrations (*rationes demonstrativae*) are required. Truths belonging to the second class transcend human reason. For this second group, no demonstrative arguments are available. This explains why the antagonist of the Christian faith can only be convinced with respect to the first class. With respect to the second one, the *ScG* gives the explicit warning that "it cannot be our intention that the adversary be convinced with arguments."[30] Accordingly, the wise man is left with the task of solving counter-arguments put forward by the antagonist: i.e., showing that these are either self-contradictory or only probable. In this way, these counter arguments are shown to have no necessary force. Consequently, not only the impossibility of the Christian faith is ruled out by Thomas, but it is also clear that for him the acceptance of this faith in itself is not a logical necessity.[31] It would be possible to give truly convincing "arguments" to the other side only on the basis of the Bible. Thomas is well aware of the fact that this step would necessarily presuppose that the other has already accepted the authority of the Sacred Text by an act of faith.[32] Indeed, Thomas sees faith as a starting point granted by Divine Mercy in order that humans should come to a knowledge of God. Like many Patristic and Medieval authors, Thomas too, supposed that man is capable of (such an act of) faith. This is a strong presupposition. In fact, Thomas even argues that man is more capable of believing than arguing.[33]

It is true that someone agreeing with Thomas's description of the deficiencies of human rationality will not necessarily embrace the Christian faith. But at least he or she will be able to understand that Thomas accepted the starting point of faith (*fides*) quite unconditional-

---

30. *ScG* I, c. 9: "non debet esse ad hoc intentio ut adversarius rationibus convincatur." According to Gauthier "convincere" here does not mean *to persuade*. Convincing someone in the sense of proving his error is one thing, whether afterwards the adversary becomes obstinate or well-disposed is another question. Cf. Gauthier, *Introduction*, 151–5.

31. Cf. the same approach in *ST*, I, q. xxxii. a. 1. There too, Thomas argues that the Trinity cannot be known and proved by natural reason. The response to question xxxii says that "sufficit defendere non esse impossibile quod praedicat fides."

32. Cf. ibid.

33. *ScG* I, c. 4 offers a detailed picture of the difficulties human rationality has to face.

ly.³⁴ It would nevertheless be a mistake to suppose that faith in this sense means for Thomas the mere acceptance of the as yet unverifiable truth claims of some obscure propositions.³⁵ Without denying this dimension of faith, it nevertheless covers more than an *argumentum non apparentium*.³⁶ The fundamental meaning and role of faith is displayed in the act of believing (*actus fidei*) itself, i.e., faith in the sense of personal trust.³⁷ Consequently, even in his theoretical account of faith in theology, Thomas does not lose sight of the relevance of this practical or existential dimension of faith. He recognizes that ultimately only someone sharing this trust of faith, the same commitment to the Christian life, is able to come to a real understanding of some certain dimensions or "contents" of faith.

This explains why Thomas restricts the applicability of arguments pertaining to truths of the second class.³⁸ Ultimately, these latter truths could not be understandable to unbelievers because these truths presuppose precisely that very faith that the unbelievers do yet not have. Thus, Thomas does not deny the existence of some probable arguments (*rationes verisimiles*) pertaining to this second class of truths, but he restricts their function to the training and the consolation of believers. He even warns his readership of the danger that when in a discussion with infidels probable arguments are employed as arguments for the truth of the Christian faith, the unbelievers will imagine that the Christian faith is based on worthless argumentation.

---

34. Ibid.: "oportuit per viam fidei fixam certitudinem et puram veritatem de rebus divinis hominibus exhiberi."

35. See *ScG* I, c. 6 where Thomas takes pains to explain why the Christian faith is not a careless belief because of its acceptance of things beyond reason. There Christian faith is contrasted with Islam and a good summary is given of medieval anti-Moslem apologetics. The upshot of the paragraph is that the Moslems are the really careless ones, lustful, and stupid in their own faith.

36. Cf. Heb 11:1.

37. In *ScG* II, c. 4, the phrase "doctrina fidei Christiana" is synonymous with "fides Christiana" and the theologian as the "fidelis" is contrasted with the "philosophus." Cf. also *ST* I, q. 1 a. 2 where Thomas claims that theology is a science in a special sense: "procedit ex principiis notis lumine superioris scientiae, quae scilicet est scientia Dei et beatorum." On God as a teacher, see *ScG* I, c. 7.

38. *ScG* I, c. 9: "Sunt tamen ad huiusmodi veritatem manifestandam rationes aliquae verisimiles inducendae, ad fidelium quidem exercitium et solacium, non autem ad adversarios convincendos: quia ipsa rationum insufficientia eos magis in suo errore confirmaret, dum aestimarent nos propter tam debiles rationes veritati fidei consentire."

The first chapters of his *ScG* also testify Thomas's sincere conviction that there cannot be any contradiction between Christian faith and human reason.[39] At least in principle any kind of objection against faith can be refuted.[40] Thomas's objective with his *ScG* is precisely to offer such counter-arguments.

The Moslems' Objections and the De Rationibus Fidei

While the *ScG* is a detailed general exposition of Christian wisdom, the *RF* addresses more specific problems. Several manuscripts and early printed editions testify to the attention the *RF* has received in the course of history. Notably, in the 14th century, Demetrios Kynodes, the translator of Thomas's *ScG* and *Summa Theologia*, also rendered the shorter treatise into Greek. Hagemann—himself one of the editors of the 20th century German translation—gives the following overall evaluation of the *RF*:

> The special attention received by the *De Rationibus Fidei* is justified, since this work is a concise summary of the content and also a more precise version of some chapters from the *Summa contra Gentiles*. As such the *De Rationibus Fidei* was promptly received with keen interest—mostly in tandem with the *Summa*. However, it remained always overshadowed by that incomparably more extensive work.[41]

As a consequence of the close association between the two works, the *RF* has been generally neglected by modern scholarship. Hence it is worthwhile examining the *RF* more closely, especially if one realizes that Islam forms the primary focus of this work. Since Thomas's confrere, the Cantor from Antioch was mainly preoccupied with the Moslems' objections to the Catholic faith, these also became Thomas's chief concern in the *RF*.

---

39. See e.g., *ScG* I, c. 7 and also c. 8.

40. Cf. his conlusion ibid.: "Ex quo evidenter colligitur, quaecumque argumenta contra fidei documenta ponantur, haec ex principiis primis naturae inditis per se notis non recte procedere. Unde nec demonstrationis vim habent, sed vel sunt rationes probabiles vel sophisticae. Et sic ad ea solvenda locus relinquitur."

41. Hagemann, *Christentum contra Islam*, 52: "Die besondere Wertschätzung von 'De Rationibus fidei' liegt in ihrer Eigenart als einer knappen inhaltlichen Zusammenfassung oder auch Präzisierung gewisser Kapitel der „Summa contra Gentiles" begründet. Als solches hat sie, zumeist in Verbindung mit ihr, rasch ein reges Interesse gefunden. Freilich stand sie dabei immer im Schatten des unvergleichlich größeren Werkes."

Title and Content

The title promises "reasons [in support] of faith." The exact nature of these reasons or arguments can be best understood in the light of Thomas's theological project as it is laid out in his *ScG*. There as in the *RF*, Thomas is not looking for necessary arguments (*rationes necessariae*) in support of faith. His intention is to offer counter-arguments meeting the infidels' objections.[42] Both the text and the structure of the *RF* demonstrates this approach. Only chapter 9 argues from authorities and this chapter is not directly related to Moslem objections.[43]

The rest of the short treatise is organized in the following way:

a. Chapter 1 explains the author's intentions;

b. Chapter 2 lays out the method to be followed in disputation;

c. Chapters 3 and 4 discuss the problems of the Trinity;

d. Chapters 5, 6, and 7 treat the mystery of Incarnation and Christ's death on the Cross;

e. Chapter 8 deals with the sacrament of the Eucharist;

f. Chapter 10 treats the problem of predestination.

The Author's Intention and Proposed Methodology

In the *RF* Thomas's main concern was the preservation of the faith of the Church—against the objections of infidels.[44] He understands this faith as essentially Trinitarian and especially linked to the historical person of Jesus Christ.[45] As the Cantor of Antioch reported to Thomas, it was precisely this faith, alongside with the expectations of Christian hope coming from it, that the infidels—among them especially the

---

42. *RF* 2:12-22: "sicut fides nostra necessariis rationibus probari non potest quia humanam mentem excedit, ita improbari necessaria ratione non potest propter sui veritatem.

Ad hoc igitur debet tendere christiani disputatoris intentio in articulis fidei, non ut fidem probet, sed ut fidem defendat ... ut scilicet rationabiliter ostendatur non esse falsum quod fides catholica confitetur."

43. This chapter deals with the question of purgatory.

44. *RF* 1:6-7.

45. *RF* 1:15-17: "Fides autem christiana principaliter consistit in sanctae Trinitatis confessione et specialiter gloriatur in cruce Domini nostri Iesu Christi."

Saracens—opposed and derided.[46] The Cantor was therefore asking for moral and philosophical arguments that would be acceptable to the Saracens. Thomas's answer to this request shows that he had no intention of grounding these arguments (*rationes*) in authoritative Christian texts.[47]

The second chapter offers a concise guide for discussions with unbelievers.[48] There, a twofold strategy is laid down, which recalls the approach followed by Thomas in the *ScG*. Negatively, Thomas states that one should not aim at "proving" faith with necessary arguments. This task is strictly impossible since the truth of Christian faith lies beyond human comprehension.[49] Positively speaking, Thomas thinks that one could prove the reasonableness (*rationabilitas*) of Christian faith by showing that it is not contrary to reason.[50]

As was said earlier, Thomas's project is based on his fundamental conviction that Christian faith is true.[51] Because the Christian faith is fundamentally true, it is impossible to refute it and it is also impossible to find necessary arguments against it.[52] On the other hand, the truth of this faith cannot be proved with necessary arguments either, precisely because it lies beyond human reason.[53] In short, the truth of Christian

46. Ibid., 25–26: "Haec igitur sunt quae, ut asseris, ab infidelibus impugnantur et irridentur." See also ibid., 26–39.

47. See ibid., "petis rationes morales et philosophicas quas Saraceni recipiunt; frustra enim videretur auctoritates inducere contra eos qui auctoritates non recipiunt."

Cf. Hagemann, *Christentum contra Islam*, 46: "So selbstverständlich dieser Hinweis klingen mag, er ist es ganz und gar nicht. Immer wieder ist nämlich in der Geschichte der Auseinandersetzung zwischen Christentum und Islam versucht worden, den Koran biblisch und die Bibel koranisch zu interpretieren. Dieser Weg führt allerdings in eine Sackgasse."

48. See chapter 2 with the title "Qualiter sit disputandum contra infidelium."

49. 2:1–8: "De hoc tamen primo admonere te volo quod in disputationibus contra infideles de articulis fidei, non ad hoc conari debes ut fidem rationibus necessariis probes, hoc enim sublimitatis fidei derogaret cuius veritas non solum humanas mentes sed etiam angelorum excedit; a nobis autem creduntur quasi ab ipso Deo revelata."

50. Ibid., 16–18.20–22: "Ad hoc igitur debet tendere christiani disputatoris intentio in articulis fidei, non ut fidem probet, sed ut fidem defendat ... ut scilicet rationabiliter ostendatur non esse falsum quod fides catholica confitetur."

51. Ibid., 9–10: "quod a summa veritate procedit falsum esse non potest."

52. Ibid., 10–11: "nec aliquid necessaria ratione impugnari valet, quod falsum non est."

53. Ibid., 12–13: "fides nostra necessariis rationibus probari non potest quia humanam mentem excedit."

faith stands in its entirety beyond proof or refutation. This does not entail that this faith is irrational or that some aspects of it cannot be elucidated or even proved by reason.[54] This understanding explains why Thomas aimed in the *RF* at a rational defense of Christianity in a humble and limited sense.[55]

Trinitarian Arguments and Patterns

In relation to one of the central mysteries of the Christian faith, the Trinity, Thomas has to clarify the proper meaning of generation (*generatio*) and procession (*processio*) to Moslems.[56] By showing how one should accept and properly understand Trinitarian terminology, Thomas wants to dissolve the Moslems' misunderstandings. His answer contrasts Moslems and Christians as respectively the "carnal" (*carnales*) and the "wise" (*sapiens*) ones.[57] Thomas also hopes that the wise—even among the Moslems—might be able to follow his argument.[58]

Thomas's arguments in defense of Divine generation are taken from analogy. It is pointed out that the term generation has no univocal meaning even in its non-religious usage.[59] However, at least one fundamental rule governing the use of these different meanings can be found, namely that which says that "in anything whatsoever generation is found according to its proper nature."[60] Since God is not of a carnal nature, divine generation must be understood spiritually or intellectually. More precisely, the exact meaning of divine generation must transcend also the intellectual dimension. Since the human intellect

---

54. Thomas may have understood the status of an existential claim as being a "fact." As such, a fact is strictly speaking always beyond the question of proving or disproving.

55. Hagemann speaks of the critical-negative function of Thomas's theological method "die erkennen läßt, daß jede Theologie vor einer letzten unüberschreitbaren Grenze steht, die weder rationalistisch einholbar ist noch rationalistisch eingeebnet werden kann." See Hagemann, *Christentum contra Islam*, 45.

56. See chapter 3 and 4 in the *RF*.

57. *RF* 3:5–6: "cum enim sint carnales, non possunt nisi ea quae sunt carnis et sanguinis cogitare." See also ibid., 75–78.

58. Ibid., 7: "Quilibet autem sapiens considerare potest."

59. Ibid., 7–14.

60. Ibid., 9–10: "in unaquaque re invenitur generatio secundum proprietatem suae naturae."

falls short (*deficiat*) of the Divine Intellect, when speaking about God, humans have to recur to similitudes found in their intellect.[61]

Such a similitude is offered by the notions of a concept or a word (*mentis conceptus, verbum*). The process of "conceiving" a concept—especially when the intellect understands itself—can serve as a similitude of the Son's generation from the Father. Just as an intellect and its concepts share the same intellectual nature, so the Son and the Father share the same Divine nature. Speaking of the Divine Word as the "Son" is also justified for "son" normally (*secundum humanae locutionis consuetudinem*) denotes something or someone proceeding from another while still bearing a resemblance (*similitudo*) to its origin and subsisting in the same nature with it.[62] The fact that the Divine Intellect, Its Word (*verbum*), and the procession of the Word are analogous to a father, his son, and the process of generation linking them together, justifies the application of the latter terms to God. But in God's case, these terms refer to an immaterial reality and must not be understood in a sensible way.[63]

Thomas also takes pains to spell out this difference more concretely from different perspectives. For example, he points out that in God Intellect equals His Being, while understanding and being are different things in humans. Consequently, a human concept is always necessarily somehow accidental and partial and cannot exhaust human understanding.[64] God's immutability and atemporality can be similarly contrasted with the human intellect's mutability and temporality. Divine Simplicity furthermore entails that only one Divine Word can exist, while human concepts are characteristically multiple. Finally, the Divine Word equals the Divine Intellect, while human concepts necessarily fall short of the possibilities of even merely human understanding.[65]

The procession of the Holy Spirit also requires defense and it is to this that Thomas dedicates his next chapter. There, another similitude

---

61. Ibid., 13–23.

62. Ibid., 69–72: "Hoc autem secundum humanae locutionis consuetudinem filius nominatur quod procedit ab alio in similitudinem eius, subsistens in eadem natura cum ipso."

63. Ibid., 77–78: "immaterialem quidem, non autem carnalem sicut carnales homines suspicantur."

64. Ibid., 34–58.62–68. Cf. 108–11.120–2.

65. Ibid., 79–129.

taken from human psychology is offered. First Thomas states that "all cognition is followed by some appetitive operation."[66] He understands love (*amor*) as the first principle among appetitive operations.[67] Because God's cognition is necessarily perfect, He too must have a "perfect love" (*amor perfecta*) or in other words a kind of procession through something like an appetitive operation.[68] God's having an appetitive operation does not imply any lack within the Divine Substance, but rather means that God's own finality exists in God Himself. Both "*ordo*" and "*motus*" denote this inner dynamic directed from God towards God.[69] Within the medieval framework of thought, it was plausible to call such an inner dynamic or a love a "spirit" (*spiritus*).[70] This Divine Love must be called a Holy Spirit (*Spiritus Sanctus*) because of its purity, since all materiality is absent from God.[71] Just as Divine Understanding equals the Divine Act of Being, so is it with Divine Love.[72] Hence, the Holy Spirit must also subsist within Divine Nature. He, too, is co-eternal, perfect and unique. This characterization justifies referring to the Word and to the Spirit as persons (*personae*).[73]

All this being said, Thomas is still left with the final task of explaining to Moslems the reason why the Christian position does not

66. Ibid., 4:4–5: "omnem cognitionem sequitur aliqua appetiva operatio."

67. Ibid., 6–7: "Inter omnes autem appetitivas operationes invenitur amor esse principium."

68. Ibid., 12–16. In Thomas's view God's perfect cognition entails His perfect love. Cf. ibid., 46–48.

69. Ibid., 23–25. On the problem of God's having an appetite see also *ScG* I. c. 72 and *ST* I, q. 19 a. 1.

70. Cf. *RF* 4:25–30 where Thomas displays the essential ancient-medieval understanding of the soul.

71. *RF* 4:41–45: "In Deo autem amor materialis locum non habet; convenienter igitur amorem ipsius non solum Spiritum, sed Spiritum Sanctum nominamus, ut per hoc quod dicitur Sanctus eius puritas exprimatur."

72. Ibid., 53–57.

73. Ibid., 67–72: "Ex his autem colligere possumus quod, cum omne quod subsistit in natura intelligente apud nos persona dicatur, apud Graecos autem hypostasis, necesse est dicere quod Verbum Dei, quod Dei Filium nominamus, sit quaedam hypostasis seu persona; et idem de Spiritu Sancto." Clearly, in Thomas's Trinitarian understanding, "being subsistent within Divine Nature" is a sufficient condition for both for the Word and the Spirit to be a "person."

Since the Ecumenical Synod of Chalcedon (in the year 415) the Greek term "hypostasis" was equated with "prosopon," i.e., "persona" in Latin. On the terms "persona" and "hypostasis," see e.g., *ST* I, q. 29 a. 1–2.

entail triple-theism. Here, the core of Thomas's argument is that one can only distinguish between the Divine Persons on the basis of their respective relations to one another.[74] For instance, Father and Son are different from each other solely with respect to paternity (*paternitas*) and filiation (*filiatio*).[75] Apart from these relations, there is no difference whatsoever between the Divine Persons—in other words, there is no *essential* difference. Precisely because there is no such difference with respect to the Divine Nature or Essence, the three Divine Persons cannot be thought of as different as, for instance, three distinct human persons can be who share the same human nature or essence while they are still numerically different.[76]

Christological Arguments

Besides the doctrine of the Trinity, another vexing problem was the Moslems' apparent misunderstanding of the mystery of the Crucifixion.[77] In order to demonstrate the proper meaning of Christ's death, Thomas first sets out to discuss the cause (*causa*) and the way (*qualiter*) of Incarnation.[78]

According to Thomas, as the human intellect necessarily works with concepts, in a similar way, the Divine Word is the means by which all of God's operations take place.[79] Consequently, both Creation and Redemption are carried out through the Word.[80] This also follows from the subsequent principle: "anything whatsoever is made and restored through the same means."[81] Since within the created universe rational beings hold the most noble place, their fall (*lapsus*) from the correct exercise of their free will is hence all the more serious (*magis estimandus*)

---

74. Ibid., 81–85.95–99.

75. Ibid., 88–91.

76. Ibid., 99–113. Thomas's argument is strengthened by the fact that numerical difference between humans is introduced by matter.

77. In *RF* 5:2–5, Thomas writes the following: "Ex simili autem mentis caecitate christianam fidem irrident quia confitetur Christum Dei Filium mortuum esse, tanti mysterii profunditatem non intelligentes."

78. Ibid., 5:6–8: "Et ne mors Filii Dei perverse intelligatur, prius aliquid de Filii Dei incarnatione dici oportet," i.e. respectively in chapter 5 and 6.

79. *RF* 5:12–20.

80. On the identity of the Son and the Word see the earlier discussion.

81. *RF* 5:21–22: "Unaquaque autem res per eadem fit et reparatur."

and must be first restored.⁸² Redemption should start with the liberation of the will of these rational creatures.⁸³

In Thomas's opinion, "it pertained to Divine Goodness to restore fallen human nature through His Son."⁸⁴ This work of restoration must be in accordance with the fallen state of human nature. God had to lead humans back to the path of righteousness without coercing their free will. Ultimately, the correct exercising of human will (*rectitudo voluntatis*) is nothing other than to respect the correct order (*debitus ordo*) of love, according to which, humans should love God above all things. Everything else must be subordinated to this love.⁸⁵ This right order of loving also entails a general preference for spiritual over corporeal things.⁸⁶

Thomas argues that the Incarnation was the most effective way to call forth human beings' love toward God. As he himself puts it: "there is nothing else that calls one to love more than when one discovers that he is loved."⁸⁷ However, Thomas is aware of the fact that for many people loving God is very difficult, since in the fallen state of humanity, both human intellect and affection are directed (*depressum*) towards sensible reality.⁸⁸ Fortunately, Incarnation opened up a way towards God even for those people who otherwise could never have loved Him because they lacked both the necessary grace and training for recognizing and loving such a high spiritual reality.⁸⁹ Furthermore, Divine Incarnation

---

82. Ibid., 24–44.

83. The possibility of a conversion of angels is excluded as a consequence of their incorporeal nature. Similarly, humans can only be redeemed while still in the flesh. See ibid., 44–81. On the immutability of spiritual nature see also *RF* 6:1–9.

84. Ibid., 82–84: "Sic igitur ad Dei bonitate pertinuit ut per Filium suum naturam humanam collapsam repararet."

85. Ibid., 93–100. On love as "principalis affectio" see the discussion in the previous chapter of the *RF*.

86. *RF* 5:98–100: "ut etiam in ceteris amandis debitus ordo servatur, ut scilicet spiritualia corporalibus praeferamus."

87. Ibid., 108–9: "nec est aliquid quod ad amandum magis provocet quam quod aliquis se cognoscat amari." Note that the term "provocare" here does not refer to a necessary cause-effect relationship.

88. Ibid., 112–18.

89. In Thomas's opinion "considerare divinam altitudinem et in eam ferri per debitum amoris affectum non est quorumlibet hominum, sed eorum qui per Dei auxilium cum magno studio vel labore a corporalibus ad spiritualia sublevantur." In the next sentence, those people who lack this "studium" and "labor" are referred to as "parvuli."

can also give hope of perfect human beatitude by showing to humans that God valued humanity so much as to have become incarnate for its sake. Finally, Incarnation can also make men realize their dignity. Thereby humans are helped not to subject themselves to any other rational or sensible creature.[90]

After tackling the cause (*causa*) of Incarnation, Thomas also highlights its proper meaning or "*qualiter.*" He insists that Incarnation should not be understood as entailing any change in the immutable Divine nature. When He became incarnate God has not been transformed into man in the way, for instance, that one material element can change into another.[91] Such a change is possible only among corporeal beings and the idea that a spiritual—i.e., non-corporeal—being can be transformed into a corporeal one is nonsensical.[92] Accordingly, the term Incarnation can only refer to some sort of union between the spiritual and corporeal natures.[93] Speaking of a union between the Divine nature and an inferior one is not nonsensical, because by virtue of His infinite power God is able to effect such a union with any kind of inferior nature—be it of a corporeal or of spiritual kind.

Still, the mode of the union between the Divine and human natures in the person of Jesus Christ must be further specified. Here the important point is that the notion of "dwelling" (*inhabitatio*) of the Godhead within the human person must be transcended. Otherwise, Moslems would be right in saying that Christ was only an exceptionally holy man.[94] Thomas, as a medieval Christian, sees in Christ more than a holy man (*sanctus*).[95] He argues that because God's power transcends everything a human intellect can understand, God is able to effect a higher mode of union than that of His dwelling in His Saints.[96] This also

---

Cf. *ScG* c.4.

90. I.e., they can avoid idolatry.

91. *RF* 6:1–6.

92. Ibid., 7–9: "corpora autem sunt quae invicem convertuntur. Spiritualis autem natura in naturam corpoream non convertitur."

93. Ibid., 9–11: "sed ei potest aliqualiter uniri per efficaciam suae virtutis, sicut anima corpori." Ibid., in 11–20, the excellence of God's spiritual nature over against any created spiritual nature is pointed out.

94. See e.g., *Surah* 3:45–59.

95. *RF* 6:78–84.91–96. Thomas argues against the Koranic view according to which Jesus was only an especially holy human person.

96. *RF* 6:85.87–91: "Quia ergo secundum quantitatem ... manifestum est quod, cum

entails that the exact mode of the union between the Divine and the human in Christ should be strictly speaking ineffable and indescribable.[97]

The most convenient example (*exemplum*) of such a union Thomas finds in the union between body and soul in the human person.[98] Notably, Thomas is aware of the ultimate deficiency even of this most convenient example and the similar inadequacy of any other possible illustrations.[99] This awareness shows how Thomas's discussion works within its own self-defined limits: objections are solved and misunderstandings clarified, but the explanations given can in no way plumb the depths of Divine Mystery.

Another important point in Thomas's Christological discussion is that God remains the ultimate subject (*subiectum*) of predication in the union of Incarnation. According to Thomas's own words, in Christ, God—or better the Son—is the ultimate *hypostasis* or *suppositum* of the union.[100] This is not to deny Christ's human nature, but only to say that this nature is possessed (*haberi*) by an ultimate subject. In other words, within the union in Christ, the Second Person of the Trinity is the more important one (*praecipium*).[101] In Aristotelian terminology, one can say that Christ's human nature is related similarly to His Divine nature as an accident is to a substance.[102] Speaking of a *hypostasis* also justifies Thomas in identifying the ultimate *suppositum* of predication in terms

---

efficacia divinae virtutis humano intellectu comprehendi non possit, sublimiori modo potest Deus creaturae uniri quam intellectus humanus capere possit."

97. Ibid., 129–31.
98. Ibid., 109–14.
99. Ibid., 115–24.

100. Ibid., 21–43. The underlying principle is that according to which "unumquodque maxime videtur esse illud quod in eo invenitur esse praecipium; omnia autem alia videntur ei quod est praecipium adhaerere et ab eo quodam modo assumi, in quantum id quod est praecipium aliis utitur secundum suam dispositionem." Both the union of a city state and the natural union of body and soul ("adunitio civilis" and "naturalis unio" respectively) serve as examples of the same principle.

For a definition of *hypostasis* or *suppositum*, see ibid., 165–8: "Id autem quod habet aliquam naturam dicitur esse suppositum vel hypostasis illius naturae sicut quod habet naturam equi dicitur esse hypostasis vel suppositum"; cf. ibid., 226: "habens naturam sit hypostasis."

101. Ibid., 132–66.

102. Ibid., 141–45: "Habet etiam unum subiectum multa accidentia, sicut pomum colorem et odorem, et non e converso; habet etiam homo aliqua exteriora, sicut possessiones vel vestimenta, et non e converso."

of a person (*persona*).¹⁰³ Though even here a note of caution is added: "we speak," he writes, "of a hypostasis or a person of Divine nature insofar as Divine things can be expressed with human words."¹⁰⁴ Nor should the union effected by Incarnation be misunderstood as a composite of Divine and human nature, which would imply in Christ a third, mixed nature. Because of God's perfection, nothing can, properly speaking, be added to Him. Within Thomas's medieval intellectual framework, having become part of a composite would have meant a degradation of God's Being. This possibility is ruled out by the fact that even after the union Christ retains two distinct natures: thus he does not have a mixed nature.¹⁰⁵

On the other hand, Thomas also argues that two distinct persons—namely, a Divine and a human one—do not exist in Christ. Since it has been already shown that, in Christ, the Divine person is the ultimate subject of predication, only the notion of an additional human person must be ruled out. Thomas recognizes that, against the idea that in Christ the human person is related to the Divine person more or less as an accident is to a substance, the objection can be raised that human nature subsists in Christ not as an accident but as a substantial being. But if Christ's human nature exists as a substantial being or *hypostasis*, this seems to entail two *hypostases* in one and the same Christ.¹⁰⁶ Christ's oneness can be nevertheless saved, since His human nature does not necessarily constitute another *hypostasis* or person. For although Christ's humanity constitutes a particular substance, only an independent particular substance would be a *hypostasis*.¹⁰⁷ As was shown earlier, the Divine *hypostasis*—i.e., God's Word—has the principal role in Christ.

---

103. Ibid., 168–70: "et si sit intellectualis natura quae habetur, talis hypostasis dicetur esse persona."

104. Ibid., 178–80: "dicitur etiam hypostasis vel persona divinae naturae, secundum tamen quod divina humanis verbis exprimis possunt."

105. Ibid., 44–62.

106. Ibid., 185–89. *Hypostasis* does not refer to a substance in general but to a particular substance (*substantia particularis*).

107. The counter-example is the hand since it can be viewed as a particular substance (*substantia quaedam particularis*), but it cannot be regarded as a *hypostasis* or person, precisely because it belongs to something more principal, i.e., to (the body of) man (*homo*). Otherwise, there would be as many *hypostases* or persons as many members a human body has. Cf. ibid., 194–99.

All this serves as a preliminary to the clarification of the right mode of predication about Christ.[108] Thomas allows for calling Christ God or Divine both abstractly (*in abstracto*) and concretely (*in concreto*). Christ can be also called man or human but only concretely and not abstractly speaking, since no single being can be simply equated with human nature.[109] Properly speaking, in Christ both Divine and human nature are possessed (*duae naturae habitae*) by the same Divine person. It is the Divine nature properly that possesses the human nature, and not the other way round. Accordingly, anything pertaining to one of Christ's respective natures can be predicated by the ultimate Divine Subject of His being. For instance, though only Christ's human nature was conceived in and born by Mary, nevertheless this conception and birth pertains to the one Christ, i.e., to the Divine Word Himself. Similarly, in virtue of His Divinity, the one Christ can be treated as one with the Father.[110] In this way, the different propositions concerning Christ can be classified respectively as being based either on His human or Divine nature. But one should not forget that these propositions concern the same ultimate subject. It must be remembered that different perspectives (*secundum quid*) are possible concerning the same subject (*de quo*) of predication, while in the Divine Subject of the Word the two sides of this distinction coincide.

Before proceeding to discuss the next chapter of the *RF*, a basic feature of Thomas's Christological and Trinitarian discussion must be identified: namely, that Thomas tries to resolve the Moslems' possible misunderstandings by highlighting the proper meaning and usage of different Trinitarian and Christological terms.[111] Such an elucidation of religious language ideally includes semantics, syntax, and pragmatics in equal measure. What Thomas could offer in his *RF* is understandably only a sketch of a religious grammar of medieval Latin Christianity. Yet, Thomas knew well that no such grammatical explanation or single definition of a meaning could be satisfactory without some conceptual

---

108. Ibid., 217–69.

109. Ibid., 204–16. E.g., even Peter can be only said "quod sit homo in quantum habet humanam naturam." On the other hand, God—and the respective Divine Persons—are, i.e., constitute Divine nature and do not only instantiate it *in concreto*.

110. Ibid., 243–50.

111. It is in the next chapter, i.e., chapter 7 where Thomas will come perhaps the closest to Nicholas of Cusa.

analysis of the theological and religious uses of the terms in question. Naturally enough, such an analysis is necessarily related to the religious practice of the believer. Because Thomas was aware of the relevance of this practical dimension, he tried to formulate what in Wittgensteinian terms can be called grammatical rules or observations about the language game of medieval Latin Christianity.

On Christ's Death and Thomas's Pious Intention

The previous discussion of the Christological question allows Thomas to resolve a basic difficulty concerning Christ's death, namely that when speaking about Christ's death, one must remember that Christ did not suffer death according to His Divine, but only according to His human nature.[112] Another objection against the Cross would be saying that a truly omnipotent God could have saved mankind in another way (*alio modo*). However, this objection in itself is too general since any work of God—for instance—Creation too could be questioned in a similar way.[113] Raising such an objection is thus not sufficient if one does not specify further in what (*quid*) other way Redemption could have possibly occurred.

However, any discussion of Redemption presupposes some faith in Divine Providence. Otherwise "all religion is excluded" and the discussion is meaningless.[114] Indeed, the text of the *RF* clearly shows Thomas's concern for a religious interpretation of Christ's death. He writes the following

> If someone should consider the appropriateness of Christ's passion and death with a pious intention *[pia intentione]*, he will find there such a depth of wisdom, that to the one who reflects on them something more and higher will always occur ...[115]

---

112. *RF* 7:1–10.

113. Ibid., 11–22.

114. Ibid., 25–26: "hac enim credulitate sublata, omnis divinitatis cultus excluditur."

115. *RF* 7:32–35: "Si quis ergo convenientiam passionis et mortis Christi pia intentione consideret, tantam sapientiae profunditatem inveniet ut semper aliqua cogitanti plura and maiora ocurrant ... " Note the employment of phrase "pia intentione." Here it means "with a pious intention"; and it also is clear that Thomas himself wrote chapter 7 with such an intention. For Nicholas's Cusa's own development and application of a whole "pia interpretatio," see his *De Pace Fidei*, and *Cribratio Alkorani* and Hopkins, 1994.

Ultimately, this growing realization of the depths of Divine Wisdom can neutralize the infidels' mockery of the Crucifixion.

Since the aim of Christ's Incarnation was the redemption of humankind, Thomas goes on to identify what he sees as the hard core of human sinfulness in the neglect of spiritual values and the fixation on corporeal goods.[116] Christ's own example suggests to humans a contrary movement. His choice of poor but virtuous men for His Apostles and His shameful death on the Cross must be also seen in the same light.[117] Besides the right conduct of a virtuous life (*conversatio recta*), also a knowledge of the truth (*cognitio veritatis*) is necessary, too, for the salvation of humankind. It was thus necessary that God Himself, in the person of His Incarnate Son should confirm men in the truth. Otherwise, i.e., in the teaching of a mere human person, truth will always be subject to doubt.[118] The meaning of Christ's miracles was to show in Him the working of God Himself.

Faith, in this way, retains a fundamental role in Thomas's discussion. As we have seen, Thomas knows well that his discourse is fundamentally religious, and that it presupposes some kind of *credulitas* in Divine Providence. He is also aware of the double possibility of either faithfully accepting or principally doubting the reports of Christ's miracles. As he himself writes: "those who were present could see His [i.e., Christ's] miracles, while those coming after them could believe them to have been invented."[119] Thomas sees in Christ's weakness a remedy for this *incredulitas*, since this apparent weakness demonstrates that people do not believe (in) Christ because of any kind of human favor or power. Indeed, Thomas sees in every moment of Christ's life—weak and powerless as this life was—a connection of human fragility with Divine power.[120]

For another, rather scornful use of the "pia intentio," see Dante, *De Monarchia*, *Liber Secundus*, XI. 8.

116. *RF* 7:47–50: "peccatum autem hominis consistit praecipue in hoc quod bonis corporalibus inhaerendo spiritualia bona praetermittit."

117. Ibid., 56–58.65–74.

118. Ibid., 81–85: "Veritati autem quae docetur per hominem non omnino firma credulitas adhibetur, quia homo et decipi er decipere potest, sed a solo Deo absque omni dubitatione veritatis cognitio confirmatur."

119. *RF* 7:96–98: "miracula eius praesentes qui aderant videre potuerunt, a posteris autem potuissent credi conficta."

120. Cf. ibid., 111–20. These points can be traced back to the Gospels. See also the next footnote.

It is not difficult today to criticize the scriptural basis of Thomas's argument. Thus, relying on modern scholarship, one can easily see that the biblical passages he referred to are strictly speaking not historical records. They were originally written as testimonies from a religious, i.e., already Christian perspective.[121] It is also a truism that Thomas can hardly be fairly criticized because of his ignorance of modern exegesis. What is more important, however, is Thomas's straightforward confession of his own pious intention (*pia intentio*). This confession actually neutralizes the question as to whether Thomas's references were to 'facts' described from an already religious perspective, or not, precisely because a pious intention implies such a religious perspective.

As was shown earlier, Thomas himself was consciously writing from such a perspective, which he retained throughout the RF. The point Thomas wanted to make concerning this particular, Christian perspective seems to be nothing other than that it is not irrational to view reality from this perspective. Thomas's arguments aim at demonstrating the *reasonableness* (*rationabilitas*) of Christianity. The question whether the literary devices of Scripture help one to accede to this perspective does not in itself constitute any argument for or against the validity of the perspective itself. Furthermore, if we discard Thomas's allusions as the outcome of a primitive Christian reading of an otherwise neutral historical reality, this presupposes a completely a-religious view of reality. It is all too obvious that such a point of view was not available to Thomas, or to most medievals—whether Christian or Moslem. Neither is there much hope that the controversy between Moslems and Christians can be settled on such a "neutral ground." If religious concepts are consciously excluded, it is difficult to see how such a discussion could arrive at, and shed light on, a genuinely religious meaning.

Apart from the miraculous signs as they are recorded in the biblical narratives, Thomas also takes Christ's infirmity and its great fruitfulness into consideration. As a medieval Latin Christian, he believed that almost the entire world had already accepted Christianity, and he saw this (alongside the miracles) as a sufficient sign of God's providence to any reasonable person. Thomas also identifies the same infirmity in Christ's Apostles and in the mission of the Church.[122] In a powerful passage he

---

121. Two examples of a special literary genre indicated would be the angels' song at Christ's birth in Luke 2:13–15, and the resurrection of the dead in Matt 27:52.

122. See RF 7:122–27.130–40.

gives an ideal picture of the mission of the Church.[123] Although medieval Christianity failed at many times and in many respects to realize this apostolic ideal, it was nevertheless sought with genuine sincerity—at least sometimes and in some respects. The fact that Thomas himself was a member of a mendicant order indicates that there is no reason to doubt his own sincerity concerning this ideal.

Returning to the theme of Redemption, Thomas states that "it was necessary for the redemption of mankind that humans should learn not to trust themselves proudly [*superbe*] but rather to trust God."[124] By trusting God, humans should subject themselves freely to Him. As was earlier shown, this subjugation must include the rejection of worldly goods. According to Thomas, Christ could not have taught this to His disciples better than by His own example: i.e., by His own sufferings and death.

One final consideration is added that is based on the concept of justice (*ordo iustitiae*).[125] Justice requires satisfaction for an offence by way of penalty: this satisfaction must be proportionate to the offence. The offence itself is always proportionate to the rank of the offended person. In relation to God, this entails that no mere human being (*purus homo*) is able to give satisfaction to Him because of His infinite dignity. The offence against infinite dignity requires an infinite satisfaction.[126] This is the reason why the Divine Word became incarnate and suffered death in the person of Jesus Christ.[127]

---

123. Ibid., 130–45.

124. Ibid., 146–8: "Hoc autem erat necessarium reparationi humanae, ut homines discerent non de se ipsis superbe confidere sed de Deo."

125. Ibid., 158–228.

126. Ibid., 194–95: "habet . . . peccatum contra legem Dei commissum quodam modo iniuriam infinitam."

127. The discussion is closed with answering two minor objections. On the one hand, it is stated that God allowed for the Fall of man because He gave him free will. On the other, the reader is reminded that Redemption did not cancel the *ordo iustitiae* but transcended it in God's mercy. See ibid., 216–28 and also *RF* 10:104–6. In this connection, one can recall Thomas's fundamental conviction according to which "gratia supponit non destruat naturam." In the *RF* 7:223–24, he writes: "providentiae autem est ordinem rerum non destruere sed salvere."

A Practical Question: The Eucharist

In the next chapter, Thomas discusses some difficulties pertaining to the Eucharist. Since the aim of this sacrament is to engrave the memory of Christ's death into the believers' soul, its discussion is placed conveniently after the previous chapter.

Thomas thinks that the infidels laughed at the Eucharist in vain, since anyone who has received even the slightest instruction concerning this sacrament (*quilibet parum instructus in christiana religione*) would easily perceive their errors.[128] The phrase employed here makes it clear that the "little instruction" concerns the nature of Christian religion itself. Nevertheless, the RF does not disclose the whole doctrine of the Eucharist. The reason for this is that the proper religious meaning of a Christian symbol is only accessible to a practitioner of the Christian religion.[129]

This observation reveals the one-sidedness of Hagmenann's following judgment:

> He [i.e., Thomas in the RF] is carrying on a monologue. Carried away by the thrust of his own theology, he will not arrive at the shore he really wants to reach. The intended translation of Christian faith for Moslems will not work this way. His apology is an *apologia ad intra*, and not an *apologia ad extra*.[130]

Thomas had no intention of completely translating the Christian faith for the infidels. More importantly Thomas was also aware of the ultimate impossibility of such a translation. As was shown earlier—and the example of the Eucharist also testifies to this point—only a Christian

---

128. Cf. RF 8:13–15: "Quam vane autem hoc sacramentum infideles irrideant, quilibet etiam parum intstructus in christiana religione de ea facili potest attendere." Contrast this with the objection of the simple Tartar in Nicholas's *De Pace Fidei* XVI, 54:9–15 and 60:1–4.

129. RF 8:66–68: "Alia vero huius sacramenti mysteria non sunt hic magis discutienda, quia infidelibus secreta fidei pandi non debent." The Biblical inspiration behind this text is evident. (Cf. Matt 7:6.) It displays a traditional, ancient religious attitude, similar to the *disciplina arcana* of primitive Christianity. It is thus understandable that in the RF, the chapter discussing the Eucharist, chapter 6 is the shortest one—not counting the introductory chapters.

130. Hagemann, *Christentum contra Islam*, 54: "Er monologisiert. Von der Strömung seiner eigenen Theologie mitgerissen, kommt er nicht an das Ufer, das er eigentlich erreichen will. Die intendierte Übersetzung des christlichen Glauben für Muslime will so nicht gelingen. Seine Apologie ist eine *apologia ad intra*, nicht eine *apologia ad extra*."

believer, i.e., a practitioner is able to come to a full understanding and appreciation of Christianity. Any rational explanation concerning this belief and this practice remains to some extent opaque as long as one is defined as a non-believer and does not already follows the Christian practice. The objections of such a person can be resolved, and he can be shown that the practice and the belief he questions is not irrational, but no argument can force him to give his assent to this belief and make him to change his own practice.

The *RF* as a whole, and also chapter 8 within it, demonstrates that Thomas basic concern is only to resolve the Moslems' possible objections—in the latter case objections directed against the Eucharist.[131] Thomas sees the Eucharist in terms of the doctrine of transubstantiation. Although the *RF* does not employ the term *transsubstantiatio*, Thomas makes it sufficiently clear that during the rite of the Eucharist the accidents of bread and wine do not change while both substances undergo a substantial transmutation.[132] Apart from the case of the Eucharist, the Aristotelian-medieval universe offers no other instance of such an extraordinary change, but this is no problem for Thomas since he is addressing himself only to believers who themselves confess God's omnipotence.[133] Ultimately it is God's omnipotence, and not the Aristotelian framework, that makes the mystery of the Eucharist possible. In this respect, the doctrine of transubstantiation must be seen as only secondary: it makes the sacrament understandable without explaining away the mystery.[134]

The very objections taken up by Thomas show the kind of errors he is fighting against. Some arguments of the Moslems are motivated by a rationalistic attitude in saying that Christ's body will be used up in consumption sooner or later even if there were a huge quantity of it.[135] Similar is the rejection of Christ's Eucharistic presence based on the ap-

131. Cf. *RF* 8:16–65.

132. See ibid., 8:56–59: "Deus qui est substantiae et accidentis creator potest accidentia sensibilia conservare in esse, subiectis in aliud transmutatis"; cf. ibid., 27–50.

133. *RF* 8:61–65: "Si quis vero Dei omnipotentiam non confitetur, contra talem in praesenti opere disputationem non assumpsimus, sed contra Saracenos et alios qui Dei omnipotentiam confitentur."

134. See ibid., 26–39 and 56–65. Cf. Moyaert, *De mateloosheid van het christendom*, 149 in connection with the Synod of Trente.

135. *RF* 8:16–20. Thus "the shore he wants to reach" is not a translation of Christian faith for Moslems, but only a clarification of some dimensions of Christianity.

parent lack of any outward sign of a transmutation.[136] Other objections are based on a lack of a proper understanding of God's omnipotence.[137] In answering all these objections, Thomas shows himself a traditional theologian in limiting the scope of a discussion concerning a Christian sacrament. Naturally, he had some confidence in the "little instruction" he offered.

A Philosophical Argument

The *RF* closes with a thoroughly philosophical argument concerning the classical question of Divine foreknowledge (*praescientia*) and predestination (*praeordinatio seu praedestinatio*). The problem was whether they would impose any necessity on human actions. In connection with this discussion Thomas reminds his reader of the double task of defending truth and avoiding error.[138]

In relation to Divine foreknowledge, the basic point is God's atemporality. The eternal God cannot be viewed as prior or posterior to any given instance of created time. That is to say: God exists completely outside the temporal order. Consequently, His knowledge cannot be properly grasped in temporal terms.[139] Thomas understands eternity not as a perpetual duration but as an "eternal now," a *"tota simul."*[140] Eternity can be symbolized by an extra-linear point (*punctum extra lineam existens*) that has the same relation to all other, intra-linear points in a similar way as eternity to the single instances (*instans*) of time. Thomas maintains that God knows everything in the same way.[141] Such a strictly

---

136. Ibid., 40–51.

137. In the *RF*, Thomas also answers yet another kind of objection, one not easily classified by the above two-fold distinction. In 52–56, he rejectes the interpretation of the Eucharistic change solely in terms of the fantasy (*phantasia*) of the spectator. The Eucharist cannot be understood as a magician's trick (*praestigium artium magicarum*), because "veritatis sacramentum nulla fictio decet."

138. *RF* 10:6–8: "In qua quaestione sic caute procedendum est ut veritas defendetur et falsitatis error vitetur."

139. *RF* 10:22–24: "Deus est superior temporis decursu et esse suum est aeternum, unde sua cognitio non est temporalis sed aeterna."

140. Ibid., 30–33.

141. Ibid., 58–61: "Sic igitur Deus qui de aeternitatis excelso omnia respicit, semper totum temporis decursum et omnia quae geruntur in tempore praesentialiter intuetur." In this sentence "praesentialiter" is a relapse into temporal language, but line 65 speaks of God as "quasi praesentia inspiciens."

speaking atemporal form of knowledge would not impose any necessity on the objects of His knowledge.[142]

On the other hand, Divine ordinance or providence (*ordinatio qua provide ordinat universa*) is at work in every being according to the special mode of that particular being.[143] As a consequence, some created beings will necessarily accomplish their proper actions such as for instance, the celestial bodies (*corporea caelestia*). Some others will act only in a contingent way and sometimes they get even frustrated in their proper activity, as corruptible bodies do: for instance a (barren) tree or a (sterile) animal. Because the proper mode of human activity is the free and rational exercise of human will, God in His providence respects this characteristic dimension of humanity. Otherwise human rationality would be impeded.[144]

A Temporary Conclusion

After having surveyed Thomas's approach towards Islam one must be impressed by the caution with which his balanced view on a possible Christian-Moslem dialogue was formulated. At the same time, one cannot fail to notice the self-imposed limits of this approach. As the discussion of the previous chapter has shown, it is advisable to contrast such a medieval approach with another one, because in this way both their respective strengths *and* limitations can appear in a clearer light. Therefore, before giving an evaluation of Thomas's enterprise, another medieval thinker, Ramón Lull, and his approach towards Islam will be examined.

• • •

---

142. Ibid., 86–88: "divina scientia contingentibus necessitatem non imponit." See also Thomas's parallel between the course of time and a journey on a way in lines 69–85.

143. Ibid., 93–95: "operatur in omnibus et movetur singula ad suos actus secundum modum uniuscuiusque."

144. Ibid., 95–109. Cf. 7:216–25.

The "Doctor Phantasticus" and Islam

> This Ramón certainly did write many true things, but his method was foreign both to the methods of philosophers and theologians.[145]
>
> —Jean Gerson

> Do not despise Lull before you should know Lull![146]
>
> —A. Olivier

On Ramón's Ideal

Throughout his life, Ramón Lull (Latin Raymundus Lullus, Catalan Llull), the famous Catalan thinker (1232/1233—c.1316) was driven by a single goal: he wanted to bring different peoples of the world together in Christian faith.[147] Perhaps the same goal even became a kind of obsession for him.[148] This latter statement may already indicate that he can be considered in some sense as a radical religious thinker. As he himself put it:

> just as there is only one God, Father, Creator, and Lord of everything that exist, so all peoples could unite and become one people, and that people be on the path to salvation, under one faith and one religion, giving glory and praise to our Lord God.[149]

---

145. "Dixit quidem et scripsit iste Raymundus multa vera; sed modus applicationis sue fuit extraneus a modis tam philosophorum quam theologorum" quoted in Vansteenberghe, "Un traité inconnu," 466.

146. "Lullum, antequam Lullum noscas, ne despicias." A. Olivier in *Raymundi Lulli Opera Medica*, quoted by Bonner in *Selected Works of Ramón Llull. Volume I*, v.

147. For this brief sketch of Ramón's life and activities see the following sources: Colomer, "Raimund Lulls Stellung," Domínguez, "Der Religionsdialog," and Lohr, "Ramon Lull und der Dialog zwischen den Religionen."

A good introduction to Ramón's philosophy is Hösle, "Einfürung." A classical work of reference is Hillgarth, *Ramon Lull*.

My analyis of Ramón's thought also profited from these works. As a primary source I relied on the English translation of *The Book of the Gentile and the Three Wise Men* (*Book of the Gentile* in the following), 91–304, in *Selected Works of Ramón Llull*. That is Bonner's rendering of the original medieval Catalan text of the *Libre del gentil a los tres savis*.

148. E.g., Hösle, "Einfürung," xvii. speaks of "Lulls monomanische Fixiertheit auf sein Ziel" and points out that Ramón was referred too by his own contemporaries as a person with a very strange fancy (*phantasticus*).

149. *Book of the Gentile*, 116, cf. also 301–2.

The divided condition of humanity spurred Ramón to search for an ideal of unity connecting all people. The Catalan phrase "*concordança en una creença*" with its Latin equivalent "*concordantia in una lege*" express well this fundamental ideal.[150] Ramón was convinced that a unified, or rather uniform social-religious project is a condition of possibility for the healing of the existing divisions among peoples. Thus he speaks of "the harm that comes from men not belonging to a single sect, and . . . the good that would come from everyone being beneath one faith and one religion."[151]

Human Reason as a Basis for Inter-Religious Dialogue

Ramón intended to argue with the Moslems for the truth of the basic tenets of Christianity, i.e., for Trinity and Incarnation. These two doctrines served him as a basis for an all-embracing view on reality. However, his own experience of non-Christian cultures taught him a clear lesson:[152] "The unbelievers do not care for the believers' declarations, but only for rational grounds."[153] Since no agreement was possible on the religious authorities of the different traditions of faith, the starting point had to be another. Ramón thought to have found such a universal starting point in the shared principles of human reason (*ratio*).[154]

---

150. Hagemann, *Christentum contra Islam*, 64. See also Colomer, *Nikolaus von Kues*, 117.

151. *Book of the Gentile*, 116.

152. Cf. Domínguez, "Der Religionsdialog," 273–74. On the Dominican preachers' failure see Chazan, "Barcelona Disputation," 77–91.

153. Hagemann, *Christentum contra Islam*, 64–65.

154. In *The Book of the Gentile* on page 170 the representative of Judaism says the following "we and the Christians agree on the text of the Law, but we disagree in interpretation and commentaries, where we reach contrary conclusions. Therefore, we cannot reach agreement based on authorities and must seek necessary arguments by which we can agree. The Saracens agree with us partly over the text, and partly not; this is why they say we have changed the text of the Law, and we that they use a text contrary to ours."

On page 116, one of the wise men says that "since we cannot agree by means of authorities, let us try to come to some agreement by means of demonstrative and necessary reasons."

Therefore, even though Ramón had a good knowledge of Arabic and was also familiar with the Koran, generally, he avoided a direct discussion of the Moslems' Sacred Scripture. Nor did he cite the Bible. This was a conscious decision from his part. Cf. Hagemann, *Christentum contra Islam*, 65 and Domínguez, "Der Religionsdialog," 275–76.

In this respect Ramón's intellectual behavior stood in clear contrast to medieval culture.[155] He recognized that the context of an inter-religious dialogue was necessarily different from medieval European intellectual discourses.[156] What is more, he believed that in such a dialogue, he had the better and more effective arguments, which he called "*rationes necessariae.*"[157] To put it plainly, Ramón saw faith as the dividing and reason as the uniting force between religions. He thought that while people of different religions believe in different so-called revelations, human reason would offer a common basis for an inter-religious dialogue.[158] Ramón thought that reason could express the content of religious truths in a more appropriate way or at least in a form more suited for an inter-religious dialogue than any traditional religious discourse did. It was precisely Ramón's lively interest for and actual knowledge of non-Christian religions that pushed him to this conclusion. This was an extraordinary conclusion for a medieval thinker.[159]

Ramón recognized that even Moslems do believe, yet this fact in itself does not guarantee that what they believe is true. A belief, namely, can be either true or false, while reason is in the truth.[160] One important

---

155. Medieval Christianity regarded the Bible both as the *medium* and the *instrumentum* of all religious and every other kinds of discourse. Consequently, there was no genuine understanding of the world possible for a medieval thinker completely separated from Biblical discourse. Cf. the *Prolegomena*.

156. Domínguez, "Der Religionsdialog," 275–76.

157. Hagemann translates this phrase with "stringente Vernunftgründe." Phrases such as "rationabilissime" and "claris rationibus" already appear in the text of Ramón's first missionary sermon preached at Tunis in 1292. For the text, see Lohr, "Ramón Lull und Nikolaus von Kues," 222–23.

158. He had a more or less Platonist conception of God and of the relationships between Him and the world. On the other hand, the *de facto* priority of reason would soon develop for Ramón into a *de iure* priority.

159. Cf. Hösle, "Einfürung," xxxiv–xxv: "Die simple Einsicht, daß der Glaube allein nicht schon Wahrheit garantiere, ist im Mittelalter gänzlich ungewöhnlich; sie berechtigt wohl dazu, in Lull einen Aufklärer zu sehen."

160. Cf. *Book of the Gentile*, 142: "the soul sometimes believes falsehood, thinking it to be truth. The soul, in itself, has no virtue by which it can believe the truth, since its understanding does not understand by necessary reasons the truth it believes. Now when the soul believes something to be true, there must exist something nobler than the soul which helps it to believe that which, by its own powers, it could not believe, and that thing is God."

consequence of Ramón's view is that all inter-religious dialogue would ultimately fail if the truth of Christianity cannot be proved by reason.[161]

Reason and Faith

Ramón focused in the first place on the *content* of faith, while the other dimension, i.e. the act of faith he largely left out of his consideration. In doing so, he overlooked Aquinas's distinction between two kinds of religious truths. As we have seen, Thomas sharply distinguished between those truths of Christian faith that can be proved rationally and those that can be only known through faith.[162] If there exist some truths that are only accessible to a believer, then the act of faith will have a more positive epistemological function. Notably, for Thomas, both crucial dogmas in a Christian-Moslem dialogue, i.e., Incarnation and Trinity belong to the second class: they can be only known to the practitioner of the Christian religion. In contrast, Ramón was deeply convinced that both of these mysteries can be positively proven by reason.[163] Ultimately, he wanted to transform faith or belief into clear rational understanding. But this circumstance alone would not make him a *rationalist*—at least not with respect to the *content* of faith (*fides quae*).[164] His position is expressed characteristically by the similitude of the oil swimming on the

---

161. Cf. Domínguez, "Der Religionsdialog" 268: "Die Apologetik Ramon Lulls setzt als einziges Kriterium die Vorstellung einer logischen Notwendigkeit des Glaubens voraus."

162. Cf. *ST* I q. 32 a. 1 in the responsum: "impossibile est per rationem naturalem ad cognitionem Trinitatis divinarum personarum pervenire."

163. Hösle, "Einfürung," xxiii calls this conviction "die philosophische Grundlage von Lulls System" and does not conceal the fact that thereby Ramón provoked many times annoyance.

In this respect the Lullian project can be seen as a consequent and extreme realization of the Anselmian project of a *fides quaerens intellectum*. Cf. Comoler, "Raimund Lulls Stellung," 224 and Hösle, "Einfürung," xxii–xiv.

164. Hösle, "Einfürung," xli–xliii tries to draw the limits of what the author calls "Lulls Rationalismus". He suggests that for Ramón, faith works as *a necessary psychological precondition*, as a motivation for understanding. As he points out "um eine logische Voraussetzung kann es sich nach Lulls Selbstverständis schwerlich handeln, da ja sonst die Bekehrung der Ungläubigen mittels »rationes necessariae« nicht möglich wäre." See also ibid., xxx where Isaiah 7:9 is referred too.

top of water: just as the rising of water would only lift the oil upwards, so understanding would only enrich faith.¹⁶⁵

However, one should not forget that the other dimension of faith, namely, the form (*fides qua*) was largely ignored in Ramón's philosophical discussion.¹⁶⁶ But if Thomas's distinction is valid there exist at least some contents of faith that cannot be fully deduced from human understanding, and religious "truths" of this second kind cannot be reduced to mere "contents" of faith. If Thomas is right then the formal dimension of faith does have an epistemological significance that cannot and should not be switched off in rational discourse.¹⁶⁷ Therefore, authorities inevitably will have a theoretical importance. Theology as a science has nothing to fear from accepting Divine Revelation. As Thomas put it: "arguing from authorities is most proper to this discipline [i.e., to theology]."¹⁶⁸ Clearly, Ramón regarded such an authoritative, traditional form of theologizing as deficient and inauthentic.¹⁶⁹

The Genre: Dialogue

The genre of the dialogue offers different advantages.¹⁷⁰ Besides the literary enjoyment it can give more insight into the social context of

165. Cf. Hösle, "Einfürung," xlii.

166. Cf. Domínguez, "Der Religionsdialog," 290.

167. Note that the distinction between *fides qua* and *fides quae* is already an abstraction. Besides, the same point can be made stronger by Thomas's observation that even some non-theological sciences are based on their acceptance of axioms coming from and authorized by other disciplines. Cf. *ST* I q. 1 a. and a. 6 ad 2. In this way, several projects for attaining knowledge do start with an act of acceptance (of authorities), in other words with a *fides qua*. On the importance of personal trust in modern science, see Polanyi.

168. Hösle, "Einfürung," xxxvi: "argumentari ex auctoritate est maxime proprie huius doctrinae"; cf. *ST* I q. 1 a. 6. ad 2 and q. 32 a. 1.

169. Hösle, "Einfürung," xxxiii. In this respect Ramón explicitly criticised the theologians of the Sorbonne. Cf. Domínguez, "Der Religionsdialog," 280–81. On page 289, Domínquez writes the following: "[D]er Schlußstein seines [i.e., Lulls] ganzen Denkens ist die Behauptung einer unbedingten logischen Notwendigkeit der Glaubenssätze."

170. From the approximately 300 works produced by Ramón about 40 could be either classified as dialogues or display dialogical features. Cf. Domínguez, "Der Religionsdialog," 263. For the brief characterisation of the dialogue form as a genre, I rely on Jacobi, "Einleitung,". Domínguez, "Der Religionsdialog" discusses Ramón's use of the dialogue.

I will treat Nicholas of Cusa's dialogues in the next two chapters.

the discussed question. It can give the extra philosophical advantage that is not to be understood in the form of a different philosophical content or a different sort of philosophy, but rather as a certain way or form of thought.[171] The dialogue can be contrasted with the other kinds of philosophical and theological literature of the Middle-Ages: the dialogue is often offered as an "oral" form, an imitation of a real exchange even if it was originally conceived as literary work meant to a readership. In other words, the dialogue can be characterized as a text that makes its reader forget that what he or she is reading is a text.[172] This somewhat paradox feature makes possible that a dialogue can as it were re-inform the praxis of discussion and re-conduct its reader to actual reality. For instance, leaving the ending open, can suggest that no philosophical inquiry can reach a definite end. In this way—precisely through its form—the dialogue teaches a formal lesson by giving hope for a continuing real dialogue. This characterization of the dialogue is directly applicable to Ramón's dialogical works, especially to his *Llibre del gentil a los tres savis*. It is to this work that I will turn now.

The Book of the Gentile and the Three Wise Men

Interestingly, Ramón himself did not write extensively on Islam. *The Book of the Gentile and the Three Wise Men* (*Book of the Gentile* in the following) can be seen as his most extensive discussion of this subject.[173] Furthermore, this work offers an easier access to the system of Lullian thought with a clearer focus on Islam than his more theoretical treatises.[174] Indeed, such a reading is encouraged by the very text of the *Book of the Gentile*.[175] Precisely because in the *Book of the Gentile* Ramón

---

171. On page 19, Jacobi speaks of "eine ganz bestimmte Denkweise."

172. Ibid., 21. Jacobi qualifies this statement adding that not all medieval dialogues can be thus characterised.

173. Bonner in note 1 (*Book of the Gentile*, 258) writes the following: "Curiously enough, Islam is not a subject Llull discusses much; aside from isolated remarks in various works, the only other extended discussion is that in *Doctrina pueril*, ch. 71."

174. In fact, Ramón intended this book as a popularization or simplification of his Art. Cf. *Book of the Gentile*, 114, note 14.

175. The Prologue, for instance, expresses Ramón's desire for finding "a new method and new reasons" and admits that "this demonstrative science needs obscure words unfamiliar to laymen." Bonner time and again points out the important correspondences between the *Book of the Gentile* and the Lullian Art.

was writing to laymen, he wanted to put things "briefly and in plain words."[176] According to Ramón's story a Gentile is looking desperately for truth and meets up with three "wise men," i.e., a Jew, a Christian, and a Moslem respectively. The books contain their discussions that are aided by Lady Intelligence and some trees representing the Lullian Art.[177] The point of the discussion is what religion the Gentile should choose out of the three.

In the course of the *Book of the Gentile*, Ramón was trying hard to deduce answers to the theological problems of the three monotheistic religions from his conceptual scheme or as he called it his Art. He was looking for what he called "necessary reasons."[178] His arguments tend have the following logical form:

$p_1 : q$ or $\sim q$

$p_2 : \sim (\sim q)$

$c : q.$

In other words a question is represented as having two alternative answers.[179] Since "contradictions cannot exist," Ramón tried to exclude one alternative $(\sim q)$.[180] Thereby, he thought to have demonstrated the logical necessity of the other one (q). The Aristotelian principle of (non)-contradiction justifies this procedure.

However, the requirement according to which q and its negation cannot be both false seems to presuppose an existential claim.[181] This

---

176. *Book of the Gentile*, 110. Within the same passage, his "new method and new reasons" are referred to as "this science and this Art." At the end of the book, on page 304, Ramón wrote the following: "[The *Book of the Gentile and the Three Wise Men*] is ... newly edited and extracted from the *Brief Art of Finding Truth*, which most thoroughly investigates the cause and the principles of all things in all fields of thought, in the liberal arts as well as in the mechanical arts ..." In his note 8, ibid., Bonner identifies the *Brief Art of Finding Truth* with the *Ars compendiosa inveniendi veritatem*.

177. It can be argued that by using such literary means Ramón wanted to communicate his message also in an indirect way.

178. On necessary reasons, cf. *Book of the Gentile*, 110, 116, 134, 142, and 170.

179. This representation of the logical form of Ramón's arguments is somewhat imprecise as it leaves open the interpretation of the 'or' in the first premise. The fact that "contradictions cannot exist" means that the same proposition (with all its terms taken in the same sense) cannot be both true and false at the same time. This entails that it is irrelevant what truth-value the logical function would prescribe for such a case.

180. Cf. *Book of the Gentile*, 163.

181. Without such an existential claim, namely, propositions would be rather empty

entails that Ramón's arguments would fail to have necessary force if the existential presupposition tacitly made by them can be seriously doubted. Additionally, this logical analysis of Ramón's "reasons" can detect another weak point of his project. Moreover, this latter weakness will fatally flaw his arguments—even independently from the question of an existential claim.

The problem can be best illustrated by generalizing the logical form given so far:

$p_1 : r_1$ or r_2 or ... r_n

$p_2 : \sim r_2$

...

$p_n : \sim r_n$

$c : r_1$.

When generalized, the first premise (p_1) is understood as an exhausting list of all possibilities (r_1 or r_2 or ... r_n). It is not difficult to see that if and only if all the following premises (from p_2 to p_n) succeed in excluding the truth of all other possibilities (from r_2 up to r_n), can the conclusion (r_1) be reached. If the first premise poses only a false alternative of, for instance two possibilities (r_1 or r_2) without excluding all other possibilities, then the conclusion stating either of the alternatives (r_1 or r_2) will not follow.

Ramón wanted to offer a neutral conceptual scheme acceptable not only to Jews, Christians, and Moslems but also to anyone with an open mind and of a sound philosophical education. The narrative framework of his dialogue also suggests that the principles and concepts of the Lullian Art should be acceptable to the human intellect.[182] However, the acceptance of Ramón's conceptual scheme also seems to imply the acceptance of its completeness. Namely, if Ramón's system cannot account for reality in its entirety, then it can be hardly expected to contribute to the solution of all questions.[183] Therefore the Lullian Art should be also

---

phrases than strictly speaking false. E.g., to the propositions "The present king of France is bald." and "The present king of France is not bald." no truth-value can be assigned.

182. The wise make a request to Lady Intelligence "to explain to them the nature and properties of the five trees, and what was the meaning of the writing on each of their flowers"; and she grants this request. *Book of the Gentile*, 113–14.

183. Ramón explicitly attributed such a universal efficacy to his Art extending to "all fields of thought." Cf. ibid., 304 n. 8.

able to handle every dimension of the respective religious faiths. If the Art is incapable of translating important features of a specific question of religious controversy into its own categories, then it is difficult to see how it can settle the same religious controversy. Notably, one important goal of the whole system was the correction of the Moslems' erroneous religious beliefs.[184]

Islam

In the fourth book of the dialogue, the Moslem proceeds in a similar manner as both the Jew and the Christian have done before him.[185] First, he lists his faith in the twelve following articles:

1. One God;
2. Creator;
3. that Muhammad is the Prophet;
4. the Koran as Divine Law;
5. the Questioning of the dead in the tomb;
6. that all things will die;
7. Resurrection;
8. Muhammad will be heeded on the Day of Judgment;
9. that all men will have to account for their deeds;[186]
10. that their merits and fault will be weighed,
11. that they will pass along the path;
12. and finally the existence of Paradise and Hell.

---

184. Ramón made that clear: "[The] conditions govern the flowers, which are principles and doctrine to rectify the error of those who have no knowledge of God nor of his works, nor even of their own beliefs." Ibid., 115.

185. For the fourth book, see *Book of the Gentile*, 258–304. When referring to the third of the wise men, Ramón employs the term Saracen meaning "Moslem." Cf. ibid., 113, 148, and 258–93.

186. Ramón's list does not include the 9th article, which he nevertheless discusses in the fourth book. Cf. *Book of the Gentile*, 258–59 and 279–82.

Out of these, Christians would agree with 5, while Jews only with 4. Naturally, none of them would accept Muhammad as a prophet, the Koran as divine law, together with 4 further articles of Moslem faith.

What is interesting is in the fourth book is not so much the arguments themselves but the disagreements arising between the participants and I will come back to this topic immediately. The other feature deserving a closer look can be found in the Moslem's references to positive dimensions of religious faith. These latter references are numerous. For instance, the 3rd, 4th, 5th, 6th, 7th, 8th, 9th, 11th, 12th articles start with a declaration of Moslem belief. Such statements concerning positive dimensions of religiosity are in themselves no argumentative mistakes, but the recurring reference to specific aspect of Islam is. The problem of the Lullian Art is that such declarations of Moslem faith necessarily include an existential claim by virtue of their referring to specific facts (e.g., different details of Mohammed's life) and there is no way of deducing these positive facts with logical necessity. The existential claim must be accepted by an act of faith.[187] Whenever Ramón's arguments for Christianity include an existential claim that is strictly speaking beyond proving or disproving, the same problem returns. Consequently, if Ramón's arguments take on the same general form that has been analyzed earlier, then they cannot have necessary logical force—precisely because of the included existential claim. This is not to say that Ramón wanted to represent the Moslem's arguments as convincing ones. On the other hand the references to positive dimensions of Moslem religiosity are also important because their presence demonstrates the extent to which Ramón was familiar with Islam.

As far as the disagreements between the dialogue partners are concerned, these are also numerous: the Gentile gives retorts to the Moslem on several occasions.[188] Some of these disagreements directly concern the application of the Lullian Art. After one proof for the 8th article, for instance, the Gentile points out that the Moslem did not respect one of the conditions of the tree and he adds "this is impossible; which impossibility proves that you do not understand the conditions of the trees as they should be understood."[189] To this, the Moslem does not have an answer; instead he goes on giving another proof. His apparent

---

187. Cf. the *Prolegomena*.
188. Cf. *Book of the Gentile,* 260–61, 263, 264, 271–72.
189. Ibid., 278.

inability to give a proper answer can be read as a tacit admittance of the truth of the Gentile's criticism that in turn presupposes the efficacy of Lullian Art.

An Example of Pious Interpretation

Before turning to the closing words of the *Book of the Gentile*, a central theme of anti-Islamic Christian apologetics is worth of a brief consideration. This is the Islamic description of heavenly bliss. Its theoretical importance lies in the fact that it is related to Nicholas of Cusa's project of *pia interpretatio*.[190] Ramón Lull did not only know the commonplace sensual images in which his Christian co-religionists' conceived the Moslem Paradise, but more importantly, he was also familiar with different versions of genuine Moslem understandings of the Koranic doctrine.

Already in arguing for the third article of Islam, the wise Moslem in Ramón's dialogue informs the Gentile that: "in Paradise there will be many great blessings" among which "there will be many beds with many beautiful women with whom one will experience agreeable bodily pleasures."[191] The Gentile, understandably, gives a retort to this, by using the "flowers" of Lullian Art. Later, the very last article of the fourth book gives a more detailed discussion about Paradise.[192] The Gentile inquires what Moslems actually believe concerning the celestial glory.[193] The Moslem's answer to this is important, because he distinguishes between two kinds of glory, namely, a spiritual and a physical one. Spiritual glory turns out to be nothing else than a *visio Dei*, while the other sort of glory will consists of pleasures through bodily senses. Of this latter sort the Moslem gives a very detailed description.[194] This description is not only interesting because of its undoubtedly poetic character but more

---

190. On *pia interpretatio*, see chapter four and five of the present study. Cf. also the previous discussion on Thomas.

191. *Book of the Gentile*, 264.

192. Ibid., 288–93.

193. There is no need of proving the existence of Paradise and Hell, since they have been already proved earlier. Cf. *Book of the Gentile*, 182–90 and 288.

194. Ibid., 288: "Spiritual glory is seeing God, and loving and contemplating God." This "vision will be so great a glory that no heart can conceive it nor any mouth describe it."

On physical glory, see, 288–91.

importantly, because it follows the five bodily senses of sight, hearing, smelling, tasting and touching.[195] Understandably, "the beautiful women and maidens" or "virgins" appear in the sections discussing sight and touch. These are the *houris* from the Moslem Paradise.[196] After hearing the Moslem's closing words pointing to even more glories to come in Paradise (glories that the Moslem is unable to describe) the Gentile is wondering about the existence of filth and corruption as a concomitant of bodily pleasure in the Paradise. To his question the Moslem replies that by God's ordinance these things will simply not exist there. Whether or not this is a satisfactory answer, is less interesting than the more serious question concerning the ultimate purpose of human existence. As the Gentile points out to the Moslem, the latter's description of a double heavenly bliss is fundamentally ambiguous and such a Paradise is inconsistent with God's plan for creation. Apparently, the Moslem and the Gentile agree on the fact that "[M]an was created principally to know and love God," in other words, "to have glory in God."[197] This agreement justifies the Gentile's question whether all Moslems believe in this kind of double heavenly bliss. The Moslem's ultimate answer to this question is worth of a long quote:

> It is true that among us there are differing beliefs with respect to the glory of Paradise, for some believe it will be as I said, and this they take from a literal interpretation of the Koran . . . , of the Proverbs of Mohammed, and of the commentators' glosses on the Koran and the Proverbs. But there are among us others who take this glory morally and interpret spiritually, saying that Mohammed was speaking metaphorically to people who were backward and without understanding; and in order to inspire them with a love of God he recounted the above-mentioned glory. And therefore those who believe this say that in Paradise there will be no glory of eating or of lying with women, nor of the other things mentioned above. And these men are natural philosophers and great scholars, yet they are men who in some ways do not follow too well the dictates of our religion, and this

---

195. Few reader would miss the inherent human character of the following sample from page 289: "you will talk with your friends and companions about anything you wish, about everything you did in this world and about the glory you are experiencing; and those with whom you talk will talk to you similarly, and speaking and hearing such words will give a person great pleasure."

196. See, e.g., *Surah* 56:6–27.

197. *Book of the Gentile*, 291.

is why we consider them as heretics, who have arrived at their heresy by studying logic and natural science. And therefore it has been established among us that no man dare teach logic or natural science in public.[198]

Those Moslems thinkers who understood the Paradise in such an intellectualistic or spiritual way were apparently Avicenna (980–1037), al-Ghazali (1058–1111), and al-Farabi (d. 950/951).[199] Their appearance at the end of the fourth book both does not only demonstrate Ramón's Christian preference for heavenly bliss in terms of a *visio Dei* and the difficulty the same spiritual ideal might causes to the Moslems, but it also shows well Ramón's familiarity with actual Moslem beliefs. Indeed, his description of the Moslem Paradise is not only more benevolent, but much more objective than the common medieval folk-fantasies. On the other hand, Ramón's reliable knowledge of Islam means no excuse for those other faults of his project discussed earlier. In spite of the fact that the fourth book offers important information about Moslem belief, the proofs given there are faulty. They are faulty even by Ramón's own standards. This negative judgment can be gathered by the Gentile's various interventions referred to earlier. This failure can be related to the general conclusion of the *Book of the Gentile* to which I will turn now.

The Closing of the Discussion as an Invitation to Dialogue

By the end of the story, the Gentile has understood and retained the wise men's words. The three wise also realize that they have not spoken to "a man without heart or ears."[200] This reference to the "heart" of human understanding suggests that for properly understanding Ramón's discourse something more may be necessary than simply reasoning.[201] Be as it may, the book tells that the Gentile's understanding was illuminated by the path of salvation, his heart began to love, he even starts

---

198. Ibid., 292.
199. Bonner's note 27 ibid.
200. *Book of the Gentile*, 294.
201. Cf. Bonner's note 1 on page 294, note 24 on page 288, and note 2 on page 299.

praying.²⁰² Moreover, he confesses his desire to "spread the word of God's honor among those who do not know God."²⁰³

Interestingly, the text does not specify which of the three faiths the Gentile has embraced. This fact is all the more enigmatic, since the Gentile explicitly speaks of the "true faith" that now enlightens his intelligence.²⁰⁴ Indeed, he does want to make his choice public to the three wise men but they prefer not knowing which religion he will choose. As they say "this is a question we could discuss among ourselves to see, by force of reason and by means of our intellects, which religion it must be that you will choose."²⁰⁵ In this way, the reader of the dialogue is also free to reflect and then to choose his true religion. At this point, the figure of the Gentile disappears from the dialogue, and the three wise men make up their mind in the following way:

> We should debate and see which of us is in truth and which in error. For just as we have one God, one Creator, one Lord, we should also have one faith, one religion, one sect, one manner of loving and honoring God, and we should love and help another, and make it so that between us there be no difference or contrariety of faith or customs, which difference and contrariety cause us to be enemies with one another and to be at war, killing one another and falling captive to one another. And this war, death, and servitude prevent us from giving the praise, reverence, and honor we owe God every day of our life.²⁰⁶

This text shows that the importance of the Gentile's figure lies in his being an ideal interlocutor in a rational discussion. His *de facto* choice is not made explicit. Instead, the text poses the question of his *de iure* choice as a topic for further discussions.²⁰⁷ Ramón himself realized that one difficulty of an inter-religious dialogue is people's religious-social attachment to their faith.²⁰⁸ As an answer to this the *Book of the Gentile*

---

202. *Book of the Gentile*, 294–99.

203. Ibid., 299.

204. Ibid., 295.

205. Ibid., 300–301.

206. Ibid., 301–2.

207. The same text also testifies Ramón's belief in a unified social project and shows that he did not tolerate but would rather banish what Nicholas of Cusa would later call the "difference in rites."

208. *Book of the Gentile*, 302: "people were so rooted in the faith in which they found themselves and in which they were raised by their parents an ancestors, that it was im-

states that truth is rooted in the mind more strongly than falsehood: "[T]herefore, if falsehood were strongly opposed by truth, continually and by many people, then truth will necessarily have to vanquish falsehood." The implication is that falsehood ought to be actively opposed by truth. It is thus not surprising that the three wise agree that they can and actually will discuss further in order to have one religion.²⁰⁹ Thereafter, the author's closing words identifies the *Book of the Gentile* as constituting

> a doctrine and method for enlightening clouded minds and awakening the great who sleep, and for entering into union with and getting to know strangers and friends, by asking what religion they think the Gentile chose in order to find favor with God.²¹⁰

Finally, Ramón poses the following question: "What religion you think the Gentile chose in order to find favor with God?" The reader is thus clearly called upon to do what the wise planned, i.e. to put Ramón's dialogue model into practice.

Yet, the question is only a rhetorical one, just as the Gentile is a rhetorical figure. With the help of these rhetorical means, the dialogue suggests that there can be only one answer to the question: the Gentile ought to choose that religion that he sees as rational, that is to say, true according to the Lullian Art. Thus the reader's own reflection on the Gentile's choice, concerns in fact the question which religion a rational human agent should freely choose.²¹¹ Even though the characteristically Lullian answer to the question is not stated explicitly, the text makes it sufficiently clear. While both the open-ending of the dialogue and the closing words testify Ramón's love for and his recommendation of a rational discussion on the topic of religion, the Catalan thinker truly

---

possible to make them break away by preaching, by disputation, or by any other means man could devise. And this is why, as soon as one starts discussing with them, showing them the error of their ways, they immediately scorn everything one tells them, saying they want to live and die in the faith their parents and ancestors gave them."

209. The text even adds that they remain faithful to this promise. See ibid., 303.

210. Ibid., 304.

211. From a dramatic point of view, this also explains why the three wise are not interested in the actual choice of the Gentile. Cf. Obrador's interpretation as referred too by Bonner in his note 4 on page 301.

believed that "the Christian arguments were more convincing, or that the Jewish and Muslim arguments are more easily refutable."[212]

A Rational or a Religious Dialogue—A False Alternative?

The tension between the rational and the religious aspects of inter-religious dialogue is not only observable in the *Book of the Gentile*, but also characterizes Ramón's entire project. The foregoing analysis has shown his tendency to be overtly neutral and rational in spite of the fact that he was writing from a Christian perspective.[213] For him, all of the different opinions should be considered true at the starting point, while by the end of the discussion only that one will be seen true which is proven to be the truest. Differing opinions are thus possible, but properly speaking, only the *maior veritas* is truth.[214]

Ramón saw Christianity as perfect truth while he thought that Judaism and Islam contained truth mixed with falsity.[215] As soon as the respective contents (*fides quae*) of different religious faiths were concerned, he required rational arguments. Precisely because the respective religious statements of the different faiths are phrased in their own religious parlance, these statements are incompatible with each other.[216] This is the reason why Ramón wanted to develop another form for dialoguing, namely one through which these respective religious statements could be translated into a philosophical discourse. In contrast to his medieval contemporaries, Ramón was aware of the cultural-linguistic barriers between the Moslem and the Christian world.[217] In order to arrive at a genuine inter-religious communication he intended to employ a genuinely new language, i.e., the universal language of reason understandable to everyone. He wanted to employ his Art in search for a better and universal understanding. He sought to replace both the

---

212. See Bonner's note 4, ibid. Cf. also the previous analysis of the Moslem's arguments.

213. Ramón was also deliberately vague both about the fact which of the three wise men proposes the rational discussion in the *Book of the Gentile* and that which one proves the shared beliefs of the three religions. Cf. *Book of the Gentile*, 116–18 etc. and Bonner's note 23 on page 118.

214. Domínguez, "Der Religionsdialog," 269–70 and 288.

215. Ibid., footnote 23.

216. Ibid., 280. Cf. *Book of the Gentile*, 116.

217. Domínguez, "Der Religionsdialog," 270–71.

sapientia of the Sacred Books and the *scientia* of the theologians with his own *ars universalis* or *generalis*. This whole project was based on a fundamental presupposition according to which the contents of the respective religious faiths are translatable to his Art.[218]

In the *Book of the Gentile*, he was able to show the very possibility of a friendly and rational exchange between different religions.[219] Generally speaking, the success of such a rational argumentation can be described as succeeding in convincing the Other.[220] As we have seen, for Ramón, in a dialogue with the religious Other the Christian believer has to be able express the contents of his faith through "*rationes necessariae.*"

For Ramón, human rationality had clearly a serving function, i.e., to serve the practical missionary purpose of converting the Moslems to Christianity.[221] His thought presupposes and implies the existence of a kind of philosophical knowledge standing over against and actually beyond any particular religious discourse.[222] Unfortunately, it is highly questionable whether this philosophical knowledge can have any specifically religious significance.

On the Relation of Theory and Practice

Theory can be seen as a form of monologue, i.e., its author ultimately conversing with his own (literary) creature.[223] In doing so, he is running the risk of becoming violent against the Other. In Ramón's writings, relying on his real but limited acquaintance with Moslems, what he in effect ventured to do was to transform the Other into his own image.[224]

---

218. In the course of the *Book of the Gentile*, each representative of the three monotheistic religions demonstrates that this translation is possible. Cf. Domínguez, "Der Religionsdialog," 282.

219. Cf. ibid., 282–83.

220. No wonder that Ramón's later dialogues tend to have a definite end. Domínguez, "Der Religionsdialog," 284.

221. Cf. Hagemann, *Christentum contra Islam*, 65. Hagemann calls it "die . . . nicht mehr überbietbare Widerlegung nichtchristlicher Glaubensaussagen." Colomer, "Raimund Lulls Stellung," 235 writes that "Raimund war kein reiner Denker, sondern ein Missionsdenker. Die Theorie ist für ihn der Entwurf einer Praxis."

222. Ibid., 290.

223. For this point, see Colomer, "Raimund Lulls Stellung," especially 231–36.

224. Colomer, "Raimund Lulls Stellung," 233. There, he also writes that "Er [i.e.,

It is small wonder that later a real encounter with the Other revealed the insufficiencies of Ramón's approach and pushed him towards the direction of a more violent dispute.[225] He even started to devise military plans and kept proposing his works to popes and petitioning for a mobilization of Christendom.[226] In relation to these developments in Ramón's approach one can only agree with Colomer's judgment according to which "thereby the opposition between theory and practice . . . only become sharper."[227] Practice in the form of actual dispute and history in the form of military failures proved much more recalcitrant and troubling to Ramón's theory than he would expect them to be. The painful historical experiences hardened his attitude towards Moslems.

On Evaluation

Although the content of Ramón's thought had always retained its intrinsically Christian character, by the strategic exclusion of the dimension of religious commitment (*fides qua*) from his intellectual discourse, he did miss a fundamental point. No matter how necessary or bright any rational argumentation could be, it could only have religious significance if it can be related to positive moments of religiosity, i.e., in relation to particular religious practices, symbols, and commitments. Religious language will necessarily include both strictly non-verbal signs such as symbols *and* practices such as rites etc. Ramón genuinely wanted to transcend the discrepancies between different religious languages with a rational, non-religious discourse. Both the exclusion of important dimensions of religiosity and his bold trust in the possibility of a rational translation of religious language—being two moments of the same movement—have a dangerous potential for religion that could destroy the subject thus treated.

Raimund] dachte den anderen so, daß dieser prinzipiell nicht vermeiden konnte, gedacht zu werden."

225. Up to the year 1285, Ramón Lull had been a pacifist clinging to the only ideal of peaceful missions. Between 1285–1292, he considered a combination of war and missions.

226. The historical reason for this change of mind was the fall of Accon in 1291.

227. Colomer, "Raimund Lulls Stellung," 235.

Ramón's idea of a general science remained under the spell of Aristotelian theory.[228] A similar failure characterized his efforts for a genuine inter-religious dialogue. While Ramón thought that his "best book of the world" would replace divine revelation, in fact, it is likely that a genuine believer would find this very idea repellent and unacceptable—if not sacrilegious.[229] As G. W. Leibniz (1646–1716) put it much later: "The Scholastic theologians had already blamed Ramón Lull for having undertaken to demonstrate the Trinity through Philosophy."[230]

• • •

The "Doctor Christianissimus" on Ramón and Thomas

> ... wherever Saint Thomas made use of arguments in favor of the articles of faith, he instantly dissolved these in order that they could not be taken as self-evident.[231]
> —Jean Gerson

At later times Ramón's thought was regarded as heretical from a Christian perspective. In 1376, it was condemned by Gregory XI.[232] Even after this condemnation was withdrawn, Lullian thought remained suspect for a long time. During the 16th and 17th centuries Ramón's works stood often on the index. This story in itself does not form a convincing argument against his position since accusations of heresy and actual condemnations were not uncommon during the Middle-Ages. Some were even leveled against some of Aquinas's statements whose teaching later became even official doctrine of the Church. In most cases, actual

---

228. I will come back to discuss Ramón's theological epistemology at the end of my third chapter in order to specify this judgment. Cf. Pindl-Büchel, "The Relationship," 87.

229. Cf. Domínguez, "Der Religionsdialog," 279.

230. "[L]es Theologiciens Scholastiques avoient déja blâmé Raymond Lull d'avoir entrepris de demontrer la Trinité par la Philosophie," in the *Discours preliminaire de la conformité de la foy avec la raison* as quoted by Hösle, "Einfürung," lxxx.

231. Cf. Vansteenberghe, "Un traité inconnu," 466: "... sicut sanctus Thomas loquitur ubicumque raciones introducuntur pro fidei articulis, quas inductas statim dissolvit ne putentur esse euidentes."

232. On the other hand, earlier, in September 1311, Ramón attained an official statement of his orthodoxy written by the hand of the chancellor of the Sorbonne. In 1419 pope Martin V even beatified him.

condemnations were as much motivated by extra-philosophical factors, i.e., pastoral and political considerations, as by academic concerns.

A survey of the polemics around Ramón's or Thomas's thought is not my goal here.[233] Although Nicholas of Cusa's mind was deeply steeped in the thought of the Catalan thinker, the Cardinal from Kues himself was apparently not interested in the question of Lullian heresy, neither had he any reason to doubt Aquinas's orthodoxy.[234] In the foregoing, Thomas's and Ramón's respective approaches toward a possible discussion with another religion have been outlined and analyzed. Their basic disagreement can be best perceived in their different attitudes towards religious authorities and necessary reasons. A fundamental difference concerns the relationship of faith and reason. Given this disagreement, the question can be asked how the very same disagreement was seen from a medieval perspective. Therefore, on the remaining pages of this chapter, I will briefly examine a medieval reaction towards Ramón and Thomas in the hope of bringing my reader closer to Nicholas's intellectual sphere. The full relevance of this step will be borne out in the subsequent chapters.

For an answer, I turn to Jean Charlier Gerson (1363–1429), a disciple of Pierre d'Ailly (1350–1420). Gerson was a respected theologian of his time, acting both as a church politician and working as chancellor of the University of Paris (1395–1429).[235] Gerson first confronted Lullism around the year 1390. Before that time, i.e., hundred years earlier, Lullism had been popular at Paris. At the end of the 14th century it was revived; and then the Parisian theological faculty launched an attack against this Lullist revival. As a result, an edict was published forbidding the propagation of Lull's doctrine. There is some evidence that Gerson himself was actively engaged in the preparation of this document.[236]

---

233. For some, especially modern details of the debate on Lullian thought, see Madre, *Die theologische Polemik*, 88–133.

234. Nicholas did have a literary debate with John Wenck, a theologian from the University of Heidelberg on his own *De Docta Ignorantia* in which he was defending Master Eckhart. For the details of their discussion, see *Nicholas of Cusa's Debate with John Wenck*.

235. Gerson was a leading figure of the conciliar movement in Constance. He valued both practical pastoral care and mystical theology more than scholastic theology. Both he and d'Ailly were influenced by William Ockham's nominalism. About 400 works are on Gerson's record. For a short discussion see Decorte, *Eine kurze Geschichte*, 307–9.

236. Cf. Vansteenberghe, "Un traité inconnu," 441–44. The text of the edict is not extant. For further details, see Madre, *Die theologische Polemik*, 81.

Even though some of Lull's writings were accessible at Paris, apparently, Gerson never engaged himself in a detailed and comprehensive analysis of these sources. Besides, the stance of a modern historian cannot be expected from him.[237] However, in the year 1423, Gerson composed a short treatise, *On the doctrine of Ramón Lull.* This text shows that Gerson had at least enough familiarity with Lullian Art and its objective to sincerely dislike both.[238] With respect to Ramón's new terminology, Gerson's judgment was overtly negative. Gerson described this doctrine as "fantastic and useless and vain."[239] Although he admitted that "this Ramón said and wrote many true things," he hurried to add that Ramón's "methodology was foreign both to the method of philosophers and theologians."

Apparently, Gerson was not so much dissatisfied with the content of Ramón's thought. More importantly he was disturbed by its unusual form. Gerson, being a conservative theologian, opposed both Ramón's new terminology and the curious intricacies of his Art. As Gerson put it, he feared a Babylonian confusion of languages in theology. This refusal of accepting Ramón's new language is not too surprising, if one recalls Ramón's own and relatively independent intellectual background. The circumstance that the Catalan thinker was a bit out of touch with the academic culture of his own time exerted a lasting effect on the controversy around his thought during the fifteenth century and would continue to determine many later reactions as well.[240] Even though Ramón had visited Paris three times, he never pursued a standard university career. He remained more or less an independent intellectual.[241]

Besides the question of terminology, however, Gerson had another, more substantial reason for opposing Lullism. In his perception, Ramón's "demonstrations" (*demonstraciones*) were only "statements with some

237. For the following, I rely mainly on Vansteenberghe, "Un traité inconnu."

238. Cf. Vansteenberghe, "Un traité inconnu," 447. For the text of the treatise, see ibid., 465-73. As it can be gathered from page 465, its alternative title may have been *Contra doctrinam Raymundi Lulli* or *Contra Raymundum Lullum*.

239. Vansteenberghe, "Un traité inconnu," 466: "fantastica et inuntilis et vana." If I am not mistaken, in this context "fantastica" can also be translated as "mad" or "crazy." Gerson indeed thought that Lullian doctrine would only disturb and damage the minds of those who busy themselves with it.

240. Cf. Madre, *Die theologische Polemik*, 146.

241. Ramón was in Paris between 1288-1289, in 1298 and finally from November 1309 to September 1311.

persuasive force" (*persuasiones*). Gerson realized that these statements can only make sense if they start with faith (*presupposita fide*) and they cannot positively prove faith, but can only serve as counter-arguments against infidels.[242] In relation to this point, Gerson recalled Thomas's procedure: "wherever Thomas made use of arguments in favor of the articles of faith, he instantly dissolved these in order that they could not be taken self-evident."

As it has been shown, Thomas had indeed a critical approach towards rational arguments in matters of faith. Both in the *ScG* and in the *RF* he tried to show that arguments induced against Catholic faith can be answered, but by distinguishing between two sets of religious truths, he maintained a difference between those articles of faith that are accessible to reason and those that are beyond proving or disproving. The systematic "deconstruction" of arguments of the latter type recalled by Gerson is a procedure also observable in Thomas's *ST*.[243] For instance, the 32nd question of the first part of this work addresses the problem whether the Trinity can be humanly known. Its first article treats the problem whether on the basis of natural human reason alone such knowledge is possible.[244] Thomas's solution sounds already familiar: "it is impossible to come to know God with the help of natural reason."[245] Indeed, as he was wont to do in the whole of the *ST*, after giving the solution to the main question, Thomas went on to dismantle the objections put forward one by one.

When Thomas was discussing the second group of such arguments (*secundo*), he consciously opposed the position of some Christian theologians. For instance, he explicitly referred to Richard of Saint Victor's (d. 1173) "necessary arguments" of whose existence and applicability

---

242. Vansteenberghe, "Un traité inconnu," 466: "putat se demonstraciones adducere, ut puta circa fidei articulos, que non sunt nisi persuasiones a sanctis patribus presupposita fide, quas voluerunt efficaces ad convincendum proteruos et incredulos reputare, neque dari intelligi quod propter huiusmodi raciones persisterent in fide …"

243. Vansteenberghe, "Un traité inconnu," note 1 referes to the *RF*, the *ScG* I, 8–9 and IV, 1, and to the *ST* I, q. 32 a. 1.

244. Concerning Thomas's influence on Gerson, cf. Vansteenberghe, "Un traité inconnu," 454: "Il est facile de reconnaître dans ce passage de saint Thomas d'Aquin, non seulement les idées auxquelles se rallie Gerson, mais jusqu'aux expression dont il sert."

245. See *ST* I, q. 32 a. 1, in the *responsum*: "impossibile est per rationalem naturalem ad cognitionem Trinitatis divinarum Personarum pervenire."

the latter had been convinced.²⁴⁶ Gerson, from his own part, made the same reference to Richard, naming him together with Ramón and Anselm.²⁴⁷ Inspired by Thomas's general approach, particularly by the arguments of the *ST*, Gerson pointed out that although the Trinity is necessary in Itself (*sibi*), this fact does not entail that a human being can arrive at a necessary knowledge of the Trinitarian God. Such a necessary knowledge is only available to God Himself. By starting with the knowledge of creation, i.e., the effects, their cause, the Trinity cannot be proved with necessary reasons. Only if the Christian faith is already presupposed, can one speak of a necessary knowledge about God.²⁴⁸ On this issue, Gerson and Aquinas clearly joined fronts against Ramón's opinion. Ramón, from his own part, seems to have been aware that his project of necessary reasons was opposed by some theologians. On the other hand, in one of his writings, he even referred to Augustine and Thomas as to theologians supporting his project, but his reference to the *ScG* testifies that—supposing he read it—Ramón completely misunderstood the intention of Thomas's work.

In his reaction against Ramón, Gerson basically agreed with the great theologians of the 13th century. This circumstance testifies well Gerson's conservative theological attitude. His reaction towards Lullism can also be related to his general view on theology. According to Gerson's vision, theology should aim at edification; it should bring fruit in and should have *practical* relevance for one's life.²⁴⁹ This practical, mainly pastoral, orientation is attested to in Gerson's whole oeuvre. Moreover, it is not without importance that Gerson's dissatisfaction with Lullist thought was phrased in ethical terms. Because of its novelty, of its non-traditional, self-made character, Gerson perceived this new doctrine as an instance of vain curiosity.²⁵⁰ It is not difficult to recognize in Gerson's

---

246. Cf. Richard of Saint Victor, *De Trinitate*, I, iv: "[C]redo . . . sine dubio ad quorumlibet explanationem quae est esse, non modo probabilia, immo etiam necessaria argumenta non deesse."

247. See Vansteenberghe, "Un traité inconnu," 467.

248. In the third part of his treatise, Gerson discussed the different meanings of necessity in relation to God and creatures. There, he did what a theologian had to do, i.e., defending God's transcendence. Cf. Vansteenberghe, "Un traité inconnu," 465 and 468–72.

249. Cf. Burger, *Aedificatio*, 1–3. On the central importance Gerson attached to the notion of *curiositas*, see ibid., 110–25.

250. In 1402, Gerson delivered two lectures against vain curiosity in matters of

concern for practical relevance and in his perception of Ramón's shortcomings the form of the general practical attitude of medieval knowing outlined in the *Prolegomena*.[251]

Naturally, the practical and the theoretical dimensions should not be simply opposed to each other, but their actual connection must be also highlighted. Practical matters such as pastoral care or church-politics do not *per se* preclude a genuine contribution to a question that is phrased theoretically in the historical records.[252] Indeed, Gerson in his short treatise is displaying all the finesse of a scholastic theologian by making distinctions in defense of his position (or better of the position of the church).[253] Gerson was not denying that Ramón also wrote true things, but he recognized the dangers the Catalan thinker's approach meant for religious faith.

It can be argued that neither thinkers within the contexts of the university nor someone—as Ramón himself—mainly external to that context were able to do justice to all dimensions of the problem of inter-religious dialogue. Thomas had drawn the limits of such a rational dialogue earlier and many were glad to accept these limitations. In spite of all his intellectual pretensions, Ramón lived closer to the context of a real dialogue, but even though he was more familiar with the Islamic problem, this familiarity did not save his project from fatal weaknesses. Earlier, this defect was identified in his attempt to reduce every aspect of religious faith to his own conceptual scheme. He thought that his theory can account for every dimension of the problem of religion, but he failed to notice the consequences of the extreme character of his project. In contrast, both Aquinas's and Gerson's approach towards the Divine Mystery was more modest. It is understandable that from their position Ramón's project could appear only vain and displaying some measure of intellectual pretension (*superbia*).[254]

---

faith. In both lectures he opposed Lullist thought. Cf. Madre, *Die theologische Polemik*, 81 and Burger, *Aedificatio*, 110–25.

251. This is not to say that Gerson's own terminology completely conforms to the *sapiential* evaluative scheme of my *Prolegomena*. Cf. Burger, *Aedificatio*, 110–25 and Oberman, *Contra vanam curiositatem*.

252. Cf. the reflection on the tacit dimension of medieval texts in the *Prolegomena*.

253. Cf. Vansteenberghe, "Un traité inconnu," 463 and 465.

254. Cf. *ScG* I, 7: "ne te inferas in illud secretum, et arcano interminabilis nativitatis non te immergas, summam intelligentiae comprehendere praesumens: sed intellige incomprehensibilia esse."

However, this agreement between Gerson and Aquinas was only partly conditioned by the former's conservative attitude. Gerson was not a Thomist himself and had no special ideological reasons for defending a Thomist position.[255] On the other hand, both of these men, as university professors of theology, had a common concern, as both wanted to defend Christian faith against possible objections and intrusions of something they perceived as a non-religious form of rationality. The medieval university offered the natural context of this defense. Thomas's and Gerson's connections with scholars from other faculties, the institution of organized debate together with their teaching experiences made these theologians sensitive both towards the dangers and limits of a rational debate on matters of faith. Ramón, on the other hand, in spite of the positive and realistic dimensions of his approach toward Islam, lacked such an intellectual sensitivity. Clearly, the Catalan thinker was not able to draw properly the limits of his Christian apologetics. His missionary zeal drove him beyond these limits. Since both Aquinas and Gerson acknowledged the fundamental importance of faith for a proper understanding of (Christian) religion, they were able to respect these limits. In this sense, their criticism of Ramón's project is thus justified.

All this being said the question is still open whether there can be yet another way of communication between different religions. Ramón had been working long to mediate and overcome religious differences through his rational Art. Both Thomas's and Gerson's approaches show the reason why his efforts were ultimately in vain. This suggests that if there exists another way of communicating the Divine Mystery to others, this way cannot be absolutely external to religious faith. Neither is a strictly Christian theological discourse—in the way Thomas or Gerson conceived it—apt for such a purpose.

Gerson saw *superbia* as the ultimate motive behind, and the origin of both vain curiosity and a desire for intellectual novelty and originality (*singularitas*).

255. The secondary literature generally refers to Gerson as a Nominalist and an opponent of the *via antiqua*.

3

On the Manuductive Strategy of Nicholas of Cusa's Mystical Theology[1]

> [I]t is necessary to use guiding illustrations in a transcendent way and to leave behind perceptible things, so that the reader may readily ascend unto simple intellectuality.[2]
>
> I will attempt to lead you by way of experiencing and through a very simple and very common means into most sacred darkness.[3]
>
> —Nicholas of Cusa

Looking for a New Perspective

Several distinguished scholars have studied Nicholas of Cusa's knowledge of and his interest in non-Christian religions, particularly his spe-

---

1. Some material from this chapter was published earlier in another form in my Hungarian article treating Ramón Lull and Nicholas's *De Coniecturis* (*"Who is wise among you?" From the limits of scholastic theology to inter-religious dialogue* in: *Korunk*, Cluj, Romania). I also discussed some images and concepts in the manuductive strategy of *De Visione Dei* in my "The Mirror, the Painter and Infinity," 231–46 in the volume *Spiegel und Porträt. Zur Bedeutung zweier zentraler Bilder im Denken des Nicolas Cusanus*, edited by Inigo Bocken and Harald Schwaetzer at Shaker Publishing, 2005. Both material is included here with the knowledge and by courtesy of their publishers.

2. *DI* I 2, 8:4–7: "Exemplaribus etiam manuductionibus necesse est transcendenter uti linquendo sensibilia, ut ad intellectualitatem simplicem expedite lector ascendat." If not indicated otherwise, English translations of Nicholas's texts are taken from Hopkins, sometimes modified for my purpose.

3. Prologue to the *DVD* 1:8–10: "Conabor autem simplicissimo atque communissimo modo vos experimentaliter in sacratissimam obscuritatem manuducere."

cial attitude towards Islam. Generally, these interpretations try to situate Nicholas more or less within his own historical-intellectual context: he is often seen as a medieval intellectual with remarkable intellectual habits and perhaps with an exceptional charity, yet someone who ultimately fails to acknowledge the Otherness of Islam.[4] For instance, it is pointed out that even in the most sympathetic passages of his *Cribratio Alkorani*, Nicholas perceives the Koran in the light of the Christian, biblical revelation thereby fundamentally misunderstanding the Koran's content, distorting its argument, and violating its religious integrity.[5]

Such a criticism is justified to the extent that it is an honest and genuinely modern approach in its concentration on the data, on what Nicholas or the Koran was actually saying. Since Nicholas knew less of Islam and was biased through his medieval Christian ideology, his attempts at a genuine understanding of the Other inevitably failed. If this is true, even the most fair-minded modern critic cannot help acknowledging both the weakness *and* the strength of Nicholas's enterprise. The best and perhaps most generous approach to Nicholas from such a modern perspective would be to take him as a source of encouragement and inspiration, but the point remains that in inter-religious dialogue one has to go further. After having heard John of Segovia's plea for a serious investigation of the 'facts,' one cannot help but appreciate this kind of criticism.

However, such a critical reading of Nicholas leaves at least two questions without an answer:

1. The first problem concerns the real strength of Nicholas's approach. It is not completely clear in what this strength precisely lies. Was it only a question of a sentimental Christian good-will that ultimately and necessarily failed? Or was it rather intellectual curiosity? Or perhaps should

---

4. For an exception, see, e.g. Hopkins, "The Role of *pia interpretatio*," 39–55. Both in his evaluation of other contemporary approaches to and in his own assessment of Nicholas, Hopkins is very subtle.

5. Cf. Hagemann, *Christentum contra Islam*, 81: "Die inhaltliche Angleichung koranischer Aussagen an christliche Vortsellungen unterschätzt, beziehungsweise verkennt die Eigenständigkeit koranischer Theologie, ihr Selbstverständnis und ihre eigene Sinndeutung." Finally, "kommt im cusansichen Glaubensgespräch mit den Muslimen jene Voraussetzung zu kurz, die für einen Dialog unabdingbar ist . . . , den Koran aus sich heraus zu verstehen, d. h. den genuin koranischen Sinn der Suren zu erfassen, von den polemischen Passagen in der „Sichtung des Korans" einmal ganz abgesehen."

Nicholas be best understood as moving towards modernity's ideals of rational inquiry and ethical engagement? In the final analysis, should his thought be appreciated as an early form of humanism and also criticized as a yet inadequate penchant for religious tolerance? All these questions are intelligible from a contemporary, modern perspective. If one approaches Nicholas from such a perspective, Nicholas's move towards modern ideals proves to be unsatisfactory. The researcher is thus left with the task of explaining the reasons for this failure.

2. The second problem concerns the direction in which Nicholas's approach should be transcended. Even if one grants his overall failure, the question can still be raised concerning what extra efforts are necessary and beneficial for inter-religious dialogue. Is this a question of acquiring more (accurate) data, for instance, through modern biblical exegesis and recent Islamic scholarship? Or is there perhaps something much more important at stake in inter-religious dialogue? Would it not be possible that salvation cannot be expected from the data alone but some extra principles are also necessary? If the answer to this last question is affirmative, then it is still possible that these principles would not be coming exclusively from modern scholarship.

It is not difficult to see how these two problems are connected with each other. To the extent that Nicholas is interpreted as a forerunner of modernity, one is likely to judge his failures according to modern standards. In such an approach, it will be highly unlikely that Nicholas could give adequate answers to problems formulated in the (post-)modern terminology of (in-)tolerance and religious pluralism. On the other hand, if the real strength of Nicholas's approach is not to be found in its preparatory, but rather in its distinctively medieval character, his thought can serve as an adjustment to (post)modern ways of seeing and approaching the same problems.

In order to avoid misunderstanding I emphasize that nothing of what I have written so far would completely discredit either form of rationality. That is to say, my aim is not to take sides in a "modern versus medieval rationality" debate. As I see it, such a step would cause as many problems as it would try to resolve.[6] But I maintain that by avoiding an uncritical surrender to either "side," one is still able to learn both from Nicholas's and from more modern approaches.

---

6. I will return to this problem in the third part of my study.

For understanding Nicholas of Cusa's dialogue with Islam, the dialogue *De Pace Fidei* has formed a natural focal point of research. Many scholars have tried to elicit answers from it to the questions of tolerance and religious pluralism. Such an interpretative work is necessarily conducted from the scholar's own perspective. In principle, every such viewpoint on a given subject is justified, provided it can make one understand more of the subject under investigation. Since it is not clear how modern research would render harmless the two problems pointed out earlier, I am justified in looking for another perspective. In the following part of my study, I will present Nicholas of Cusa from a new perspective without, however, leaving modern research completely out of consideration.

A new perspective does not necessarily lessen the merits of previous efforts. To the extent that modern approaches confront the reader with the inadequacy and insufficiency of Nicholas's data, these approaches must be taken seriously. The data have a relative importance instead of having no importance at all.[7] However, the concentration on the data has its own dangers as sometimes it can jeopardize a better understanding. It is possible to miss the forest because of an exclusive attention to the individual trees. In the following, the emphasis will be on the way, the mode or *knowing-how* of Nicholas's enterprise. Since the formal aspect of Nicholas's thought forms the focus of my inquiry, I am going to examine Nicholas's enterprise from the perspective offered by Jos Decorte's own approach to medieval thought. Thus I hope to be able to show that such an exercise can make two related achievements. One would be a better understanding of both Nicholas's enterprise and of its lasting importance, while the other demonstrates how a new interpretative tool for medieval philosophy actually works.

---

7. While the distinction between the "what" and the "how" of knowledge is a real one, all knowledge necessarily shares both dimensions. Cf. Ryle, *Concept of Mind*, 48: "The ability to do things in accordance with instructions necessitates understanding those instructions. So some propositional competence is a condition of acquiring any of these competences." While knowing–how always presupposes a knowing–what, the former cannot be reduced to the latter. See also the *Prolegomena*.

Nicholas of Cusa as a Medieval Thinker

Nicholas was a truly medieval thinker in several different respects. Paul Sigmund showed this, for instance, with regard to his conciliar theory.[8] Koyré demonstrated similarly to what extent Nicholas's cosmology in the second book of the *De Docta Ignorantia* was based rather on metaphysical speculation than on an anticipation of the experimental method of modern science.[9] Such specific points could be further multiplied. Instead of doing so, I would like to make a more basic observation: Nicholas's use of knowledge is truly medieval in one crucial respect, namely, for him, knowledge should lead humans towards God.[10] To say it in traditional terminology, knowledge has an *anagogic* function or to employ a more Cusanian term it is a sort of *manuductio*.[11]

In what follows, I will examine Nicholas's thought precisely with the help of this latter concept. My aim is to trace the concept of *manuductio* and its employment in some important Cusanian texts.[12] My working hypothesis is that an understanding of the *manuductio* will help the reader achieve a better understanding of the formal aspect of Nicholas's thought.

---

8. Nicholas was thus no forerunner of modern liberal democracy. See the Sigmund, "Introduction."

9. Koyré, *From the Closed World*, 5–24.

10. See my "Recovering Nicholas's early ontology: A reading of the *De concordantia catholica*," where I explore this in relation to the *CC*.

11. Cf. Decorte, "Ter inleiding," 36: "A handbook [Dutch "handleiding," Decorte's term for "manuductio"], as Nicholas explains it in the *De Docta Ignorantia* and also in the prologue to the *De Visione Dei*, always leads the believer from the sensible to the intelligible, and from the intelligible to the unfathomable mystery of the Godhead. Such a *manuductio* is always intended as a guidance [Dutch "handleiding"] into *mystical theology*, that is to say into a vision of the Divine—to the extent that this is possibile in this life (*visio Dei*)." In the following I will justify Jos Decorte's claim with the help of Nicholas's works. I will also extend his statement philosophicaly.

12. I leave his sermons completely out of consideration. The choice of the actually examined works will be justified in the particular sections treating them.

The Motive of *Manuductio*

Basic Semantics

Before discussing Nicholas's own usage of *manuductio*, first a semantic clarification is necessary. *Manuductio*—or alternatively *"manualis inductio"*[13]—means literally *"leading by the hand."* It can be translated in many ways: in English as *guidance*, or *guiding*; in German as *"(handgreifliche) Anleitung," "Hinleitung,"* or *"Führung."*[14] The verbal form *"manuducere"* is rendered with English *to lead* or with German *"führen."*[15] *Manuductio* does not refer to a manual or to a handbook in the first place. While a handbook contains the written "recipe," the "blueprint," stating the method or the procedure of a complex practice, the meaning of *manuductio* is rather situated on the practical level and it has a more dynamic aspect. By way of anticipation it can be said that in Nicholas's own usage, *manuductio* became very close to the literal meaning of a *handbook*.[16]

"Leading or guiding someone by the hand" can mean several things: one can help a blind man across the street or one can take a child's hand while teaching her how to write.[17] That is to say, the Other is either guided to another place (a way) or the Other gets acquainted with a certain practice (a knowing-how). As it will be clear from the following both of these dimensions are present in Nicholas's work.

The basic meaning of the term *manuductio* can be perhaps best illustrated with the help of an example taken from Catholic liturgy. Within the context of the Holy Mass, *"manuductor"* designates that person—usually a priest—who is standing at the side of a newly ordained minister during his first service at the altar.[18] The task of such

---

13. C I, Prologus, 4:1.

14. Cf. *DI* I, 2, 8:4–5; 8, 29:17; 25, 84:21; C II, 12, 132:3. See also the table of content in *CA* 17:28, 18:9.11.12.15.

15. Cf. *DI* I, 18, 52:2.

16. Cf. Happ, "Einführung," xi: "Nach Nikolaus' eigenen Worten will „De coniecturis" eine Anleitung geben, eine Formel sein, eine Kunst lehren." ("Anleitung" is Happ's translation of manuductio.)

17. Hugh of Saint Victor speaks of "caecus manuductione utens" in his *In hier. Dion.* (*Commentarium in Hierarchiam caelestem S. Dionysii libri* X.) 2, c. 948 A.

18. Blaise, *Dictionnaire* defines the manuductor as a "guide" and "prêtre assistant de celui qui dit sa premiere messe." See also Radó, *Enchiridion*, 478.

a *manuductor* is to help the beginner in performing his liturgical duty. Evidently, his role is only a temporary one, since sooner or later every priest is supposed to become able to lead the service by himself.

In sum:

a. *manuductio* is a transitory activity;

b. it is necessary because of human weakness;[19]

c. *manuductio* is showing the practical way how things can and should be done. It is the rule acted out in practice.

d. The success of such *manuductio* presupposes that during the learning process the Other (the pupil) is determined to learn, i.e., he or she is ready to accept (the *manuductio* of) the *manuductor*.[20] In the last analysis one must (learn how to) walk the way by himself.

Ancient Origin and Medieval Usage

The term *manuductio* itself can be found in several medieval authors, for instance, in John Scotus Eriugena (c.800–c.877), Richard (d. 1173) and Hugh of Saint Victor (d. 1141), Albert the Great (1193–1280), Bonaventure (c.1217–1274) and Thomas Aquinas alike. Its ultimate source seems to have been Pseudo-Dionysius the Aeropagite's (fl. c.500) *De Caelestia Hierarchia*. The original Greek word was χειραγωγια and even Aquinas's own use of *manuductio* is ultimately taken from a Latin version of the Dionysian text.[21] All of the aforesaid authors composed commentaries on Dionysius's works.[22] Nicholas was familiar with this long tradition: he knew of the different Latin translations of the *De*

---

19. E.g., a child is not able to know at once how to write, just as no one is born as a perfect liturgical minister.

20. This dimension of personal trust and inner determination can be aptly illustrated with the help of Beierwaltes's translation of *manuductio* as "Handreichung" (i.e., reaching the hand) in Beierwaltes, *Der verborgene Gott*, 17. I will return to the theme of trust later.

21. It is not unlikely that originally Pseudo-Dionysius was inspired by the language of the New Testament where χειραγογεω and χειραγογος appear in *Acts* 9:8, 22:11 and 13:11 respectively. These biblical passages connect the term with both physical and spiritual blindness.

22. E.g., Eriugena both translated the *De Caelestia Hierarchia* and composed a commentary on it. Later, Hugh of Saint Victor commented on Eriugena's commentary.

Hierarchia—among them Eriugena's and most importantly the commentary from Albert the Great.[23]

The limited framework of my study leaves no place for a detailed philological cum historical exploration of the term and the usage of *manuductio*. However, even the short summary in the previous paragraph is clearly pointing toward the ultimate origin and context of *manuductio*, i.e., to the tradition of mystical theology. Nicholas's familiarity and intellectual affinity with this tradition strongly suggests that the Cusanian *manuductio* must be situated and contextualized within his own version of mystical theology. Therefore it is appropriate to examine Nicholas's works from the point of view of *manuductio* with a clear emphasis on its proper context, i.e., on mystical theology.

Nicholas of Cusa's Manuductive Strategy

Manuductio *and Metaphysical Speculation in the* De Docta Ignorantia

One of the first and most important works written by Nicholas was his *De Docta Ignorantia* composed in the year 1440 and dedicated to his former teacher, the Cardinal Julian Cesarini (1398–1444). In the first book, the notion of *manuductio* comes more clearly to the fore, and it is there that Nicholas is developing the basics of his metaphysics.[24] However, in order to elucidate Nicholas's overall view on the role of *manuductio*, after the examination of the first book, I will turn briefly to the third book.

The second chapter of the first book of the *DI* clarifies the author's intent. Since Nicholas was going to discuss learned ignorance (*docta ignorantia*) he wanted to speak of the maximum learning of ignorance. Consequently, he had to treat the notion of maximum. In his opinion, this maximum is at once absolute maximum (*maximum absolutum*),

---

23. Wilpert, "Vorwort de Herausgebers," xii reminds the reader that before the composition of the *DI*, "Nicholas bereits Ps.Dionysius Aeropagita, und zwar in der erst 1436 gefertigten Übersetzungen des Ambrosius Traversi kannte." (Cf. Nikolaus von Kues, *Vom Nichtanderen*, xxi.) On the relation between Nicholas and Dionysius see Beierwaltes, *Der verborgene Gott*; Hoye, "Die Vereinigung," and Senger, "Die Präferererenz." On Nicholas and Eriugena, see Beierwaltes, "Eriugena."

24. The remaining parts of the *DI* treat more specific issues, i.e., cosmology (II) and Christology (III) respectively.

Absolute Being (*absoluta entitas*), and the (absolute) One (*unum, unitas*). All things are in it, nothing is opposed to it.[25] This maximum is beyond understanding and cannot be grasped by a human intellect. The question is how this Maximum can be understood, if It is incomprehensible. Nicholas's answer is that one should not understand his text at a superficial level: it is not sufficient to attend to the proper significations of words (*proprietates vocabularum/verborum*).[26] Nicholas is conscious of the fact that the examples he has employed are all *manuductiones*: he reminds his readership that these examples must be taken according to a figurative meaning by leaving behind their perceptible elements.[27]

The term *manuductio* reappears in chapter ten of the *DI*.[28] The title of this chapter already signals the direction of Nicholas's thought, as it refers to a transcending movement towards the Trinity.[29] Later, *manuductio* will be revealed as a means for this movement. Precisely because the Maximum or the One stands beyond all things, the reader must leave behind all things that are attained by the senses. In order to understand that maximal Oneness is triune, one must transcend human imagination and reason to the simplest understanding (*ubi omnia sunt unum*).[30] Nicholas states the following methodological point: "[P]hilosophy, which endeavors to comprehend, by a very simple understanding, that the maximal Oneness is only triune, must remove all things imaginable and rational."[31] The difficulties a reader has to face with respect to this very simply understanding are characteristically acknowledged in the text.[32] The author of the *DI* is ready to offer a sure guidance, that is to say a *manuductio* to his reader.[33] At the same time, the reader is admonished to rise from the signs upward to truth by understanding

25. Otherwise, it would not be maximum.

26. *DI* I 2, 8:1–3.

27. Ibid., 8:4–7: "Exemplaribus etiam manuductionibus necesse est transcendenter uti linquendo sensibilia, ut ad intellectualitatem simplicem expedite lector ascendat."

28. *DI* I 10, 29:16–19.

29. Ibid., 27:2–3: "Quomodo intellectus trinitatis in unitate supergreditur omnia."

30. Ibid., 29:1: "Adhuc cum dico: 'Unitas est maxima', trinitatem dico."

31. Ibid., 29:8–11: "emovere omnia imaginabilia et rationabilia necesse est philosophiam, quae unitatem maximam non nisi trinam simplicissima intellectione voluerit comprehendere." Cf. ibid., 27:4–6.

32. Cf. ibid., 27:15–16.

33. Ibid., 29:16–19: "Unde, ut acuetur intellectus, ad hoc te facilius indubitata manuductione transferre conabor, ut videas ista necessaria atque verissima."

the words of the book symbolically. Only then will one arrive already in this life at a blissful vision of the Trinity. In this way, the *DI* identifies both the aim of metaphysical speculation and of *manuductiones* with a *visio Dei*. It can be added that the *manuductiones* function as a concrete means for such a speculation. This feature of Nicholas's thought also characterizes his other works. As it will be shown, the *manuductio ad mysterium*, which is quite literally a *manuductio ad Trinitatem*, forms a permanent structure in the Cusanian enterprise.[34]

Nicholas's employment of mathematical examples must be understood in the same light.[35] Like the whole Platonic tradition going back to antiquity, Nicholas also saw in mathematics a precious tool for doing philosophy and mathematics offered good illustrations for his thinking.[36] Since its region lies the closest to the world of ideas, mathematics can also give the best guidance in speculative theology.[37] Generally speaking, divine things can only be investigated by way of symbols.[38] By virtue of their abstraction, mathematical symbols have the advantage of being purer, more certain, and thus closer to the divine truth.[39]

Nicholas also tried to interpret the ancient Platonic metaphor of participation with the help of mathematical examples.[40] His discussion again employs the term *manuducere*.[41] With the help of mathematical signs Nicholas wanted to pursue a symbolic investigation (*symbolice*

---

34. Nicholas speaks of this vision in terms of "quantum studioso secundum humani ingenii vires elevato conceditur," and this may be a sign of Nicholas's intimation of the limitations of his own enterprise. See ibid., 29:22–23.

35. On mathematics, see *DI* I, 11–23.

36. According to Nicholas, all the great ancient thinkers employed mathematics when they discussed the most difficult subject matters. He names Pythagoras, the Platonists (=Neoplatonists), Augustine, and Boethius as thinkers asserting the priority of numbers in inquiring about reality, and he includes even Aristotle within this tradition. See *DI* I, 11, 31:13–17 and 32:1–13.

37. Here, the term "guidance" (manuductio) is not used, although the employment of mathematics is is referred to as a way (via). *DI* I, 11, 32:16.

38. Ibid., 30:5–7: "visibilia veraciter invisibilium imagines esse atque creatorem ita cognoscibiliter a creaturis videri posse quasi in speculo et in aenigmate."

39. Ibid., 32:26–29: "cum ad divina non nisi per symbola accedendi nobis via pateat, quod tunc mathematicalibus signis propter ipsorum incorruptibilem certitudinem convenientius uti poterimus." See also ibid., 31:4–11.

40. See *DI* I, 17–18.

41. *DI* I, 18, 52:2–3: "Quomodo ex eodem manuducimur ad intellectum participationis entitatis."

investigare).[42] In his opinion, a beginner's (*incipiens*) inquiry into the maximal truth should start by relying on the help coming from respected former thinkers.[43] The beginner's appearance here is clearly related to learning process and both of these concepts belong to the basic semantic field of *manuductio*.

Besides the general features of *manuductio*, the *DI* also identifies a specifically religious context of this notion. Both Nicholas's explicit reference to a symbolic investigation and the fact that throughout the "mathematical part" of the first book terms denoting a transcending motion abound strongly suggest that the Cusanian *manuductio* must be understood within the framework of symbolic thinking.[44] This observation makes clear the inherent connection of Nicholas's *manuductio* with a fundamentally religiously inspired language.[45] Moreover, the penultimate chapter of the first book of the *DI* employs this key-term in relation to the question of religion. There, the notion of *manuductio* is explicitly placed at the heart of a discussion of non-Christian religions.

The penultimate chapter of the first book demonstrates Nicholas's good command of ancient sources. The text lists several different modes of pagan worship. What is remarkable is not the exhibition of a classical renaissance erudition, but more importantly Nicholas's sympathetic approach to some forms of pagan religiosity.[46] Being a medieval Christian thinker, Nicholas does not spare pagans from criticism: paganism is compared with the Jewish religion and the text notices the ironies of pagan religiosity. Nicholas points out that pagans derided the Jews whose God was unknown to them, yet, in fact, pagans and Jews worshipped the same God. While the Jews worshipped Him in His most simple unity, the pagans worshipped Him in the creatures (*in explicationibus—*

---

42. See *DI* I, 12, 33:6–7. While 33:17–18 speaks of those "labouring in enigmas" (in aenigmate laborantibus), the title of chapter twelve, "Quomodo signis mathematicalibus sit utendum in proposito" is also worth of noting because of its clear emphasis on the knowing-how.

43. *DI* I, 12, 34:1–3. The subsequent section refers to Anselm and other unnamed thinkers.

44. See e.g. *DI* I, 14, 37:3.13 for "transcendere," 12, 33:13 and 16, 42:2.6 for "transferre" (translative). 12, 33:14 has "transumere," 16, 45:2 "transumptive," and 19, 55:2 together with 23, 70:2 have "transumptio."

45. On the connection of the symbolic and the religious dimensions, see the *Prolegomena*.

46. Cf. *DI* I, 25, 83 and 84:1–11.

divina opera). These pagans were partly unaware of the real object of their religious worship.

Interestingly, the fundamental mistake of pagan worship is intimately connected with the proper meaning of *manuductio*. Creatures, namely, as perceptible things are meant to serve as a sort of *manuductio* leading towards the one Beginning and Cause that is beyond any perception.[47] Created beings must be accepted in a special sense for religious worship. By taking them not as images but as the (transcendent) reality itself, paganism forfeited their real religious importance. This was the beginning (*principium*) of idolatry. Thereby, pagans missed the whole point of Creation. By concentrating exclusively on the visible dimension they were not able to see the invisible. They actually reduced the transcendence of the Transcendent to mere immanence.[48]

This short investigation of the manuductive passages of the first book of the *DI* demonstrates the central role of *manuductio* in Nicholas's thought. It also shows the intimate connection with religious language and with Nicholas's own approach to different religions. At the end of the first book of the *DI*, besides the motive of *manuductio*, several other Cusanian notions can be identified that are important for a possible dialogue with other religions:

a. those outside the Biblical revelation had some legitimate sense of transcendence and religious worship;

b. this awareness was somewhat unconscious on their part;

c. unfortunately, they were led astray;

d. the wise among them still retain a clearer vision, i.e., one closer to Christianity.

Concerning these points many questions are possible, but most of them cannot receive a definite answer yet. For instance, what are the exact criteria for a legitimate religion (a)? In what sense can a religion be both legitimate and nevertheless followed unconsciously (b)? Who or what led people astray in their worship (c)? Finally, how can the 'wise' referred to be further characterized (d)?

---

47. Ibid., 84:20–21.

48. This traditional criticism of pagan worship comes from Saint Paul, see Rom 1:19–25, especially verses 20–21.

My main concern being Nicholas's own confrontation with Islam, in the following, I am inquiring whether and to what extent these points from the penultimate chapter of the first book *DI* (together with others elicited from the same work) are applicable to and can be developed further in relation to the Muslims' religion. Fortunately, answering this latter question would at once offer answers to the more specific question listed in the previous paragraph—at least as far as the Moslems are concerned. However, before trying to do so, however, it is advisable to gain a better understanding of Nicholas's manuductive project. The discussion of the Islamic question (even with respect to the treatment of Moslems in the *DI*)—will be postponed, so that other important Cusanian works may be examined as possible instances of and variations on the theme of *manuductio*.[49]

Before turning to Nicholas's other works, however, I would like to emphasize the fact that Christian faith plays an essential role in the *DI*. Its third book discusses the main doctrines of Christian faith such as, for instance, Christ's birth and death, His Resurrection and Ascension. After having treated these, chapter eleven (one of the longest in the third book) is devoted to "the mysteries of faith."[50] As a matter of fact, the subject-matter of chapter eleven is not Christian dogmatics, but the "mysteries" of faith itself.[51]

The discussion of chapter eleven is related both to *fides quae* and *fides qua*. In a typically medieval vein, the first sentence of the chapter already asserts what "[A]ll our forefathers unanimously maintained," namely "that faith is the beginning of understanding."[52] In this respect one can refer back to Anselm and also to the ultimate biblical source of this idea in *Isaiah* 7:9 of the Vulgate—a text Nicholas quotes explicitly.[53] The context of the quotation makes it clear that "faith" ought to be taken here in a broader sense than only denoting an acceptance of truth

---

49. See the following and my next chapter.

50. Cf. the title of the chapter. According to Senger, there is some evidence that Nicholas inserted this chapter later into the previous discussion. See Senger, "Anmerkungen," 141.

51. Ibid.: "Es geht jezt nicht mehr um Glaubensgeheimnisse und (dogmatische) Inhalte des christlichen Glaubens, sondern es geht hier um die Geheimnisse, die der Glaube als Glaube selbst schafft."

52. *DI* III, 11, 244:3–4: "Maiores nostri omnes concordanter asserunt fidem initium esse intellectus."

53. Ibid., 244:8–9.

claims.⁵⁴ It is surely an acceptance of specific truth claims, but it is also an act, necessarily involving the dimension of *fides qua*.

This latter dimension of faith is important for the following reason. If one reduces the notion of faith to the question of specific truth claims, then the project of the *DI* aiming at an increase of faith will appear absurd and perhaps even paradoxical.⁵⁵ Namely, if someone has already accepted Christianity as a true doctrine, there are no more doctrinal points to be accepted. But even such a person can have more (or less) faith, in the sense of having a more (or less) intense personal trust. Furthermore, chapter eleven speaks of different possible degrees of faith. Maximal faith is not equated with the acceptance of the greatest number of truth claims but with the highest certainty excluding all hesitation (*summa certitudo absque omni haesitatione in aliquo quocumque*).⁵⁶ The intrinsic relation between faith and the personal dimension of trust can also be seen from the fact that, for Nicholas, *caritas* is the essential form-giving aspect of faith.⁵⁷ Faith in the sense of an exclusive *fides quae* would be pointless as it would forfeit its own form, that is to say its proper teleology.

The increase of faith goes parallel to an increase of learned ignorance as the believer has to recognize that he cannot really know Jesus Christ.⁵⁸ Because of His Divinity, Christ remains hidden from the wise.⁵⁹ Christ as God has to be approached via symbols that serve the only goal of leading the believer to the realization that God in His Infinity cannot be comprehended—not even in Christ. In relation to this point, the example of Saint Paul is referred to.⁶⁰ According to Nicholas's in-

---

54. Senger, "Anmerkungen," 142: "Wie sich aus dem Kontext ergibt, bezieht Nikolaus diese Aussage nicht allein auf den religiösen Glauben, sondern auch auf Glaube schlechthin als jedewedes anerkennedes Für–wahr–halten." Cf. *DI* III, 12, 244:12–13: "Ubi ... non est sana fides, nullus est verus intellectus."

55. Cf. *DI* III, Prologus 181:4–6 and 11, 244:10–12.

56. Ibid., 248:20–21. Paradoxically, this highest certitude also appears as minimal faith, to the extent as it differs from an ordinary form of faith wrought with doubts. See also ibid., 12, 257:1–2.

57. Ibid., 250:12–15: "Non enim est viva fides, sed mortua et penitus non fides, absque caritate. Caritas autem est forma fidei, ei dans esse verum, immo est signum constantissimae fidei." Cf. 248:9–11.

58. Ibid., Prologus 181 and 12, 245:1–3.

59. Cf. Matt 11:25: "abscondisti haec a sapientibus, et prudentibus, et revelasti ea parvulis."

60. For the following, cf. Senger, "Anmerkungen," 143–4.

terpretation, the Apostle himself had thought that he knew Christ, but his knowledge crumbled in the face of a new Divine Revelation. Through recognizing his former ignorance, Paul became a man of *docta ignorantia*.[61] Paul's example suggests that positive knowledge concerning Christ proves to be unsatisfactory because He is revealed in and through faith.

The point is that faith does not simply stem from the inadequacy of positive truths of faith (*fides quae*) but also from a reflection on the status of such a positive knowledge and the intimation of the existence of God's immensity. The outcome of such a reflection is *docta ignorantia*, for the more someone recognizes that he is unknowing, the more learned he will be.[62] In this way, learned ignorance leads the believer to Christ.[63] Ultimately, God cannot be known via sense-perception, imagination, reason or intellect, not even through Christ. He can only be seen with the "eye of the intellect" (*oculus intellectus*), which is able to realize His presence even in His absence.[64] This intellectual faculty—in fact the highest activity of the highest human faculty—enables the human subject to see and properly understand signs and traces as pointing toward the Divine.[65] Faith and learned ignorance function together as important moments of coming to know God as God.

Even though Christology is apparently an important topic for the whole of the *DI*, it cannot be treated properly here.[66] Nevertheless, my short analysis of faith in terms of *docta ignorantia* demonstrates that Christology has an important role in Nicholas's thought. The connection between Christology and *docta ignorantia* is especially clear. As a medieval intellectual, Nicholas of Cusa was convinced that Christ

---

61. *DI* III, 11, 245:20–24. Cf. 1 Cor 2:2–4 and 2 Cor 12:2. Senger points out that Nicholas's understanding of these Pauline passages is parallel with Dionisius's treatment thereof. For the reference, see my previous foonote.

62. Cf. *DI* I, 1, 4.

63. *DI* III, 11, 246:1–2: "Ducimur igitur nos Christifideles in docta ignorantia ad montem, qui Christus est." The mountain is a biblical image invoking both the Mount Sinai and the (symbolic) location of Divine Revelation. Cf. Exod 19:9–25. On the parallels between Exodus and Platonic thought, cf. Turner, *Darkness of God*, 11–18.

64. *DI* III, 246:4–5: "scientes intra ipsam caliginem montem esse."

65. Nicholas speaks of "vestigia," "characteres," "organa," and "signa." E.g., 247:17–18 states that "omnia . . . creata signa sunt verbi dei."

66. On Christology, see *DI* III, 1–10. I will come back to some aspect of Nicholas's Christology in my fourth chapter.

was the Word of God (*verbum dei*), the very intelligibility (*logos*) of reality. However, for Nicholas, every kind of knowledge—surely mediated by Christ—must be transcended. If knowing God is a question of *docta ignorantia*, then Christ's role is to lead the believer to this learned ignorance.

Manuductio, *Self-knowledge, and Difference in the* De Coniecturis

Nicholas's other early work, the *De Coniecturis* (1440–1444)—dedicated also to Cesarini—presents itself as good example of the Cusanian *manuductio*. Its German translator reminds the reader that, "According to Nicholas's own words, the "De Coniecturis" wants to give a guidance, to be a method, to teach an art."[67]

In the dedication to his teacher, cardinal Cesarini, Nicholas speaks of this work as "a new formula" of arts.[68] Here, the term "formula" should be understood as meaning a (small) pattern, prescribing[69] a rule or a method regulating the way of one's research into different forms of "art."[70] The alternative term "art" (*ars*) can mean just any possible kind of knowledge implying a skill, a *knowing-how*, (*familiarity* in English), a certain way of doing things.[71] Art or skill, in the sense of a practical knowing-how could be applied as well to morals, designating character, manner of thinking so far as these are made known by external actions.[72]

---

67. Happ, "Einführung," xi. Cf. footnotes at the beginning of this chapter.

68. *C* I, 1:14: "hanc novam indiganarum artium formulam..."

69. Hence, Happ translates it as "Vorschrift."

70. Originally, the Latin term also signified *a conduit or a pipe of an aqueduct*. In legal language, it referred to the form or rule for regulating juridical proceedings its usual meaning being not far from that of "norma," "regula'" or "praescriptum." E.g., the phrase "formula cognitionis" meant the rule of evidence on which the legal inquiry is conducted. In the publicists' language, formula could designate any form of agreement or regulation, and, generally speaking, was taken in the sense of a *rule* or a *principle*. See Lewis and Short, *A Latin Dictionary*.

71. Originally, the Latin term "ars" had to do with manual, i.e., physical activity. (Cf. "arma.") It referred to a skill in joining something, in combining, working it, etc. in the sense of French "adresse." Later its meaning was extended entirely beyond the sphere of the common pursuits of life, both in relation to artistic and scientific action, and also to mental-spiritual cultivation. See ibid.

72. "Doctrina," "prudentia," "virtus," "industria," "ratio," "via," "dolus" can be its synonyms. On art see also *DP* 34:1–10.

It is important that as such, *ars* not only designated a skill—e.g., in producing any material form, handicraft, trade, occupation or employment—in the sense of the Greek τεχνη or English-French *technique*. In this respect, the text of the C makes clear that *ars* also refers to any physical or mental activity, in so far as it was practically exhibited—such as gymnastics, the art of war, politics, jurisprudence, rhetoric, grammar, music or medicine.[73] The employment of the terms "ars" and "formula" indicate that Nicholas was concerned with the formal aspect of knowledge. This emphasis on the knowing-how does not entail that the theoretical dimension of knowledge is absent from the C. This will become clearer in the following, where the meaning of *ars* is examined in more detail.

The Prologue to the first book of the C expresses Nicholas's conviction that precise truth is unattainable. No positive assertion can be absolutely precise.[74] The meaning of any proposition can always be refined and made more accurate and more explicit. Assertions are "true," i.e., they reflect truth, but only to some extent and formulated from a limited perspective. Truth itself is inexhaustible and there remains always something more to be grasped.[75] Even the meaning of a single proposition can only be fully understood if it is related to the meaning of the whole and finite human beings usually do not have a clear insight into the totality of meaning.[76] Hence, truth claims are only partial and thereby human statements only conjectures.[77] Furthermore, the actual form of the limitation of human understanding is different in every being and consequently, no single person can have precisely the same per-

---

73. The same Latin word could also mean science or knowledge. In a derivative sense, it can denote the theory of any art or science.

74. C I, Prologue, 2:4: "praecisionem veritatis inattingibilem intuitus es..." Nicholas wrote his *DI* with the same conviction. Thus, *DI* II, 1, 91–93, successively shows that there is no exact precision or agreement either in *astronomy*, *mathematics* or *music*; and that absolute precision is an exclusively divine attribute. Ibid., 90 n. 11–12.

75. Ibid., 2:6–7. C I, 2:4–5: "consequens est omnem humanam veri positivam assertionem esse coniecturam."

76. Cf. ibid., 3:1.

77. Cf. Kolakowski, *Religion*, 88: "No partial truth can carry absolute certitude unless it is related to the whole truth; otherwise the meaning of the partial truth must always remain in doubt: the owner of a partial truth can neither know how the truth behind his reach can alter the sense of the truth he has taken possession of nor what the latter's scope of validity is."

spective on any given issue as someone else and no one can understand with absolute precision the meaning of another person's utterance.[78]

However, this criticism of human cognition does not make Nicholas a skeptic. Neither was he advocating a thoroughgoing relativism.[79] In C, he expresses his hope that his former teacher, Cesarini, with his sharper intellect, would catch his meaning and would be even able to formulate it more clearly than Nicholas did. Nicholas, with his book was offering intellectual food (*quasi cibum*).[80] This "spiritual food"—as any kind of substantial food—needs digestion, that is to say both intellectual chewing and regular rumination (*diligentiore masticatione atque crebra ruminatione*) are necessary. Only by such a process could C be turned into clearer thoughts (*in clariores intellectualitates*).[81] Every intellectual inquiry implies the thinking of new thoughts so far not thought. In such an activity, intellectual experience can serve as a guiding light as it helps to see things more clearly. Since the beginner is precisely lacking such a light, therefore he needs a *manuductio*,—in as much as he or she wants to be led to see hidden things. During this learning process, the beginner will gradually learn unknown and see hitherto unseen things.[82] As in *DI*, also in his *C*, Nicholas promises to provide examples for the sake of such a beginner.[83]

So far, the following important aspects of a *manuductio* can be identified in the *C*:

78. C I, 3:1-7.

79. *DVD* 15, 67:4 states that God imparts every form: "a te recipit id quod est." This rules out the possibility of a relativistic "perspectivism." Arne Moritz makes this point examining both the *C* and the *DVD* in Moritz "Das Sehen des Papstes," 147-58. On the distinctions between different perspectives and relativism, cf. Taylor, "*Gadamer on Human Sciences.*"

80. C I, Prologue, 3:12. Cf. C II, 8, 116:16-17: "rationabilibusque doctrinis, quae alimenta quaedam sunt." Happ, "Anmerkungen," 218 reminds the reader that Nicholas is following here the rhetorical convictions of his age. However, this does not entail that Nicholas was only paying lip service to an ancient standard or that he merely intended to flatter Cesarini, since there is no a priori reason why the very practice of employing these rhetorical convictions should not be taken seriously.

81. The point made for Cesarini is that a brighter intellect can catch other people's meaning and even formulate it in a clearer fashion. Obviously, this truth is not restricted to the person of Nicholas's former teacher.

82. C I, 4:1-3: "Oportet autem quadam manuali inductione iuniores quosque, experimentali luce carentes, ad latentium ostensionem allicere, ut gradatim ad ignotiora erigantur."

83. C I, 4:7-8.

a. youth without experience,

b. the revealing of hidden things,

c. the gradual learning process,

d. and the role of examples.

It is not difficult to see how these points are connected to the general characterization of *manuductio* given earlier. According to Nicholas's own words, the whole of the *C* was written with the explicit intent of refreshing those who have a thirst for the truth (*famelicas animas*). The success of this work presupposes a certain desire or zeal for knowledge as a precondition of the learning process from its readers, and that is the reason why *manuductio* features throughout the *C* as a fundamental underlying motive.[84] After having explained the basics of his art, for instance, Nicholas continues to give examples of its practical applications.[85] These are explicitly meant as a help for the *"tardiores,"* i.e., for people with a slower, more reluctant understanding. By demonstrating the employment of the same idea in various contexts, Nicholas intended to lead his readers to the conjectural art. The aim of these intellectual exercises was quite simply the appropriation of Nicholas's conjectural *ars*.[86]

This last observation brings me back to the question of *ars*. Art in *C* is as an imitation of nature and is contrasted with nature.[87] An important consequence of the view according to which no precision is attainable is that nothing can exist that does not have a share in both nature and art.[88] Still, the two domains of reality remain different from each other. Consider, for instance, human speech. It clearly transcends the merely natural dimension. Although it comes forth from an art, speaking itself is a natural characteristic of humanity. Different languages can be called natural in different degrees. Logical reasoning (*ars racionandi*)

---

84. Ibid., 4:12–17. Nicholas already speaks of a natural desire for knowledge in *DI* I, 1, 2–4. I will come back to the theme of intellectual desire when discussing the *DVD* later.

85. Cf. *C* II, Prologue, 70:8–9: "in praxi partim explicare curabo."

86. Ibid., 70:9.13–15.

87. *C* II. 12, 131–33.

88. Ibid., 131:6–9.

can be another example. Doing logic is a thoroughly natural human activity, but it is not possible without any art.

In the *C*, the meaning of art is also connected with that of *"factibilitas,"* a term referring to the possibility of producing or making things.[89] This *ars* is a productive activity, such as for instance speaking (producing speech), weaving (producing a texture), sawing (in order to produce grain), cooking (producing a meal), and the like.[90] All these activities have both a natural and an artificial or productive dimension—and they have this in different degrees. Furthermore, all the named activities are related to human rationality. They belong to the *"ars rationalis"* and all have their goal in sensible nature. Throughout this discussion of art, the practical dimension of the term *ars* rings through.[91] Nicholas is giving Cesarini the advice that if he wants to investigate the themes of art, nature, and their connection, he should employ the *manuductio* already familiar to him from the foregoing.[92]

So far it has been amply demonstrated that the *C* must be understood as a *manuductio* into conjectural art. Even though the Lullian Art may have inspired it, Nicholas's art was clearly a different enterprise. The basic difference between the two intellectual projects concerns an epistemological point to which I will come back later, at the end of this chapter. Here, it must be emphasized that Nicholas did not think that he arrived at a closed system of logical principles with a complete conceptual catalogue in *C*. His subsequent writings testify a continuous search for ever-new alternatives for thinking.

Even on the basis of such a brief examination of *manuductio* in *C*, it is worthwhile to point out the differences with the *DI*. In this respect, the last chapter of *C* deserves special attention.[93] Its title (*De cognitio sui*) already indicates that the goal of Nicholas's exercise was self-knowledge. It is not difficult to recognize in this *finis libelli* the *finis intellectus* par excellence. Self-knowledge as the aim of intellectual inquiry has been

---

89. Ibid., 132:12–13.15.

90. Ibid., 133:9–10.

91. Nicholas makes a distinction between intellectual, rational, and sensible arts, without giving examples of the latter.

92. *C* II, 12, 132:1–3: "Si . . . naturae differentias investigare volueris atque artis et conexionis utriusque, ad saepe apertam figurarum manuductionem recurrito." Cf. *C* I, 9, 41:7–8: "ut sensibili manuductione ad arcana coniecturam convertere possis." Right after this sentence Nicholas gives a "figura" for an example.

93. *C* II, 17, 171–84.

a traditional theme both in Platonic and in Christian thought. For Nicholas, self-knowledge meant the recognition of one's own self both as a limited, finite being, but also as a being participating in the Divine Light and sharing God's triune nature. This self-knowledge cannot be for its own sake and it is connected to one's life (morals) and its ultimate finality (God). That is to say, Nicholas thought that genuine *cognitio sui* should help one to give direction to one's life, to integrate it into a unity, to direct it toward its proper end.

As the German translator of *C* reminds the reader "the conjectural art is not meant to be a philosophy of being, rather it focuses on the doctrine concerning unitas."[94] It can be added that according to this "doctrine concerning the *unitas*" everything comes from the One and should return to this same One. The One posits the end of human life and the *cognitio sui* functions as a practical condition for a (re-)integration of morals and (re-)unification of life in view of this One. The whole importance of the cognitive-ethical movement lies in the Great Return to the One.

The invisible *unitas* humans ought to return to is compared to light in *C*.[95] Light makes things visible by letting them participate in light according to various modes. Thereby, light establishes a unity within the diversity of all different visible things. Different colors are nothing else than different modes of (participation in) visibility—that is to say of light. Colors are *per definition* multiple and it is always either this or that particular color that appears in experience. Every color instantiates a particular mode of visibility, an aspect of light. Speaking in Kantian terminology, one can say that light functions as the condition of possibility of (seeing) visible things. In Cusanian terms, light is the unity all things and all colors share with each other. Precisely by virtue of this unity things can appear as visible.

The important point is that Divine Nature relates Itself to human nature in the same manner. The One Creator created all humanity and this One God gives humans a true unity. Every human being participates in the Divine Nature although in a contracted way. Divine Nature is tri-

---

94. Happ, "Einführung," xx: "Die Mutmaßungskunst ist keine Seinsphilosophie, sondern sie stellt die Lehre von der unitas in den Mittelpunkt." For a criticism of opposing *Seinsmetaphysik* with *Einheitsmetaphysik* in Nicholas's thought, see Hopkins in *Nicholas of Cusa on God as Not–Other*, 10–11.

95. For the following, see C II, 17, 172–4.

une: infinite unity, equality, and connection. Similarly, in its contracted way, every human being is structured according to this triune principle. Nicholas is emphasizing that (infinite) unity, equality, and connection are not three numerically different principles. Within the Godhead they are completely within each other.[96] Hence, the light of unity, equality, and their connection is the same light. The light of understanding (*intelligere*) brings unity to diverse propositions and to sense data. It functions as the unifying light of knowledge. The light of justice brings unity (balance, harmony, peace) into one's moral, practical actions, while in its judgments it relies on understanding. The more someone participates in (divine) understanding and the more this understanding is revealed in his just acts (life), the more godlike one becomes.[97] The light of love also gives a certain unity to one's life and understanding can help this love.[98] Indeed, love should work *intellectualiter* not as a merely sensual love.[99] This kind of spiritual or intellectual love will act out (more than) justice (equality). In short, the more one participates in any of these three aspects of divine life, the more divine one becomes, that is to say the closer one will be to his or her own end.[100]

Since unity, equality, and connection cannot be without each other, truly participating in the one means in effect participating in the two other aspects as well. An important consequence is that understanding is not without loving.[101] The C explicitly states that the intellect cannot work without loving: loving itself belongs to the perfection of the intellect.[102] However, there cannot be any perfection of understanding without the lower faculties of reason and the senses. This suggests that all these dimensions of one's humanity must be integrated into the same human perfection. What *cognitio sui* brings about is ultimately nothing else than the unification of a human life. Nicholas's own intellectual in-

---

96. Ibid., 173:13–16. Traditionally, the same idea is expressed by the doctrine of perichoresis.

97. Ibid., 174:24–25.

98. Since love accepts everything it will accept any good advice from the intellect. Cf. 1 Cor 13:7.

99. C II, 17, 174:27–30 and 176:1–8.

100. Ibid., 174:10–30.

101. Ibid., 176:22–23: "amat enim intellectus intelligere suum . . ."

102. Cf. ibid., 176:23–24: "Intellectualis enim amor intellectum et ipsum intelligentem supponit." See also ibid., 177:12–14: "Inclinatur igitur intellectus ad intelligere et amare, ut perficiatur natura eius, ita ratio ad ratiocinari, sensus ad sentire."

quiry finds its teleology within the same movement of divinization and the *manuductio* of *C* functions as a concrete means for this movement.

The last chapter of *C* also gives an important warning to the reader.[103] Cesarini is reminded of what he has learned before. In the course of the book, all the different regions of being—the sensible, the rational, the intellectual, and the divine—have been surveyed. It is emphasized that every one of these regions must be respected and treated differently. Their differences must be taken into account and this is *a fortiori* true of God. The different modes of speaking must conform to the different modes of (participation in) being and it is important that none of these modes could be completely reduced to another.

By now, the direction into which the *C* has developed the idea of *manuductio* must be evident. *Manuductio* retains its relation to intellectual inquiry and to the use of examples. The other basic features familiar from the *DI* are present as well. Nicholas's fundamental teleology remains the same transcending movement towards the One Trinity. Instead of being completely transformed, *manuductio* has become more concrete and practical through the employment of new ideas and examples in the course of the *C*. The *manuductio* is revealed here as a path leading the reader toward self-knowledge and moral (re-)integration. The full meaning of this *cognitio sui* implies a (re-)discovery of the Trinitarian structure of one's own being. In this way the *manuductio* towards the mystery of the Trinity of the *DI*, is made more concrete in the *C*, by an extra attention both to more practical-moral dimensions and to the actual form of its Neoplatonic-Christian itinerary.

However, as far as Muslims are concerned there is no explicit reference to them in the *C*—not even in the context of discussing the different forms and degrees of religiosity. It is yet to be seen what their exact place could be within Nicholas's flexible scheme. The answer to this question must be postponed until I have provided a detailed examination of Nicholas's approach to Islam in the next chapter. So far, it has been shown that both the *DI* and the *C* point towards the original philosophical-theological context of the concept of *manuductio*. Since both of these works can be read as following the tradition of mystical theology, I will show in the next two chapters that this mystical theol-

---

103. Ibid., 175:1–3: "Sis autem attentus in his omnibus, ut terminis secundum traditas regulas utaris. Dum enim de divinitate per terminos locutus sum, eos ad eius naturas transumas."

ogy forms an important background for Nicholas of Cusa's approach towards Islam. Before turning to Nicholas's treatment of Islam, I will discuss the actual form of the Cusanian mystical theology in the remaining sections of the present chapter.

Manuductio *and the* Mystical Theology *in* De Visione Dei

No discussion of Nicholas's mystical theology can forego his *De Visione Dei*. This work in its entirety is dedicated to the subject of mystical theology and it was composed together with the *De Pace Fidei* in the year 1453.[104] Nicholas of Cusa's letter to John of Segovia, written on December, 29 1454, makes clear that the first version of the latter work was already completed by that time, that is to say the *PF* must have been finished by the middle of September 1453.[105] In a letter, addressed to the abbot of the Tegernsee monastery and dating from September 14th, Nicholas himself had spoken about his plan of writing *DVD*, which work must have been completed by November 8th of the same year.[106]

Chronologically speaking, the compositions of the *PF* and *DVD* are only separated by some months. While Nicholas had been speculating on the themes of mystical theology and after hearing the news from Constantinople, he composed the *PF* in a rush. Later, he returned to actually writing *DVD*. This may indicate more than a mere temporal coincidence of the two works, but only a closer examination of both texts can adequately demonstrate the existence of a thematic connection between Nicholas's mystical theology and his approach to Islam. These are the very themes I am going to confront in the following.[107]

---

104. My analysis of the *DVD* is based on the text translated and edited by Hopkins in *Nicholas of Cusa's Dialectical Mysticism*, 107–269.

105. See Klibansky and Bascour, "Praefatio," xii.

106. See *Nicholas of Cusa's Dialectical Mysticism*, 16–17.

107. There is another feature common to the *PF* and *DVD*. Both of their titles can be read either as a *genetivus objectivus* or a *genitivus subjectivus* and this fact may have some bearings on the interpretation of both works. Cf. Decorte, "Ter inleiding," 11–12. Cf. also Biechler and Bond, "Introduction," xxxvii, and *Nicholas of Cusa's Dialectical Mysticism*, 17. Bocken and Decorte, "Inleiding," 29–31 points out both the temporal and thematic connections between *DVD* and the *PF*.

The Saint Quirinus Abbey

The author of *DVD* intended to teach a group of Benedictine monks about the accessibility of mystical theology.[108] This group of monks belonged to the Tegernsee Abbey in Bavaria and Nicholas had a close relationship with this community, especially with Abbot Caspar Aindorffer and Prior Bernard von Waging. These men were familiar with Nicholas's thought both from correspondence, personal conversations, and from their reading of Cusanian works. They knew both the *DI* and the *C*—Bernard even composed a book under the title "*Laudatorium Doctae Ignorantiae,*" i.e., "*A Praise of Learned Ignorance.*"[109]

The Saint Quirinus Abbey at Tegernsee became a centre of spirituality and learning partly because of the close relationship between its community and Nicholas of Cusa.[110] The monastic community at Tegernsee was deeply influenced both by the *devotio moderna* and the mystical theology of Dionysius Aeropagite. They were confronted with the question of how exactly knowing and loving relate to each other in mystical theology. In his answer to this question, Nicholas tried to avoid the extremities of a merely affective mysticism. He both emphasized the necessary role of knowledge in loving and underlined the importance of loving for knowledge. Nicholas understood love as the desire for the unknown dimensions of everything already familiar to the human subject.[111] This fascination with the yet unknown is intellectual desire or a desire with an intrinsic intellectual dimension to it. In other words, knowing as an intellectual activity necessarily has a dimension of engagement.[112] In short, love and knowing do not contradict, oppose

---

108. Cf. *DVD* Preface, 1:1–2: "Pandam nunc quae vobis dilectissimis fratribus ante promiseram, circa facilitatem mysticae theologiae." As it can be gathered from the note to the Latin text on page 268 in Hopkins's edition, the explicit of one codex identifies the *DVD* as "tractatus N. cardinalis de praxi seu manuductione in misticam theologiam" while another one calls it simply "theoria."

109. Bocken and Decorte, "Inleiding," 20.

110. On this relationship, see Endres, "Nicolaus Cusanus" and also Bocken and Decorte, "Inleiding," 17–21.

111. Cf. Endres, "Nicolaus Cusanus," 139 and Bocken and Decorte, "Inleiding," 20–21.

112. Bocken and Decorte, "Inleiding," 20–21: "»Being familiar« (Dutch 'kennen') is precisely coming to know ('leren kennen') that what one does not know from the reality with which one is engaged ('betrokken')." My analysis in this passage is based on Bocken and Decorte.

or exclude each other. These dimensions of human life are mutually presupposed by and included in each other,[113] and *DVD* confirms that Nicholas was thinking along these lines.[114]

The Author's Intention

Before examining this Cusanian treatise on mystical theology it will be beneficiary to characterize the author's intention in more precise terms.[115] First and foremost, *DVD* does not give an objective analysis of the Divine Mystery, in the sense of offering a speculative rational theology. Neither did Nicholas intend a thoroughgoing relativism by making any human perspective on the Divine only relative. Nor was the *DVD* composed as a description of the concrete technique for personal prayer. This work was certainly a speculative enterprise—what can be called a philosophical *manuductio* into mystical theology.[116] The author's intention was not that of transmitting a special doctrine but rather leading his reader by the hand (*manuducere*) along the speculative exercises of his own intellectual journey.[117] This is not to deny the theoretical dimensions of a work from which almost every page can be read as a testimony of Nicholas's intellectualism. *DVD* is a speculative project that retains a necessary relation to a certain kind of (intellectual) practice. Only a reader actually thinking along the lines offered by Nicholas can come to insights intended by the author of *DVD*.[118]

---

113. Cf. the discussion of love and intellect in the *C*.

114. See *DVD* 16, 71–74. 71:4–5, which states that "qui es forma omnis desiderabilis est veritas illa quae in omni desiderio desideratur." Human intellect, thus, has the following ambiguity: on the one hand, it is not satisfied with what it can fully understand and, on the other hand, it is not satisfied with what it cannot understand at all. Accordingly, only God in His Infinity can be a fitting object for the intellect's desire. In 74, Nicholas treats God's richness in terms of intellectual food.

115. On the author's intention, see Bocken and Decorte, "Inleiding," 22–23.

116. See ibid.: "This work must be rather seen as a philosophical practice [praxis] or a 'practical philosophy' where the reader/viewer is led from the known to the unknown and he or she comes to the insight that the unknown can only be seen from the known." Also ibid., 10: "The most interesting example [of Nicholas's mystical theology] is the *De Visione Dei* from the year 1453. This [work] demonstrates the connection between theory and practice [praxis] within mystical theology."

117. Cf. Bocken and Decorte, "Inleiding," 23–24.

118. Ibid., 32–33: "There is a quest for truth going on here and the reader gets an insight into the very process of thought [Dutch 'denkgebeuren'] preceding the formula-

Mystical Theology

A key feature of any kind of mystical theology can easily be recognized in *DVD*. According to this basic tenet, God alone can make Himself known.[119] This is the ultimate reason why Nicholas intended "to explain ... the wonders which are revealed beyond all sensible, rational, and intellectual sight."[120] Accordingly, the Prologue identifies Nicholas's intention explicitly as "*manuducere*," that is to say, "leading the readers by way of experiencing and through a very simple common means into most sacred darkness."[121] Once the disciples have arrived there, they will try to approach God ever nearer.

In connection with this *manuductio*, Nicholas admits that he has to speak about the Divine by using *similitudo*, i.e., likeness.[122] An essential feature of a picture, a portrait or any other kind of likeness is that it is both like and unlike the original: it is a *Zusammenspiel* of *similitudo* and *dissimilitudo*.[123] This can be called the epistemological ambiguity of the *similitudines*. Nicholas knew well about this ambiguity. He saw that every religious image and symbol leads one astray inasmuch as it is only a human means for attaining the *visio Dei*.[124] Through creatures, God can be only known in an enigmatic way.[125] When the human subject is confronted with enigmas, symbols, and the like, what he first and foremost needs is not so much a theoretical knowledge about these, but more importantly, a practical knowing-how concerning their usage

---

tion of doctrinal propositions. Therefore is the book [i.e., the *DVD*] is no coursebook, but a book with instructions [aanwijzingen] to start one's quest for truth—addressing not only the monks from Tegernsee."

119. E.g., *DVD* Preface, 1:6.

120. Ibid., 1:7–8: "enarrare queam mirabilia, quae supra omnem sensibilem, rationalem, et intellectualem visum revelantur."

121. Ibid., 1:8–10. See note 3 above for the Latin.

122. Cf. ibid., 2:1–2.

123. Cf. Decorte, "Middeleeuwse," 551, where a brief analysis of the portrait is given. The subject of the picture can be further examined with the help of Wittgenstein. See Churchill, "Rat and Mole's Epiphany."

124. Cf. the earlier discussion of the *DI*.

125. Cf. *DVD* 6, 22:1 and the following. There, expressions such as "velate et aenigmate," "secretum et occultum silentium," "caligo, nebula, tenebra, seu ignorantia," "supra omnia velementa," "omnem visibilem lucem transilire," "lucem quam videre non potest," and "excellentia lucis solis" all point both towards the impossibility of such a vision and the necessity of a transcendent movement.

in and for religion.¹²⁶ This observation points toward the special importance *manuductio* has for *DVD*. In the context of mystical theology, *manuductio* is connected with the idea of using or teaching the usage of a *similitude*. Such a *manuductio* is thus nothing else than the (teaching of) knowing-how concerning this or that sensible image.

The *manuductio* is strictly speaking a concession to human weakness. Because humans are sensible, material creatures, attached to and immersed in material, sensible reality, they cannot rise toward the pure spiritual realm otherwise, except with the help of such sensible, material guidance.¹²⁷ What was called earlier the epistemological ambiguity of images cannot be superseded by an explanatory theory, because every explanation finds its ultimate context in (the acquisition of) a practical skill of its own employment.¹²⁸ To say the same thing in Polanyian terms, an explanatory theory is only understandable at the background of the tacit knowledge of a practical knowing-how. Accordingly, the *DVD* should be characterized as a theoretical treatise on mystical theology retaining its (necessary) relation to (religious) practice. It is an intellectual reflection on the use of religious concepts.

My reading makes clear the reason why the idea of image plays an important role in this work. Nicholas employed several different images or similitudes in this work and it is not necessary to discuss them here in all their diversity. It will be more fruitful to turn to one specific image that is both easily identifiable and plays a central role and also has further implications for understanding the whole of *DVD*. This central image is a picture of an omnivoyant face, and it forms the starting-point of Nicholas's spiritual-intellectual journey.¹²⁹

126. Cf. Bocken and Decorte, "Inleiding," 22: "Nicholas . . . wants precisely to show that the insight into the necessity of the image commands a special treatment of that image." Note the presence of the practical dimension.

127. Cf. *DVD* Preface, 5:1–2: "Ex hac tali sensibili apparentia, vos fratres amantissimos per quandam praxim devotionis in mysticam propono elevare theologiam." Here, the original Dionysian meaning of manuductio rings through. Cf. e.g., Eriugena's Latin commentary on Dionysius.

128. Cf. Bocken and Decorte, "Inleiding," 23–27. See also Decorte's exposition of Polanyi's analysis in *RA*, 206–11 and a discussion of Wittgenstein in Churchill, "Rat and Mole's Epiphany," 158–61.

129. Similar pictures were abundant around that time. Nicholas listed four of them and sent one such picture to the Tegernsee monks. He called his exemplar "eicon dei." Later, he himself referred sometimes by this phrase to *DVD*. (Cf. *Nicholas of Cusa's Dialectical Mysticism*, 18–19 and Decorte, "De fascinatie," 118, 120–23. See also *DVD*

As far as this central image is concerned it is sufficient to say that:

1. the omnivoyant face beholds each monk at once,

   and

2. consequently, its gaze accompanies the moving monks as well.

In this way, the gaze will accompany even persons walking in opposite directions. The epistemologically important point is that one can only be certain concerning this simultaneous opposition of the movements of the gaze, if one believes (*credet*) the other person's report on his own experience.[130] In a typically medieval fashion, personal trust in the form of faith is revealed here as a "condition of possibility" for attaining knowledge.[131] Only after this necessary epistemological requirement is fulfilled can the contemplating individual start his own reflection and follow the way shown by Nicholas.[132]

Three Preliminary Considerations

Nicholas himself was aware of the anagogic function of this image.[133] Since his enterprise is of a speculative-intellectual kind, it is appropriate that after the prefatory discussion on the use of the image, three important premises are put forward.[134]

Preface, 2:2–11, *DP* 58:20–21.) Unfortunately, the picture sent by Nicholas is no longer extant. The same is true about Roger van der Weyden's (1400–1464) painting mentioned in *DVD*. A copy of this latter picture has been preserved in a Flemish tapestry. Nicholas could have seen the original when he was visiting Philip the Good in Brussels at the end of 1452. Cf. Nicholas of Cusa, *Selected Spiritual Writings*, 235 n. 10.

I cannot refrain from noting that in a rather amusing way, Jos Decorte called this picture as an "audio-visual handbook" (Dutch "audio-visuele handleiding"). Cf. Decorte, "De fascinatie," 118.

130. *DVD* Preface, 4:9–12.

131. Cf. *WW*, 319–21 and Bocken and Decorte, "Inleiding," 24–25. The latter text calls belief (Dutch "geloof") a necessary precondition of understanding ("noodzakelijk voorwaarde voor het begrijpen") and a necessary structure preceding all meanings ("een noodzakelijk structuur die aan alle betekenis voorafgaat"). Both *WI*, 314 and Decorte, "De fascinatie," 119 equally emphasise the importance of mutual trust and believing.

132. Bocken and Decorte, "Inleiding," 24 emphasises that this faith is not a Kierkegaardian "jump" and does not entail any kind of fideism.

133. Cf. *DVD* Preface 4.

134. Cf. ibid., 5:3: "praemittendo tria hoc opportuna." See also chs. 1, 2, and 3 respectively.

1. The first one is the assumption that whatever is *apparent* with regard to the icon-of-God's sight is more true (*verius*) with regard to God's true sight. God's sight is the Absolute Sight (*absolutus visus, visus abstractus*) viewed abstractly, that is to say sight as seen apart from every eyes and organs. In contrast to the contracted human viewpoint, God's perspective is not limited by anything whatsoever (*verus incontractus visus*).

2. The second consideration is intimately connected with the first one: God's Absolute Sight embraces all modes of seeing (*omnes modos*). Since God is above all limitation and contraction, His perspective positively transcends all other possible modes of seeing.

3. Finally, as a third consideration, it is stated that different things that are said of God do not differ in reality, because of His highest simplicity. Different names can be attributed to God, according to different limited human perspectives, but in Himself, God is fundamentally one and simple. Therefore His seeing equals His being "and so on with the remaining attributes" (*et ita de reliquis attributis*).[135] The rest of *DVD* is written in the form of a prayer that the omnivoyant image arouses in the contemplative. This text spells out some important speculative dimensions of the *visio Dei*.[136]

Using Different Images

Even though the image of the omnivoyant face has functioned as a starting-point for Nicholas's more speculative enterprise, this does not restrain Nicholas from employing other images in order to elucidate Divine things. This strategy is not extrinsic to his enterprise. If images are at once similar and dissimilar of what they are the images of, this means two things. On the one hand, the dissimilarity signals the ultimate

---

135. Nicholas has at least two reasons for especially speaking about sight in relation with God. On the one hand, he points to the etymology of the Greek word θεος in *DVD* 1, 6:4–6 and 8, 31:1–2. (Cf. *NA* 23, 104:12–14 and *DA* 14:1: "Deus dicitur a theoro, id est video.") On the other hand, the idea that God sees everything was familiar to Nicholas also from the Bible. See e.g., 2 Chr 16:9 and Ps 139:1–12.

136. Cf. *DVD* 4, 9:1 and Nicholas of Cusa, *Selected Spiritual Writings*, 239 n. 20. Bocken and Decorte, "Inleiding," 45 refers to this part of the *DVD* as a "witnessing" ("getuigenis").

shortcomings of any image in representing the signified reality. On the other hand, the similarity of any particular image to that reality indicates that an image can positively show something of the Divine.[137] God is radically transcendent, i.e., different from creatures and at the same time He is radically immanent as the Creator of the very same creatures. In the former sense, He is nothing since there can exist no proportion between His Infinity and finite Creation.[138] In the latter sense, however, God can be said to be everything. This means that He is visible and invisible at the same time.[139] Precisely because God is fundamentally visible in and to all creation, there can be no *a priori* objection to seeing Him through different images taken from this Creation, provided one does not forget the epistemological ambiguity of the particular image in question. Furthermore, if different images, names or concepts are necessarily articulated from different perspectives, their diversity can even have a positive role, namely, that of pointing towards God's Infinite Mystery (as seen) from different perspectives. Nicholas thus refers to God as to the Divine Painter (*pictor*) wanting to produce an image of Himself.[140] It can be argued that the likeness of God's Infinity cannot be unfolded in any other way, than in creating many images. As a consequence, Nicholas is able to accept several different images both in nature and human art.[141] As he confesses, all things induce the contemplative to turn toward God.[142]

Another important image, the metaphor of the wall of Paradise (*murus Paradisi*) captures well the ambiguity of the images.[143] This met-

---

137. Bond distinguishes between an evocative and a descriptive function of what he calls the coincident method of Nicholas's theology. Cf. Bond, "Introduction," 48–55. Bond's entire discussion is connected with the notions of an iconographic language, images, metaphor, and analogy. On the evocative function of images, see also Decorte, "De fascinatie," 127.

138. In Bond's interpretation, the key to understand Nicholas's position concerning analogy resides in the term "nulla." Between the finite and the Infinite there cannot exist any kind of proportionality but this does not exclude a non–proportional employment of analogy by way of using images or metaphors. Cf. Bond, "Introduction," 54.

139. Cf. *DVD* 12, 47:3–13.

140. *DVD* 25, 111:10–16.

141. Ibid., 113:14–15.

142. Ibid., 3–4: "Omnia me excitant ut ad te convertar."

143. In *DVD* the metaphor of the wall appears 22 times—10 times as "murus coincidentiae" and 12 times as "murus paradisi." Decorte, "De fascinatie," 129.

aphor, in fact, sets up the ultimate limits of discursive thinking (*ratio*).[144] This wall, also called "the wall of absurdity," delimits an impossibility—an invisible vision (*invisibilis visio*).[145] Names, similitudes, and any possible means of understanding (e.g. images) also remain necessary on this side of the wall.[146] Although they point towards the Divine, none of them actually reaches God since "no intelligence can scale that wall by its own power."[147]

Human intellect can only begin to really see (something of) God's transcendence in becoming conscious and acknowledging its own shortcomings and limitations. That is to say, God can be effectively approached only through *docta ignorantia*.[148] Only when one has seen and understood that he cannot see and understand God properly, does he or she actually come closer to seeing and understanding Him, because God can be positively understood as surpassing all possible images and names.[149]

The recognition of this "fact" gives one insight into negative theology. For Nicholas, such an insight was apparently not a purely theoreti-

---

144. For the biblical inspiration behind this image, cf. Gen 3:24: "Ejecitque Adam, et collocavit ante paradisum voluptatis Cherubim, et flammeum gladium atque versatilem ad custodiendam viam ligni vitae." In the tradition a cherub was understood as "the fullness of knowledge" or "spiritus altissimus rationis" in *DVD* 9, 39:9.—As such the cherub does not belong to the highest rank of the celestial hierarchy, i.e., the seraphim who are united to God. Hence, the guarding cherub forbidding the entrance to paradise is a suitable symbol of the ultimate shortcomings of analysing human reason that is unable to enter the Divine mysteries. See Decorte, "De fascinatie," 129–30. On the different ranks of angels, consult Pseudo–Dionisius's classical *Celestial Hierarchy*.

145. *DVD* 12, 48:1–49:2.

146. Ibid., 13, 52:6–9.11–15. The problem with names is that they are taken from limited beings. Therefore they can have contraries, e.g., light vs. darkness. When referring to infinity such a finite name will lose its limited signification and also its well-defined meaning. In this way, any analogy between the finite and the Infinite will ultimately break down.

147. *DVD* 12, 49:4–5: "murum . . . quem nullum ingenium sua virtute scandere potest."

148. Ibid., 13, 53:6–10: "Oportet . . . intellectum ignorantem fieri et in umbra constitui, si te videri velit. Sed quid est, deus meus, intellectus in ignorantia? Nonne docta ignorantia? Non igitur accedi potes, deus, qui es infinitas, nisi per illum cuius intellectus est ignorantia, qui scilicet scit se ignorantem tui."

149. *DVD* 12, 51:4–8: "absolutam cum te video infinitatem . . . , tunc revelate te inspicere incipio et intrare ortum deliciarum, quia nequaquam es aliquid tale quod dici aut concipi potest, sed infinitum super omnia talia absolute superexaltatus." Note again the connection between the intellectual and the affective aspect.

cal question. In other words, the assertion "I know that God is greater than I can think of Him" is not a first order proposition. Otherwise it would contradict other propropositions of the same order and it would also contradict itself. It would give the impression as if, ultimately, God could be defined in human terms.[150] The attitude of *learned ignorance* ought to be situated on a *meta-level* since it prescribes a certain way of dealing with limited propositions from the first order.[151] This observation shows the importance of the fact that *DVD* offers *manuductio* into a kind of speculative self-reflection that is necessarily related to the practical dimension of knowledge.

Nicholas's reflection on the "facial vision" of God (*facialis visio*) confirms this interpretation.[152] A face (*facies*) is a symbolic surface as it reveals one's thoughts, emotions, and feelings.[153] For Nicholas, God's Face is the example of all human faces. Therefore, every human face looking at the Divine sees nothing else in God, than the truth of his own face. Humans cannot judge otherwise than in a human way.[154] Thus, every person will necessarily take his own face as a starting point in attributing a "face" to the Infinite God.[155] If animals would be able attribute a "face" to God, they too, would similarly ascribe to him an animal face such as their own.[156] However, God's true Face transcends all these finite images. This entails that His Face can only be seen through a learned ignorance, for as long as someone conceives of something, he or she is far removed from the Divine Face. Neither God nor His Face (both names denoting in reality God) is a finite object of human

---

150. Bocken and Decorte, "Inleiding," 23: "Yet, this cannot be pure theoretical insight. Otherwise it should contradict itself and the definiability of God [Dutch 'bepaalbaarheid van God'] should be smuggled back unnoticed: God is then 'after all' nevertheless knowable, namely as unknowbale."

151. Bocken and Decorte, "Inleiding," 26: This attitude [Dutch "houding"] means in the first place a practice wherein one must practice him– or herself and beyond which there is no knowlegde thinkable." The authors refer to the example of wine tasting. Cf. *DVD* Prologue, 1:12–15 and 5, 14:1–10. I will return to these issues later.

152. Cf. *DVD* 6, 19–22.

153. Chapter 26, 95:15–16 calls the face "cordis nuntius," i.e., messenger of the (human) heart. Similarly, the eye or the gaze can function as a symbolic indicator. Cf. *DVD* 4, 11:3: "ibi amor ubi oculus." For everyday examples of symbolic practices, see *DVD* 26, 95–96.

154. *DVD* 6, 20:14–15: "Homo non potest iudicare nisi humaniter."

155. Ibid., 20:15–18 and 21:1–2.

156. Ibid., 20:18–19.

cognition as any other being (*aliquid*) could be. Nevertheless, by virtue of His Infinity (that is to say also of His Exemplary Being) God is visible in all faces.[157]

HUMAN PERSPECTIVES ON THE DIVINE

To make a general point, one can say that Nicholas's speculations based on seeing as a paradigm for human knowledge make understandable that human knowledge of the Divine necessarily comes from a particular and limited perspective.[158] Without such a perspective it would be even meaningless as human knowledge. This also means that in principle every human being is able to 'see' something of God.[159] As mentioned earlier, different human names only name God from respectively different human perspectives.[160] Furthermore, because God's seeing equals God's caring, not only does He see every creature equally, but He cares for all of them in equal measure.[161] Thus, God is present to every single being, because it is He who imparts them with their own being.[162]

When one recognizes this ontological presence, when one consciously encounters this Divine sight, care, and loving presence from one's own viewpoint, then that person will be naturally inclined to think that God does not care for any other being more than for himself.[163] The reason for this natural inclination does not exclusively lie in an egotistic preference for one's own being. The error is also conditioned by the fact that the human subject in question does not yet realize the Infinity of

---

157. Ibid., 22:1. It is clear from the following that a necessary precondition of this universal visibility is (learned) ignorance.

158. Cf. ibid., 8, 32:13–15: "Quod enim oculus noster se ad obiectum flectit, ex eo est quia visus noster per angulum quantum videt." See also Bocken and Decorte, "Inleiding," 28.

159. *DVD* 10, 41:8: "Ab omnibus creaturis es visibilis, et omnes vides."

160. *DVD* 3, 9:3–5: "omnia quae de deo dicuntur, realiter ob summam dei simplicitatem non posse differre, licet nos secundum alias et alias rationes, alia et alia vocabula deo attribuamus."

161. Cf. *DVD* Preface, 4:15–21 and chapter 5, 15–18. The equation of God's gaze with his loving care is all the more telling since a human gaze (*visus*) can naturally be the expression of attention, affection, care, and mercy (or of the lack of these).

162. *DVD* 4, 10:9–12: "Sic quidem ades omnibus et singulis, sicut ipsis omnibus et singulis adest esse, sine quo non possunt esse. Ita enim tu, absolutum esse omnium, ades cunctis, quasi non sit tibi cura de quocumque alio." See also 11:10–13.

163. Ibid., 10:11–12 and 11:1–3.

God's gaze, but he or she still tries to think the Infinite— i.e., the Divine Gaze—in terms of the finite human gaze. As a result, every person prefers his or her own mode of being to any other modes and wishes to let the being of all other beings perish rather than to see his or her own being destroyed.[164]

On the Task of Interpretation

It is possible to relate the earlier account of different human perspectives and self-love to the problem of different religions.[165] Such an interpretation appears all the more attractive, since—as a consequence of Nicholas's third premise—God's seeing necessarily coincides with His speaking. Therefore, one can also say that God is actually speaking to all creatures at one and the same time.[166] Furthermore, *DVD* points out that every human being is attached to his own—otherwise justified—religious images concerning the Divine.[167] More importantly, the claim is made that "all intellectual spirits are useful to each intellectual spirit" because they can reveal to one another what they respectively see from the Divine.[168] As a result of such a mutual dialogue, both their knowledge of and love for God is increased and "the sweetness of their joy is aflame."[169]

However, for a moment, I will withstand the temptation of explicitly relating these points to the question of different religions. Such a reading of *DVD* must necessarily go beyond the letter of this work. As its opening passage demonstrates, Nicholas addressed this treatise on mystical theology to a group of Christian contemplative monks. Small wonder then, that *DVD* contains no explicit reference to people not sharing Christian faith. On the other hand, against this *caveat* it can be pointed out that the account of *DVD* can be fairly called ontological. This ontological character is observable in the employment of such

---

164. Ibid., 10:12–18. See also 13:1–3; 15, 70:4–5, and 17, 79:5–7.

165. Cf. Bocken and Decorte, "Inleiding," 29–33.

166. See *DVD* 10, 40:12–14: "Id quod mihi est ecclesia, hoc tibi, domine, est totus hic mundus et singulae creaturae, quae sunt aut esse possunt. Sic igitur singulis loqueris et ea, quibus loqueris, vides." See also ibid., 40–42.

167. Cf. *DVD* 6, 20:14–19; 15, 67:1–2, and 15, 70:2–7.

168. *DVD* 25, 111:16–22.

169. Ibid., 111:22. Cf. 113:1–4.

general terms as, for instance, "thing" (*res*), "being" (*esse*), "whatever that exists" (*quodlibet quod est*) and creature (*creatura*).[170] Even though this account of being was inspired by and is actually written from a Christian perspective, it is presented as applicable to the entire universe (*totius universi*).[171] Therefore an interpretation developing further the aforementioned points is in principle not impossible.

Such an interpretation has to fulfill at least two conditions. First, it should not come into open conflict with other Cusanian works or it ought to able to resolve such a conflict. Secondly, this interpretation must be able to shed new light on those works by making them more understandable. The question whether this reading could actually render a consistent and useful interpretation of Nicholas's thought, can naturally be answered only in the course of its actual execution. Therefore, I will return to this question, when treating the *De Pace Fidei* in my next chapter.

INFINITY

For now, I would like to return to a previous point, namely, to God's Infinity. As it is clear from *DVD*, in Nicholas's opinion, God is not only infinitely greater than that which a human can think of, but one cannot even escape positing this Infinity. Thinking and knowing subjects necessarily have some awareness of Infinity. This Infinity must be presupposed before (thinking or coming to know) any form of otherness (*alteritas*).[172] This *otherness* is naturally a relative term, since it is only understandable as a reference to another. In this way, otherness derives its being from non-being, i.e., from the fact that its being is not (like) the being of the other.[173] Consequently, otherness cannot be a *principium*

---

170. Cf. e.g., *DVD* 10, 41:7–8.

171. *DVD* Preface, 4:19–21.

172. *DVD* 13, 56:8–10: "si non foret infinitas, neque tunc foret finis neque tunc aliud nec diversum, quae sine alteritate finium et terminorum non possunt esse."

173. *DVD* 14, 61:4–5: "Quod enim unum non est aliud, hinc dicitur alterum." Logically speaking, otherness presupposes negation. In modern formal logic, negation in itself is only a function, i.e., a formal procedure without a variant (content). Ontologically speaking, however, such a negation cannot stand on its own: there must be *something* to be negated.

positivum.[174] In contrast, Infinity is a positive principle.[175] Infinity is not opposed to or limited by anything else. Because Infinity is defined by Infinity— i.e., by Itself and Itself alone—Infinity has no otherness and consequently, no name is applicable to It.[176] However, any form of otherness can only appear at the background of this Infinity.

This idea of Infinity in *DVD* is important because it can be connected to the notion of non-otherness, which Nicholas would more fully elaborate later in his famous *De Directio Speculantis seu De Li Non Aliud* (1462).[177] This latter work is another speculative *manuductio* in the course of which Nicholas consciously takes up and develops some Dionysian themes.[178]

My short examination of *DVD* has shown how similar motives that have already been working in the *DI* and *C* are also operative in Nicholas's mystical theology. All three works display Nicholas's manuductive strategy from the sensible towards the Divine as a permanent structure of his intellectual-spiritual practice. The Trinitarian concern of these works is also manifest.[179] Further evidence of the Cusanian manuductive concern may be gathered when one turns to Nicholas's other works. Examples of *manuductio* can be further multiplied almost at will: Nicholas's famous *Idiota* (1450), for instance, can be read as the simple layman's *manuductio* of the schoolman into divine wisdom.[180] The term *manuductio* also returns in Nicholas's *De Possest* (1460) and in his own "Retractations," in the *De Venatione Sapientiae* (1462-3). As

---

174. *DVD* 14, 61:1-2.4.5-7: "dicis alteritatis non esse positivum principium. . . . Alteritas enim dicitur a non esse. . . . Alteritas igitur non potest esse principium essendi, quia dicitur a non esse. Neque habet principium essendi, cum sit a non esse."

175. Nicholas does not call infinity a "principium positivum." On God as Absolute Infinity, see *DVD* 13, 52-59.

176. Cf. *DVD* 13, 52:12-14, and 14, 60:3-5.

177. On the coincidence of opposites, see e.g. *DVD* chs. 9-13. *DVD* equates this coincidence with the wall of Paradise. The text makes clear that God is not simply equal to the coincidence of opposites, but He is even beyond that coincidence, i.e., He is to be found beyond the wall.

178. Cf. Beierwaltes, Werner. *Der verborgene Gott*, 24: "Die trinitarische Entfaltung des non–aliud . . . kann . . . schon von sinnlichen Erscheinungsbild her als ›*manuductio*‹ gelesen werden." The term "directio" in the title confirms this reading.

179. For a discussion of the Trinity, see *DVD* chs. 17-18. For the essential role of Christology, see chs. 19-25.

180. Beierwaltes, *Der verborgene Gott*, 17-18 names the "ludus globi" as an instance of manuductio.

has been pointed out earlier, the *Non Aliud* is another late Cusanian *manuductio*.

Before delving into other instances of the Cusanian *manuductio*, attention should first be paid to the dialogue *De Deo Abscondito*. This text places Nicholas's manuductive concern within the context of other religions.[181] Afterwards, *De Possest* and *De Li Non Aliud* will be briefly examined. The first of these two treatises directly preceded, while the second one followed up the completion of the great apologetical treatise, the *Cribratio Alkorani*. With respect to these three works, my working-hypothesis is similar to the one in relation with *DVD* and *PF*: Nicholas's own struggles with mystical theology in *DP* and *NA* formed the general theoretical framework for his approach towards Islam in the *CA*. This hypothesis can be verified after a respective examination of all three of Nicholas's *Spätwerke*.

Manuductio *as a Way of Talking to a Religious Other in the* De Deo Abscondito

Both the genre and the actual form of this very short text are not without significance. The *DA*—completed before 1445—is composed as an imaginary dialogue between a pagan and a Christian. In its course the pagan is confronted with a devout and rather obstinate Christian who keeps answering his puzzled questions with more and more mysterious replies. However, the pagan neither gives up his inquiry nor loses his temper. Throughout the discussion, he will remain both extremely polite *and* interested thereby indicating that he is really eager to learn.[182]

The starting point of the text is a twofold fact: the Christian's devout religiosity and his strange confession of consciously worshipping whom he does not explicitly know. Apparently in Nicholas's view, the problem is not so much that Christians worship God whom they do not know,

---

181. This work is not far from the *DI* in time. For the English translation, see Hopkins, *A Miscellany*, 131–37, notes 284–87. For the Latin text, see the Heidelberg edition. (Bond offers another translation in Nicholas of Cusa, *Selected Spiritual Writings*, 207–13.)

182. He addresses the Christian twice as "frater" and repeatedly employs phrases such as "quaeso" and "rogo." (Cf. *DA* 2:6, 7:1, 8:1, 13:14.) The entire dramatic framework emphasises the pagan's sympathy and readiness for a dialogue, as it starts with the pagans's recognition of the Christian's devotion (1:4–5) and it concludes with the former's philosophical–religious confession and praise of the One God.

but rather the opposite would be the mistake. As already indicated in *DI*, pagans worship God whom they only think they know.[183] Thereby they are fundamentally deceived. The real problem does not concern worship per se, but the confusion between the absolute, unintermingled, eternal, and ineffable Truth (Creator) with its works (creatures) in the course of worship. Nicholas's point is that "absolute truth" or the ultimate meaning of reality cannot be possessed properly speaking. It can be only approached and participated through the religious practice itself.[184] This explains the reason why pagans are mistaken in their worship and thought. More importantly, the same point entails that Christianity's claim of "possessing" absolute religious truth ultimately turns out to be a question of learned ignorance.

According to Nicholas, no one single essence can be fully grasped and known by a human intellect. Much less can one understand God or Truth itself. Thus, "knowing the absolute" can only mean that one realizes that one does not know Him, that is to say, that one does not know God as a limited, finite object of human cognition. In the final analysis, human knowledge in the form of propositional knowledge concerns these limited objects. The Infinite/Truth/One cannot be an object of this kind of knowledge since it cannot be equated with any finite being. Because of His exceptional ontological status God is not an object (among other objects) in the world. In these respects God's relation to objects parallels the subject's relation to objects. Just as (subjective) sight itself cannot be seen and traced as an object of seeing and thus relates itself to objects as a *non*-object, so it is with God. Sight is not a thing in the (visible) world but—to use again Kantian terminology—a condition of possibility for seeing (in order to encounter visible objects). Neither is God an object of human cognition.[185]

Hence, the epistemic value of religious statements cannot lie in their 'objectivity,' that is to say, religious and theological statements do not belong to the class of ordinary propositions. Nor are they empty

---

183. The pagan asks the Christian "to lead him to the point of being able to understand." Cf. *DA* 8:1–2.

184. Cf. *DA* 6:5–6.

185. Cf. the analysis of light in the *C* or the speculation on the Divine Gaze in *DVD* along similar lines. Modern parallels can be found in the three so-called Kantian ideas (God, world, I), which are all conditions of possibilities for objects to be thought and encountered. For Kant these ideas offer a perspective or horizon that makes any objective encounter possible.

phrases. They are more like pointers, arrows, indicators, signs, metaphors or symbols.[186] They show the seeker the direction of transcendence without making this transcendence an object of (objectifying) cognition. The text of the *DA* testifies that for Nicholas, the Christians' religious and theological position is superior to the pagan's, precisely because the former realizes the limitations of his knowledge. At the end of *DA*, the Christian succeeds in communicating to the courteous gentile the right sense of his theological discourse. The latter has come to see God's transcendence.

In another important respect, however, the *DA* leaves much open. Namely, it is not the Triune God of Christianity that is defended in this dialogue, but the One God, One Truth, without any composite and alterity, in His uttermost Simplicity and Perfection, a neo-Platonic-Aristotelian God rather than a Christian one. This fact should not come as a surprise if one remembers the dramatic setting of the *DA*. As its scenery shows, the goal of Nicholas's dialogue was to lead the courteous pagan to genuine monotheism. The pagan had to learn that he should not worship any limited image, but—in and through those images—the One truly transcendent God. Earlier in the present chapter, the crucial importance and the fundamental role of the Trinitarian doctrine both for Nicholas's thought in general and for his *manuductio* in particular have been pointed out. Approaching the *DA* from this perspective, it becomes clear that this text cannot be possibly meant as a guidance to the Trinity: at best, this dialogue could be read as an incomplete form of Trinitarian *manuductio*, in other words, a first, preparatory step of a longer and difficult process. The full significance of this observation will be born out only in my next chapter. Here, I would like to point out that the apparent lack of a full-fledged Trinitarian *manuductio* from the *DA* forms no argument for denying that in Nicholas's perception, non-Christians were in need of a specifically Trinitarian *manuductio*. It seems only that—at least in this dialogue—Nicholas was ready to make some necessary concessions in a manuductory process.

However, in relation to the strict monotheism of Islam a merely monotheistic *manuductio*—such as the one in *DA*—is at best superfluous. After all, the monolithic God of the *DA* and the God of the Muslims are very close to each other. It remains yet to be seen what Nicholas could offer to Muslims in terms of a full-fledged Trinitarian *manuductio*. This

---

186. Cf. Hopkins, *A Miscellany*, 287 and *RA*, 189–218.

problem will be treated in the course of the next two chapters, while the remaining sections of the present chapter aim at a deeper understanding of the Cusanian *manuductio* and mystical theology.

Manuductio *and the Cusanian Project in* De Possest

Nicholas composed *De Possest* in 1460, before writing his great apologetic work on the Koran.[187] *DP* is presented as a dialogue between Nicholas and his two friends, Bernard and Abbot John.[188] In its course, several important Cusanian ideas reappear: for instance, the *docta ignorantia*, the *via negativa*, and the *coincidentia oppositorum* alongside themes of mathematical symbolism and that of mystical vision.[189]

How Can One See God?

The discussion starts with Bernard's request. He wants Nicholas to explain *Rom* 1:20, a key text of medieval epistemology: "The invisible things of Him, including His eternal power and divinity, are clearly seen from the creation of the world, by means of understanding created things."[190] The answer to the question as how to interpret this particular passage from Paul is given by way of a reference to another text from the Apostle where visible and invisible things are contrasted as being respectively temporal and eternal things.[191] The first ones are images

---

187. For the translation and Latin text, see Hopkins, *Concise Introduction*.

188. According to Hopkins' note on page 178, Ms. Cusanus 219 calls the work *stella*, meaning "guiding star." It is possible to see this label as indicating the fundamental manuductive character of *DP*.

Bernard was chancellor of the archbishop of Salzburg and he is not to be confused with the Prior at Tegernsee. John Andrea Vivegius was abbot at the monstery of St. Justine of Sedazium, he also appears as one of the interlocutors in the *NA*.

189. Cf. Hopkins, *Concise Introduction*, v: "After much study, I finally came to recognize that the dialogue *De Possest* provides the easiest access to Nicholas' basic ideas." In my reading, *DP* is also an important witness of Nicholas's fundamental manuductive concern. The fact that this work can clarify some other essential Cusanian ideas obviously helps my interpretation.

190. Hokpins's translation of *DP* 2:3–5. "Invisibilia enim ipsius a creatura mundi per ea quae facta sunt intellecta conspiciuntur, sempiterna quoque virtus eius et divinitas." Hopkins, *Concise Introduction*, 173 n. 3 points out that the original Latin text is ambiguous.

191. 2 Cor 4:18: "non contemplantibus nobis quae videntur, sed quae non videntur; quae enim videntur temporalia sunt, quae autem non videntur aeterna sunt."

(*imagines*) of the second ones.[192] Through understanding them, humans can understand eternal "things." In this way, creatures can manifest God.[193]

Even if one is ready to accept this answer, the question is still open as to what manner (*quomodo*) one will be able to see the invisible truth of the Creator.[194] *DP* suggests the answer by the example of reading. The truth of every written text is, namely, "invisible" in a certain sense. Written characters do not convey a real vision, but they make the reader understand the message of the text. As signs, they are actually pointing beyond themselves. The meaning of the text is the object of the intellect and not of the senses. Therefore, this meaning cannot be seen otherwise than in an intellectual manner. For Nicholas, a similar point holds about perceptible things in general. In encountering and seeing them as perceptible, final, and temporal humans can arrive at the insight that these beings cannot exist on their own. They are dependent on a higher power. What is "seen" in this way is ultimately the invisible God Himself.[195] Here, *DP* provides the sketch of an itinerary already familiar from the *DI* and *DVD*, i.e., an ascending movement mounting up from creatures, through their *ratio*, to their Beginning.

Such an apprehension of the Divine *invisibilia* through the *visibilia* of Creation can actually start with any being whatsoever. Every existing thing is able to be what it is and this fact, for Nicholas, presupposes that Absolute Actuality must actually exist. However, this Absolute Actuality is also able to exist and thereby its actual existence presupposes Absolute Possibility. Since these two concepts mutually presuppose each other, they not only stand and fall together, but they necessarily coincide. Because no limited, temporal being can exist without them, Absolute Actuality, Absolute Possibility, and their Union are coeternal, or even better they *are* Eternity, i.e., God Himself. God must be prior to any actuality and possibility. God is alone what He is able to be and He is able to be what He is. Absolute Possibility, Absolute Actuality, and the Union of the two are Nicholas's own terms for the Divine Persons of the Trinity of Christianity. The text of *DP* especially emphasizes the differ-

---

192. *DP* 2:8–9: "Temporalia imagines sunt aeternorum."
193. Ibid., 2:11: "Ita a creatura mundi fit dei manifestatio."
194. Ibid., 2:12—3:2.
195. Ibid., 4:1–6.

ence between this God and His creatures. Concerning God's greatness it is said that He is infinite and indivisible greatness.

This lack of proportion between God and His creatures signals a serious difficulty. Namely, if God is infinitely different from every creature it is not clear how it is possible to speak about Him using human terms.[196] In *DP* this problem is fully acknowledged. For Nicholas, every name or concept taken from creatures forms a disproportionate likeness to God who is actually both the possibility and the actuality of the existence of every determination. God is not able to exist otherwise than He does. This fact gives Nicholas the occasion to coin a new name for God: Nicholas thought that *Possest* is a sufficiently approximate name for God. On the one hand, it can be the name of every thing. On the other hand, it is no name at all. In this way, the name *Possest* makes the epistemological ambiguity of our human cognition manifest.

As *Possest*, God is everything that He is able to be: only He is Being in an unqualified sense.[197] He differs infinitely from any creature. Nevertheless, God can be referred to by any name taken from creatures, provided that the limits defining that particular name with respect to possibility are mentally removed.[198] Clearly, Nicholas had already been struggling with the same problem of naming Infinity in his *DVD*. In *DP*, he explicitly drew the consequence according to which, ultimately, "one must not insist upon the words themselves."[199] This is an important phrase and will reappear at a crucial point in the inter-religious discussion of *PF*.[200]

It can be argued throughout his life, as a Trinitarian thinker, Nicholas was trying to form ever new names for the Holy Trinity.[201] His continual struggle for naming the Divine Mystery was intrinsically connected to Nicholas's creative use of language. His intellectual ascent toward God relies on the help of language. By a transference of meaning, words undergo a transformation in taking up a metaphorical meaning. In this way, even the name *Possest*—when taken properly—will lead

---

196. Hence Bernard's remark in 10:1–5.

197. Cf. ibid., 14:18–19: "Solus deus perfecte et complete est."

198. Ibid., 11:10–12: "Non refert igitur quomodo deum nomines, dummodo terminos sic ad posse esse intellectualiter transferas."

199. Ibid., 11:1: "Non est vocabulis insistendum."

200. See my next chapter.

201. Cf. e.g., *DI* I, 9, 25 and *NA* 5, 19.

one unto a mystical vision which vision can be a beginning of Divine Revelation.[202] According to Nicholas, Saint Paul did not intend another meaning in Rom 1:20: if someone apprehends the world as created he or she transcends the world in order to seek its Creator. *DP* makes it again clear that no natural human power suffices to understand God, since His Infinity cannot be comprehended by a finite mind.[203] Nicholas's appreciation of this fact is related to the positive possibility of human intellect's self-transcendence.[204]

In the *DP* both mathematical illustrations and sensible images play a necessary role.[205] For instance, the example of the top (*trochus*) is taken up.[206] Similarly, the example of the line is elaborated with the help of the concept of *Possest*. In relation to the same example it is pointed out that by applying the concept of *Possest* to a finite, nameable object that object becomes a symbolism (*aenigma*) of that which is beyond all names. When it comes to naming the Almighty, all names such as oneness, singularity, plurality, multitude, and being or non-being are ruled out. Ultimately, there can be found no name that is applicable to God "with complete truth and complete distinctiveness."[207]

The problem of naming the unnamable is already familiar from the previous discussion. In *DP* it is phrased through the question as to how a finite intellect can grasp Actualised-possibility. Abbot John points out that the human intellect is never Actualised-possibility Itself,

---

202. *DP* 15:1–4: "Ducit ergo hoc nomen speculantem super omnem sensum, rationem et intellectum in mysticam visionem, ubi est finis ascensus omnis cognitivae virtutis et revelationis incogniti dei initium."

203. Understanding something means becoming similar to it and this is impossible in this case. Cf. *DP* 17:1–16.

204. Cf. ibid., 15:15–16.

205. In 18:3–6, Bernard is asking for a manuductio by a sensible image precisely in order to transcend all images. In the next line, his request is accepted.

206. From my perspective, the unusual interpretation of this sensible image is less interesting than the fact that it is employed only as an illustration and not as an argument. See *DP* 19:28–29: "Satis sit ergo hoc phantasmate posse ainigmatice aliquiter videri quomodo." In 24:2–3, Bernard calls the example of a top as a most fitting symbolism.

Hopkins, *Concise Introduction*, 176 n. 38 points out that Nicholas used the Latin "aenigma" in the sense of a "symbolism." (Cf. also 1 Cor 13:12.) On Nicholas's use of the top, cf. ibid., 175 n. 32.

207. *DP* 26:4–5: "verissime et discretissime nullum nomen nominabile per nos invenis."

consequently, it cannot grasp Actualised-possibility. However, the intellect glimpses Actualised-possibility from afar.[208] The exact way or mode of this seeing can be better understood when one remembers that God cannot be naturally viewed except through symbolism. "He who remains ever invisible" can become visible only through Divine Revelation, that is to say, only God Himself can reveal Himself. More precisely, God's true and only Revealer is Jesus Christ.[209] In and through faith in Him, humans can attain a divine vision. Christ must dwell in the believer through faith and this is only possible through the indwelling of the Holy Spirit who is the spirit of love and truth. Ultimately, it is this Spirit who enlightens the seeker who in turn "acquires sight through faith."[210] *DP* clearly states that concerning the exact mode of this vision there is no further explanation possible.[211]

Just as in *DVD*, the way towards this vision is described as a way of desire.[212] The human desire to know, i.e., the desire to see God will be satisfied only by Him. What is at stake in this vision is an insight into God's own *logos*, which is at once the *logos* of everything. In *DP*, knowing the Word turns out to be a necessary precondition for real self-knowledge while the purity of heart is a necessary preparation for attaining the Divine Vision.[213]

Beyond Trinity?

When coming to discuss the Trinity, *DP* acknowledges that "in various ways many things can always be said, although most inadequately."[214] The text refers back to Nicholas's previous writings.[215] His many meditations and readings resulted in his conviction according to which the

---

208. Ibid., 30:6–7: "licet a remotis videat, non capit."

209. Ibid., 31:9–13.

210. Ibid., 32:9–10.

211. Ibid., 32:10–12: "Neque dici potest quomodo hoc fiat. Quis enim dicere posset hoc? Nec qui ex non–vidente factus est videns." In the following, the story of the blind man is referred to. Cf. John 9:1–41.

212. *DP* 35:3–5; 38:6–8.

213. Cf. *DP* 34:8–11 and 38:1–5. Note that in 38:7–15, the "scientia dei" is called "scientia scientiarum," which is in turn equated with "verbi dei notitia."

214. *DP* 40:6–8: "Semper varie multa dici possunt, licet insufficientissime, haec quae praemisi et quae in variis libellis mei legisti ostendunt."

215. For references to *DVD* and *DI*, see respectively *DP* 58:11–21 and 60:1–7.

ultimate and deepest contemplation (*consideratio*) of God is boundless (*intermina*), infinite (*infinita*), and in excess of every concept. In the final analysis, by no name or term can humans limit or define God's infinite Absolute Concept. He—and His concept—is not conceivable. To the attentive reader of *DI*, *C*, and *DVD*, these points sound already familiar.

DP draws out an important consequence from the foregoing by explicitly stating that God is neither one nor three.[216] Considering Nicholas's basic Trinitarian concern throughout his manuductive project this is a remarkable statement. Its striking character can be somewhat neutralized by pointing out an important reason for holding such a view. *DP* also states that there is no proportion between (infinite) possibility and (finite) actuality.[217] God as *Possest* is above both possibility and actuality just as He is also above every human concept. Seeing from a human perspective, rational entities (*rationis entia*) such as mathematical figures and numbers can be known with precision since these are construed by human reason.[218] In contrast, real things (*realia*) are constructed solely by the Divine Intellect and thus only God can know them with precision. The distinction between these two realms of being is important. While mathematical notions are necessary for human life (for instance in the form of building or measuring) when applied to the *realia*, they can indicate them only in a metaphorical way (*per assimilationem figurae*) or symbolically (*ex aenigmate*).[219]

The epistemological point is that there exist aspects of being—such as, for instance, expressed by the concept of human species—that cannot be accounted for in purely quantitative terms.[220] Outside proper mathematical knowledge, there cannot exist exact knowledge. God—who cannot be greater or smaller—is beyond any (quantitative)

---

216. *DP* 41:5–7: "Sic neque ipsum nominamus unum nec trinum nec alio quocumque nomine, cum omnem conceptum unius et trini et cuiuscumque nominablis excedat."

217. *DP* 42:13–15.

218. In Nicholas's words, mathematical entities have their origin (*principium*) in humans. For a more detailed discussion of the different realms of being and the respective investigations pertaining to them, see *DP* 62–64.

219. E.g., the concept of the form is analogous to a geometrical figure, without being a figure properly speaking. While a mathematical form is imaginable (as it can be represented with an image), a form (in the sense of an idea) is beyond representation.

220. That which lacks quantity cannot have a (mathematical) figure. Being as such, it cannot be captured through a mental image.

concept, thus He is beyond every number too.[221] Mathematics can only offer symbolism for theology.

Nicholas naturally knew that human understanding necessarily works with the help of quantitative concepts such as the concept of number. But he insisted that although God is three, He cannot be quantitatively, that is to say numerically three.[222] The same point must hold true for Divine unity as well.[223] God is beyond any *substance*, *res* and *ens*. As Beginning (*principium*), He is prior to any alterity and plurality and as such also prior to the concept of number. In relation to creatures, the Creator must be called triune but taken in Himself, God remains ineffable with respect to every mode of discourse. In short, Nicholas saw the doctrine of the Trinity ultimately as both relative and justified at the same time. Whoever thinks that he or she has apprehended God, must know that this belief results from the deficiency and meagerness of his or her intellect. Therefore, *DP*'s mystical theology—even in its Trinitarian passages—points again toward the Cusanian *docta ignorantia*. The text acknowledges that it is really difficult "to see" a God who is above all opposition. He is at once everywhere and nowhere.[224] He can reveal Himself in every tiny creature, yet He surpasses (*excedens*) all images—even those of a Trinitarian discourse. The relevance of this point for a possible dialogue with Islam will be borne out later.

As far as *DP* is concerned, this work states clearly that negation is the best way to see God.[225] This does not entail that images are useless, but rather that they should be taken in a special sense or mode when used for seeing the invisible God. When applied to the Divine, all human concepts should be transferred transcending every limit.[226] However, ultimately, sensible, imaginable, and even intelligible knowledge is of

---

221. Cf. *DP* 43:27–30: "Omne ... quod non cadit sub multitudine nec magnitudine, non potest nec concipi nec imaginari nec de eo phantasmata fieri, sic nec praecise intelligi."

222. Cf. *DI* I, 19, 57:10–11. According to Nicholas this point was already made by Augustine. Senger adds in his notes that though this is not a direct quotation, some passages from Augustine and from the commentaries of Pseudo-Beda and Thierry of Chartres come close to its meaning.

223. Cf. *DP* 46:1–2 and 50:4–6.

224. Ibid., 74:4–5: "totaliter undique et nullibi."

225. See e.g. *DP* 67:11–15 and 70:2–5.

226. Cf. ibid., 68:21–23: "Si ... aufers terminum et videas esse interminum seu eterminum sive aeternum, utique tunc vides ipsum ante non-esse."

no avail in spiritual things.[227] During this ascending movement towards God's Mystery the believer will necessarily lose his or her sense of direction, that is to say he or she will arrive at darkness and ignorance. God remains completely (*penitus*) unknown to all who seek Him by way of reason and intellect. That is the reason why the reader of *DP* is reminded of the absolute necessity of Divine Revelation.[228]

DP makes a strong point against any rationalistic theology or philosophy aiming to understand God fully.[229] Nicholas was convinced that Christ revealed the way to God. This a way of faith, hope, and desire: the way as shown by the words and deeds of Christ Himself. At the end of *DP*, Nicholas clarified his intent by clearly stating that "all statements we have made aim only at making us understand that our Creator surpasses all understanding." The next sentence makes clear the connection of this negative move of mystical theology with Christian religious practice.[230] At the end of *DP* the practice of *imitatio Christi* and Divine Grace are revealed as the ultimate horizon for understanding God's transcendence.

To the reader of *DI* and *DVD* all this should not come as a surprise. In both of these works Christology has played a crucial and manuductive role. As *DVD* states:

> a free student, who is under his own guidance, is not perfected unless he subjects himself by faith to the word of a teacher; for he needs to trust and hearken unto a teacher.[231]

---

227. *DP* 74:12–15.

228. Cf. ibid., 75:1–3 and also earlier.

229. *DP* 31:9–11: "Est enim deus occultus et absconditus ab oculis omnium sapientium, sed revelat se parvulis seu humilibus, quibus dat gratiam." Cf. Matt 11:25.

Cf. *DVD* 21, 92:3–10: "Ihesu, ... Tu es omnibus huius mundi sapientibus penitus ignotus, quia de te contradictoria verissima affirmamus, cum sis creator pariter et creatura ... Stultitiam asserunt id credere posssibile. Fugiunt igitur nomen tuum; et lucem tuam, qua nos illuminasti, non capiunt. Sed cum se putent sapientes, stulti et ignorantes et caeci manent in aeternum." See ibid., 9, 39:1–5: "deus meus, qui patefacis mihi quod non est via alia ad te accedendi, nisi illa quae omnibus hominibus, etiam doctissimis philosophis, videtur penitus inaccessibilis et impossibilis, quoniam tu mihi ostendisti, te non posse alibi videri quam ubi impossibilitas occurit et obviat." Cf. 1 Cor 1:20–21.

230. *DP* 75:8–9: "Quaecumque igitur per nos dicta sunt non ad aliud tendunt quam ut intelligamus ipsum omnem intellectum excedere."

231. *DVD* 24, 108:9–11: "discipulus liber qui sui iuris est, nisi se verbo magistri subiciat per fidem, non perficitur; oportet enim quod confidat et audiat magistrum."

Christ, by virtue of His being the Word of God and a human person at one and the same time, proves to be the Teacher (*magister*) of humanity *par excellence*. Only a person accepting Christ's guidance can arrive at a proper knowledge of God.[232] *DP* points out that "just as the artist who is untrained cannot do those things which belong to the art, so neither can the believer who is unprepared."[233] This preparation or teaching process starts with the necessary moment of personal trust (*fides qua*).[234] The ultimate aim of this act of faith is the *visio Dei*.[235] Through the actual *imitatio Christi*, the believer gradually becomes more and more Christlike.[236] Leaving behind all (sensible) hindrance, he or she assimilates to himself or to herself the Divine knowledge that was revealed in Jesus Christ's words and deeds.[237] In this way, the human intellect recognizes in itself God's Truth, i.e., the Word.[238]

Mystical Theology versus Aristotelian Reason in the NA

Nicholas wrote his *De Non Aliud*—or *Directio speculantis*—directly after the composition of his great apologetic work on the Koran.[239] The

---

232. *DVD* 24, 108:15–18 and 25, 113:6–8.

233. *DP* 34:7–8: "Et sicut non potest indispositus artista operari ea quae artis sunt, ita nec indispositus fidelis."

234. Cf. *DVD* 24, 109:12 speaking of "credere deo."

235. *DP* 39:1.3–4: "videre fidem esse videre deum ... Nam fides est invisibilium et aeternorum. Videre ergo fidem est videre invisibile, aeternum—seu deum nostrum." Cf. Heb 11:1 and 2 Cor 4:18.

236. Cf. *DP* 32–33.

237. *DP* 39:7–14; 75:8–11. Cf. *Epistola auctoris* in *DI* III, 264:5–17. These references to the indwelling (habitare, mansionem facere) of Christ or the Spirit point toward a personal interiorisation of the religious doctrine without entailing a thoroughgoing subjectivism. Cf. Dupré, "Truth in Religion," 40: "Believers assume that what they know of the divine object they know through that object itself. Christians have traditionally expressed this in the doctrine of the indwelling Spirit who teaches them 'entire faith.' . . . this kind of evidence provides no scientific support for its truth, nor does it increase our knowledge of the world. But it opens up a different *perspective* on metaphysical insight as well as on empirical investigation, and brings with it a unique yet highly personal justification of its own truth."

238. *DVD* 24, 109:4–5.

239. The *CA* was composed during the winter of 1460–1461, while the *NA* was completed before January 18th in 1462. Cf. Nikolaus von Kues, *Vom Nichtanderen*, xix–xx and *Nicholas of Cusa on God as Not-Other*, 3.

title already suggests that the *NA* is a speculative *manuductio*.[240] It is written in the form of a dialogue between Nicholas and three of his friends: Ferdinand appears as a traditionally Aristotelian thinker, while both Abbot John—already familiar from the *DP*—and Peter Balbus are more or less Platonists.[241] Nicholas himself is presented in the *NA* as an enthusiast reader of the works of Pseudo-Dionysius Areopagite.[242] After the introductory chapter, Ferdinand converses with Nicholas in chapters 2-19, while in chapters 20-21 and 22-24 Peter and John take up the role of the dialogue partner.

According to Wilpert, its German translator, the *NA* is probably one of the most abstract works written by Nicholas's hands.[243] However, just as in all of his writings, Nicholas was also here struggling with the question of God.[244] The *NA* grew out of a single intuition and all the technicalities of its discussion should be understood as clarifying and justifying this basic intuition.[245] Much the same can be said concerning other works such as, for instance, the *DI*, *DVD*, and *DP*.[246] The proximity of the *NA* to the entire Cusanian project is also shown by the fact that this late work offers—alongside with new speculations on the concept of God—a general presentation of Nicholas's philosophy.[247] If this is true, then it is not altogether clear in what way an examination of

---

240. Nikolaus von Kues, *Vom Nichtanderen*, 199n1: "Hier haben wir den Titel unserer Schrift: Anleitung zum Schauen. Die Abhandlung ist also eine Methodologie, sie will vom rationalem Denken zum intuitiven Schauen führen." Cf. also ibid., 107 n. 3: "Immer wieder erscheint als Motto seiner [i.e., Nikolaus's] Schriften, daß er einen leichteren Zugang zur mystischer Theologie—diese blieb immer das Ziel—gefunden habe." The *NA* employs quite often words such as "dirigere," "ducere," and the like. Cf. *NA* 24, 113:1-10.

241. Cf. *NA* 1, 1:2-6. Ferdinand Matim of Portugal was Nicholas's personal physician; Peter Balbus of Pisa was a translator of Proclus and later became bishop of Tropea.

242. Ibid., 1, 1:6-7: "tu vero, cum vacat, in Areopagita Dionysio theologo versaris." In the *NA*, Dionysius is the Theologian par excellence. Nicholas did not only call him as "theologus," but also "magnus theologus," and even "theologorum maximus." Cf. *NA* 14, 53:12-13 and 54:2 respectively.

243. Nikolaus von Kues, *Vom Nichtanderen*, xv: "Die Schrift Vom Nichtanderen erscheint äußerlich vielleicht als das abstrakteste unter allen Werken des Cusanus."

244. Cf. ibid., xv-xvi.

245. Ibid., xxv-xxvi

246. For the *PF*, see my next chapter.

247. Nikolaus von Kues, *Vom Nichtanderen*, xxvi.

the *NA* could add to my investigation. That is to say reiterating previous points of the Cusanian mystical theology such as those concerning *manuductio*, Divine invisibility, sensible images, and *visio Dei* seems to be superfluous.

The Theologian and the Philosopher

In any case, the *NA* strikes the eye as the most emphatically Dionysian work from Nicholas: Dionysius the Areopagite is meant to be the intellectual hero of this book. The *NA* quotes several extended passages from *The Celestial Hierarchy*, *The Ecclesiastical Hierarchy*, *The Divine Names*, *The Mystical Theology*, *The Letter to Gaius*, *The Letter to Hierothus*, and also comments extensively on these texts.[248] Moreover, Nicholas saw himself as a serious follower of Dionysius, and he interpreted other thinkers in the light of his own understanding of Dionysius.[249] In sum, the *NA* takes up and consciously develops different themes of (Nicholas's interpretation of) the Dionysian mystical theology offering thereby the clearest statement of Nicholas's relation to Dionysius. This also means that the *NA* gives a general Dionysian perspective on Nicholas's manuductive project. What is especially important for my purpose is that the *NA* confronts and openly criticizes Aristotelian epistemology and logic. Inasmuch as Dionysius can be called the positive hero of the *NA*, Aristotle plays an exceedingly negative role.[250] In this way, the *NA* offers at the same time perhaps the best introduction to Nicholas's criticism of Aristotelian thought.[251] As will be clear from this criticism, far from

---

248. See *NA* 14, 53–71. Wilpert points out that chs. 15–17 are explanations of the Dionysian quotations.

249. Cf. *NA* chs. 18–21.

250. Even though Aristotle's achievements in "rational and moral philosophy" are acknowledged in *NA* 19, 89:14–16.

251. Nikolaus von Kues, *Vom Nichtanderen*, xxii: "Seinen besonderen Reiz . . . erfährt das Gespräch dadurch, daß in Ferdinand ein Vertreter des Aristotelismus eingeführt wird. Als Mediziner gehört er der konservativen Richtung des Humanismus an; er ist der Repräsentant des gegenwärtig in den Schulen herrschenden aristotelischen Nominalismus. Deutlicher als in jeder anderen seiner Schriften zeigt Cusanus hier, daß er die Schule kennt, aber ebenso klar wird, daß er dem Aristotelismus nichts abzugewinnen weiß." Cf. Nikolaus von Kues, *Vom Nichtanderen*, 197 n. 2.

See also ibid., 198 n. 3: "In der Grundhaltung . . . empfindet Cusanus das Trennende stärker als das Gemeinsame, und die schroffe Ablehnung der Schulphilosophie, wie sie die Apologie zum Ausdruck bringt, hat sich nicht geändert."

being a simple denial of Aristotelian epistemology, it is also a constructive one. Thus, instead of looking for further details on or variations of *manuductiones* in the *NA*, in the following I will concentrate on the criticism of Aristotle. This can both shed light on the manuductive project of Nicholas's mystical theology and will help to show the differences from Ramón Lull's thought.

With the help of Dionysius, Nicholas was trying to articulate a higher kind of human discourse. The examination of Nicholas's manuductive project so far confirms Carlos Steel's observation, according to which Nicholas developed

> in an ingenious way, manifold strategies, (mathematical examples, conjectures, coincidences of oppositions) to make us say something about what is beyond all discourse. In fact, we should not too easily stop thinking and speaking about what is One. This complex supra-rational discourse is in his view the real mystical theology.[252]

After an exploration of the Theologian—i.e., Dionysius Areopagite—the dialogue of the *NA* turns to Aristotle.[253] Until the end of chapter 17, Ferdinand, the representative of the Aristotelian school, has been paying careful attention to Nicholas's speculations concerning the Not-Other (*non aliud*). In the subsequent chapter, the same Ferdinand turns the discussion to Aristotle.[254] While chapter 18 discusses the deficiency of the Aristotelian theory of substance, chapter 19 treats the limits of rational thinking. It is these two chapters that will be examined briefly in the following.

Substance

To begin with, the *NA* states that Aristotle had been searching for the *quidditas* but he never found it.[255] As Nicholas puts it,

252. Steel, "Beyond the Principle of Contradiction?" 599.

253. See *NA* 18–19.

254. Nikolaus von Kues, *Vom Nichtanderen*, 197 n. 1: "Die Opposition der Renaissance gegen die scholastische Tradition war begreiflicherweise auch eine Ablehnung des scholastischen Aristotelismus. Ferdinand, der Vertreter der Tradition, der sich bisher so gelehrig der neuen Betrachtungsweise des Kardinals erschlossen hat, wünscht nochmals eine zusammenfassende Würdigung seiner bisherigen für unantastbar gehaltenen Autorität."

255. Cf. *Metaphysics* 996 a 5–9 and 1028b 2–4.

at last, it seemed to him that no one had named it correctly. For whoever named it, named it something other and not that most simple quiddity-of-things, which Aristotle saw not to be able to be anything other.[256]

Moreover, Aristotle

did not stray in this matter; but he stopped there, as had other men. For he saw that no rational mode of pursuit sufficed for acquiring that wise and so greatly desired knowledge.[257]

In short, Aristotle was not able to recognize that the proper object of his inquiry—the *quidditas*—cannot be cognized in terms of ordinary knowledge, because it forms itself the condition of possibility of all knowledge. Being as such the *quidditas* lies outside of the domain directly accessible to human knowledge.[258] Just as light cannot be seen by a mere effort of the eyes, neither can the condition of possibility of human knowing be known in the ordinary way. The same parallel can be stretched a bit further, by saying that in the way light can be recognized with an insight into its functioning, so the *quiddity* can be recognized by a simple intuition.[259]

Logic

Secondly, the *NA* also emphasizes the limits of Aristotelian logic.[260] It is argued there that in spite of all his efforts, Aristotle was neither able to

---

256. For the Latin text, see the next footnote.

257. *NA* 18, 84:14–20: "Et demum illi visum est, quod illam bene nemo nominavit; quia, quicumque eam nominarunt, aliquid aliud sive quid aliud, non ipsam simplicissimam rerum nominarunt quidditatem, quam utique vidit non posse esse aliud aliquid. Et in hoc quidem non erravit, sed ibi, sicut alii homines, cessavit. Videt enim, quod omnis rationalis venandi modus ad capiendum ipsam tantopere desideratam et sapidam scientiam minime sufficit."

258. See *NA* 18, 85:1–5: "qui quaerit videre, quaenam visibilium sit substantia, cum visu illam inter visibila quaerat, lucem se anterioriter percipere non attendit, sine qua nec posset quaerere nec reperire visibile.... nempe sic philosopho accidit."

259. Nikolaus von Kues, *Vom Nichtanderen*, 198 n. 7 (taken from the marginal notes of Nicholas's own copy of a Latin text of the *Metaphysics*): "Patet quod in theologicis debet esse maior certitudo quam in mathematicis; et non est verum quod prima certitudo est in mathematicis, nisi addamus ad quam ratione attingimus. Contemplatio vera certitudo est, quia visio intellectualis, illa enim nihil praesupponit nec arguit aut inquirit, sed est simplex intuitio."

260. On this point, see *NA* 19, 86–87 and Steel, "Beyond the Principle of Contradiction?" 581–5.598–9. Cf. also the title in Wilpert's translation.

complete his own elaborate logic nor the art of definition. The reason of his shortcomings was that he relied exclusively on reason (*ratio*). He is criticized for making the principle of (non-)contradiction absolute. Aristotle, namely, wanted to develop a universal method based on reason (*via rationis*) for attaining the substances of things. This logic proved to be insufficient to reach a reality that precedes reason and is not accessible to it. With the notion of *non-aliud*, Nicholas was able to show that the first principle of rationality (*primum principium*) will never allow the human mind to contemplate truth beyond reason (*supra rationem*). Thus, the *NA* contrasts reason with the mind's eye (*oculi mentis acie*). While the latter is able to embrace even seemingly contradictory statements in a single intuition, reason holds to the principle of (non-)contradiction. Naturally, this brings up the whole question of the *coincidentia oppositorum*, which also plays an important role in other important Cusanian works such as *DI* and *DVD*. I cannot properly survey the whole problematic of this notion here, instead I will at least avoid a possible misunderstanding.[261]

On the Coincidence of Opposites

Nicholas of Cusa did not want to simply explain away contradictions. As Dionysius pointed out affirmations and negations are equally and simultaneously employed in theology. Nicholas recognized that the Aristotelian majority still regarded this Dionysian principle as a heresy, although this principle should be the starting point for the ascension towards mystical theology.[262] Against Nicholas's criticism of Aristotle, any school theologian could object that the destruction of the principle of (non-)contradiction will, in effect, destroy the very possibility of every science. Thereby even theology as a science, as a rational enterprise would be rendered impossible. This point was in fact explicitly stated by the theologian John Wenck's in his criticism directed against Nicholas's *DI*.[263]

---

261. Cf. Steel, "Beyond the Principle of Contradiction?" 599. Steel points out that Nicholas of Cusa was not a "speculative" thinker, and that the coincidence of opposites is only a discursive strategy.

262. Cf. the English text of the *Apologia* 6:8–10 *Nicholas of Cusa's Debate*, 46.

263. For this debate, see *Nicholas of Cusa's Debate with John Wenck*. Cf. Nikolaus von Kues, *Vom Nichtanderen*, 198 n. 7.

Nevertheless, the Aristotelian insistence on the principle of (non-)contradiction is not an absolute starting point for thinking, because it presupposes at the least that statements and terms have a clearly defined meaning. This is a reasonable requirement but it cannot be always realized in practice. Although the requirement of (non-)contradiction presupposes a completely univocal usage of language, human language will always remain imprecise and approximate, and thus, the ideal language is not attainable.[264] If this is true about ordinary language, it is also true of the language of religion. Indeed, Nicholas realized that in the case of theological language, the meaning of the employed terms cannot be exhausted by absolutely exact definitions. As *DVD* makes it clear, different religious statements concerning God are formulated from different human perspectives. The relevant point of the *coincidentia oppositorum* is that often these respective statements cannot be reduced to a language of one univocal theological discourse. It is not always possible to point out exactly, to separate and in a very nice scholastic way to reconcile the different perspectives of *"secundum quid"* from which differing theological statements are phrased.[265] That is the reason why Nicholas of Cusa was so critical concerning school-theology: he saw its rational project flawed from the very beginning. In contrast, Nicholas's thought was to achieve with his *manuductiones* what Aristotelian science was not able to do, namely, to show the Mystery of God from a limited, human perspective.

Nicholas of Cusa and Ramón Lull

From the foregoing discussion Nicholas of Cusa's thought emerges as a critical reaction against more traditionally styled forms of theologizing. As will be clear in the following, Ramón Lull reacted in a similar way against the methodology of Aristotelian science. A comparison between the two thinkers' theological epistemology can also shed light on the difference of their respective approaches to the question of other religions. In this section, I will address this question.

---

264. Leibniz's mathesis universalis is thus an impossible project. For Nicholas's criticism of school theology see my discussion of the wise in the *C* at the end of this chapter.

265. For Nicholas's criticism of Albert the Great concerning this point, see Steel's article.

On Ramón's Theological Epistemology

To begin with, one reason for Ramón Lull's reaction against scholastic theology was coming from his missionary perspective.[266] As far as this missionary project was concerned, he did not want to employ Aristotelian science but rather the means of Islamic theology.[267] Traditionally, both Islamic and Christian theologies were thought to be based on revelation. Islamic theology was not seen as a theoretical or speculative science, but as a practical one intrinsically bound up with the believer's praxis. Ramón himself did not deny the intellectual dimension of demonstrative theological work, but he emphasized its connection with the positive phase of theology that has to do with the human will.[268] For Ramón, theology had to retain its relation to the praxis.

On a more theoretical level, however, Ramón was also able to show the insufficiency of Aristotelian science and its epistemology.[269] Ramón's basic epistemological point against Aristotelians was that they confounded sense-knowledge with reason. But sense perception cannot form a valid argument for truth, consequently it is not possible to comprehend intellectual things with discursive, rational categories derived from sensual knowledge alone.[270] For Ramón, knowledge of sensible things belongs to the positive grade of making assertions concerning sensible objects (*obiecta sensibilia*). A human intellect is able to transcend sense-perception. Thus it can arrive at the comparative grade and cognize intelligible reality (*obiecta intelligibilia*). Both Aristotle and Averroes arrived at this point. In Ramón's opinion, however, real science must lay beyond this insight, because God Himself is beyond both the sensible and the intelligible dimensions. In order to arrive at real knowledge of the Divine, it is not enough to transcend the sensible dimension, but also a second transcending moment (*secundus trancensus*) is necessary: the second grade of intellectual knowledge must also be transcended. In other words, the human intellect has to transcend itself.

---

266. On Ramón's epistemology, see Lohr, "Ramón Lull," and Pindl-Büchel, "The Relationship."

267. Lohr, "Ramón Lull," 219.

268. Thus, for Ramón, love illuminates cognition and contemplation leads to action.

269. Pindl-Büchel, "The Relationship," 87.

270. Lohr, "Ramón Lull," 220–1 and Pindl-Büchel, "The Relationship," 85.

Ramón clearly rejected the one-dimensional concept of Aristotelian epistemology. He postulated different types of knowledge for different types of reality and kept these different levels of knowledge strictly separated from another.[271] Ramón recognized that when confronted with God's infinity, humans are completely stupefied because they are not able to think or even to imagine infinity. In trying to comprehend infinity, human beings are thrown back onto their own finitude. Indeed, if some finite created beings familiar to humans already exceed the mind's capacity for understanding, then infinity must be even much more incomprehensible. Indeed, the notion of absolute infinity would be contradictory, if it could be reached by way of a finite judgment with the help of Aristotelian categories.[272] The important point is that the limits of human reason must be recognized. Somewhat paradoxically, when the human subject becomes conscious of this finitude, his or her intellect has in a way already transcended its own limitations.[273]

Ramón, naturally, subscribed to the Scholastic axiom according to which "nothing can be in the intellect without first having been in the senses." In his view, the contact with an external object serves to reveal the constitutive activity of internal knowledge, that is to say the self-knowledge of the human intellect. Although knowledge from our human perspective *quoad nos* begins at the lowest degree of sense-perception, but *quoad se* knowledge consists in self-reflection. Speaking in Kantian terms, one can say that only from its highest, that is to say intellectual degree is human knowledge able to perceive the very conditions of its own possibility.

In Ramón's opinion, truth and certainty can be solely found in the first, simple principle. Hence, the necessary importance of a second transcending movement of the intellect from contingent multiplicity to the One. By rising above sense perception, imagination, and even beyond reason (*ascensus*) the intellect will come to the realization that all oppositions that appear when one is thinking are transcended in God. On this third grade of knowledge, none of the previous distinctions will apply. Afterwards, in descending, the mind will see its own truth as a representation of the absolute and its reflection—penetrating

271. Pindl–Büchel, "The Relationship," 85.

272. For Ramón, the idea of the divine infinity must not be understood quantitatively. Ibid., 77.

273. Ibid., 78.

all the multiple forms encountered in the world. In relation to this point, Pindl-Büchel reminds the reader that "[T]here is only one fixed given in the dialectic between the finite and the infinite, the dialectic itself."[274] Since God is infinite and God's unity is Trinitarian, any attempt to comprehend God's essence as it is in itself must be abandoned. "[T]he dynamic between the finite and the infinite never comes to rest, a notional comprehension . . . of the infinite is impossible."[275]

Important Differences between Ramón and Nicholas

The previous sketch of Ramón's theological epistemology anticipates several important Cusanian themes. It is all the more important to point out the differences between Ramón Lull's and Nicholas of Cusa's approach to the Divine Mystery.

To begin with, both Ramón's criticism of Aristotelian science and his whole intellectual project produced a considerable effect on Nicholas.[276] In relation to Ramón's epistemology one can recall the fact that Nicholas made detailed notes on Ramón's critical remarks concerning human knowledge and also recognized its paradoxes.[277] The basic epistemological point, i.e., the recognition of the limits of human thought and knowing shared by Ramón and Nicholas, is especially important and can serve well the purpose of a comparison.

Docta Ignorantia

The recognition of the limits of thinking is, formally considered, a judgment about a judgment.[278] This higher level of reflection leads one further to the insight that the absolutely infinite can only be grasped by a judgment that transcends natural judgments. In Nicholas's terminology, the knowledge based on this recognition may be properly called *docta ignorantia*. That is to say, one could transcend the very limitations of

---

274. Ibid., 81.
275. Ibid.
276. See Colomer, *Nikolaus von Kues* and Pindl-Büchel, "The Relationship." Hösle, "Einfürung," xxiii states that in Ramón's thought Nicholas of Cusa's system was already "vorgeformt."
277. Pindl-Büchel, "The Relationship," 78.
278. Ibid.

his human way of knowing by recognizing his own fragility. In relation to Nicholas of Cusa's *De Pace Fidei*, Jos Decorte made the same point using the terms of "formal attitude" and humility.[279] In his analysis of Nicholas's thought, the expression formal attitude corresponds to the second order judgment in Pindl-Büchel, while the notion of *humility* points to the recognition of one's own (intellectual) fragility.[280]

This formal attitude or the judgment of the second order does not directly concern the content of the first order judgments. It is not a knowledge about things, but a knowledge concerning the knowledge about things. This kind of knowing can be understood as a *knowing-how* related to the limited status of human knowledge. It can best be seen as a rule prescribing how to handle the knowledge of the first degree—that is to say, how to *live* with it. Once one tries to think the second order in terms of the first one, one will actually reduce it. As a consequence (the possibility of thinking and thereby respecting) transcendence will be lost.

This distinction—both as between first and second order or as between the form and the content of knowledge—solves the paradoxical character of human knowledge. Precisely because the first order is separated from the second order, the partial truth-claims of the first one do not contradict the universal judgments of the latter, because real contradictions can only arise on the same logical level.[281] While the distinction between different orders of predication makes the point clear logically, the notion of a formal attitude suggests a necessary link between knowledge and the lived practice itself.[282] Both analyses suc-

---

279. See Decorte, "Ter inleiding," 36–40. Although Decorte intended to do some research with respect of the Catalan thinker I am only aware of the following explicit reference to Ramón in his published writings: "First of all, it is this one [i.e., Ramón Lull] . . . who is exerting a significant influence on Nicholas's thought. The mystical–mathematical speculations as well as the strife for unity and reconciliation between different religions are standing in the first place for Lullus and for Nicholas of Cusa. Both of them are endeavoring via an 'ars generalis' to find the divine name (the 'verbum praecisum') and through this to discover the structure of the divine. In the library at Bernkastel-Kues the most typical author to be found is Ramón Lull." See Bocken and Decorte, "Inleiding," 12.

280. On humility and knowing, see especially *RA* and Decorte, "Middeleeuwse."

281. Logically speaking, judgments of the second order belong to a meta-level.

282. The attitude of intellectual humility does not convey additional truth claims with contents identifiable in the form of first order propositions. Rather, it offers a way of treating the contents of human knowledge.

cinctly demonstrate the importance of the formal dimension of knowledge for the ideal of *docta ignorantia*.

Nicholas not only took over Ramón's criticism of Aristotelian science, but he also developed the idea of intellectual ascent in a characteristically different way.[283] While Ramón arrived through an ascent at his *Ars*, an encyclopaedia of the sciences, Nicholas would emphasise the subjective power of the intellect. Nicholas kept clearly in view the dialectic involved in the ascent and the descent of the intellect. He distinguished not only *de facto*, but also terminologically—though not always consequently—between the two higher degrees of knowledge as *ratio* and *intellectus*. As Pindl-Büchel observes:

> Cusanus alone formulated explicitly the necessity of a third, highest degree of intellectual knowledge which constitutes the basis of the lower degrees of knowledge.[284]

According to Nicholas, a human intellect cannot comprehend but only apprehend the absolute *maximum*. In order to do so, one must "spit out" sense perception, imagination, and reason.[285] At this very point of the epistemological itinerary, Ramón characteristically started his mystical philosophy of love. In contrast, Nicholas postulated a mystical theology beyond the principle of contradiction on which Aristotelian science was based.[286] Ultimately one can agree with Pindl-Büchel's judgment:

> [I]t was in the attempt to go beyond Aristotelian epistemology that Nicholas's originality lay. Lull was able to show the insufficiency of Aristotelian science and its epistemology.... But he did not really go beyond the first principle of Aristotelian science—the principle of non-contradiction. The elaboration of the doctrine of the *coincidentia oppositorum* as an attempt to overcome this principle remains the specific historical achievement of Nicholas of Cusa.[287]

---

283. Pindl-Büchel, "The Relationship," 86–87. See also Hösle, "Einfürung," xxii–lxxxii.

284. Pindl-Büchel, "The Relationship," 86.

285. Cf. *DI* I, 10, 27:11–18 and also *DP* 17:1–16; *DP* 17:3 explicitly states that God "nullo gradu cognitionis attingitur."

286. Cf. Colomer, *Nikolaus von Kues*, 118: "Es wäre auch zu untersuchen, inwiefern die Mystik des Raimund Llull ihre Spure in der 'theologia spiritualis' des Cusanus hinterlassen hat."

287. Pindl-Büchel, "The Relationship," 87. Hösle, "Einfürung," xvii recalls the Cusanian distinction of ratio and intellect.

This brief comparison between Ramón Lull's and Nicholas of Cusa's theological epistemology so far indicates some of the special strengths of the latter by showing some defects in the former. Philosophically speaking, Nicholas's own theoretical strength lies in the fact that he thematized and systematized his own alternative to Aristotelian theory more explicitly than Ramón did. On the other hand, it can be argued that Nicholas's approach also stayed closer to religious praxis itself. At this point it can only be anticipated that in his discussion with Islam, not only did Nicholas employ Biblical authorities, but he did not even refrain from sieving the Koranic text.

After the investigation of the present chapter, my working hypothesis according to which Nicholas's speculative—and not merely affective—mysticism could shed light on his approach to Islam has gained some plausibility. It has been shown that this mystical theology can bridge the gap between the theoretical and the practical dimensions of religion. It remains to be seen in what way such an understanding can be fruitful for a Christian-Muslim dialogue. Accordingly, in my next two chapters Nicholas's approach towards Islam will be investigated from the same perspective, that is to say, within the manuductive context of his mystical theology.

However, before tackling the details of Nicholas's manuductive itinerary in relation to Islam, I would like to return briefly to the problem of different religions. This move will not only confirm my results of the present chapter, but it will also anticipate some important notions from the following one. In this way, this last section is intended to make clearer the transition from discussing Nicholas's mystical theology to investigating his approach towards Islam.

Who Are the Wise?

Nicholas addresses the theme of different religions in chapter 15 of the second book of the *C*.[288] On the one hand, this text suggests that Nicholas was convinced of the existence of something like an inherent human religiosity promising a higher immortal end.[289] On the other hand, the text also makes clear that he regarded the actual forms of human religiosity as different degrees of *participation* in that one underly-

---

288. See *C* II, 15, 146–54.
289. Ibid., 147:6–8.

ing religion. In his view, every group participates in but none actually possesses "that" religion.[290]

In describing the different modes of this participation, a general threefold scheme is employed. Within this scheme the *"sapientes"* are placed as the first ones, then the rational ones follow up, and the line is closed by the sensible people.[291] Nevertheless this is not a rigid classification as the evaluative scheme leaves place for further refinement by virtue of its conjectural status.[292] In addition, Nicholas allowed for the possibility of temporal "fluctuations" within a particular religion.[293]

What is important for my purpose is not so much the application of Nicholas's general threefold figure for picturing the differences in humanity, but rather his evaluation of the different degrees of human religiosity. According to this evaluation, the highest ones are those who give themselves to contemplation. They already abide, as it were, in a kind of highest human heaven (*in supremo humanitatis caelo*). These *sapientes* clearly correspond to the faculty of intellect. Therefore, Nicholas's clearly figurative or metaphorical 'heaven' can be also referred to as "intellectual."[294]

Hence, the *sapientes* are those who have time for submerging themselves in speculation concerning truth. The terms "speculation," "contemplation," and "religio" are used here interchangeably. This usage demonstrates the intimate connection between medieval intellectualism and the aim of all kinds of religiosity in the form of a *visio Dei*.[295] From such an intellectualistic and spiritual perspective—for Nicholas, these two terms have almost exactly the same meaning—it is evident that the sensible people attached to sensual pleasure deserve only the lowest place. Their behavior is regarded as absurd (*absurdissime*) and animal-like.[296]

---

290. Ibid., 147:8–16.

291. Ibid., 146:13–18.

292. Ibid., 147:15–16: "Adhuc primi triniter distinguuntur, ita et secundi et tertii." In my reading the threefold division points only to a general (generaliter) pattern. Cf. 146:19–20 and 148:1–2.

293. See ibid., 148–49.

294. Nicholas does not employ here the expression "caelum intellectuale."

295. Cf. Happ's German translation of 146:11–12 and 147:1–2.

296. Cf. *C* II, 15, 147:15 and 146:15–16. In the *DI* III, 8, 229:4–5.7–8.12–17 Muslims are characterised along very similar lines. On this question, see my fourth chapter.

It is equally important to see what place those people occupy who rely on their reason: they hold a middle position between the inferior sensible ones and the superior intellectual ones. Not surprisingly, many school theologians of Nicholas's own time are placed here. They are explicitly criticized because of their limited vision of rationality.[297] In contrast to these theologians, the reader of the *C* is urged that he or she should strive to transcend a mere rational mode of inquiry towards the simple understanding of the intellect because in Nicholas's opinion, a rationalistic theology necessarily blocks the road to real theological knowledge.[298] My investigation has indeed shown that Nicholas tried to overcome the difficulties posed by such a rationalistic theological approach with his own of kind mystical theology.

In addition, the appearance of the wise (*sapientes*) and the sensible people in the *C* also sheds light on Nicholas's discussion of the Islamic problem. Anticipating the following discussion, here it can be said that the sensible ones will be equated with the majority of the Muslims while the wise with some exceptional figures. Because of the shared ideal of *sapientia*, Nicholas appreciates the latter group best. His criticism of the rational school-theologians of his own day indicates that when speaking about the Divine, Nicholas himself wanted to tread another path— that of wisdom. It remains to be seen to what extent he could achieve what he set out to do in relation to Islam.

---

297. Cf. *C* I, 8, 34:14–17: "Et haec est paene omnium theologorum modernorum via, qui de deo rationabiliter loquuntur; multa enim hac via admittimus in schola rationis, quae scimus secundum regionem simplicis unitatis neganda." Cf. *C* I, 5, 20:1–4 and 21:1–4.

298. *C* I, 10, 53:12–14: "Ad quae philosophantes atque theologi ratiocinantes hactenus sibi sua positione principii primi ingrediendi viam praecluserent." Nicholas made it thus clear that these people cannot have a genuine appreciation of what he called "mysteries" (*arcana*). Cf. *C* I, 5, 18:11–20; 9, 41:7–8, and 10, 53:8–9.

4

Manuductio in the *De Pace Fidei* and the Beginnings of *Pia Interpretatio*

> So that the most simple may be guided by a perceptual example through which, from afar, they may see to some extent the Father, the Word, and the Spirit[1]
>
> —Nicholas of Cusa

IN THIS CHAPTER I WILL ATTEMPT TO INTERPRET NICHOLAS OF CUSA'S approach to Islam in terms of *manuductio*.[2] In this way, by continuing the discussion of the previous chapter, I will apply the formal perspective of the *Prolegomena* to a specific question. What has been said so far suggests that such a "formal" interpretation of Nicholas's thought does not lack some plausibility. Whether it can be verified with respect to the Islamic problem in detail is still an open question.[3]

Thus I will extend my reading experiment from the previous chapter to those Cusanian works that directly address the issue of non-Christian religions or specifically treat the Islamic problem. These works have been already identified in my first chapter. Therefore, after a brief introductory reflection, I examine the *PF* and Nicholas's letter to John of

---

1. *CA* I, 20, 82:1–2: "Et ut simpliciores exemplo sensibili ducantur, per quod patrem, verbum et spiritum aliqualiter a remotis videant ..."

2. Cf. Haubst, "Die Wege der christologische manuductio," Hopkins, "The Role of *pia interpretatio*," and Kremer, "Die Hinführung." Decorte, "Ter inleiding," 7–42 proposes such a manuductive interpretation of the *PF*. My present chapter can be read as a detailed justification of this proposal.

3. Cf. ibid., 39: "The opinions about the ... text [of the *PF*] and the project Nicholas is working out therein differ from each other.... we have tried to give an interpretation pointing towards a truth understood more *formally*. Our reader has to form his or her judgment on the issue."

Segovia in this chapter and I dedicate my next chapter to the discussion of the quite extensive *CA*.[4]

Manuductio in Relation to the Muslims?

Nicholas's knowledge of Islamic religion goes back at least to the time of his conciliar activities at Basle. It was there that he befriended John of Segovia and the two men often conversed with each other—among other subjects—regarding Islam.[5]

Thus it should not be surprising that the Muslims had already found their way to the third book of the *CC* (1433) and made an appearance also in the last book of the *DI*.[6] However, from the perspective of a possible inter-religious dialogue, neither of these two accounts are very promising. Admittedly, the picture offered in the *CC* is more balanced, but its immediate context is (church) politics. The third book of the *CC* makes clear that the goal of political rule is peace. The basic precondition for attaining this peace is taking and keeping the right direction to the Eternal by way of observing religion's rule. Hence, the care for religion is crucial for the ruler. Even though politics and religion are connected in this way, the *CC* does not discuss the theological difficulties of Islam. Surely this is what one can expect from a work not directly concerned with Christian apologetics.[7] Neither is the rather harsh and negative treatment of Muslim faith in the *DI* encouraging. There, the reader learns that Muslims acknowledge Christ as the greatest and most perfect man, yet they deny His Divinity. Muslims simply do not see the truth. What is perhaps even worse, they persecute the cross and they are excluded from salvation. In fact, they do not even expect true salvation since Mohammed's law, i.e., the Koran promises them only the fulfillment of their own sensual desires. This treatment

---

4. Jos Decorte had already pointed out that the *CA* can be read as a more detailed application of Nicholas's manuductive program. Cf. Decorte, "Ter inleiding," 33: "Nicholas has apply put this program into operation in his *De Pace fidei*, but excuted it in even more detail in his *Cribratio Alkorani*."

5. See *CA* I, Prologue 2:9–14 and the opening passage of John's letter to Nicholas as quoted in Klibansky and Bascour, "Praefatio," li: "de quorum (*scl.* Sarracenorm) ritibus observantiaqe, moribus ac modo conversionis multa diebus illis conferebamus." See also Nicholas's letter to John, ibid., 93:21–94: and 97:22–25.

6. See *CC* III, 7, 348:6–11 and *DI* III, 8.

7. Cf. *CC* III, 7, 348:12–16 and 349.

of Islam hardly rises above the ordinary level of traditional Christian anti-Muslim literature.

Nevertheless, right before the passage concerned with the Muslims, the *DI* expresses Nicholas's conviction that no perfect religion would be able to lead man to the ultimate end of peace that does not embrace Christ, i.e., the way, the truth, and the life. This statement not only reveals the explicitly Christological context of the discussion of different religions, but also signals clearly its teleology. Concerning this teleology it can also be observed that both accounts—of the *CC* and *DI*—are connected to the topic of peace. In Nicholas's view peace is the ultimate end of one's human existence. This is true for humans both as individuals and as social beings. In light of this observation the meaning of the "perfection" of a religion can be better understood. A *perfect* religion, namely, is the one that helps humans in a better or the best possible way to reach the aim of their existence.[8] Nicholas, as a medieval Christian, saw Christ as the way, the truth, and the life; thus, he had hardly another option than assigning to Muslims the category of an *imperfect* religion. Hence the harsh treatment of Islam in the *DI*.[9]

As said earlier, in spite of Nicholas's bitter experiences with the Basle assembly, the concern for peace and reconciliation had remained a constant in his life. The following discussion will also demonstrate that while the Christological credo remained Nicholas's fundamental conviction until his last day, in the course of time his treatment of Islam would undergo significant modifications.

De Pace Fidei

The *PF* with its 19 chapters is a relatively short work when compared to the *DI* or *DVD*. The chapters have no original titles, so the structure of the book may not be completely clear from the beginning:[10]

---

8. Within the Aristotelian medieval world-view the idea of perfection is always connected to the idea of attaining a goal: the Aristotelian *form* is both the *first perfection* as the starting point of a development of a particular being and its *second perfection* as its fulfillment in attaining its goal. E.g., a *perfect* society is the one that is able to attain its goal.

9. As far as I can see, at this point of Nicholas's oeuvre there is no explicit connection between *manuductio* and Islam.

10. For the table of contents, see Kremer, "Die Hinführung," 126–63 and Haubst, 164–91, "Die Wege der christologische manuductio."

a. Chapters I–II–III form a *Prologue*;

b. chapter IV to chapter XIX: the main discussion of the problem of religious plurality in dialogue form;

c. chapter XIX is the *Epilogue*.

The central part can be divided into three main manuductive steps:

1. Chapters IV, V, VI, and VII: a *manuductio* to One Wisdom, i.e. to God;

2. chapters VIII, IX, and X: Trinitarian *manuductio* (already introduced in chapter VII);

3. chapters XI, XII, XIII, and XIV: Christological *manuductio* (already introduced in chapter X).

These manuductive steps are connected with each other, since they are introduced in such a way that the second step is a natural continuation of the first one. In like manner, the third step comes as continuing the second one. The discussion of Christological mysteries is linked to the following part:

4. chapter XV on celestial happiness and a Christian reading of the Koran anticipating Nicholas's *pia interpretatio* in the *CA*.[11]

5. chapters XVI, XVII, XVIII, and XIX on the question of religious rites.

Scenery, Genre, and the Author's Intention

As the opening passage quoted earlier makes clear, the *PF* is an expression of Nicholas's Christian faith and hope.[12] Within the framework of a heavenly vision, he sees the wise men of different peoples and religions assembled. Under the guidance of the Divine Logos accompanied by His apostles, Peter and Paul, these wise men arrive at a common understanding (of religion), i.e., at a *concordantia* with a relative ease.[13]

---

11. This latter chapter strictly speaking belongs neither to the previous Christological discussion nor to the subsequent treatment of rites.

12. See my first chapter.

13. *PF* XIX, 68:11–12. For the evaluation of this work, cf. Watts, Pauline M. "Talking to Spiritual Others" and other essays in the same volume. See also Biechler and Bond,

However, it would be wrong to suppose that with this celestial peace-conference Nicholas was only aiming at emotional comfort. The very title of the dialogue makes it clear that his whole project starts with faith. In a literal rendering the Latin title can be translated into English as "*On Peace of Faith.*" Notably, the term faith (*fides*) has here a twofold meaning. On the one hand, it refers to the (faith of) different religions. According to this meaning, Nicholas was concerned with the mutually peaceful relationship between the diverse forms of human worship. Hence the title might be paraphrased as "a peace in faith" or "a peace between faiths." On the other hand, Nicholas also thought that this kind of peace can only be reached *in* faith, that is to say through religious commitment. According to this second reading, the title can be understood as referring to a "peace coming through faith." The point of this double reading can be summed up by saying that the "pax fidei" is both a *genitivus objectivus* and *genitivus subjectivus* since faith functions at one and the same time as the starting point, the concrete means *and* the constitutive moment in the process of attaining peace. This double reading of the title encompasses both dimensions of faith: the *fides quae* in the form of the different religious faiths (1st meaning) and the *fides qua* of the actual religious commitment (2nd meaning). In Nicholas's case, it was beyond doubt his Catholic faith that gave him hope and made him think that peace is possible between the different religions in spite of the scandal of war and disagreement.[14] It was this deep, personal conviction he wanted to communicate to his readers—among them those bearing political responsibility in the confrontation.[15] If one takes Nicholas's theological starting-point seriously then he or she must read this dialogue with the double meaning of "pax fidei" and with the double dimension of faith in mind.

It must also be remembered that Nicholas was far from being naive in matters of international and inter-religious peace: being a man of (church) politics and diplomacy he knew all too well that Western Christianity must answer a military offensive such as the capture of

---

"Introduction," ix–xlviii. Biechler and Bond's bilingual edition of th *PF* with its concordance of the Latin terms (*Nicholas of Cusa on Interreligious Harmony*) offers an excellent tool for research.

14. Biechler and Bond, "Introduction," xxxvii.

15. Cf. *PF* I, 1:12–14: "ut haec visio ad notitiam eorum qui hiis maximis praesunt aliquando deveniret, eam quantum memoria praesentabat, plane subter conscripsit."

Constantinople with armed force, unless it wants to run the risk of being accused of weakness and cowardice.[16] I would like to emphasize, however, that there is no trace of that sort of military consideration in the *PF* itself. As the opening passage makes clear, armed conflict is acknowledged as a pitiable reality but not as a means for a final solution to the problem. Later, while preparing the crusade, Nicholas would not regard war as the ultimate solution to the problem either but as a necessary act of self-defense. Realistically speaking, Nicholas can hardly be condemned for holding such a view while facing the real danger of the absorption of (all) Christian countries by the Ottoman Empire and being terrified by Mehmed's constant military advance.

The opening passage of the *PF* places Nicholas's "meditations" within the context of a vision thereby taking a certain distance from actual political reality.[17] More precisely, this vision should be called a "double vision." First the author—in his own rapture (*raptus*)—is granted with a vision about the meeting of heavenly beings as he sees God, His angels and saints. Thereafter, as a result of this first "conference," a second meeting is organized together with the most judicious or most important men of this world (*graviores huius mundi*).[18]

In the subsequent parts of the dialogue 17 figures appear representing all tongues and nations.[19] Eight of them are easily recognizable as coming from Augustine's *De civitate Dei* VII 9: an Ion becoming a Greek in the *PF*, then an Italian, an Indian, a Chaldean, a Scythian, a Frenchman, a Persian, and a Spaniard. To these, Nicholas of Cusa is adding four other figures. Two of these latter figures have already appeared in Ramón Lull's *The Book of the Gentile*, while the two other ones can be found in other works of the Catalan thinker: these four are the Saracen called an Arab by Nicholas, the Jew, the Jacobite referred to in the *PF* as a Syrian, and finally the Tartar.[20] The five remaining figures in the *PF* can be related to Nicholas's own lifetime: the Turk, the

---

16. As it was shown in chapter one this awareness of the real military-political dangers made Nicholas labor with the practical preparations for a crusade in the aftermath of Constantinople's fall.

17. Cf. *PF* I–II–III.

18. *PF* III, 9:4. For the different translations, see *Nicholas of Cusa on Interreligious Harmony*, 11, *Godsdienstvrede*, 55, and *Nicholas of Cusa's De Pace Fidei*, 37.

19. For the following, see *Godsdienstvrede*, 55 n. 27 and Haubst, "Die Wege der christologische manuductio," 165.

20. The term "Saracenus" is not used in the *PF*.

German, the Armenian, the Bohemian, and the Englishman. Not only are all these men called in the *PF* as "wise" (*sapientes*) or "experientially knowledgeable" (*peritiores*), but their literary origin also confirms this description. For instance, the chapter where the first eight figures appear in Augustine's *De civitate Dei* is entitled as "On that philosophy that comes closer to the truth of Christian faith" (*De ea philosophia, quae ad veritatem fide Christianae propius accessit*).[21] In a similar way the dialogue of the wise may be recalled from *The Book of the Gentile* and other Lullian works. It is also important that the phrase *"peritiores"* reminds the reader that the question under discussion cannot be solved by mere theoretical thinking, but real familiarity with the issue of "the different rites" is required too.

These wise men in the *PF* come together by way of a rapture (*quasi in extasim rapti*) and their task appears to be preparing another meeting that will take place in Jerusalem.[22] Commentators point out that here the city of Jerusalem has a symbolic significance. Indeed, Jerusalem was considered to be at the centre of all countries (*quae in medio terrae est*) both by Europeans and Arabs: it was placed in the middle of medieval maps. Hence, it could be seen as the most fitting place for an international meeting of all peoples gathering "as in a common centre" (*quasi in centrum commune*), as Nicholas put it.[23] Jerusalem or Zion, the Lord's elected city had an explicitly religious meaning: Jew, Christian, and Muslim alike regarded it as a meeting-place between heaven and earth. Furthermore, as Nicholas's works also attest, it was not uncommon to connect Zion with the idea of the (final) *visio Dei*.[24] Jerusalem was also connected with the idea of peace and the Paradise in Heaven was considered as the "heavenly Jerusalem." By taking all these features together, Jerusalem offered the 'perfect' site for Nicholas's theological peace-conference.[25]

Just as the idea of "(heavenly) Jerusalem," also the literary genre of a celestial vision comes from the Christian tradition.[26] Out of these

---

21. Haubst, "Die Wege der christologische manuductio," 165.

22. Cf. *PF* XIX, 68:11–18.

23. Ibid., 68:15 and III, 9:1.15–16.

24. Cf. *Psalm* 83:8 and *NA* 24, 113:10–12. The term "Zion" is not employed in the *PF*.

25. Cf. Klibansky and Bascour "Adnotationes," 69–70 and *Godsdienstvrede*, 56 n. 30.

26. Cf. 1 Kgs 22:19, Isa 6:1–13, Job 1:6, and Rev 4. All these are examples of a subgenre of celestial vision showing a "heavenly conference" (*concilium excelsorum*). Cf.

heavenly visions and utopias one of the most ancient and most influential ones is the Book of Revelation. In the literary culture of the Middle-Ages, this biblical book could serve as a model for any other similar work. It must be remembered that the intention of the author of that biblical book was not so much to chart the course of future events or to offer an accurate recipe for solving the pressing difficulties of his present. Rather, his aim was to awaken believers, to warn and exhort them and to give hope to the desperate. Both the Book of Revelation and the *PF* were written in a hopeless and threatening situation—respectively at the time of the first persecutions of the Christians and in the aftermath of the "culture shock" caused by the capture of Constantinople. Hence it is reasonable to suppose a similar general orientation in both works. This similarity, however, should not blind the reader toward the differences between the two works. While the Book of Revelation relates a visionary narrative with some dialogues, the *PF* is a dialogue placed within the framework of a visionary narrative. The biblical book nowhere advances anything that comes close to Nicholas's speculative, philosophical arguments.

Furthermore, in the *PF*, the leader of the dialogue is Christ (*Logos*) with his two apostles in heaven. The final agreement (*concordantia*) at the end is not reached by the direct intervention of the pope, the general council or any other representative of the militant church. This stylistic feature of the dialogue intensifies the speculative dimension of Nicholas's text and underlines the role of (Catholic) faith. The reader is reminded that what he has in his hands in the first place is neither rationalistic Neo-Platonist speculation nor a kind of naive affective mysticism. Quite simply, the *PF* is a speculative expression of Nicholas's Christian faith. To the attentive reader of the *DI*, it should not come as a surprise that only trust in the one *Logos*—and His revelation symbolized by the figures of His apostles—can lead to a peace between religions. As its title has already made clear, the whole of the *PF* manifests the fundamental role of faith in Nicholas's discourse. This in no way entails that this work is a celestial caricature of a real dialogue. To say that the *PF* is written out of and is based on faith, to emphasize its religious or theological dimension is not to deny that the same work displays a certain type of rationality. According to his own words, Nicholas's vision takes place

---

Godsdienstvrede, 47. In order to understand the *PF* the more general genre of vision should also be taken into consideration.

"on an intellectual height" (*ad quandam intellectualem altitudinem*).[27] Although the meaning of this expression is somewhat unclear, it signals that the dialogue makes a claim on rationality and intelligibility.

An Exercise in Cognitio Sui

As other Cusanian works, the *PF* also testifies to Nicholas's intellectualism. In order to better appreciate the importance of this intellectualism, I would like to emphasize the reflexive character of the *PF*. Nicholas, like many medievals, was convinced that reflection can lead humans to (a knowledge of) God. As shown in the previous chapter, already in the *C*, he offered a discussion of self-reflection within the context of spiritual life. The *PF* testifies that Nicholas was convinced that when humans reflect on reality they will come to a recognition of their own being as creatures and thereby they will arrive at a knowledge of the Creator.[28] This "knowledge" of God is an indirect one, having a symbolic structure. This knowledge can and should become operative in spiritual-moral life. *DVD* manifests that the same fundamental conviction formed a constant in Nicholas's intellectual life. The abiding presence of the idea of *docta ignorantia* in his thought also points toward the importance of reflection. All this evidence notwithstanding, the *PF* indicates that Nicholas was realistic enough to admit that for most people life is simply too hard for such a genuine intellectual-spiritual journey. Because of their constant labor and being subject to superiors they could hardly find time for sincere reflection.[29] Only a few people (*pauci*) are granted spare time (*otium*) enough for refection leading to self-knowledge (*notitia sui*).[30] This explains people's need for divine teachers, i.e. prophets.[31]

The phrase "a few" (*pauci*) serves as a rhetorical device in the *PF*. It is hardly conceivable that Nicholas thought that those people actually exist, i.e. the *"few"* who can dispense with revelation as it is mediated through prophets. On the other hand, the phrase recalls the wise (*sapientes*) to whom there are many references in Nicholas's works. For

27. Cf. *PF* I, 2:1 and XIX, 68:11.
28. Cf. ibid., I, 3:1–12.
29. Ibid., 4:7–8: "ita te, qui est Deus absconditus, quaerere nequeunt..."
30. Ibid., 4:4–6.
31. See ibid., 4:8–9.13–14.

instance, as the reader has seen, the C, while discussing the different forms of religiosity, contrasts the *sapientes* both with people attached to sensible reality and with the rational theologians of Nicholas's own time.³² The *DI* calls those pagans who retained a vision on religion closer to Christianity than the sensible ones *sapientes*. The wise will also reappear in the *CA*. As far as the *PF* is concerned, it has already been pointed out that this work is written in the form of a (fictional) dialogue between the wise men.³³ According to its scenery, these wise men were chosen by God and summoned to the heavenly conference. Throughout the dialogue they are depicted as either philosophers and theologians, or alternatively simple, but wise persons.

One can further ask the question concerning what the author's exact relationship with these wise men might be. Two dangers of misinterpretation should be avoided here. At first sight it is tempting to see Nicholas as one of the wise—without qualification. After all, the author of the *PF* is depicted in the opening passage as a spiritual person, giving himself to long meditations. Nicholas's intellectual career and his fondness for intellectual inquiry can make this reading more convincing. Against such a reading it can be objected that Nicholas was well aware of the dangers of regarding oneself a wise person *simpliciter*. The most important reason for such a caution is to be found in the idea of *docta ignorantia*: if real wisdom is a result of a continual reflection on one's own ignorance, then no one can be called wise *simpliciter*.³⁴ Wisdom cannot be acquired once and forever, but instead it is a continual act of spiritual and intellectual asceticism.³⁵ On the other hand, one can also recall the fact that Nicholas as church-politician and reformer was living a rather busy life.³⁶ Thus it may be tempting to go to the other extreme in thinking that he had nothing to do with (this) wisdom at

---

32. See my discussion at the end of the previous chapter.

33. Cf. *PF* I, 1:8–9: "paucorum sapientium omnium talium diversitatum quae in religionibus per orbem observantur peritia pollentium . . ." (Biechler and Bond have "ediversitatem" in Latin, which must be a printing error.)

34. Cf. *DI* I, 1 and the *Apologia*.

35. His *Idiota* testifies that although Nicholas was a lover of books, he did not think that wisdom was exclusively to be found in them.

36. Cf. *DI* I, 1: 9–11 where Nicholas wrote to cardinal Cesarini the following "quasi tibi pro tuo cardinalatus officio apud Apostolicam Sedem in publicis maximis negotiis occupatissimo aliquid otii supersit . . ." By the year 1453, Nicholas himself had the busy life of a cardinal.

all. Instead, I suggest that a middle-course should be taken: the passage about the "few" recalls Nicholas's experience of absorption in everyday business but also his love of reflection and desire for self-knowledge. Certainly, Nicholas would not consider himself a wise man *simpliciter*, i.e., as a possessor of wisdom. His intellectual attitude can be more aptly described as one of searching for wisdom (*venator sapientiae*). Wisdom in the form of a learned ignorance involves self-reflection. A "learned ignorant" is someone who has reflected on himself or herself: a person who learned about his own ignorance, recognized his own (intellectual) limitations and the meaning of these limitations.

Characteristically, self-reflection also plays an important role in *DVD*—a work written almost parallel with the *PF*. *DVD* presents the different religious perspectives as relative perspectives. Its reader is called to reflect on the limitation of his or her own perspective. No human being can pretend to step outside his or her own perspective, but this does not entail that particular human perspectives have absolutely no value. Human truth, i.e., truth in relation to humans, is always and necessarily seen form a perspective, but this does not entail a thoroughgoing relativism. This fact and its full meaning can only be recognized with the help of (self-)reflection.[37]

In the previous chapter, I consciously withheld connecting these points to the question of different religions. Now, turning to the *PF*, one can easily recognize in this dialogue the concrete form that the general sketch of *DVD* takes. From a chronological point of view it can be argued that since *DVD* was composed after the *PF*, in the latter work Nicholas was able to draw a general ontological picture of what he had treated in more concrete terms in the former work. Although *DVD* was actually written after the composition of the *PF*, Nicholas had been earlier occupied with the themes of mystical theology as the documents of his contacts to the Tegernsee community amply testify. Thematically the question of different religions is only tacitly present in *DVD* where a general account of different human perspectives is given. This fact in itself is probably hardly surprising in a treatise on mystical theology. On the other hand, as a work explicitly concerned with the vexing question of religious enmity, the *PF* sets out to discuss the different religious perspectives in considerable detail. Within the framework of the

---

37. Just as the different optical perspectives in relation to the one icon of God are all relative and thus justified (as limited perspectives) at the same time, so it is with the different religious perspectives of different people.

dialogue, different religious doctrines and rites are presented by and to the wise, i.e., by and to those who are both familiar with their plurality and able to reflect on them. In this way, the dialogue partners are called to reflect on the doctrines and rites of a religion alien to them (i.e., alien to Christianity) and try to understand it better. Furthermore, they are equally called to reflection in the more original sense of the word, namely, to reflect on their own respective religious points of view and to see these as limited perspectives. The same point can be pushed further by saying that the *PF* is a reflexive work throughout: its author reflects on the real meaning and significance of Christianity and its relation to other religions.

Generally speaking, if someone is not ready to reflect on his or her own perspective and to see it as a relative one, then he or she will not be able to appreciate the (Otherness of the) Other. By simply taking one's own perspective as absolute, one necessarily excludes all other perspectives from the discussion. From the different medieval approaches examined so far, both John of Torquemada's and Ramón Lull's project comes close to such an *exclusive absolutism*. In the following, I will try to show that in his approach, Nicholas was neither rejecting nor simply making his own (form of) religion absolute. This will be especially borne out with respect to the question of the Trinity and of religious rites. The *PF* calls also the (religious) Other to reflect on his or her own beliefs and practices. The dialogue is Nicholas's reflection on religious difference, i.e., a reflection on the question of how to think this difference and how to live with it peacefully. Since the difference in question is both doctrinal and practical, both of these aspects must be examined.

The Doctrinal Enigma: Monotheism vs. Trinity

Nicholas was aware of the central religious-theological differences between Christianity and Islam. Not surprisingly, in the *PF* he approached the essential problem through the figure of the Arab, i.e., the representative of Islam's true monotheism.[38]

While philosophers may agree in the existence of one God, the Arab clearly has a problem with the worship of a plurality of gods. The Word's answer to his question is that all the worshippers presuppose

38. *PF* VI, 16–18.

implicitly one deity, "[F]or in all the gods, they adore the deity one and the same in all its participants."³⁹ It is even said that "[N]o race was ever so obtuse that it believed there to be a plurality of gods each of whom was the universe's First Cause, Beginning, or Creator." Philosophically speaking, the sheer plurality of gods cannot account for the universe.⁴⁰ In a typically Cusanian turn the next speaker, the representative of Indian wisdom and religion, accepts the necessity of worshipping one God while at the same time retaining the worship of idols as sacred objects related to the same one God.⁴¹

To a reader already familiar with the discussion of the *DA* and Nicholas's Platonically inspired thought, it is hardly surprising that the real problem of the *PF* is apparently not monotheism but the doctrine of the Trinity.⁴² It is admitted that with respect to this central doctrine of Christianity, "it will be very difficult for a harmony to be accepted everywhere," as Trinity seems to imply plurality.⁴³ This implication goes against the previous statement concerning only one absolute deity. This has been a traditional Muslim argument against Christianity, namely, that the latter equals a kind of polytheism.

At this point of the discussion, Nicholas employs Meister Eckhart's famous distinction between God in relation to us (as Creator) and God in Himself (as Infinite).⁴⁴ In the first respect God is triune and one. However, any name—even Trinity as a name—referring to God is taken from creatures. God in Himself stands beyond any names: He is ineffable. Afterwards follows a Cusanian discussion of Oneness, Equality of Oneness, the Union of Equality, and Oneness. To this the Chaldean⁴⁵

---

39. *PF* VI, 17:9–10: "Illam enim in omnibus diis tamquam in participantibus eandem adorant."

40. Ibid., 17:15–17.

41. *PF* VII, 19–21.

42. Cf. the Chaldean's objection in *PF* VIII, 23:26–27: "quod Deus habeat filium et participem in deitate, hoc impugnant Arabes et multi cum ipsis." See also my discussion of the *DA* in the previous chapter.

43. *PF* VII, 20:18–19: "Sed de trino Deo difficillimum erit concordiam undique acceptari..."

44. *PF* VIII, 21:1–2. Cf. *DVD* 13, 58:9–12.

45. It is not clear whom the Chaldean represents. In Augustine, this figure refers to the Old Testament. Thomas Aquinas uses the same term with the meaning "the wise man of the Orient." For Nicholas this term can also denote the Nestorians from Cyprus.

aptly replies: "Even if the wise (*sapientes*) can to some extent grasp these, they exceed the common folk (*vulgus*)."[46] After having agreed with the philosophical interpretation given there, the Chaldean gives another reminder: "the Arabs—and many others—call this into question."

The reader can be spared from most of the technicalities of Nicholas's Trinitarian discussion. In the *PF*, Nicholas himself stated that even the names Oneness, Equality, and Union are not proper terms; nonetheless they signify the Trinity suitably. Although throughout his intellectual career Nicholas was looking for fresh ways of articulating this basic doctrine of the Trinity, in a sense, he was not really troubled about finding the proper terms. According to his general conviction, if simpler terms could be found, they would be more fitting, such as e.g. Oneness, Itness, and Sameness.[47]

The same point can be also phrased in another way. For Nicholas, the point of any Trinitarian discourse was "to explicate (better) the most fecund simplicity of the essence." In the *PF*, this fecundity is revealed as a fundamental structure of all being.[48] However, without God's fecundity nothing could exist and nothing could be fecund.[49] This idea of Divine Fecundity became a constant in Nicholas's later thought. It indeed reappears in the *CA* and the *NA*.[50] In the *PF*, even the Jew—another monotheist par excellence—is ready to accept this image of the Trinity as Divine Fruitfulness Herself. The point is made clear by the Word:

1. to deny the Trinity is to deny the divine fecundity and creative power;

2. to confess the Trinity is to deny the plurality and an association of gods.

The text adds that

> in the manner in which Arabs and Jews deny the Trinity, it ought to be denied by all. But in the manner in which the truth

---

46. *PF* VIII, 22:1: "Haec et si sapientes aliquantulum capare possent, tamen vulgum communem excedunt."

47. See *DI* I, 9, 25–26 and *NA* 5, 19.

48. *PF* VIII, 24:8 etc.

49. Ibid. 24:18–20, cf. X, 27:3–9 and *DI* I, 25. Notice here the theme of *love* in the discussion.

50. For the latter, cf. Beierwaltes, *Der verborgene Gott*, 24.

of the Trinity is explained above, of necessity it will be embraced by all.⁵¹

It is no exaggeration to say that the *PF* displays a certain appreciation of the Jewish and Muslim insistence on monotheism. It seems that Nicholas tried to understand those aspects of a Trinitarian discourse that may justify criticism coming from the non-Christian camp of monotheistic religions. Notice in this respect the emphasis on the different modes (*modi*) of the respective utterances (i.e., of denial and confession) in the quotation. These different modes of expression are articulated from respectively different religious perspectives. The *PF* makes it clear that the Muslim and Jewish arguments against the Trinity make sense even to a Christian.

Naturally, Nicholas, as a Christian, would not stop at simply accepting this kind of monotheistic criticism. He would phrase his own criticism of Islam and Jewish religion instead. However, in his opinion, both Muslims and Jews participate in the truth. Christianity does not appear in the *PF* as monotheism without qualification. That is the reason why the question can be raised whether Christians actually understand this monotheistic criticism. Namely, it is not clear whether they see the reason why Jews or Muslims object to the Trinitarian doctrine. The traditional reference to moral or cultural inferiority—one of the basic constants of anti-Muslim polemic literature—is present in Nicholas's work, albeit not in the *PF*.⁵² This dialogue offers ample evidence that in Nicholas's perception this medieval common-place was not a sufficient explanation of the Muslims' attitude towards the doctrine of Trinity. This is the reason why he made an effort of making sense of the anti-Trinitarian objection. Nicholas was also aware of the fact that Muslims were rather badly informed and did not understand the basics of the Christian faith. As we have seen, his friend, John of Segovia attributed the responsibility for this to the Christians themselves. It is important to recognize that within the context of medieval anti-Muslim polemics Nicholas let the Muslims make a point about (their insistence on) monotheism in the *PF*. Perhaps Christianity needs the *correctio fraterna* from Judaism and Islam in their uncompromising dedication to uncon-

51. *PF*, IX, 26:23–25: "Modo autem quo negant Arabes et Iudei trinitatem, certe ab omnibus negari debet; sed modo quo veritas trinitatis supra explicatur, ab omnibus de necessitate amplectetur."

52. Cf. the earlier discussion of the *DI*.

ditional monotheism. On the other hand, Nicholas also insisted that strict monotheists, such as the Muslims, have to learn from Christianity. Indeed, in the *PF* "a primitive stranger," the Scythian seems to appreciate what Christianity can offer in terms of love.[53]

Another Doctrinal Difficulty: Incarnation

The next speaker, the French theologian explains the Trinity in terms of Eternity either Unbegotten or Begotten or neither Unbegotten nor Begotten. However, he also confesses that the troubles are not over: "there still remains in the world the greatest contradiction," namely, with respect to the question of Incarnation.[54] As pointed out earlier, the Muslims also traditionally attacked this doctrine. What is more, the doctrine of the Trinity and the Incarnation stand or fall together. While the first one forms the ontological foundation for Incarnation (and thus personal faith in Christ), the historical fact of Incarnation is the way the Sacred Trinity actually reveals Itself. Without the epistemological foundation provided through and in Incarnation, there would be no way of coming to know the Divine Trinity. Small wonder, then, that after having discussed the question of Trinity, the *PF* turns next to the doctrine of Incarnation.[55]

The figure of the Frenchman not only reminds the reader of this crucial problem but at once recalls the series of great theologians of France, starting with Hilary of Poitiers (c. 315–367) and ending with the late scholastics such as for instance Jean Gerson.[56] This fact is perhaps not without some irony since it testifies Nicholas's own intellectual-spiritual debt to scholastic theology. The next speaker, the apostle Peter also behaves more as a scholastic intellectual from Paris rather than a simple fisherman from biblical Palestine.[57] He takes over the leading of

---

53. *PF* X, 27. What follows seems to be reiterating and reaffirming a previous point.

54. *PF* X, 28:11–13: "maxima restat contradictio in mundo, asserentibus quibusdam Verbum caro factum ob redemptionem omnium, aliis aliter sentientibus . . ."

55. The letter to John of Segovia also mentions the same problem. See Nicolaus de Cusa, "Epistola," 98, 18etc.

56. Cf. *Godsdienstvrede*, 77 n. 72.

57. Cf. *Godsdienstvrede*, 78 n. 73, where Decorte points out that in a sense Peter is a better witness to the Incarnation of the Word than Christ himself. Peter is giving a testimony not of himself but of another (i.e., of Christ). Decorte also suggests that

the dialogue from the Word.[58] If Peter appears as a scholastic master, he certainly finds his match in the figure of the Persian that recalls the great Islamic theologians such as Avicenna and Al-Ghazali (1056–111).[59] In the course of the ensuing exchange, Peter's answers are met with more and more questions because the Persian keeps on demanding a clear explanation.[60]

This debate makes clear a methodological point: it is said that no similitude (*similitudo*) can be precise, i.e., absolutely exact.[61] Nevertheless, this is no reason to give up similitudes.[62] On the contrary: by giving more intelligible examples, the other can more easily grasp the truth.[63] In the light of Nicholas's previous use of sensible examples in his theological discourse, it is clear that the examples of the *PF* do have a manuductive role.[64]

The Symbolism of the Magnet

An examination of one sensible example can confirm this interpretation. An interesting manuductive illustration is offered in the *PF* with the help of the magnetic stone (*lapis magnes*).[65] Its usage goes back to the Church Father Saint Ambrose and was almost a common place in medieval theology.[66] Magnetism illustrates Christ's power through

---

another reason for the change of the speakers could be the fact that Nicholas was not satisfied with the arguments of this passage.

58. *PF* X, 28:15–18 and the following lines.

59. Respectively Ibn Sina and Al-Ghazali. Cf. *Godsdienstvrede*, 79 n. 75. As will be shown later, Nicholas had a special appreciation for Avicenna.

60. *PF* XI–XII.

61. *PF* XII, 36:3: "non possunt fingi similitudines praecisae..."

62. The clause quoted in the previous footnote introduces the example of the substance and the concept of wisdom. (The latter is related to the Koran.) Nicholas would come back to this in the *CA*. See my next chapter.

63. Cf. *PF* XII, 36:1–2.

64. Cf. the Persian's words in XII, 39:19–21: "Videtur quod, postquam unio illa quae in altissimo est necessaria bene consideratur, quod Arabes ducibiles sint ad recipiendum hanc fidem..." The term "ducibiles" points toward a possible *manuductio*. (Cf. XII, 41:4.12 where both "duci" and "conducere" appear). The term *manuductio* itself does not come up in the *PF*.

65. *PF* XII, 40:1–9.

66. *Nicholas of Cusa on Interreligious Harmony*, 230 n. 50 points out that the example of the magnet "had a long and distinguished pedigree."

which He draws everything and everyone to Himself. Nicholas himself often made use of this similitude.[67]

The real significance of this "scientific" example, however, easily escapes the modern reader.[68] Within the medieval-Aristotelian world-view magnetism was seen as a special instance belonging to the category of the so-called "specific forms." The concept of "specific form" was related to a special kind of celestial influence.[69] In medieval cosmology, it was a limit notion applicable to any natural phenomenon whose explanation remained yet hidden. Magnetism formed an instance of a special form since it did not square with the Aristotelian theory of movement.

Since Nicholas could suppose that Arabs shared the same scientific framework, he had some hope that they would grasp the point of this similitude: Incarnation was an exceptional instance somewhat similar to magnetism as conceived by medievals. Granted that all similitudes necessarily fall short of (this divine) reality, the example of the magnet could at least draw one's attention to the uniqueness of this event. Strictly speaking, Incarnation is not an instance of a special category, since Incarnation was in no way a natural phenomenon. Yet, Incarnation manifests the working of the Divine in a similar way as a magnet shows the special influence of a celestial sphere. Thus, both the notion of Incarnation and a special category pose a limit to human understanding. As a limit notion, Incarnation points toward the Mystery—a Mystery, ultimately ungraspable by finite human minds. If this is true, then even the modern reader who rejects both the Aristotelian scientific framework and medieval cosmology is able to appreciate the point of the limit notion.

This observation shows how the manuductive employment of the magnetic stone is connected with Nicholas's "Christological bias." On the one hand, both Nicholas's argument sketch in the *PF* and his subsequent intellectual struggle in his letter to John of Segovia and the *CA* can be read as an attempt to defend (medieval) Christianity's claim for possessing absolute truth. However, Nicholas's vision on his own faith

---

67. Cf. *Godsdienstvrede*, 89 n. 85. See also *CC* I, 2 and *CA* III, 21, 237:1–10. Klibansky and Bascour "Adnotationes" 81 points out that magnetism appears especially in the Sermons.

68. On magnetism, see Auty, et al., *Lexikon des Mittelalters*. I am grateful to Jason McBride for drawing my attention to the notion of "special form" and magnetism.

69. On the scientific notion of heavenly influence, see C.S. Lewis's short introduction to medieval cosmology: "Imagination and Thought," esp. 55–57.

was much more subtle and intricate than a simple exclusive absolutism. While it is beyond argument that he never gave up his basic Christian credo, it is also equally clear from his employment of the magnetic stone, that neither would his faith allow for complete rationalization. By pointing towards the Mystery of Incarnation, Nicholas was both pointing out the limitations of finite human understanding and suggesting a genuine appreciation for a real sense of transcendence. By the same gesture, he invited the Other to share his (i.e., Christian) vision on transcendence and at once acknowledged the limitations of the very same (i.e., his own) vision.

It may well be that this gesture will not necessarily convince the Other. Nicholas felt rightly that his "argument" in the Christological part of the *PF* was not completely convincing. The magnetic stone offered him a weak parallel for Incarnation—ultimately falling short of the Divine reality since no magnetic stone could ever have infinite power.[70] All the same, the point remains that such a manuductive gesture can achieve something more than mere rational persuasion of the Other to the extent that it makes one's own perspective relative. Indeed, in Nicholas's opinion, all human perspectives are necessarily relative. As the discussion of *DVD* and the *DA* also made clear, by one and the same manuductive gesture Nicholas did not pretend to be able to see (transcendent, Divine) truth without or outside of any (limited, human) perspective. This circumstance not only explains but also to some extent justifies what was referred to earlier as Nicholas's "Christological bias."

The Practical Nuisance: The Variety of Rites and the Human Condition

The lofty theological discussion of the *PF* continues with the treatment of Christological doctrines such as the hypostatic union, Christ's death and resurrection, virginal birth, human desire, and heavenly happiness.[71] The discussion is sketching out similitudes in order to convince the dialogue partners that a basic concord can be reached in these matters of (Christian) faith. Since the (post-)modern reader is less optimistic concerning such a concord between the all too different contents of di-

---

70. Cf. *CA* III, 21, 237:1–10.

71. See *PF* XIII–XV. I will return to the question of heavenly happiness when discussing Nicholas's letter to John and the *CA*.

verse faiths, he or she is probably also less interested in the discussion. However, when the question of different rites (*varietas rituum*) comes up even a (post-)modern reader can learn again from the formal aspect of Nicholas's approach.

The question of different rites is central to the *PF* as signaled by the opening passage—the apropos of the work being "the persecution that was raging more fiercely than usual on account of the difference of rite between the religions." The same passage also makes clear that the ensuing heavenly conference issued as a solution to religious conflicts is a meeting of a "few wise men who are rich in the experimental knowledge of all such differences," i.e., of differences of rites.

In the course of the dialogue, after the long philosophical-theological disputation, it is the figure of the simple Tartar that addresses the question of different rites.[72] Afterwards, in the closing part of the dialogue, at least the most important Christian rites are touched upon and even circumcision—common to Jews, Muslims, and even to some Christians—is discussed.[73] A rite (*ritus*) can mean a sacrament, ceremony or ritual.[74] Thus, circumcision, baptism, the different arrangements concerning marriage and sacrifices are all instances of a ritual. Further, one can also elicit a more general meaning of the *ritus*, which points toward distinguishing features of particular religions.[75] However, if religion is understood as a certain human practice, this conceptual distinction is only of relative importance as the specific instances of religious rite(s) can be subsumed under the general notion.

This is obviously not to deny the doctrinal dimension of religions—only emphasize their practical side. This emphasis on the practical dimension is in accordance with my overall focus on the formal aspect of medieval knowledge. If one sees religions in terms of a human practice, one can say that what makes a real difference between two religions is

72. *PF* XVI, 54:1, etc.

73. In the discussion with the Arab and the Indian, some forms of non-Christian worship also receive theoretical treatment. Cf. *PF* V–VI.

74. Hopkins, *Nicholas of Cusa's De Pace Fidei*, 218 n. 8. For the first meaning, see *PF* XVI, 54:2–4 etc. and XVIII, 65. The latter text discusses the Eucharist and uses the term "sacramentum."

The *PF* employs the term "ritus" 13 times: 4 times in singular and 9 times in plural. Out of its appearances 9 times the word clearly refers to the difference of religious rites.

75. See *PF* I, 1:5–8 and also *CA* III, 8, 184:8–9 and III 16, 218:1–2. Hopkins points out that the second notion is a collective one used in the singular.

the different "things" done or the different ways the same "things" are done in those different religions. Different religions thus may either have completely different rituals such as circumcision and baptism or they can practice the same "thing" in very different forms such as marriage in the form of monogamy and polygamy. Seen from a practical point of view, difference is always a practical difference: a difference in doing or not doing some things. Doctrinal explanations of differences are only secondary. Rite, in this general sense of the term, can refer to any kind of religious practice, i.e., anything that is done in a particular way while having religious significance.

Nor is this consideration completely out of place in a discussion of the *PF*. It can be argued that in the dialogue, this practical viewpoint is offered through the figure of the "simple Tartar."[76] This Tartar is not so much interested in theoretical questions, but in the real differences of rites. His figure represents a primitive people believing in the One God but apparently without a sophisticated theology. In his first words, he admits that he has heard several points in the course of the lofty theological discussion that were so far unfamiliar to him.[77] As being thus unsophisticated, the Tartar makes no move at contesting the various theological doctrines exposed so far. Instead, he addresses the practical question thereby touching the real issue. No matter what kind of intellectual concordance would be achieved between the wise, the practical issue of tolerating different rites still remains. This is the Tartar's concern: there are so many diverse rites and his people are amazed or even

---

76. Cf. *Godsdienstvrede*, 102 n. 111.—Decorte, "Tolerance," drew my attention to the figure of the Tartar and the practical dimension of the issue.

77. Cf. *PF* XVI, 54:1-2: "Audivi multa in hoc loco prius incognita mihi. Tartari multi et simplices, unum Deum ut plurium colentes . . ."—Nicholas knew of the Tartars from his reading of Marco Polo's famous work (*Il milieno*) in the Latin translation of the Dominican Friar, Francisco Pipino de Bononia, from the year 1445. Cf. Klibansky and Bascour "Adnotationes," 86, Biechler and Bond, "Introduction," xxx, and especially their note on page 234: "Nicholas apparently received conflicting information on the religious beliefs of the Tartars but he preferred to regard them as monotheist." From the quotations as given by Klibansky and Bascour, it is not clear why the two claims should be conflicting. Since Nicholas was ready to accept the idolatry of the Indians as an expression of a monotheism, he could do the same with the Tartars' religion. Monotheism with a kind of primitive "idolatry" was acceptable to him. As can be elicited from Klibansky and Bascour and Biechler and Bond's respective notes, both Marco Polo and John de Plano Carpini (c. 1180-1252) called the Tartars *idolaters and worshippers of one god*. They solely differed in attributing different names to that *one god*.

shocked by some of them.⁷⁸ The Tartar rightly points out that such a diversity of religious practice can be a source of conflicts.⁷⁹

It is no exaggeration to say that Nicholas realized that one can well find the Other's practice astonishing or even abhorrent. This realization has to be taken all the more seriously as Nicholas made this clear on the example of Eucharist, i.e., the central sacrament of Christianity.⁸⁰ It was shown earlier that Thomas Aquinas also knew about the Muslims' mockery and misunderstanding of the Eucharist.⁸¹ In answering the objections leveled against the Eucharist, on the one hand, Thomas showed himself a traditional theologian in limiting the scope of his discussion concerning a Christian sacrament, while on the other hand, he had some confidence in the "little instruction" he was giving. While it would be an exaggeration to call Thomas' view on the problem optimistic, it can be argued that Nicholas took this practical nuisance more seriously. In the *PF*, the function of the simple Tartar is to introduce a perspective to the reader from which the Eucharist and generally the question of diverse rites can better be perceived. The point is that even if one accepts that the Other worships the same One God, the Other's practice can be still disturbing.⁸² In the dialogue, the Tartar introduces this observation in neutral terms and not as a mockery. His statement according to which this variance of practices is inevitable due to historical circumstances and geographical differences suggests a matter-of-fact approach.⁸³ The Tartar even adds that it is very sad that "diversity begets divisiveness and enmity, animosities and wars." But as Nicholas's former teacher, Henry van de Velde (†1460) also recognized, this fact belongs to the human condition.⁸⁴

In the ensuing discussion, Paul takes over Peter's leading place and tries to answer the Tartar's and others' vexing questions concerning the

---

78. *PF* XVI, 54:3–4: "admirantur varietatem rituum aliorum etiam eundem cum ipsis Deum colentium." Later, in line 12, the Tartas calls the Eucharist "abhominabilius."

79. *PF* XVI, 54:15–16: "Diversitas enim parit divisionem et inimicitias, odia et bella."

80. Ibid., 54:9–13. Cf. Nicolaus de Cusa, "Epistola," 100, 9–10.

81. On Thomas, see my discussion in the second chapter.

82. Cf. *PF* XVI, 60:1–4.

83. Ibid., 54:13–14.

84. According to Klibansky and Bascour, 51, Henry placed the following note in his own copy of the *PF*: "Hec diversitas est connaturalis homini in orizonte eternitatis et temporis constituto."

difference of rites. Here, Paul's figure as the apostle of the Gentiles seems to be an obvious choice. It was chiefly due to Paul's missionary and literary activities that primitive Christianity liberated itself from Jewish religion. This "liberation" consisted in the different way Christians read the Hebrew Bible—or more precisely its Greek version, the Septuagint. Emancipation from Judaism also implied a different religious practice. In this transition from Judaism to Christianity, a central issue was whether and to what extent Christians still should keep the Jewish Torah and perform accordingly Jewish rituals such as for instance circumcision. Paul himself was encouraging the change and preached giving up Jewish observances. Moreover, he can be seen as the first theoretician of that movement, in effect, the first great theologian of Christianity. The biblical texts relating his life and work still communicate the sense of anxiety and tension in the first Christians' struggle for what Paul called their "freedom" in Christ.[85] What I would like to emphasize is that the issue at stake was very much practical, i.e., the legitimacy of a form of Jewish observance, religious practice itself. With the intellectual leadership of Paul, primitive Christianity defined its own practices very much through this movement of liberation and abandoned large parts of Jewish observance.

Keeping this biblical background in mind, it appears somewhat ironical, yet from a historical perspective perhaps necessary that later Christianity developed its own observance with its own set of very strictly defined rites. Only a passing glance at medieval Western Christianity can show how ritualistic it was. My employment of the term "ritualistic" is strictly descriptive and thus neutral, as I do not feel entitled to enter into an evaluative discussion of late-medieval Christian rituals nor do I need to do so. My point is simply that rituals played an important role in medieval Christianity. On the other hand, both Paul's fundamental theological contribution and the Gospel records of Christ's own behavior to (Jewish) rituals had become very much part and parcel of the Christianity's religious legacy.[86]

Approaching the *PF* from this perspective, one can better appreciate the special nuances of Nicholas's own view of the question of

---

85. See especially Phil, Gal, and Rom.

86. Some hundred years after Nicholas's death, the Protestant movements in support of their own criticism of the excesses of medieval Christian rituals will pick up this issue.

rites. It is interesting to see Nicholas evoking a critical attitude towards Christian rituals in a context completely different both from Paul's and the Reformers. As a cardinal of the Roman Church and a man of personal piety, Nicholas could hardly be expected to give up medieval Catholic practice or even truncate it in the way some Reformers would later do. Nor could he be as radical with respect to Catholic sacraments as the historical Paul was towards Jewish circumcision. Finally, Nicholas certainly did not want to fully rationalize these practices either, if rationalization means a rationalistic explanation that is independent from the religious tradition, i.e., from the practice itself.

The Cusanian positive attitude towards the diversity of rites comes to the fore when Paul discusses the problem of different Christian rites. Although it is stated that circumcision is not a sacrament necessary for salvation, this rite is accepted for the Ethiopian Jacobites and other Eastern Christians.[87] Historically speaking, the very same question had already been discussed at the council of Florence (1439–1443). The official decision fell against circumcision either before or after baptism and in this respect the *PF* shows Nicholas more "tolerant" of this practice than the Catholic Church officially was.[88] It is equally clear that while Nicholas would accept the practice of circumcision he would (re-)interpret it in his own, Christian terms, by giving it another, Christian explanation.

The *PF* also acknowledges the fact that such a sympathetic attitude in itself does not render the question as "how peace can be maintained among believers if some are circumcised and others are not" completely harmless.[89] Earlier I referred to the irony of Paul's appearance in this discussion. The irony of the entire issue with circumcision is all the more apparent from this text since the historical Paul explicitly warned Christians from circumcising themselves.[90] The fact that Nicholas approves of the rite of circumcision and that his approval is displayed in the *PF* through the figure of the Apostle Paul may indicate Nicholas's own embarrassment with regards to the problem of circumcision.

---

87. *PF* XVI, 60:5 etc.

88. Cf. *Godsdienstvrede*, 109 n. 128.

89. *PF* XVI, 60:13–14: "Sed quomodo possit servari pax inter fideles, si qui circumciduntur et alii non, est maior dubitatio."

90. See Gal 5:1–13, e.g., verse 2: "Ecce ego Paulus dico vobis, quoniam si circumcidamini, Christus vobis nihil proderit."

To generalize an earlier point it can be said that even if the basic concord in faith is already reached, in the sense of a common theological understanding of the rite, there still remains the problem of harmonizing or tolerating each other's (different) practices. One of the strengths of the *PF* lies precisely in the discussion with the simple Tartar addressing this very issue. Nicholas explicitly states that if there is both a majority not practicing circumcision and a minority holding on to this practice, a common theory does not exclude the possibility of a conflict. As a possible solution to the problem, he considers several alternatives.⁹¹ On the one hand, it would be beneficial if the minority could give up its own practice for the sake of peace (*ob pacem servandam*). Yet, Nicholas recognized that this solution is somewhat unrealistic. Hence, he also proposed that the majority might still accept the practice of circumcision on the condition that the other party also accepts baptism. Such mutual concessions (*mutuae communicationes*) may offer a practical solution, though admittedly, even this solution would be very difficult to realize.⁹² Ultimately, nothing remains to be done, than to confirm the unity of faith by the law of love (*in fide et lege dilectionis firmari*). To establish peace would mean concretely 'tolerating' (*tolerando*) the Other's practice.⁹³

On Toleration

Notably, this is the only instance in the whole text where the reader finds the term *"tolerare."* Since the general question of the *PF* consists in the problems posed by religious diversity, it is tempting for the modern mind to interpret Nicholas as an advocate of toleration *avant la lettre*. But modern religious tolerance is a modern answer to a modern question, therefore it would be a gross mistake to attribute such an attitude to Nicholas of Cusa.⁹⁴ One basic philosophical difference

---

91. *PF* XVI, 60:14 etc.

92. Ibid., 22–23: "Arbitror autem praxim huius difficilem."

93. Ibid., 23–24: "Sufficiat igitur pacem in fide et lege dilectionis firmari, ritum hinc inde tolerando." In interpreting this sentence I am following Decorte's translation. (For the philological and theological justification of the translation see Decorte, "Ter inleiding," 10–17.) I read the clause "et lege dilectionis firmari" as an *et explicativum* while being aware of the possibility of a simpler reading (Cf. *Nicholas of Cusa's De Pace Fidei*, 66: "faith and the law of love.")

94. *Godsdienstvrede*, 116 n. 142.

is the modern rationalistic approach that lies behind the idea(l) of religious tolerance. No such attitude can be expected from Nicholas. As Colomer points out:

> Nicholas was no Enlightenment thinker before Enlightenment. His ideal was not universal religion of reason, but a toleration (*Duldung*) of the different religious practices in its essentially Trinitarian and Christological fundamental doctrines by all peoples freely accepted, universal Christianity.[95]

When the reader turns to the text of the *PF*, he or she finds that the meaning of the word *"tolerando"* is rather neutral. Perhaps it can be even called negative as denoting an unpleasant and inconvenient activity. Such a negative semantic dimension was not uncommon to this term during the Middle-Ages.[96] Precisely through this negative moment of the term, the passage under discussion brings forth an important point. As the last sentence makes it clear, the solution to the question of different religious rites turns out to be a question anchored in Christian charity.[97]

The *PF* also makes clear the necessary connection between charity and faith. The foregoing discussion actually by-passed the first part of the exchange between the Apostle Paul and the simple Tartar.[98] There, Paul unequivocally stated that "salvation comes from faith." To the Tartar's question whether faith in itself is sufficient, the Apostle replies by saying that "[W]ithout faith it is impossible for anyone to please God, but faith has to be a formed faith; because without works faith is dead."[99] This answer is interesting as it actually connects two conflicting lines of biblical theology, i.e., Pauline thought and the teaching of the Apostle

---

95. Colomer, *Nikolaus von Kues*, 115: "Nikolaus . . . war kein Aufklärer vor der Aufklärung. Sein Ideal war nicht eine universale Vernuftreligion, sondern ein durch Duldung der verschiedenen religiösen Gebräuche in seinem wesentlichen trinitarischen und christologischen Grundlehren von allen Völkern frei angenommenes, universales Christentum." Colomer himself refuses an anachronistic interpretation of Nicholas's project, while expresses its strengths in terms reminiscent of toleration.

96. On the meaning of the term "toleration," see my *Appendix*.

97. For Nicholas, the question of different religious-ethical laws can similarly be reduced to the same problem. Cf. *PF* XVI, 59.

98. *PF* XVI, 53–58.

99. Ibid., 58:23–24: "Sine fide impossibile est quem placere Deo. Oportet autem quod fides sit formata; nam sine operibus est mortua."

James.[100] More importantly, the expression "formed faith" (*fides formata*) makes clear the connection between faith (*fides*) and love (*caritas*). As Thomas Aquinas puts it in the *ST*, "love is said to be the form of faith, in as much as the act of faith is perfected and receives form through love."[101] Nicholas's *DI* attests that he was familiar with this concept of "formed faith."[102] Formed or perfected faith is a faith qualified by love. Its moments include an attachment to (*adhesio*) and a personal trust in (*fiducia*) God as well as a living praxis of loving and believing.[103] The historical Paul himself already declared that "faith ... works through love."[104] This suggests that love (*caritas*) functions as an essential aspect of faith. The reference to its perfection in love expresses the teleology of the act of faith. Charity as the form of faith, that is to say its essential aspect prescribes that this faith must be lived out in practice.

Earlier in this study I tried to highlight this essential connection between *fides* and *caritas* in my discussion of the *DI* and *DVD*. Taking all the evidence together and applying it to the problem of differences in religious rites, one can say that this form of faith prescribes that Christian faith must be acted out concretely by enduring or bearing with (*tolerando*) the Otherness of the Other's practice. It is also clear from the *PF*, that this concrete form of Christian charity has its own intellectual counterpart in the Cusanian idea of a learned ignorance. In this way theory and practice meet in trying to answer the challenge of the situation when they are confronted with a practical nuisance. Nicholas's answer to the practical nuisance can be summed up by saying that faith and charity (*fides quam lex dilectionis*) are two intrinsically related dimensions of the same reality prescribing an ethical as well as an intellectual engagement with the Other. In the following, I hope to show that this intellectual engagement takes the concrete form of a *"pia interpretatio,"* when I come to discuss Nicholas's letter to John of Segovia and his *CA*.

---

100. The first half of the answer is a quotation from Heb 11:6, while *PF* XVI, 58:24—59:1-3 can be read in connection with Jas 2:17.

101. *ST* IIa IIae q. 4, a. 3 (under the title "Utrum caritas sit forma fidei"), in the response: "caritas dicitur forma fidei, inquantum per caritatem actus fidei perficitur et formatur."

102. Cf. *DI* III, 6, 217:16-17 and 11, 248:9-10.

103. Cf. Senger, "Anmerkungen," 122.

104. Gal 5:6: "fides, quae per charitatem operatur."

Is the PF a Manuductive Work?

After discussing the different rituals, the heavenly conference of the *PF* is closed with a kind of "rational" or "intellectual-speculative concord."[105] After having studied ancient sources on the question of different religious observances, the wise men of the world arrive at an agreement.[106] Thereafter they are called upon to return to their respective peoples in order to teach them and lead them (*inducant*) to a religious unity of different cults.[107] Although the expression *"unitas veri cultus"* (unity of the true religion) employed in this passage may suggest a unitary cult, the foregoing discussion made it clear that no such uniformity is necessary or beneficiary.[108] In the very last later chapter of the dialogue, Saint Paul plainly states that "to seek exact conformity in all respects is rather to disturb the peace."[109]

With the task of leading different peoples to a peaceful unity, the dialogue of the *PF* opens up a perspective on a practical learning process for the followers of different religions. The text also emphasizes a further specific task for the wise, namely, a preparation of the final theological peace-conference or assembly in Jerusalem.[110] As pointed out earlier, the image of Jerusalem is linked to the idea of perpetual peace. This Christian image anticipates the coming of an eschatological peace (in the heavenly Jerusalem), while the question whether permanent peace can be realized in this world (in the earthly Jerusalem) is left open. Through this way of closing his dialogue, the author reminds his readership of the fact that the heavenly assignment is a task for him or her to realize.

In the last analysis, one has to agree with Hopkins's statement that in this dialogue, "Nicholas did not attenuate the teachings of Christianity in his quest of a single faith which all nations could accept."[111] Offering

---

105. PF XIX, 68:11–12. Cf. *Godsdienstvrede*, 118n146 and also *Nicholas of Cusa on Interreligious Harmony*, 236n82.

106. PF XIX, 68:1–10.

107. Ibid., 12–13: "Et mandatum est per Regem regum ut sapientes redeant et ad unitatem veri cultus nationes inducant ..."

108. Apart from the discussion with the Tartar, see PF XVII–XIX.

109. PF XIX, 67:4–5: "exactam quaerere conformitatem in omnibus est potius pacem turbare." Cf. PF XVIII, 66:7–11.

110. PF XIX, 68:15–17.

111. Hopkins, "Introduction," 12.

another religion than Christianity was never his aim, since such a goal could not have been a rational aim for a medieval Christian thinker at all. For Nicholas, the 'core' of the unitary faith (i.e., of the *"unitas veri cultus"*) remained his Christian faith explained in terms of medieval Catholic doctrine. Interestingly, Nicholas did not only admit but also endorsed some variety with respect to religious rites as he saw no theoretical conflict between such a variety and his own Christian faith.[112] Thus in the closing words of the *PF* he expressed his opinion that "the entire diversity among religions lay in the rites rather than in the worship of one God."[113]

Nicholas's argument in support of his statement that religions have always presupposed one God sounds a bit implausible to the (post-)modern mind. However, the (post-)modern reader must be reminded of the fact that Nicholas's statement does not *per se* entail a devaluation of the importance of religious practice itself. As the discussion between the Tartar and Paul makes it clear, Nicholas saw the difference between rites as a serious problem that can only be "solved" through one's benevolent personal attention in everyday life. The theoretical reflection offered by the *PF* would be pointless and ineffective without a practical engagement with the Other. Thus, in spite of its overtly optimistic closing words, the *PF* is not a work born out of a religious naiveté or intellectual daydreaming, but rather a book challenging its readership both intellectually and practically.[114] Some of the "optimistic" features of the dialogue can be better viewed when related to Hopkins's observation according to which Nicholas's aim was the creation of an intellectual atmosphere. The unrealistic features (such as politeness and neutrality) play a similar role in the *PF* as in Ramón Lull's work.[115]

Therefore, one can only agree with the following overall appraisal:

> Perhaps *De Pace Fidei* is best viewed not as an argument but as an invitation—as a work, that is, which invites the leaders of all religions to identify what they regard as the essence of their respective faith and to see whether they think that Christianity

---

112. Ibid. See also the earlier discussion on Paul and rituals.

113. *PF* XIX, 68:5–6: "omnem diversitatem in ritibus potius compertum est fuisse quam in unius Dei cultura..."

114. This is the reason why Hopkins's judgment according to which Nicholas was overly optimistic or even "parochial" needs some qualification.

115. On Ramón, see my second chapter.

and the faiths other than their own can be reduced to that one essence.... In all fairness, Nicholas should not be criticized as being myopic but should rather be recommended for his efforts to peer beyond the perimeters of Western Christendom and to "proselytize" in a way that, prima facie, did not affront the intellect of those whom he addressed—a way that emphasized the inherence of truth in religions other than Christianity.[116]

The previous examination of Nicholas's works has shown his enduring intellectual concern for different forms or application of *manuductio*.[117] This general observation places Hopkins's judgment according to which Nicholas's main concern in the *PF* is identified as *manuducere*, within the context of Nicholas's overall intellectual project.[118] In the *PF* this manuductive project takes up the concrete form of guiding the adherents of other religions to truth—thereby guiding Others who are not seen as antichrists, but as potential allies in the religious-theological quest for more explicit truth.[119]

The truth is not only meant to guide the imaginary figures of the dialogue, but Nicholas's contemporary Christian readers as well. Through the rhetorical and reflexive structure of the dialogue, its readers are called upon to reflect on the discussed topics in a similar way (*modo*) as the author himself did.[120] Just as earlier the employment of Nicholas's conjectural art was offered as in principle open to any ardent student, so it is with the rational or intellectual heaven (*caelum rationis sive altitudinis intellectualis*).[121] This intellectual dimension of human

116. Hopkins, "Introduction," 12–13.

117. The following quotation from *PF* I, 3:6–12 testifies the basic *manuductive* continuity between the *DI* and the *PF*: "quamvis spiritus ille intellectualis, seminatus in terra, absorptus in umbra, non videat lucem et ortus sui initium, tu tamen concreasti eidem ea omnia per quae, excitatus admiratione eorum quae sensu attingit, possit aliquando ad te omnium creatorem oculos mentis attollere et tibi caritate summa reuniri, et sic demum ad ortum suum cum fructu redire."

118. Cf. Hopkins, "Introduction," 13: "Though the word '*manuductio*' is not used in the *De Pace Fidei*, the concept is operative throughout." In the previous chapter I argued that *manuductio* was operative in Nicholas's whole oeuvre.

119. Hopkins, "Introduction," 13.

120. Cf. *PF* XIX, 68:11–12 etc. See Hopkins's statement mentioned earlier and the earlier discussion of the literary genre and reflexivity in my second chapter.

121. *PF* 68:11 has "in caelo rationis" while *PF* I, 2:1 speaks of "ad quandam intellectualem altitudinem." Both Decorte and Hopkins point out that it is possible to read these two expressions as synonymous, because Nicholas did not always consequently distinguished between reason and intellect in his terminology. *DVD* 25, 111:7–8 refers to human intellectual nature as to "caelum veritatis."

life is open to anyone—at least to those having enough spare time for study and reflection. The dialogue of the *PF* suggests that if an intellectual readership would willingly take up the burden of serious reflection in similar way to Nicholas, then there is hope that they could lead the different nations closer to a peace between religions. In Nicholas's opinion such an intellectual reflection must be both mediated by faith and prayer and conducted through a theoretical effort of study and understanding.

Manuductio and Pious Interpretation in Nicholas's Letter to John of Segovia

Now I turn to the second text crucial for Nicholas's approach to Islam, i.e., to his letter to John of Segovia. As other aspects of this letter have already been discussed in my second chapter, here I will only examine the theological-philosophical material contained in the second part of the letter.[122] This part of the letter gives a good summary of what Nicholas thought about a possible dialogue with Islam. The text both states points already made in the *PF* in a very clear and concise manner, and also anticipates the exegetical approach of the *CA*. The letter explicitly refers to the *PF* as a work already written and makes clear that Nicholas's aim was not so much offering additional information to John but rather reflecting on the Islamic question.[123]

The second part of the letter starts with Nicholas's confession that he and John had the same understanding of the Islamic problem. Nicholas basically agreed with John in preferring a peaceful rapprochement of Islam and saw a real possibility for John's (theological) conference as a way to peace. In Nicholas's opinion, Christian faith would certainly profit from such an encounter as it could mitigate hostility and let the truth manifest itself.[124] As shown earlier, with respect to such an intellectual exchange, Nicholas suggested to John that it would be worth bringing into the discussion some Christians living under

---

122. For the text, see Nicolaus de Cusa, "Epistola," 96–100.

123. Ibid., 100, 11–13: "Ista ergo non informando doctissimum scripsi, sed occasionem praestando cogitandi; licet credam nihil restare quod non sit in opere digestum."

124. Ibid., 97, 13–15: "ad colloquia posse perveniri, et ex illis furor mitigabitur et veritas se ipsam ostendet cum profectu fidei nostrae." Cf. ibid., 100, 13–14.

Muslim dominion.¹²⁵ This proposal recalls the wise of the *PF* who are said to have experiential knowledge (*peritiori*) in matters of religions. In his letter, Nicholas also diplomatically confesses that he sees some hope that John's rational theological arguments concerning the Trinity could persuade the Turks. He also admits that many similar arguments can be formed, but he does not further elaborate on this question. He only states that these arguments can sufficiently demonstrate that God cannot be viewed as the most perfect principle unless He is conceived of in relational terms.¹²⁶

While Nicholas was convinced that both Jews and Turks can easily be convinced that the Trinity does not contradict Divine Unity, he pointed out the difficulties he will face at other crucial points of Christian doctrine. Most importantly, both his *PF* and his letter testify that Nicholas was aware of the problems of explaining the *unio hypostatica*. In Nicholas's opinion, the Christological problem is related to the fact that there is no proportion between the finite and the infinite. Hence, any attempt at apprehending Christ at the same time as finite creature and as Infinite God must be problematic. Nevertheless, Nicholas thought that Muslims can be brought at least to understand that Christians do not believe that Divinity, which is per definition beyond sensible reality, was present in Christ in any sensible way.

I have already briefly looked at the *PF*'s Christological discussion. Here, I would like to show how this discussion is related to Nicholas's own interpretation of the Koran. Namely, Nicholas was convinced that by arguing that Christians do not believe of Christ what the Muslims think they believe, one can demonstrate how the Koranic message concerning Christ should be properly understood.¹²⁷ As far as Christ is concerned, there is a special sense according to which the Prophet's words are true (*vera*). If rightly understood, the Koranic texts refer to Christ as a human being, but the very same words have nothing to do with Christ's Divinity. This interpretative move prefigures an exegetical rule that Nicholas would consequently apply in the *CA*. The next para-

125. Ibid., 97, 16–18: "qui et mores atque fundamenta eorum optime sciunt et semper student ipsis obviare . . ." Cf. *PF* I, 1:8–10; III, 9:1–3, and 68:1–5.

126. Nicolaus de Cusa, "Epistola," 97, 25–98, 4: "Possunt et plures aliae formari, quae ostenderent sufficienter fidem Trintatis ad summam notitiam unius Dei accedere, in quo non potest natura summe perfecta videri uti in principio nisi correlationes divinae admittantur."

127. Ibid., 99, 9–15.

graph of the letter elaborates another means for a consciously Christian reading of the Koran by way of an interesting example.[128] The particular passage provides a good summary of the essential strategy of Nicholas's way of reading the Koran—an interpretative method he already employed in his *PF* and would more fully develop and apply in the *CA*.[129]

The particular example of pious interpretation is related to a commonplace of medieval culture, which also continues to live in popular understanding today. As the earlier examination of Ramón Lull's work and Nicholas's *DI* show, it was generally assumed during the Middle-Ages that the Koran's description of Paradise is one of carnal, sensual pleasures.[130] Such an idea was repellent to medieval Christians, especially intellectuals coming for the most part from a celibate clergy.[131] It was precisely this group of intellectuals that formed popular imagination to a considerable degree with their devotional works and preaching activities. They very much defined also the epistemic field of a more philosophical discourse. Hence, it is only understandable that within medieval culture the image of a lustful Heaven could be easily targeted and condemned by the same group of intellectuals—or by anybody else—as immoral, animal or even diabolic and absurd. The previous examination of John of Torquemada shows a clear example of such an overtly negative approach. Nicholas, himself a celibate cleric, was both familiar with the image of a lustful Muslim Paradise and the harsh criticism leveled against it from his fellow Christians. Nor did he differ from this majority in his spontaneous reaction in terms of repulsion and disgust.[132] Interestingly, in spite of his discontent with the Koranic description of Paradise, Nicholas tried to approach the same question from a different perspective.

Nicholas's view concerning the correct interpretation of the Koranic description of a sensual Paradise can be summarized by pointing out that the author of the Koran simply employed bodily images (*similitudo*).[133] This kind of approach perfectly fits with Nicholas's

---

128. Later Nicholas would call this kind of an interpretative strategy "pious interpretation" (pia interpetatio).

129. Cf. *PF* XV, 50:3–14 and *CA* II, 18–19.

130. Cf. *Surahs* 44, 52 and 55.

131. Cf. Southern, *Western Views of Islam*, 7.

132. Cf. *PF* XV, 51:3–14 and *CA* II, 19, 154–55.

133. Nicolaus de Cusa, "Epistola," 99, 19–20: "Etiam videtur sciptorem Alchorani

overall thought according to which religious language is necessarily symbolic.¹³⁴ More specifically, both in his letter and in the *PF*, Nicholas explicitly refers to Avicenna who in his *Metaphysics* offered an intellectualist interpretation of (Muslim) religion.¹³⁵ Avicenna wrote that because a prophet has to speak of divine things according to human understanding, he will use rhetorical devices.

Besides Avicenna's text, Nicholas studied Richard of Montrecroce's and Dionysius the Carthusian's account of Islamic doctrine. Alongside with his own reading of the Koran, all the evidence taken together led him to the conviction that many wise (*intelligentes et sapientes*) among the Muslims basically agree with this intellectualist or spiritual interpretation of the Koranic promises concerning celestial happiness.¹³⁶ The genuine Koranic promise consists in intellectual happiness, i.e., in a *visio Dei*.¹³⁷ Muhammad, however, while preaching to the simple Arabs (*rudi populo*) was forced to do concessions to their level of understanding. The Prophet employed sensual *similitudes* in order to indicate that the heavenly beatitude is the fulfillment of all human desire. In this way, those who were not able to understand that the most basic human desire is of an intellectual kind were still encouraged by the carnal imagery to seek happiness through keeping the Divine Law. In this way Muhammad could achieve his main goal: he was able to lead away (*avertere*) those people from idolatry and guide them further to embrace the worship of the One only God.

It is not difficult to see in this rhetorical move a genuine example of *manuductio*. Nicholas clearly read the Koran as a religious *manuductio*. Through this reading he both could justify the employment of sensual imagery in the Koranic descriptions of Paradise and would also solve the apparent disagreement between Muslims and Christians concerning celestial happiness. This reading makes also clear the reason why it is not difficult to reach an agreement between Christianity and Islam

---

locutum per similitudinem corporalium deliciarum de futuris deliciis." Cf. *PF* XV, 51:9–10.19–21.

134. See my third chapter.

135. Nicolaus de Cusa, "Epistola," 99, 16–22 and *PF* XV, 52:7–9. For Avicenna's text see Avicenna Latinus, *Liber Philosophia*, book X, ch. 2.

136. Cf. *PF* XV, 52:4–9.

137. *PF* XV, 52:7–8 employs the phrase "felicitatem intellectualem visionis seu fruitionis Dei et veritatis."

with respect to this problem.¹³⁸ Nicholas drew from this example the following more general moral:

> Hence, it is apparent that we always have to strive for this, i.e., that this book [=the Koran] that holds authority for them should aid us in the argumentation. For we find therein things useful for us—and those that are contrary to us we shall interpret by the former ones.¹³⁹

Taken in isolation, these two sentences might puzzle or perhaps scandalize the (post-)modern reader. It is tempting to see them as nothing other than expressions of intellectual violence forcing the Other into a meaning alien to him- or herself. On the previous pages of the present study, I have gathered sufficient evidence for challenging such a simplistic reading. On the other hand, if this short passage gives the general direction of Nicholas's approach, then it should be related to the actual execution of the same approach. The question to what extent his approach is justified must be postponed before a detailed examination of the *CA* is given in my next chapter.

In his letter Nicholas offered his own considerations on the question as to how to convince the Muslims that Christians do not confess absurdities. What one can read here concerning the Cross and the Eucharist recalls the similar manuductive approach of the *PF*.¹⁴⁰ With respect to these points it should be emphasized that both the *PF* and the letter to Segovia bring into play at least some Koranic material without, however, examining Muhammad's Law in its entirety.¹⁴¹ Nicholas also considered the possibility that his reasoning would not convince Muslims. He thought that at least it could be made clear to them that they should not persecute or harass the followers of Christ because the Koran also praises Him.¹⁴² This statement demonstrates Nicholas's sin-

---

138. Cf. ibid., line 10. See also Nicolaus de Cusa, "Epistola," 99, 16.

139. Nicolaus de Cusa, "Epistola," 99, 22–25: "Unde videtur quod semper ad hoc conandum sit quod liber iste, qui apud eos est in auctoritate, pro nobis allegetur. Nam reperimus in eo talia quae serviunt nobis; et alia quae contrariantur, glosabimus per illa." For the interpretation and translation of this passage I am especially indebted to the late Jos Decorte for his kind assistance.

140. Cf. Nicolaus de Cusa, "Epistola," 99, 26–29.

141. Ibid., 98, 15–17.19–23 etc.

142. Ibid., 99, 13–15: "vel acquiescerent, vel saltim ostenderemus ex Alchorano ipsos non debere contra nos saevire, si illum mediatorem recte colimus quem ipsi tantum laudant."

cere and practically oriented preoccupation with the question of peace. On the other hand, it points towards his method of pious interpretation (*pia interpretatio*) already signaled in the *PF* and to be more fully developed in the *CA*.

Thus, the examination of Nicholas's letter to his friend shows this text as the link connecting the *PF* with the *CA*. The letter at once continues the thought of the *PF* and also lays the foundations for the method of "pious interpretation."

5

Manuductio and *Pia Interpretatio* as a Way of Giving Glory to God

> If, as they claim, there were other gods besides God, they would surely seek to dethrone Him. Glory be to Him! Exalted be He, high above their falsehoods![1]
>
> —Koran

> in order that those who use their reason may see that we who believe in the Trinity are reasonably moved, let me proceed with another illustration toward the same conclusion.[2]
>
> —Nicholas of Cusa

THIS CHAPTER CONTINUES MY INVESTIGATION, BY EXAMINING Nicholas of Cusa's third and probably most important work in relation to the Islamic problem. I will first discuss Nicholas's intention and his overall hermeneutical conception. The subsequent two sections will deepen the understanding of this hermeneutical conception and develop it in relation to Nicholas's Koranic exegesis.[3] All this naturally leads the reader to the discussion of "pious interpretation." Afterwards, I will examine the manuductive aspect of the *CA* in more detail and I will attempt to connect it to the project of "pious interpretation." Since Nicholas's entire thought, especially his *CA*, provides evidence of his central Trinitarian concern, the chapter will be closed with a reflection on the Trinity.

---

1. *Surah* 17:42–43.

2. *CA* II, 7, 103:2–3: "Adhuc ut ratione utentes videant nos qui trinitatem credimus rationabiliter moveri, alio exemplo ad idem procedamus."

3. The following discussion of Nicholas's Koranic exegesis is fundamentally indebted to Hopkins, "The Role of *pia interpretatio*," 39–55.

The Author's Intent and His Overall Hermeneutical Conception

My earlier discussion highlighted the extent to which the cardinal from Cusa was dependent on and misinformed by his medieval sources concerning Islam. However, in the first prologue to the *CA*, Nicholas consciously demarcates his intent from the listed authors': "But I applied my mind to disclosing (*ostenderem*), even from the Koran, that the Gospel is true."[4] This intention is grounded in Nicholas's general understanding of reality. According to this characteristically medieval framework of his thought, every human being shares an intellectual desire (*appetitum*) for the Good, this Good being both the Beginning and the End (*principium pariter et finis*) of the intellect.[5] This End of human intellect is not present in the human spirit as an object known, yet, "the intellectual spirit by its nature desires to understand (*comprehendere*) the Good."[6] The symbolic structure of knowledge is particularly important for our human intellectual teleology. The *CA* clearly states that the Good is not known by the intellect as to its "what" or essence, although the intellect certainly knows "that" it exists. Neither can the name of the Good be known nor can a proper concept be formed of it; this Good positively transcends all human concepts and names.[7]

The mysterious Good is not present to the intellect through the senses. It cannot belong to sensible reality. The Good is, however, not completely absent from human intellect. The very structure of human intellectual desire, namely, points towards the Good. Because of the intimate relationship between the human intellect and the senses, all human knowledge necessarily starts with sense-perception. This holds true even for intellectual knowledge.[8] Sense perception is essentially

---

4. *CA* First Prologue, 4:8–11: "Ego vero ingenium applicui, ut etiam ex Alkorano evangelium verum ostenderem."

5. Ibid., 5:1–7. For a the similar discussion of the *PF* IV–VI, see Kremer, "Die Hinführung," 127–35.

6. *CA* First Prologue, 5:12–13: "Appetit ergo spiritus intellectualis in sua natura comprehendere bonum illud."

7. *CA* First Prologue, 6:1–4: "Et cum intellectum, quid sit hoc bonum, quod esse non dubitat, ignoret, non habet etiam scientiam nominis eius et conceptum de ipso facere nequit, quem non haesitat omni conceptui maiorem et meliorem." Cf. *DI* I, 26, especially 87:1–6 and 88:15–20; and also *DI* I, 25. For the following cf. also *PF* IV, 4.

8. *CA* First Prologue, 6:4–5: "nihil experimur in nostro intellectu comprehendi,

linked with a bodily existence within the sensible world and it functions as a positive condition helping humans on their way towards the Good.[9] This still leaves open the possibility that humans can fail on their intellectual-spiritual journey towards their proper end, i.e., the Good. Not only does Nicholas's picture leave room for such a failure, but it also identifies its two origins. The potentially seductive character of the sensible dimensions is one possible source of failure, while another equally important factor is the free choice of the individual human being.

All this being said, there still remains the practical question concerning the proper way (*via*) leading to the Good Itself.[10] For Nicholas, the way in question must obviously be a good way: "[T]o anyone with understanding, it is clear that these points are true," he writes.[11] The practical problem is precisely how one finds and identifies this good way. As a matter of fact, there exist different ways and each of these seem to be good at first sight. The existence of the ways of different religions as described respectively by Moses, Christ, Muhammad, and many other wise men and prophets leaves one perplexed and makes one hesitate concerning the good way.[12]

This introductory discussion shows that on the one hand, Nicholas identified God as the universally accepted and understandable aim of human life (the Good), and on the other hand, he intended to find a discourse concerning the way leading to God that could be similarly acceptable and understandable universally.[13] Nicholas was convinced that the different ways of religions aiming at the Good all presuppose and tacitly acknowledge that their basis is the Good, which is maximal, one, and ultimately must be equated with God. Nonetheless, he had to explain how one can decide which one of them is the (good description of the) good way. This question was all the more vexing to him, because he realized that "no one who is merely a man can conceive of God" and therefore no one can be certain concerning what is stated by any wise

---

quod per sensum in ipsum non intrat..." Cf. *PF* I, 3:6–12.

9. *CA* First Prologue, 6:11–13: "Verum nisi ad hoc nostrae intellectuali naturae iste mundus conferret, frustra intrassemus in ipsum." Nothing would be less 'un-medieval' then supposing an intrinsic futility of worldly human existence. See also ibid., 7:1–3.

10. Ibid., 7:3–5. Note here the term "seducit" and later, in line 8 the term "ducit."

11. Ibid., 7:5–6. Cf. Decorte's discussion of the way in the *Prolegomena*.

12. *CA* First Prologue, 7:6–15. Note the clause "manet haesitatio" in line 7.

13. Cf. ibid., 7:5–10.

man or prophet as divine revelation.[14] If the ultimate End of human existence is unknown to every human being, how can anyone ever come to know the way thereto?

Nicholas's thought would not allow for an objective knowledge of this End. God (or the Good) can be present only symbolically to human cognition. Therefore, even the Divine message of revelation necessarily requires a symbolic interpretation, but this reference to a symbolic reading offers no solution to the problem, because symbols are notoriously difficult to decipher, they originate in particular contexts, and are not always interchangeable between cultures. They need an interpretation, and the possibility of different interpretations cannot be excluded. This entails that, at least in principle, every interpretation of religious symbols is open to further discussion and criticism.

This may even seem to suggest that no one could be able to understand and explain such a symbolic message of revelation. Nicholas himself recognized that even a divine and symbolic revelation (*sermones . . . qui figurabant seu significabant deum et viam ad ipsum*) cannot be understood by human beings—not even by the prophets receiving it.[15] In the final analysis, only God Himself is able to explain His own revelation. This entails that only a prophet who is at the same time human and divine could solve the interpretative crux:

> if that man were not omniscient Divine Wisdom through which God works all things, then surely he would not be able to reveal that which would be unknown to him.[16]

Consequently, if a real person has manifested (*manifestare*) the way leading to the Good, he must be the greatest man of all men and must be equal to God's own Wisdom.

It can be argued that this "solution" only replaces the difficulty of interpretation of the divine message with the mystery of Incarnation and that of hypostatic union. Surely, the *CA* offers no independent

---

14. Ibid., 8:4–10: "Clarum est autem, quod cum nullus purus homo deum concipere possit, quod non habeamus certitudinem qualemcumque purum hominem nobis posse viam ad sibi ignotum terminum pandere. Unde si nec Moyses nec Mahumetus umquam, dum in hoc mundo essent, saepe dictum bonum viderunt—deum enim nemo vidit unquam—quomodo tunc aliis iter ad ipsum pandere potuerunt?"

15. *CA* First Prologue, 8:11–12.

16. Ibid., 8:15–17: "Quod si ille homo non foret ipsa omnisciens divina sapientia, per quam deus omnia operatur, utique, quod sibi incognitum esset, revelare nequiret."

philosophical argument for proving Christological doctrine. In this respect, Nicholas's discourse is strictly speaking theological. As a good Christian, he believed that once there lived a person both human and divine, the Wisdom of God in person.[17] In light of the previous discussion of Thomas and Ramón, it is not difficult to see that such a claim can never be proved with logical necessity. However, as far as Islam is concerned, it is also important to realize that Nicholas thought that Christ was not only foretold by Moses—and the other prophets—but he became also convinced that even Muhammad attested that Christ had revealed most perfectly the good way.

This is important, because if the Good is present through the same structure of human intellectual desire, then—at least in principle—every human being is able to recognize and acknowledge this good way. Without participation in the Good, a Divine Teacher cannot even teach the good way, because there would be no guarantee of a correct recognition of the Good. The metaphor of participation does not involve circularity, since participation in the Good makes possible the recognition of the Good, but does not necessarily make one a teacher.[18] In this way, the importance of teachers, prophets, and interpreters of Divine revelation is not lessened. The point is rather that they must have a more eminent teacher who is Divine Wisdom himself.[19]

With respect to the proper interpretation of the Koran, Nicholas drew an important and interesting double consequence from his basic Christian understanding of reality and Christian faith. He came to the conclusion that this other prophet, Muhammad, disagrees with Christ. Whenever the Koran contradicts the Gospel, in principle there are two possibilities:

a. either Muhammad was ignorant and did not know or understand Christianity;

b. or he was of "perverse intent" (*perversitas intentionis*), i.e., seeking his own glory under the guise of a religious goal.[20]

---

17. Ibid., 9:1–5.

18. Cf. Kremer's analysis of the *PF* in Haubst, "Die Wege der christologische manuductio," 131, 133–35. One can also say that the participation in and the understanding of the Good together form a genuine hermeneutical circle.

19. About the wise, see the discussion of the two previous chapters.

20. *CA* First Prologue, 9:5–9. The clause "non intendebat homines ducere ad illum finem quietis" shows that, in Nicholas's opinion, Muhammad failed as a *manuductor*.

In the *CA*, Nicholas took both of these presuppositions for granted. Keeping them in mind he set out to compare the two respective "Laws," i.e., the Koran and the Gospel. He hoped that this comparison would amply demonstrate that both *a* and *b* were true. Furthermore, Nicholas believed that "ignorance was the cause of error and malevolence," hence the alternative *b* can be reduced to *a*.[21] In the last analysis, both Muhammad's religiously masked malevolence and his misapprehension of Christianity resulted from his ignorance.

Accordingly, when writing the *CA* Nicholas presupposed the Gospel of Christ (as true revelation) and he set out to analyze (*cribrare*) the Koran. To say it with his own words:

> My intention is ... having presupposed the Gospel of Christ, to analyze (*cirbrare*) the book of Muhammad and to show (*ostendere*) that even in it there are contained those teachings through which the Gospel would be altogether confirmed ... and that wherever it disagrees this has resulted from Muhammad's ignorance and following his perverse intent.[22]

The theological inspiration behind Nicholas's intention is clear. This circumstance certainly places the *CA* into the long tradition of Christian anti-Islamic polemics.[23] As Hagemann points out, Nicholas's originality lay in his intention and method.[24] The title "Cribratio Alkorani" summarizes well both this intention and the method of the work. This phrase refers to the form of his analysis, in the sense of "passing to a sift" or "sifting."[25] The "sieve" or the filter through which the Koran should pass is nothing else than the Christian message as contained in the Gospel. With the help of the Gospel—the message of Divine Wisdom—Nicholas ventures to winnow the wheat from the

---

Cf. *CA* III, 8, 184:1–22.

21. Cf. *CA* First Prologue, 9:11–13.

22. Cf. ibid., 10:1–7.

23. Cf. Hagemann, *Christentum contra Islam*, 68.

24. Ibid.: "Besonderheit und Originalität in der eigenen Intention und Methode liegt."

25. Cf. the Latin "cribrum" (a sieve, a sift, riddle) coming from the same root as "cerno." Both Latin words are cognate with Greek "χρινω" and "χρισις" originally referring to separating, dividing, picking out or choosing. Hopkins translates the title *Cribratio Alkorani* as "Scrutiny of the Koran." (Cf. Hopkins, "Introduction," 14.)

weeds. He wants to separate truth (the finer and more subtle points of the Koranic message) form falsity (the coarser parts of the same text).[26]

The Structure of the Work and the Basic Exegetical Problems Posed by the Koran

In the Second Prologue, Nicholas's confesses that he did not manage to give a clear-cut structure to the *CA*: "I must be forgiven if I do not seem to hold everywhere to a suitable ordering when I discuss the contents of this most disorganized book [i.e., the Koran]."[27] One reason for this lack of a suitable order might have laid in the very text of the Koran. Nicholas—himself a non-Muslim reader—found the law of Islam a most confused book (*confusissimum librum*) and recognized that its chapters, the *Surahs* do not form a continuous sequence with one another. Although each *Surah* builds a poetic unity, the proper connection between the *Surahs* is not immediately clear to the reader.[28] The following overview sufficiently reveals the structure of Nicholas's work:

I. First book:
- general comparison between the Koran and the Gospel,
- showing that the Koran is not divinely inspired,
- proving Christ's Divinity and refuting the Islamic denials of it.

II. Second book:
- on the principal articles of Christian faith that are denied by the Koran, i.e.,
- on Trinity,
- crucifixion,
- death and resurrection of Christ,
- Incarnation,
- redemption of man,

---

26. Cf. Hagemann's *Einleitung*, viii–ix. Compare Nicholas's intention with the task of the wise in Aquinas's *ScG* I, c.1 and c. 2.

27. *CA* Second Prologue, 16:8–10: "Hinc ignoscendum mihi, si non videbor undique congruum ordinem tenere, quando confusissimi libri continentiam discutio."

28. Cf. *CA* Second Prologue, 16:3–8.

- and eternal life in Paradise.

III. Third book:

- refutation of more-narrowly-focused Muslim doctrines,
- ending with a discourse directed toward the Sultan and toward the Caliph of Bagdad.[29]

Hopkins describes Nicholas's hermeneutical approach to the Koran and the respective evaluations of its various interpretations.[30] He maintains that Nicholas paid tribute to the Koran's elegance of style and treated the Koran as a religious text, in addition to treating it as a theological one.[31] It can be argued that the metaphor of "cribratio" reflects Nicholas's deep and genuine interest for the Koran. Since examining the Koranic text, and then separating the grain from the chaff, i.e. winnowing one's way through this rather confused and confusing book means first of all a piece of really hard work.[32]

Hopkins also maintains that Nicholas's approach to the Koran is both dismissive *and* appreciative at the same time as he recognizes a double intent at work therein. These two intents were respectively Muhammad's own perverse and selfish purpose of self-glorification inspired ultimately by the Devil and God's own intent with the Koran.[33] Double-intent means ultimately double authorship and this makes understandable Nicholas's own project of separating the texts coming from different—i.e., divine and diabolical—origins.

Thus, Nicholas took up a definite and critical stance towards the Koran. Yet, in this criticism, Nicholas aimed to deal with its texts fairmindedly.[34] Even when Nicholas repudiated certain Koranic statements where they contradict Christian doctrines, he sought to attenuate their force by arguing that, if rightly understood, they do imply the truth of

---

29. Hopkins, "Role of *pia interpretatio*," 39.

30. Ibid., 39–55. Hopkins quotes Santinello reminding the reader that sometimes Nicholas's discussion "could assume a hermeneutical tone."

31. Ibid., 40 n. 9.

32. Ibid., 43. Cf. also 40.

33. Hopkins, "Role of *pia interpretatio*," 40–41. Concerning the authorship of the Koran, Hopkins refers to CA I, 1; III, 5, 178:3–5; III, 14, 212:6; and III, 7, 183. I will return to the question of double intent later.

34. Hopkins, "Role of *pia interpretatio*," 40.

the Gospel.³⁵ Such attempts are not necessarily successful and it is not certain that all discrepancies can thus be neutralized. This very general objection, however, in itself does not forbid a more detailed examination of Nicholas's argument. Moreover, Nicholas was conscious of the possibility that some Koranic passages are more easily reconcilable with the Gospel than others. This circumstance obviously called for an explanation, which Nicholas thought to find in the idea of double authorship. Nicholas believed to find within the Koran both an explicit denial (of Christianity) and an implicit (Christian) message or intent: he attributed the explicit denial to the perverse intent and ignorance from Muhammad's part and ultimately to the Devil, while the implicit message Nicholas saw as coming from Divine Providence.

An implicit meaning can be hidden in two ways. It may be not explicitly stated but only implied by the Koranic text or the apparent self-inconsistencies of the Koran can point toward the fact that only in the light of the Gospel can they properly be interpreted and as it were explained away.

Hopkins identifies three reasons for this fair-minded, Christian approach. First of all, he observes that on several occasions Nicholas was misled by Ketton's Latin text.³⁶ Secondly, he points out that Nicholas was eager to find the hidden Gospel even in the Koran and this attitude led him to over-interpretation.³⁷ Thirdly, Hopkins reminds us that Nicholas was also convinced that some Koranic passages do imply Christian doctrine.³⁸

Hopkins gives the following example. In Nicholas's view, the Koran nowhere denies that God has a son; rather, it denies that He has a son who is another God.³⁹ Other Koranic passages imply just the opposite. As a result, in Nicholas's perception the Koran is doing three things:

---

35. Ibid. Cf. *CA* I, 4, Surah 3:35–36 and *CA* III, 2 167:2–5, Surah 7:157.

36. *Nicholas of Cusa's De Pace Fidei*, 44 n. 33: "Nicholas is at the mercy of Robert of Ketton's Latin translation, which he interprets through the eyes of Ricoldo of Montecroce's *Contra Legem Sarracenorum* and in terms of his own predisposition to disavow the divine authorship of the Koran."

37. E.g., *CA* II, 12, 117:3–5.

38. Cf. *CA* III, 9, 185:4–5; II, 12, 117:7–9; and 118:1–7.

39. *CA* I, 9, 52:1–2.

1. explicitly denying that Christ is the Son of God;

2. making other statements, which imply that Christ is the divine Son of God;

3. by still other statements implying that Christ is not the divine Son of God.

When Nicholas was confronted with the self-contradictions in the Koran, he did not reject the Koran in its entirety simply because of these inconsistencies.[40] Rather, he sought for an explanation. Ultimately, he only rejected those texts that do not cohere with the truth discernible throughout the Koran.[41]

As far as the Koran was concerned Nicholas had to address three basic issues:

1. the Koran was contradicting the Bible (i.e., both the Old and the New Testament);

2. the Koran was contradicting itself (i.e., both expressly and by implication);

3. and finally, the Koran was speaking vaguely and ambiguously in order to accommodate conflicting opinions and to appeal to the widest audience possible.

Nicholas sought to remedy these incongruities because he regarded them as largely responsible for the hostility and open conflict between Muslims and Christians.[42] With Hopkins, Nicholas's conviction and hope can be summarized in the following way:

> Nicholas harbors the conviction that if he can help the Arabs to see the truth of the Gospel within their own scripture—and can help Christians to see that that scripture when rightly understood, is not at odds with Christianity's sacred books—then mutual persecution will cease and Christianity and Islam will

---

40. For inconsistencies, see e.g., *CA* III, 1, 159–62; 7, 182–83; 9, 185–89; 10, 190–94. Note also that *Surah* 3:7 makes a difference between two parts of the Koranic message. While one is said to be precise in their meaning, the other is referred to as ambiguous. The Koran also states that only God knows the meaning of the latter.

41. Hopkins, "Role of *pia interpretatio*," 43–44.

42. Ibid., 44. Cf. *CA* II, 13, 121:11–15.

come closer to actually being *religio una in rituum varietate*, the watchword of his previously written *De Pace Fidei*.[43]

In spite of the more polemic context of the *CA*, the presence of the idea(l) of one religion is still operative in Nicholas's project. At least some texts form the *CA* can be seen as pointers to this Cusanian idea. It can even be argued that while sifting the Muslims' sacred scripture Nicholas believed to recognize his own ideal in its text and reproached Muhammad precisely for not following this ideal in his own practice.[44] However, before forming a judgment on the exact role of the *PF*'s ideal in the *CA*, Nicholas's exegetical approach must be examined in more detail.

The Exegetical Rules of the CA

Hopkins lists the following exegetical rules as elicited from the *CA* for interpreting the Koran:[45]

Rule 1. Attempt to interpret the Koran in such a way as to show it to be compatible with the Bible. If a given text cannot be rendered thus compatible, reject it's teaching as false.[46]

Nicholas thought that only if the Gospel is included within the Koranic message could the Koran itself disclose the right way.[47] Nicholas understood the Koran as "via seu lex," i.e., a (religious) law prescribing a way of life.[48] He saw the three different "laws" of the Old Testament, the New Testament, and the Koran as different descriptions of one and the same Divine Law. Naturally, for Nicholas, the New Testament offered a spiritual understanding of the Old Testament Law. As other Christians, Nicholas was convinced that both according to Christ's and Paul's teaching, the Old Testament must be read with

---

43. Hopkins, "Role of *pia interpretatio*," 45.

44. Cf. *CA* III, 8, 184:1–8 and 17, 218:1–2.

45. Hopkins, "Role of *pia interpretatio*," 45–50. Cf. also Decorte, "Ter inleiding," 33–35.

46. Cf. *CA* I, 4, 34:11–13; II, 13, 122:19–20; and I, 6, 40:5–7; 41:1–3; II, 15; 132:15–17; I, 6, 39:3–4. As *CA* II, 12, 116:5–6 attests, Nicholas was convinced that "Alkoranus . . . evangelium et prophetas approbet."

47. Hopkins, "Role of *pia interpretatio*," 46. Cf. *CA* I, 6, 39:1–4.

48. *CA* III, 11, 196:4. Cf. Hopkins, "Role of *pia interpretatio*," 47 n. 47.

a strong symbolic understanding and one must look beyond its letter.[49] For Nicholas, this one Divine Law was most fully disclosed in the teachings of Christ. It was already shown that he identified this law in the *PF* as "the law of love."[50]

Rule 2. Attempt to interpret the Koran in such a way as to render it self-consistent.[51]

This is a fairly general rule of interpretation and no one genuinely trying to understand any text whatsoever can simply bypass it. However, this rule, when taken in isolation can clearly lead to over-interpretation: one may try to save the apparent contradictions of a text by forcing the same text into an understanding that may be consistent in itself, while being alien to the text. The previous discussion already indicates that Nicholas was also prone to this danger. At least he was realistic enough to see that this second rule is not always applicable to the Koran.[52]

Furthermore, Nicholas pointed out that Muslims themselves profess that the Koran ought to be construed as not contradicting itself.[53] Consequently, Christians should also make out the best possible case for the consistency of the same book. Any other approach would imply violence to the Other.

Rule 3. Where *prima facie* conflicts exist between the Koran and the Gospel or within the Koran itself, look for Muhammad's true intent,

---

49. Cf. *CA* III, 11, 195:10–14 and *PF* XII, 41:11–15.

50. Cf. Hopkins, "Role of *pia interpretatio*," 46 and *PF*, XVI, 59:13–14: "Dilectio igitur est complementum legis Dei, et omnes leges ad hanc reducuntur." In the next line the simple Tartar speaks of "lex dilectionis."

51. Hopkins, "Role of *pia interpretatio*," 46. Cf. *CA* II, 12, 116:4–7: "secundum libri sequaces Alkoranus non debet intelligi, quasi sibi contradicat, et cum evangelium et prophetas approbet, ideo intellectus quaerendus, quid in his praedictis intelligi velit."

52. Cf. *CA* III, 7, 183:14–16. In relation to this rule, Hopkins, "Role of *pia interpretatio*," 47 makes the following comment: "fairness ... demands that an interpreter not be quick to ascribe self-contradictions to a work into which its author does not introduce contradictions programmatically (as Plato seems to do in the second half of the *Parmenides* and Moses Maimonides admittedly does in the *Guide for the Perplexed*.)" This seems to hold true only for Muhammad's own intent. In relation to God's intent, it can be argued that God "programatically" allowed for contradictions within the text of the Koran.

53. *CA* II, 12, 116:4–7; III, 7, 183:14–16.

hidden beneath his use of symbolism and his accommodation for the uneducated.[54]

This rule was prefigured in the discussions of Muslim Paradise both in the *PF* and in Nicholas's letter to John of Segovia. In his manuductive concern, Nicholas recognized that parables play an important role in religious discourse and this is true both of the Gospel and of the Koran.[55] Nicholas was tempted to attribute the apparent or superficial meaning of the Koran directly to Muhammad, while the deeper, symbolic meaning he would ultimately ascribe to God.

Rule 4. Interpret the Koran as intending to give glory to God without detracting from Christ.[56]

This rule again implies the distinction between the two intents. Thus, in his reading of the Koran, Nicholas distinguishes between Muhammad's overt purpose and another implicit one. The first one is to be identified with Muhammad's own self-glorification (*sui ipsius gloria quaesivit*),[57] while the second intention was secretly working in the Koran. This second intention is referred to in terms of giving glory to God (*dare deo gloriam*).

This rule is very important, because it has a wider applicability, although it is invoked explicitly only in one particular passage of the *CA*.[58] Book one already addresses the problem of the right understanding of the Trinity in terms of giving glory to God (*ad glorificandum deum*):

> let me ask whether everything written in the Koran tends toward the glory of God. For the Koran attests that all men are created for glorifying God. But he who posits numerous gods seem to will to obscure God's brightness and glory. And so, as the Koran states, according to the interpretation that the Arabs give to it: to posit—for God—associates, and participants, and sons, and also to posit other gods, is to detract from the glory of the Great God.[59]

54. Cf. *CA* II, 18, 152:7-9; II, 12, 120:6-11; and II, 13, 124:11-12.

55. Hopkins, "Role of *pia interpretatio*," 48. Cf. *CA* II, 12, 120:6-11.

56. Cf. *CA* First Prologue 10:1-7.

57. Ibid., I,9:5-9: "Mahumetus . . . non intendebat homines ducere ad illum finem quietis, ad quem Christus viam ostendit, sed sub colore illius finis sui ipsius gloria quaesivit."

58. Hopkins, "Role of *pia interpretatio*," 259 n. 54. Cf. *CA* I, 14, 63:13-15.

59. *CA* I, 8, 48:2-8: "Nunc descendentes inquiramus, an omnia, quae in Alkorani

The quoted passage is important for several reasons. First of all, it recalls the Cusanian discussion of polytheism in the *DI*. Secondly, it finds a parallel in the dialogue of the *PF* where Nicholas's appreciation for the Muslims' insistence on monotheism is displayed. Here in the *CA*, the Arabs directly relate the same appreciation to the Koranic message and its interpretation. Nicholas recognized that even according to the Koran, human beings should give glory to God and those who endanger God's unity are in fact detracting from His glory. In his polemics, he asked the important question as to whether the Moslems themselves give God His glory in due manner and extent. This question of giving glory is placed in the middle of a Christological discussion. What was at stake for Nicholas in this question was a practical religious principle. He was convinced that if one wants to take both the biblical and the Koranic messages seriously, this question of giving glory cannot be avoided. The question of who gives proper glory to the Trinitarian God would thus prescribe an exegetical rule for the Christian reader of the Koran, because the problem of the Trinity is standing at the same time in the heart of Christian theology and in the focus of the Christian-Muslim controversy. Since Nicholas was convinced that God could make use even of Muhammad's vainglory, he thought that while reading the Koran he had to struggle to look beyond the Prophet's own intent of self-glorification. In order to give proper glory to God Nicholas was trying hard to discover the intention of Divine Providence even in what he found a most confusing book.

Rule 5. Work, insofar as possible, with the interpretation that the wise (*sapientes*) among the Arabs assign to the Koran, and attempt to show that even their interpretation implies Christian doctrines.[60]

---

scribuntur, tendant ad gloriam dei. Omnes enim homines creatos esse ad glorificandum deum Alkoranus attestatur. Videtur autem qui plures deos ponit velle deo suam claritatem et gloriam obfuscare. Ideo ponere deo socios, participes, filios, alios deos est gloriae magni dei detrahere . . ." Note the final clause of the pragraph in 9–10 "ut Alkoranus declarat secundum intellectum, quem Arabes libro attribuunt." Cf. the *Surahs* 2:116, 4:171, 9:30, 10:68, 17:111, 18:4, 6:100, 16:57, 17:40, 37:149, 43:16, 52:39, 112:1–4.

60. Cf. *CA* I, 9, 51:1–3. *CA* II, 12, 119:1–8: "patet secundum piam interpretationem Alkoranum haec secreta non nisi sapientibus voluisse revelare. Ideo ait illum nihil secretorum subticere et solis sapientibus facilem esse Alkoranum, aliis autem difficilem. Non erant enim rudes Arabes, quos Alkoranus ait omnium incredulorum pessimos, aperte de secretis in illo principio informandi. Quod si Mahemetus simpliciter ipsis evangelium praedicasset et non dedisset propriam legem, non accessissent ad legem Christianam, quam paene sescentis annis refutarunt." Cf. *Surah* 3:7.

This rule too, was prefigured in Nicholas's discussion of Muslim Paradise in the *PF* when Nicholas referred to Avicenna's interpretation of the Koran. The letter to John of Segovia made the same interpretative move more explicit. In the interpretation that the wise among the Arabs practice, Nicholas found a general interpretative tool not limited to the specific question of ultimate happiness. He saw in this rule a means that can help him clarify to the Arabs those central Christian doctrines that were so problematic for them, i.e., the Trinity and the Incarnation.[61]

These five exegetical rules spell out Nicholas's exegetical approach to the Koran. Hopkins summarizes this approach in the following way:

> several different exegetical rules are applicable to one and the same passage, or text.... neither from today's vantage point nor from the perspective of Nicholas's own day do these rules strike one as merely commonplace. Rather, they are controversial to the extent that they depend upon the conviction that the Gospel is contained tacitly within the Koran and that the Koran approves of the Gospel and exalt Christ above all prophets.[62]

One reason for this special attitude towards the Koran can be explained through the fact that Nicholas made use of and thus was also sometimes misled by Robert of Ketton's translation. However, this circumstance alone hardly explains the uniqueness of the Cusanian approach. Hopkins identifies two additional reasons.[63] One was Nicholas's own Christian commitment. Within the context of the *CA*, this commitment is phrased in terms of giving glory to the Trinitarian God and also in terms of wisdom, i.e., by way of reference to the acquisition of the proper knowledge concerning one's own spiritual-intellectual destiny. Both of these motives can be similarly discerned in the earlier work, the *PF* and the (re-)appearance of the Trinitarian and *sapiential* dimension in the *CA* is not accidental. These themes are essentially related to the other reason for Nicholas's Christian hermeneutics, namely, to his humanist belief according to which religious truth is readily discernible to those who know how to look for it.[64] The *PF* has already shown that Nicholas was convinced that the "wise" are not only able to converse about religious truth in an intelligent and peaceful manner, but they can

---

61. Hopkins, "Role of *pia interpretatio*," 49–50.
62. Ibid., 50.
63. Ibid., 55.
64. Hence, on page 55, Hopkins speaks of Nicholas's Christian humanism.

effectively come to an agreement. The CA spells out the specific consequences of this conviction with regard to the problems posed by the sacred book of Islam. Nicholas was looking for a proper interpretation of the Koran that was likely to be accepted by the wise—i.e., by Christians or Muslims alike. This proper way of reading the Koran Nicholas calls *"pious interpretation"* (*pia interpretatio*).

The Pious Interpretation

The *pia interpretation* is the proper way of Koranic exegesis as it is spelled out in Nicholas's five rules.[65] The essence of this approach is especially captured by Rule 4—the central issue at stake being that of giving glory to God.

In connection to this point, Hopkins especially stresses that *"pia interpretatio* is not quite the same thing as charitable construal, though it involves charitable construal."[66] The interpretation of any given text always includes an active moment of (re-)construction. This is also true in the seemingly simple case, when one is looking for the logical structure of an argument. Contemporary logicians and philosophers agree that Leibniz's quest for a *mathesis universalis* cannot be realized. That is to say, human language cannot be rendered completely univocal—hence, the necessary moment of reconstruction. Additionally, it can be argued that a reasonable interpretation will also necessarily have an ethical dimension.

These remarks do not yet sufficiently specify Nicholas's pious interpretation. Hopkins, when evaluating different approaches to Nicholas's pious interpretations, judges in the following way: "[M]uch of what commentators on CA have written about pia interpretatio is correct as far as it goes—though it usually has not gone far enough."[67] There is a special methodological reason for this statement, which is worth a closer look. The previously mentioned passage (together with others) evoking the notion of giving glory to God usually goes unnoticed since

---

65. For this point, see Hopkins, "Role of *pia interpretatio*," 51–55.

66. Ibid., 50. The principle of charity prescribes that the interpreter must seek for the most plausible interpretation of any statetemnt (of any text) and—if possible—must not to ascribe falsehood (in the form of a lie or mistake) to its author.

67. Hopkins, "Role of *pia interpretatio*," 51.

it does not explicitly speak of *pia interpretatio*.[68] Those passages speaking explicitly of *pia interpretatio* are important, but Hopkins rightly points out that they alone cannot disclose the whole meaning of this phrase—"only a look at Nicholas's examples and at his overall strategy" can achieve this.[69]

That is to say, no rule can be understood without the context of its actual application and no method can ever be defined with absolute clarity and precision. The real meaning of the rule will become only intelligible during the process of its application. Having this in mind, it is not difficult to recognize that Hopkins's remark is pointing towards a *tacit knowledge* or a *knowing-how*, i.e. to the actual way Nicholas carried out his Koranic exegesis. Nor is the reason why such an obvious fact escapes the commentators' attention is without any importance for the present study. Hopkins identifies this reason in the commentators' *"unduly focus"* on those passages of CA where the phrase *pia interpretatio* actually occurs and he makes it clear that such a narrow focusing can hinder the recognition of the rich employment of Nicholas's method.[70] In other words, an exclusive attention to the data can effectively blind the interpreter by making him unable to see the actual knowing-how of Nicholas's enterprise.

Earlier it was emphasized with Hopkins that the *pia interpetatio* concerns giving glory to God, i.e. witnessing to Christ. Hopkins calls this observation *"obvious and most natural."* He also maintains that Nicholas's pious interpretation is theologically charged, one that gives glory to God without detracting from Christ:

> For in engaging in *pia interpretatio* Nicholas is not dealing principally with texts that strike him as morally offensive or as lacking insight or as in some way alien . . . rather, he is dealing with texts that he deems to be theologically erroneous.[71]

This is not to deny that pious interpretation has also a moral dimension, but Hopkins rightly emphasizes Nicholas's theological interest and the religious dimension of the whole discussion. Together

---

68. Hopkins's example is CA I, 7, 44:1–19.
69. Hopkins, "Role of *pia interpretatio*," 51.
70. Ibid. Cf. Hopkins's note 71: "Hagemann makes CA II, 19 (154:8) the touchstone for understanding the phrase *"pia interpretatio."* He is therefore an example of those who too narrowly focus upon the passages in CA where the phrase actually occurs."
71. Hopkins, "Role of *pia interpretatio*," 52.

with other scholars, he identifies *pia interpretatio* as pious or devout interpretation in the given sense.[72] Hopkins's analysis also shows that *pia interpretatio* is a rather intricate procedure having different layers and different practical applications. He maintains that for Nicholas the program of devout interpretation was not a uniform procedure. This opens up the possibility that a *pious interpretation* could be significantly different for Muslims and Christians.

Variations of Pious Interpretation Acknowledged

It should be granted from the beginning that *pia interpretatio* can work both for Muslims and Christians. The way Christians should conduct this approach when they encounter the Koran has been amply demonstrated above with Nicholas's five exegetical rules.

It can be argued that not only Christians such as Nicholas of Cusa and his European readership, but also the Muslims will need to *"winnow their way"* through the Koran. Nicholas thought it necessary to make use of devout interpretation in accordance with their belief that the Koran approves of the Gospels. However, such a pious interpretation will not necessarily mean exactly the same thing for Christians and Muslims. For as a Christian, Nicholas presupposed the truth of the Gospel and required that the Koran should be accessed in light of this presupposition. By contrast, from their own part, Muslims too have their particular presupposition: they maintain the truth of the Koran, while insisting that the Gospel be assessed in the light thereof.[73]

Nicholas held that adherents of the Koran affirm that their book does not contradict any of the prophets but rather endorses them and confirms the books transmitted by God.[74] Nicholas thought that with the help of a devout interpretation, the wise among the Arabs ought to and may be led to resolve discrepancies between the Koran and the Bible in favor of the latter. Therefore, Nicholas was able to regard some Muslims as utilizing devout interpretation in the full sense of the phrase.[75] As

---

72. Cf. *CA* First Prologue, 10:1–7.

73. Hopkins, *A Miscellany*, 258 n. 39. Cf. *CA* I, 2, 26:9–12.

74. That is to say, the testament of Moses, the Psalter of David, and the Gospel transmitted by Jesus Christ. See Hopkins, *A Miscellany*, 261 n. 73. Cf. *CA* I, 2, 26:9–12.

75. Hopkins, *A Miscellany*, 261 n. 74.

Hopkins points out, besides *pia interpretatio*—i.e., Rule 4—this would mean also accepting Rules 1 and 5.

Variations of Pious Interpretation Ignored?

Hopkins writes that Nicholas failed to realize that both Muslims and Christians can apply the same principles of a devout interpretation not only to the Koran but also to the Bible. This means that while still complying with the principle(s) of devout interpretation, one can turn the table and venture to "sift" the text of the Bible.

As far as the *CA* is concerned as a Christian apologetic work, Hopkins is obviously right. Probably no one can reasonably expect a full-fledged *Cribratio Biblica* from a work bearing the title of *Cribratio Alkorani*. The fact that in the *CA*, Nicholas was not applying the same method to the text of the Bible should not be seen as a lack of attention, rather simply as a question of economy. Neither can a complete change of perspective be expected from a medieval thinker. With other medievals, Nicholas upheld the axiom according to which the Bible was the Word of God and hence not only true, but Truth Itself.[76] It is equally evident that Nicholas did not pay attention to textual problems of the New Testament in the same way as these can be approached and resolved by modern critical exegesis.[77] Neither can this be expected from him.

Even so, it is not altogether clear that modern scholarship can mend all the problems. This becomes apparent when one turns to a central point of Nicholas's Koranic exegesis. In the *CA*, namely, when Nicholas speaks of the Muslims' own pious interpretation as a method for understanding the Koranic message, he finds it important that Muslims too were looking for a symbolism.[78] Already the *PF* was pointing towards Muhammad's use of a symbolic language. Starting from this understanding, Nicholas thought that—in employing or interpreting religious symbols—Muslims were doing nothing else than effectively confirming the truth of the Gospel. Characteristically, he worried little about the question whether or not Muslims actually intended to do so. His theory of the double authorship made him even free from contradictions. With

---

76. Cf. the *Prolegomena*.
77. Cf. Hopkins, *A Miscellany*, 258–59 n. 39.
78. Cf. *CA* II, 18 and 19.

this theory at hand, he could easily counter any part of the Muslim religious discourse that stood in clear opposition to Christianity.

However, this is only one possible conclusion of the devout interpretation. My investigation of the two previous chapters demonstrates that Nicholas's emphasis on the symbolic dimension of thought is crucial for understanding his attempt at an inter-religious dialogue. This circumstance is connected with Nicholas's overall appreciation for the symbolic dimension of religious language and religious knowledge. If religions can only speak of the Divine through a symbolic language, then these symbols cannot be simply evaluated according to their objective truth-value.[79] It is precisely the sensitivity to this symbolic understanding of reality that can correct the "undue focus" of much modern scholarship.

Hopkins's understanding of pious interpretation is a good starting-point for this change of focus. The importance of the symbolic dimension for Nicholas's thought suggests that a symbolic interpretation of the Biblical message must be expected from him. This is not exactly what Hopkins considers as a non-acknowledged variation of devout interpretation in relation to the Bible. Nevertheless, I will show in the following that Nicholas's project comes very close to a devout interpretation of the Bible—without, however, ever acknowledging the superiority of the Koran. I would like to show that it is possible to modify both Hopkins's understanding of and his evaluation of Nicholas's Koranic project. What light such a revaluation can shed on the practice of *manuductio* will become clearer from a closer reading of the *CA* with a special attention to the symbolic dimensions of the discussion.

A Manuductive Work

A cursory look at the table of contents can already reveal to the reader Nicholas's manuductive concern at work in the *CA*.[80] This overview, placed at the end of the second prologue, promises the first *manuductio* in the title of chapter twenty of the first book ("a digression for guidance to (the triune) God") indicating the connection with Nicholas's Trinitarian concern. Hagemann's German translation of this title as "Übergang: Hinfürung zur <christliche> Theologie" catches well the nu-

---

79. Logically speaking, this is not to deny that religious symbols have any truth-value, but to say that their meaning cannot be rendered completely univocal.

80. Cf. *CA* I, 17–19.

ance of the Latin original, "Digressio ad manuductionem divinorum."[81] The divine things (*divina*) are those that can be said concerning the (triune) God of Christianity and they make up the subject matter of Christian theology.[82] Thus, chapter twenty of book one of the *CA* offers a proper "manuductio ad Trinitatem."[83]

Chapter three and four of the book make especially clear the Trinitarian context of the discussion. They discuss respectively the way in which the Divine Trinity can be seen and the way in which humans can be elevated to the Divine Nature. The respective titles of chapter five, six, seven, and ten from the same book promise further manuductive moves.[84] The issue of mystical theology as Nicholas's main concern is present in the second book of the *CA*: before the detailed manuductive discussions, chapter one sets out to tackle precisely the problem of mystical theology and God's ineffability.[85] Chapter nine offers a remote symbolism for the Trinity.[86] All this evidence shows that the *CA*, from chapter twenty of book one to chapter eleven of book two, is an embodiment of Nicholas's manuductive concern. In the following I will examine some important instances of the Cusanian *manuductio* in more detail.

The Example of the Glassblower

The first occasion for a *manuductio* for Nicholas was offered by the different translations of the Arabic term "*ruhella*" as God's breath (*flatum*), spirit (*spiritum*), word (*verbum*) or soul (*anima*).[87] Nicholas regarded all

---

81. Hopkins's rendering of the title as "a digression for guidance with respect to God" is somewhat indeterminate.

82. Cf. the English phrase "doctor of divinity."

83. Hagemann in his note 1 to *CA* II, 1, 86:3 reminds the reader that the first eleven chapters of book two of *CA* serve exclusively the purpose of leading to the belief in the Trinity.

84. *CA* I, 18:9–12.15: "Manuductio ex his, quae in mundo sunt, ut videatur deus trinus"; "Manuductio de intellectuali trinitate ad divinam"; "Manuductio eiusdem per amorem"; "Iterum ex tribus personis manuductio."

85. Cf. ibid., 18:2 and II, 1, 86–89.

86. Cf. *CA* I, 18:5–8.14.

87. *CA* I, 20, 81:2–6. Hagemann warns that the phrase "ruhella" does not appear in the Koran. Neither could one find the phrase "flatus dei" in Robert of Ketton's translation. However, the Latin text does contain the phrase "animam insufflavimus" in *Surah*

of these justified because these words do not really differ in their proper meaning, but he preferred the rendering "(intelligible) word," i.e., "concept." The reason for this preference is that this latter translation "agrees (concordat) with the most sacred Gospel."

The *CA* explicitly states that Nicholas's manuductive aim was

> that the most simple may be guided by a perceptual example through which, from afar, they may see to some extent the Father, the Word, and the Spirit.[88]

This statement recapitulates Nicholas's strategy in a form of a "manuductio per sensibilia ad Trinitatem"—a strategy already familiar to the reader from the previous discussion.[89] Note also that the manuductive example in chapter twenty is offered for the sake of the "simpliciores," in other words to those who are in need of such a *manuductio*. The aim of the Cusanian enterprise is again revealed here as that of all medieval knowledge par excellence. Even in the course of his "cribratio," Nicholas's intention was to show the invisible God in visible beings by pointing towards a presence of an absence. The *CA* testifies that he was still concerned with a *visio Dei* in the form of a *visio Trinitatis*.

From a modern perspective it is tempting to see this *visio* in terms of pure theoretical knowledge and Nicholas's intellectualist outlook may reinforce this impression. However, if one carefully examines the way the sensible example is employed, one may actually modify such an intellectualist understanding. I will show that the knowledge at stake in this passage should be called *existential* including both a theoretical *and* practical dimension. In other words, Nicholas's goal was *therapeutic*: he wanted to cure the Muslims' of their ignorance and help them see God.

The example used in chapter twenty of book one of the *CA* is one of Nicholas's favorite ones: it concerns the proceedings of a craftsman who makes glass objects (*vitra*). Nicholas saw glassblowing (*vitrifictura*) as a work of the intellect (*opus intelligentiae*) since any person devoid of an intellect will not be able to grasp this art.[90] This observation shows

---

21:91 and 66:12.

88. *CA* I, 20, 82:1–2: "ut simpliciores exemplo sensibili ducantur, per quod patrem, verbum et spiritum aliqualiter a remotis videant."

89. Concerning sensible examples, see *CA* II, 2, 93; II, 4, 97; II, 5, 99–100; II, 7, 103–6; II, 9, 109–10; and II, 10, 111.

90. *CA* I, 20, 82:5: "carentes intellectu eam artem non capient."

that while Nicholas's picture is rather intellectualist, for him intellect is connected to a knowing-how as he is speaking of the intelligent activity of glassblowing itself.[91]

In relation to the actual breathing out (*flatus*) of the glassblower two different moments should be considered. First, there is an external, perceptible breathing out (*ventus seu aer*). Secondly, there also exists an internal intellectual dimension. This latter is not perceptible directly, but can be grasped or understood indirectly by those who have intellect or understanding.[92] Nicholas claims that:

> [the glassblower's] intellect would not understand either itself or that which it is making unless it begat from itself the concept of the vessel that it is making.[93]

This statement fits the chosen example in the following sense: every craftsman has to have a clear idea (*conceptus*) of what he is going to do with his material. Otherwise he would not be a good craftsman.[94] When this concept or plan of the craftsman is actualized in the practice of his craft, it is nothing other than the explication of the craftsman's intellect.[95] The same is true of human speech: the intelligible concept (*conceptus*) and the audible word (*sermo*) have a similar relationship as the one between the craftsman's plan and its actual execution. When the intellect generates or conceives a concept, it explicates itself in (the form of) a concept. The concept, on its own turn generates speech and speech explicates itself in a sensible breathing out (*flatus*). In this way, metaphorically speaking, speech can be referred to as the breathing out

---

91. Cf. the example of the farmer (agricola) in *CA* II, 2, 93:9–10: "seminare enim est opus intellectus." *CA* II, 2, 97:4–10 identifies the many cities, sanctuaries, boroughs, buildings, garments, paintings and ornaments, languages, sciences, arts, books, harmonies, dishes, polities, and laws as "opus simplicis atque trini intellectus invisibilis et nullo sensu perceptibilis." Nicholas already recognized both the speculative and the practical dimensions of intelligence or understanding in his *C*.

92. *CA* I, 20, 82:12–14: "in intrinseco illius considero intellectum quia artifex ad finem faciendi vas vitreum operatur. Intelligit enim id, quod facit."

93. Ibid., 82:14–15: "Hic intellectus non intelligeret nec se nec id, quod operatur, nisi de se generaret conceptum vasis, quod efficit."

94. Ibid., 15–16 adds: "et hunc conceptum intellectuale verbum dicimus." Cf. *CA* I, 13, 60:1–16.

95. *CA* I, 20, 83:1–2: "Loquitur enim intellectus suam intentionem et conceptum, quem intra se videt et sensui visibilem facit."

of a human concept and a concept as the breathing out of the intellect.[96] All this is meant as a description of a(n intellectual) *process*—the motion or the operation of the intellect (*intellectualis motus*). Nicholas sees in the audible word or the perceptible breathing an invisible reality at work, i.e., human intellect itself.[97]

There are two important points to be kept in mind with respect to the example of the glassblower. The first is that spirit (*spiritus*) was generally understood in the first place in terms of *motion* both in Antiquity and in the Middle-Ages.[98] Furthermore, it can be argued that intellect itself necessarily exists in motion, that is to say, in actually performing the act of understanding. A completely inactive intellect would not be an intellect properly speaking. The second point is that the metaphorical description of the intellect is apparently misleading to the extent that it speaks of physical breath and physical motion. Nicholas knew well that after being produced, the actual breath will be gone, while a concept is not exhausted in a similar way after its generation. Once the intellect has conceived a concept, this concept can be employed time and again. In this way, a concept is characteristically different from the fleeting nature of physical exhalation.[99]

There is yet another difference between the working of the Divine Intellect and the glassblower's activity. Since God is not restricted in any way whatsoever (in Cusanian terminology: He is free from all contraction), He does not need any medium for His activity. The *CA* makes this point even stronger with the help of an image taken from the Old Testament.[100] There, God is described as neither present in the strong wind, nor in the earthquake, nor in the fire, but in a gentle breeze (*in*

---

96. Ibid., 83:4–6: "potest sermo flatus appellari humani conceptus et conceptus pariformiter dici potest flatus intellectus."

97. This intellectual motion can be seen as a parallel to the procession of the Holy Spirit from the Father and the Son. However, the theological context does not concern here directly the inner–Trinitarian movements, but rather the external workings of the Trinity, i.e., Creation. Nicholas saw in the human craftsman's own creative activity a "remote likeness" of Divine Trinitarian Creativity.

98. Cf. the *Prolegomena*.

99. *CA* I, 20, 83:13–16 points out that intellectual operations such as glassblowing are always connected with a physical operation or motion: "fiunt omnes operationes intellectuales licet non corporali efflatione, sed intellectu, verbo eius et motu seu spiritus utriusque in sensibilibus per sensibilia in sensibili materia mediante medio et organo sive instrumento sensibili."

100. *CA* I, 20, 84:1–6. Cf. 2 Kgs 19:11–12.

sibilo aurea tenuis or *in subtili sibilo tenuis aeris*).[101] The biblical passage in question employs sensible images, because all descriptions must ultimately rely on our sense perception. Nevertheless, the language of this particular biblical passage serves Nicholas's purpose well. This Old Testament passage is most fitting to God, because with the help of the *similitudo* of the gentle breeze it recalls the sense of a presence that is hardly perceptible. Nicholas concludes

> the Lord's being present in the subtle whispering of the gentle breeze shows that He is a Spirit more subtle than any other most rarefied spirit whatsoever.[102]

The importance of the manuductive use of this *similitudo* can be summarized in the following way. Since God is not a perceptible being, He cannot be present in something perceptible. Therefore His presence is necessarily of a symbolic nature.[103] The first thing one needs to learn in order to be able to see in such a symbolic way is the right employment of the similitudes. After such a learning process, he or she who knows how to see will see what God is really like.

The discussion in the *CA* moves on turning toward God's Spirit. Since God's Spirit cannot be an accident of the Divine Substance, this Spirit is identified as a Substantial Spirit or Substantial Motion.[104] It is present in every substance. The substance of everything is a spirit and thus a likeness of God.[105] The idea that the substance of everything is a spirit comes from Pseudo-Aristotle and can also be found in Albert the Great. For a Christian, biblical understanding a spirit comes from God. Since it creates everything, it must ultimately be God's Spirit.[106]

---

101. The neo-Vulgate has "sibilus aurae tenuis." Note that the biblical passage in question does not explicitly say that God was "in the gentle breeze." After hearing a noise, the Prophet Elijah does not see anything, but only hears a mysterious voice that is identified as God's.

102. *CA* I, 20, 84:5–6: "Dominum igitur in subtili sibilo tenuis aeris esse ipsum spiritum esse omni spiritu quantumcumque tenuissimo subtiliorem ostendit."

103. Cf. ibid., 84:6–8: "Non est autem deus spiritus in sibilo tenui aliter quam spiritualiter sine loci occupatione sicut intellectus in sermone." Hopkins translates "spiritualiter" as "invisibly," while Hagemann renders it with "auf geistige Weise."

104. On God's Spirit, see also *CA* II, 2–4.

105. *CA* I, 20, 85:1–2: "Substantiam igitur spiritum esse et deo similiorem, qui spiritus est, patet." The underlying idea is that every spirit participates in God's Spirit.

106. See e.g., Ezek 37:1–10, John 3:6–8.

At the end of chapter twenty, the basic points of the manuductive chapter are listed:

1. God, i.e., the Spirit is imitated by every substance;[107]
2. substantial things are to be preferred by far to perceptible accidents;
3. in theology (*in scholis divinis*) a comparison of incomparable things must be avoided. Therefore, divine begottenness is not to be compared with perceptible begottenness nor can the joys of divine life (*gaudia vitae divinae*) be related to mundane pleasures (*gaudia vitae mundanae*).[108]

So far, the meaning of the first point has been sufficiently clarified. The second one is in line with Nicholas's medieval intellectualism according to which intellectual things are to be preferred to mere sensibility. The third statement that relies on the Cusanian presupposition that intelligible things exceed the perceptible ones incomparably carries the same issue further. The third statement connects the discussion to mystical theology.

The Role of Mystical Theology

At the end of chapter twenty of book one, the reason for the previous lengthy digression (*digressio*) is stated as the following: "in order that the less well educated (rudiores) who are subject to the Koran may elevate their minds unto spiritual matters."[109] In Nicholas's view, the

---

107. Hagemann translates the first statement as "der Geist durch alle Substanz hindurch Gott nachahmt," while Hopkins renders it with "God the Spirit is imitated by every substance." Remembering that every spirit('s motion) comes from God, thus ultimately from God's own creative Motion or Spirit, one can say that Hagemann's solution is not only more theological, but it also keeps better the proper context. Nicholas's *Pseudo-Aristotelian* reference speaks of the spirit as a necessary condition for fecundity (fecunditas). Thus, the Divine Spirit or motion makes every being to be what it is. To make the same point in Aristotelian-scholastic terminology, one can say that God's Spirit makes (up) the substance of every being. Hence, a being and its activity is defined by the special working (or motion) it receives from the Divine Spirit. The grain's fertility and the craftsman's creativity are both revealed here as *ontological similitudes* of Divine Fecundity and Creativity. Cf. *CA* I, 85:2–4. On Divine Fecundity, see also the ealier discussion of the *PF* in my fourth chapter.

108. *CA* I, 20, 85:12–13: "improportionabiliter intellectualia excedant sensibilia..."

109. Ibid., 85:5–6. The "simpliciores" have been already referred too in *CA* I, 20, 82:1.

Koran was written for the uneducated (*rudiores*), while the Gospel was intellectual and divine.[110] While the Gospel is wholly intelligible and divine, the Koran has much more concession to human sensibility and is only partly or indirectly inspired by God. In this way, Muslims are in need of a proper *manuductio*.

This "elevation" of the minds of the simple Muslims is achieved through a manuductive procedure that would teach them to prefer the intelligible to sensible reality. Once this movement of ascension has been completed, the uneducated "may pass (recedunt) from the Koran back to the Gospel of Christ which is wholly intelligible and divine."[111] In Nicholas's opinion, the simple Arabs should "return" from the Koran to the full truth of the Gospel, because only there will they find their proper place. Since Nicholas saw Islam as originating in the Christian heresy of Nestorianism, he could reasonably expect Muslims to turn away from the corrupted form of the Gospel contained in the Koran and rediscover God's true revelation in Catholic Christianity in a similar manner as for instance the Hussites were expected to learn from their mistakes and rejoin the Church at the council of Basle.[112]

This Cusanian project of persuasion is carried further in book two of the *CA*.[113] The subsequent two chapters—chapter one and two of book two—promise respectively a discussion of mystical and affirmative theology.[114] In this way, through Nicholas's manuductive concern the pious interpretation of the Koran is connected with a special emphasis on a symbolic reading of the Christian doctrine.[115] This symbolic reading entails that the "reduction" of the Arabs to the Trinitarian God of Christianity is not simply a question of exchanging one religious parlance for another: this *reductio* turns out to be a sort of *manuductio* into mystical theology.[116] The general importance of mystical theology for Nicholas's thought and in particular for his *manuductiones* suggests

---

110. Cf. *CA* I, 85:5.

111. Ibid., 85:13–14: "ut sic de Alkorano recedant ad evangelium Christi totum intellectuale et divinum."

112. Cf. the discussion on John of Segovia in my first chapter.

113. Cf. Hagemann's reminder referred to in my note 83.

114. *CA* II, 1, 86–89 and 2, 90–93. Cf. *DI* I, 24–26.

115. Cf. *CA* II, 1, 86:2–5 employing the phrase "pia interpretatione."

116. Cf. Decorte, "Ter inleiding," 36.

that it may be fruitful to investigate the exact role assigned to mystical theology in Nicholas's dialogue with Islam.

The first chapter of book two of the *CA* takes up the theme of mystical theology. Nicholas's own understanding of the mystical or negative theology of Dionysius the Areopagite offers a means to counter the Muslims' claim that Christian faith in the Trinity equals thri-theism.[117] As in the *PF*, the *CA* displays an appreciation for the Muslims' insistence on monotheism. The latter work clearly states that "the Gospel not only condemns any plurality of Gods but also affirms it to be impossible."[118]

Nicholas of Cusa never thought of Trinity in terms of plurality or number. The *DI* shows that the concept of God as Absolute Beginning excludes from Him any plurality and composition whatsoever.[119] The concept of God as Principle (*principium*) when considered in Itself without any relation to things (*sine respectu principiata*) necessarily forbids intelligible speech concerning God.[120] Ultimately (*proprie*) nothing meaningless can be said about the Divine Mystery. Taken in Himself, God is Infinity Itself.[121] In His Infinity, God is beyond any determination and definition, beyond human speech and comprehension.[122] This entails that even the Trinitarian discourse of Christianity will ultimately break down in front of the Divine Mystery. As both *DVD* and *DP* point out and also the *CA* admits God will necessarily remain hidden even from the eyes of the wise.[123] Nicholas thought to recognize the same emphasis on God's absolute transcendence in the Koran as one Surah calls Allah "the God of whom there is no end," while in another Koranic

---

117. Cf. *CA* II, 1, 88:1–14. For references to Dionysius, see Hagemann's apparatus.

118. *CA* II, 1, 88:1–2: "Evangelium omnem deorum pluralitatem non solum damnare, sed impossibile affirmare."

119. Cf. *CA* II, 1, 88:3–4: "Pluralitas quomodo esset principium, cum ante pluralitatem sit unitas seu singularitas." In relation to *CA* 88:1–19, one can refer with Hagemann to Proclus, Dionysius, Eriugena, Hugh of Saint Victor, and even to Nicholas's own works such as to *DI* I, 24, 74–75, 82 and 26, 86–89; *DI* II, 4, 114; *C* I, 5, 17:5–6; *DVD* 12; *DA*, and *PF* I, 5:6–12; VI, 18 and VII, 19–20.

Even though Nicholas did not identify his sources, the ensuing philosophical discussion of the *CA* is problematic to the extent that "Califae in Bagdad ... inhibent evangelium et philosophiam publice legi" Cf. *CA* II, 1, 87:8–9. Perhaps this is intended as a warning for the "sapientes" referred to ealier.

120. Cf. *CA* II, 1, 88:6–8.

121. *DVD* 13 and *CA* II, 1, 88:15–17.

122. *CA* II, 1, 88:8–9.

123. Ibid., 88:15–16.

passage, the Countenance of God is said to be boundless (*interminabilis*) in comparison with limited mundane beings.[124] It is understandable that Nicholas could expect that the Arabs would come to realize the Transcendence of God who is only known to Himself and He "surpasses every created intellect."[125] From the point of view of negative theology, both Christians and Muslims have to agree that no positive utterance, only respectful silence can properly answer to the Divine Mystery.[126]

It is already possible to see what direction Nicholas's inter-religious dialogue is taking. Negative theology taken in itself not only justifies the Muslims' denial of the Trinity, but it also destroys all possibility for an inter-religious dialogue. The aim of the examined chapter on mystical theology of the *CA* is to show that there is an understanding of the Koran according to which it does not contradict the proper "mode" (*modus*) of Christian Trinitarian discourse.[127] This understanding is identified by Nicholas as "pious interpretation." The employment of the term *modus* is important, since it shows that Nicholas was concerned with the proper mode or way of religious discourse.[128] The "mode" of negative theology is to emphasize God's ineffability. Without any respect to creation God is ineffable.[129] This ineffable dimension can be recognized by Christians and Muslims alike. Precisely this is the proper 'mode' of an abstract discourse concerning God. From the point of view of negative theology, God will always remain a hidden God, a *deus absconditus*.[130]

Thus the "mode" of a negative theological discourse radically distanciates itself from the language of religious worship—be it Christian or Moslem.[131] Yet, the fact that the *CA* was composed as an apology for the Christian faith suggests that its author did not mean to abolish

124. *CA* II, 1, 89:4–7, cf. *Surah* 20:98. Hopkins notes that the Latin translation of these Koranic verses is misleading.

125. *CA* II, 1, 88:15–17.

126. Ibid., 88:18–19.

127. Ibid., 86:3–6: "Nunc accedamus ad elucidationem trinitatis, quam in divinitate colimus, et ostendamus Alkoranum pia interpretatione non contradicere trinitati, modo quo nos de ipsa loquimur, qui evangelio inhaeremus."

128. Ibid., 88:18–19: "Eo modo, cum de ipso nihil proprie dici et affirmari possit, quod non excedat, in silentio ipsum admiramur et contemplamur et colimus."

129. Ibid., 88:6–17.

130. Cf. *CA* II, 1, 88:15.

131. Cf. the discussion of the *DI* in my third chapter. The context of religious worship is hinted at through the word "colimus" in *CA* II, 1, 86:4.

Christian religious worship. The question is how affirmations concerning God can be justified without forfeiting the fundamental importance of Nicholas's mystical theology.

The Role of Affirmative Theology

After arriving in reverent silence at the unspeakable mystery of Divine Being, one necessarily has to change one's own perspective. For Nicholas such change of perspective is made possible by the fact that humans can only perceive truths from particular, limited, human viewpoints. Within human possibilities there is simply no absolute viewpoint available that would enable the human subject to see reality *simpliciter* as it is. Only God can see both creation and Himself in this way. Nicholas articulates these points already in *DVD*. However, our limited human vision entails that even negative theology cannot arrive at an absolute viewpoint. In principle even an affirmative discourse is justified and can work as a corrective in relation to a mere negative discourse. The *DI* already makes clear that within the context of religious worship a similitude is justified, if and only if it is employed in the right way, that is to say as a *manuductio* leading the human subject to realize the Divine Mystery.

Thus it should not be surprising that chapter two of book two of the *CA* returns to the theme of affirmative theology. According to this mode of speaking God will be rightly called triune. Affirmative theology speaks of the same God but from a different point of view. The changing of perspectives is from negative to positive theology.[132] The *CA* is not concerned as much with a detailed discussion of affirmative theology, but nevertheless makes clear that affirmative theology offers another point of view on the question of God. This other perspective is related to the (created) visible world (*mundum iste visibilem*) and its contingent beings.[133] Affirmative theology looks at the same God by looking through the visible world, i.e. through God's work in Creation. When looked at in a proper, manuductive manner contingent and dependent beings of this visible world refer to a principle of being. That principle is prior (*senior*) to the world, and cannot be necessitated from yet another

---

132. This change of perspectives is signalled by the phrase "alio modo" in *CA* II, 2, 90:3. Hagemann translates it as "aus einem anderen Blickwinkel heraus."

133. Cf. *CA* II, chs. 2–8.

principle; there is nothing prior to it and thus it is free (*liberum*) to create or not to create.

The Similitude of Human Intellect

The *CA* thus far recalls the discussion of *DP* and displays a fairly common move in Christian neo-Platonic metaphysics. From a manuductive perspective, Nicholas makes use of the similitude of the human intellect in order to shed light on God's creative activity. In the *CA*, God's absolute freedom to create or not to create is paralleled by the freedom of the human mind in its workings (*in suis operationibus*).[134] This similitude offers a dynamic picture because it concerns the working intellect and is also related to human (intellectual) experience.[135]

According to Nicholas's analysis, the working (active) intellect necessarily has three distinctive moments, which nevertheless form an operative unity:

- what is working is mind (*mens*) or comprehension (*comprehensio*),
- what is working is knowledge (*scientia*) or art (*ars*), aptitude or skill (*ars operandi*)[136]
- what is working is will or willingness (*voluntas*).

If anyone looks at his or her own intellectual nature, at the way he or she experiences his or her own intelligent activity, then that person will understand what is being said here.[137] As in the glassblower's example earlier, the similitude is also spelled out in more concrete terms through an analysis of the painter (*pictor*).[138] The three different mo-

---

134. *CA* II, 2, 90:10–11. This is not to say that human freedom is infinite.

135. Cf. ibid., 91:1–7. There the verb "operari" appears 6 times and the gerund "operandi" is employed once. Hagemann translates "operaretur" as "tätig sein," thereby emphasising the dynamic aspect. (The *CA* also makes use of the expression "producere oparationes" and the verb "facere." Cf. 91:6, 93:5–6 and 94:1.3.9–10.)

136. Hagemann's mindful translation for the last expression is "das Können, etwas zu tun" and Hopkins's is "know-how for work."

137. *CA* II, 2, 91:6–7.

138. The painter has that which he paints in his mind (in mente) as well as the proper expertise (scientia pingendi). Finally he has the will (voluntas) to paint. Another example at the end of the same chapter is the farmer (agricola).

ments listed thus far concern the same intellectual movement. They are different aspects of the same intelligent (*per intelligentiam*) operation.[139] These three are part and parcel of the same intellectual nature, while being different aspects of it.[140] An inner hierarchy exists among these three aspects: without proper understanding there is neither skill nor will since no-one can be able to or intend something that is completely unknown to him; without understanding and ability there is no proper will, because beside such a prior acquaintance, proper willing also presupposes some sort of ability or competence to execute one's own project. In this last case will is specified as a free will capable of choice (*voluntas libera et electio*). A mere act of volition disconnected from any aspect of a *knowing-how* would remain blind and cannot be free. Thus, no one can make a free choice without understanding and without the skill no one is free to achieve what he or she intends to do. In this way *knowing-that* (*mens, comprehensio*), *knowing-how* (*scientia, ars, ars operandi*), and *willing* (*voluntas*) belong together as three distinct moments in the hierarchy of the same intellectual operation.[141]

Nicholas worked hard to explain that these three moments are neither completely different from each other nor are they completely the same. In their essence (*essentialiter*) they are fundamentally the same (*idem*), since they are all essential to any display of intelligence. In spite of this, they are not interchangeable among themselves (*non convertibiliter*). Their operative unity is a unity of three different moments within the same process.

Ordinary, sensible beings can be thought of either as substances or accidents: they are either independent things or else they depend on another independent thing. In both of these cases, it is usually not difficult to identify these beings. In contrast to them, an intellectual being cannot be so easily caught with the help of same categories. Neither can it be identified in a similar way. When speaking of different regions of being,

---

139. Nicholas successively showed that will does not imply skill, ability or power to accomplish that which is willed. Neither does mind or comprehension imply skill or ability. Finally, possessing the proper skill does not entail full comprehension. Cf. *CA* II, 2, 91:10–14.

140. Ibid., 91:14–18.

141. To put it with a simple formula: mens → scientia; mens + scientia → voluntas. Cf. *CA* II, 6, 101:12–14: "sicut enim id, quod non scitur, non amatur, ita non potest non procedere a mente et notitia voluntas."

one has to conform to different modes of speaking.[142] Consequently, to say that an intellectual operation, as a process, cannot be properly understood in substantial terms—since these were devised for sensible reality—is not to deny that its different aspects can be analyzed. Rather, the point is that such an analysis has to be understood in a special sense and must not be confused with those categories that are only applicable to the sensible realm. Nicholas's analysis of the intellectual process helps one to distinguish three different moments, but one should not forget that in reality these three moments function together. All three are necessary for a perfect intellectual operation (*una perfecta operatio*).[143] The analysis makes clear that only together can the three moments accomplish their proper function. This does not entail that they are accidents to each other, but their proper being is not substantial since they exist only in relation to one another.

The *CA* continues along the same line of thought in explicating further the similitude of the intellectual nature.[144] The reader learns that the intellect works in the likeness of its Creator, because human intellect as a created reality is the image (*imago*) of the Creator.[145] Hence, intelligent activity or understanding can serve as a similitude expressing the Creator's creative activity. While God calls things into being by giving them their respective essence (*essentiare*), the intellect grasps these beings by assimilating (*assimilare*) them into itself. Just as God brings forth real things (*verae res*), the intellect produces their similitudes (*similitudines verarum rerum*). The point of this intellectualist discourse is clearly Trinitarian: if human understanding is an image of its Creator and it possesses a fundamental threefold structure, then seen from a human perspective God can also be called threefold. Since God understands everything, He is capable of doing everything and also positively wills things (to be). Therefore, there must be a Divine Mind, a Divine Knowing-How, and finally a Divine Will coming forth from these two. Christians call these three moments or aspects of the same Divine Mystery respectively Father, Son, and Holy Spirit.

---

142. Cf. the discussion of the *C* in my third chapter.

143. Cf. *CA* II, 2, 92:1–4.

144. See *CA* II, 3, 94–96 with the title "Quomodo ex operatione intellectualis naturae videmus divinam."

145. Ibid., 94:2–3: "quoniam intellectualis natura hoc et hanc nobilitatem non habet nisi a creatore suo, nam operatur in similitudine creatoris sui ..."

Nicholas's discourse is consciously Christian while at the same time understandable and accessible to Muslims. As we have seen, in a (possible) dialogue between Islam and Christianity, the very essence of Trinitarian faith is at stake. Nicholas thus argues that by denying the Holy Trinity, Muslims in effect deprive God from His most essential characteristic: they make Him sterile and love-less.[146] The rest of chapter four marshals "proofs" or indicators of the Trinity both from the Old Testament and the Koran.[147] Interestingly enough besides the employment of Cusanian metaphysics and the traditional Trinitarian interpretation of reality, Nicholas also refers to such experiences of subjectivity that are universally available to humans—thus to Muslims and Christians alike.[148]

Fecundity as Intellectual Productivity and Love

The similitude of the intellect already employed a fairly universal experience of intellectual operation or understanding. The next manuductive chapter interprets intellectual creativity in terms of fecundity (*fecunditas*).[149] The PF already revealed the idea of fecundity as the fundamental structure of all beings and it was also said that fecundity must be applicable a fortiori to God Himself.[150] The manuductive movement of intellectual elevation staring with sensible things arrives at the experience of intellectual fecundity, and from there it goes on to Divine Fecundity Itself.[151] In this way, the reader of the CA is called upon to reflect on the innumerable works (*innumera opus*)

---

146. Cf. *PF* IX, 25 and Isa 66:9, and 1 John 4:8.16.

147. Cf. Gen 1:1.26; Exod 20:5 and *Surahs* 51:47; 15:49.

148. *CA* II, 3, 96:1–2.

149. Cf. *CA* II, 4, 97:1–2: "Quomodo de fecunditate intellectualis ad fecunditatem divinae naturae elevamur."

150. Hagemann's bilingual edition (*CA* II, 87 n. 24) demonstrates that Nicholas placed the following note on the margins of his example of Denys's *Contra perfidiam*: "Quomodo tolli potest fecunditas a deo, qui dat pro maximo munere omnibus perfectis creaturis fecunditatem? Nonne sterilitas defectus est? Utique deo defectum attribuere insanire est."

151. *CA* II, 3, 97:3–4: "Et ut per sensibilia in fecunditatem intellectus et de illa in divinam eleves fecunditatem, attende" Note the expressively manuductive language in phrases such as "quomodo ... elevamur"; "ut ... eleves, attende"; "vides ... tunc ascende," and "Et videbis deum."

of the human intellect and recognize in them the creativity of the human intellect. In these works, the threefold structure of the human intellect albeit invisible in itself, becomes visible. Once this truth is recognized and well understood, the next manuductive step can follow. One should look to the Divine Intellect, which is infinitely more creative and fecund than any (creative and fecund) human intellect. The fecundity of Creation is the (self-)manifestation of the One God and Creator. It attests that God Himself cannot be otherwise than the most simple and most fecund. This Divine self-manifestation in creation cannot have any other reason than God Himself. God as the Good only gives, because of His infinite Goodness.[152] To say it in plain language, God creates only out of pure love.

The equation of God with the "bonum diffusivum sui" is a commonplace of Christian neo-Platonic theology. Within the medieval context one could perhaps reasonably expect that Muslims would also accept it. From the point of view of a Christian-Muslim dialogue it is, however, equally important that the Good forms the ultimate motive of human intellectual activity. In relation to the C and *DVD* it was shown that for Nicholas, intellectual activity necessarily shares the dimension of love. This connection forms the background for the discussion of the *CA* where the parallel between Divine and human intellect is made even stronger.[153] Both divine and human intellectual activity is said to be an "ostensio," a self-communication or self-manifestation. Both are of the same nature because both are good and the Good per definition gives a share from itself (*se diffundat*). Thus, love forms the foundation for both activities. The subsequent manuductive chapters of the *CA* will spell out this theme of love in more detail. Chapter five first states that Muhammad believed in the same God as Christians do in as much as he believed Him to be the Creator. The important consequence is that Muhammad (and with him every Muslim) must necessarily assert the

---

152. Cf. *CA* II, 4, 98:4–5: "deus benedictus, qui "divitias gloriae suae" ex mera bonitate sua ostendit..."

153. Cf. ibid., 98:5–6.8–9: "dives intellectus ad ostensionem gloriae suae se in operibus suis ostendit et communicat... ut... iuxta naturam boni se diffundat et participalem faciat."

same things of God.¹⁵⁴ The whole created world is full of fecundity, birth, and love. Moreover, without these, the world cannot even exist.¹⁵⁵

Clearly, Nicholas cherished the hope that even Muslims would be able to understand the language of fecundity, offspring, and love precisely since all creatures participate in these dimensions of being. Thus Arabs could also arrive at the insight that created beings cannot have this threefold dynamics except from their Creator.¹⁵⁶

The (post-)modern reader could object that the threefold structure is willfully imposed on the world by a Christian doctrine. There can be no doubt that the influence of Trinitarian thinking is apparent not only in the *CA*, but also in Nicholas's whole oeuvre. This does not entail, however, that Nicholas as a medieval, Christian thinker was not aware of his special starting point.¹⁵⁷ One must say that hardly any medieval theologian would have denied that only a person trained in orthopraxis and orthodoxy can properly "see" the Holy Trinity. The dedication of the *CA* explicitly states its author's intention to convert Muslims to the Trinitarian faith of Christianity. As Nicholas perceived it, Muslims' strict monotheism originated from a Trinitarian heresy. Chapter five of book two of the *CA* testifies that Nicholas wanted to show the Arabs the Trinity "to the extent that it is sufficient for faith."¹⁵⁸ What he really wanted to share with the Muslims was not mere intellectual insight or metaphysical propositions, but a kind of faith: his Christian, Trinitarian faith. In other words, not only the *PF*, but also the *CA* aimed at the "peace of faith" (*pax fidei*): Nicholas's longer treatise was meant to serve this religious peace by helping to convert the Muslims to Christianity. Thus proposing necessary arguments for a merely rational interpretation of reality was not an objective of the *CA*.

The Trinitarian structure of being is intrinsically related to the description of a process. The discussion of the *CA* strongly suggests that this threefold structure should be thought of in terms of activity,

154. Cf. *CA* II, 5, 99–100.

155. Ibid., 99:5–7: "iterum dicimus: mundum istum sine fecunditate, prole at amore non posse perseverare et subsistere certissimum est." Later, the term "partus" is also employed. It means in the first place both the active and the passive aspect of procreation, bearing or begetting and birth respectively. Figuratively, "partus" can refer to a beginning or origin.

156. *CA* II, 5, 99:1–16.

157. Cf. the *Prolegomena*.

158. Cf. *CA* II, 5, 99:5: "quantum sufficit fidei."

creativity, production, and preservation. The reader is called upon to self-reflection recalling similar experiences of his or her own activities. One example of such an experience is intellectual activity. The experience of fertility, bearing, and love is revealed as another fundamental human experience. Nicholas clearly regards fecundity, parturition, and love as forms of "perfection" (*perfectio*). Furthermore, God as Creator cannot lack any perfection possessed by creatures, but He must be infinitely more perfect than any creatures. Thus, for instance, God must be fecund. That is to say, He must be Love and therefore exist in Trinity.

Trinitarian language is still a language taken from creatures.[159] As the *DI* already testified, Nicholas was well aware of the fact that any positive statement concerning God has necessarily the same characteristics. As finite and sensible beings, humans necessarily have recourse to terms taken from their sense experience. These terms are in the first place devised for denoting finite and sensible beings. When applied to the Divine Mystery of Being, such terms will necessarily have a fundamentally symbolic character. This entails two things. On the one hand, the created world interpreted through Trinitarian religious language can serve as a sufficient guide, that is to say, a *manuductio* for proper religious worship. On the other hand, creation can offer only images of the uncreated Trinity, because ultimately nothing meaningful can be said of God in Himself.

After accepting both of these implications the question can still be asked why any specific image—such as for instance the world or human intellect—should be preferred over against other images. Nicholas was aware of the positive dimension of human religiosity and both *DVD* and the *PF* make clear that in principle infinitely many images, metaphors, and symbols are possible for a "manuductio ad Trinitatem." For any genuinely manuductive process always has to begin with the reality of the world as presented to sense experience. Or else one can start with the more intimate experience of his or her own subjectivity, that is to say in the medieval philosophical idiom: one can reflect on his or her intellectual nature as a reality connected with and more closely present to one's own being. If these answers are accepted, the further question then arises of how one is to read and interpret a particular image. This is a real issue for interreligious dialogue, since different people are coming

---

159. Cf. *CA* II, 5, 100:8–10: "Trinitas igitur, quae in creatura videtur, est a trinitate increata tamquam imago ab exemplari et causatum a causa."

from different religious backgrounds will necessarily see the same symbols differently. Followers of different religions are not familiar with the way other religions use their symbols, thus naturally they will try to understand these symbols according to their own background. They will thus be prone to misunderstand these symbols. The previous discussion shows that the manuductive chapters of the *CA* are concerned with this problem. Nicholas's question concerned the know-how of harmonizing or deciding between conflicting *ways* of different religious interpretations of the world and the human life within.

Fecundity and Self-Knowledge

The next Trinitarian *manuductio* demonstrates again the connection of knowledge with desire or will and also shows Nicholas's clear awareness of the fact that the human language of Sameness and Otherness breaks down *in divinis*. Both of these themes have already featured in Nicholas's discourse and the second one will be pursued further in the subsequent chapters. Both the problem and Nicholas's terminology in chapter six anticipate the later treatment of God as *non-aliud*.[160]

While chapter four of book two of the *CA* has already offered a reflection on the fertility of the practical intellect (*intellectus practicus*), chapter six turns to the speculative intellect (*intellectus speculativus*).[161] The fecundity of this latter, speculative intellectual dimension is revealed in the many books of the reflective thinkers (*libri innumerable contemplativorum*).[162] While Hagemann translates "contemplativorum" as "der Philosophen" (*of the philosophers*), Hopkins renders it with "*of the contemplatives*" and equates them with the mystics. These diagonally opposite renderings show that it is not easy to identify these "contemplatives." It is clear from the text that for Nicholas speculative knowledge (*theoremata*) does not equal pure theory for theory's sake, since

---

160. God as *non-aliud* has already made its appearance (at least conceptually) in *DVD* and the meaning of this new term was to be more fully developed in the *NA*. See *DVD* 14, 60–64 and my third chapter. *VS* 14, 39–41 offers a very concise discussion.

161. *CA* II, 6, 101–2. For the distinction between speculative and practical intellect, cf. ibid., 101:2–9.

162. Cf. Hagemann's note 32 on p.88 : "Gleichsam als Sonderfall der allgemeinen natürlichen Fruchtbarkeit ... zieht NvK hier die geistige Natur im besonderen heran, um von der Fruchtbarkeit der geistigen Selbsterkenntnis her die Trinität wiederum mittels der analogia proprotionalis ... zu erhellen." (See *CA* II, 2, 91; II, 3, 94–95.)

it has the fundamentally manuductive function of turning away the contemplative person from sensible reality and leading him or her to contemplate and enjoy the invisible God. Still, it is not completely clear that the text equates these contemplatives with the mystics *simpliciter*.[163] Perhaps, one had better speak of "speculative mystics" here.[164] As was shown in relation to the *C*, self-reflection has a manuductive function and self-reflection also plays an important role in the inter-religious dialogue of the *PF*. The reflective strategy returns in the manuductive chapters of the *CA*: its reader is called upon to reflect on his or her own experience of intellectual creativity and love. He or she has to realize that because God Himself has undeniable self-knowledge, the example of the intellect can lead one to the knowledge of the Trinity.[165]

On Love and the Limits of Metaphysics

The next chapter of the *CA* employs love (*amor*) as another manuductive example (*alium exemplum*). Nicholas also expresses his hope that by this move the Muslims can realize the rationality of Trinitarian discourse.[166] Not surprisingly, in the course of this discussion love (*amor*) is revealed as a universal principle of all reality. With the help of this principle, the rationality of Trinitarian faith is illustrated.[167] This does not mean a rationalist theological explanation of the Divine Mystery. In apparent contrast to Ramón Lull's enterprise, Nicholas never intended to prove the Trinity with coercive arguments, but only wanted to show that belief in the Trinitarian God of Christianity can be called rational in two senses. In the first sense, Christian faith is not plainly irrational. In the second sense, this faith is rational to the extent that it has some plausibility.[168] Earlier it was shown how the manuductive example of

163. That is to say if the term "mystic" refers to a person with a special kind of spiritual experience.

164. It can be argued that Nicholas considered himself to be a speculative mystic or "reflective thinker," since the Cusanian enterprise is fundamentally reflective.

165. *CA* II, 6, 102:1–2.

166. Cf. *CA* II, 103:2–3. For the notion of "rationabilitas," see Thomas's *RF* 2:16–18.20–22 and my second chapter. Cf. Hagemann's *Einleitung* X–XI, and Hagemann, *Christentum contra Islam*, 70–71.

167. *CA* II, 7, 103:3–5: "Nemo est, quin videat amorem omnino necessarium ad hoc, quod mundus subsistat, quoniam eo sublato penitus nihil subsistere potest."

168. See Hagemann, *Christentum contra Islam*, 70: "Das heißt nun nicht, daß das Dogma der Trinität als denknotwendig erwiesen werden soll. Von dieser vermeint-

love could make the Christian case plausible.[169] In relation to the idea of perfection and Divine Simplicity, chapter seven of book two of the CA adds a further point. Namely, since love unites, God's Trinitarian Being does not endanger, but rather makes stronger the case for Divine Simplicity.

However, the connection between love and union means that the emphasis on Divine Simplicity must be taken in a special sense. The language of substance metaphysics positively breaks down in the experience of love.[170] The fact that in Nicholas's opinion, the highest form of love was not merely sensual love, but intellectual love makes this point stronger. If this love necessarily has an intellectual dimension, then it cannot be thought of in categories devised for understanding sensible things. That is to say in Aristotelian categories love is neither a substance nor an accident, but love is a relation. Its very essence exists in being in a relation with another.[171]

Nicholas thought of love as a unifying power, producing a kind of symmetry and balance between the loving one and the beloved one. Hence, love is continuously creating an ever stronger bond between its two poles.[172] These three aspects or moments of love are identified respectively as unity (*unitas*), equality (*aequalitas*), and the connection (*conexio*, *nexus*) of the two. If God is fundamentally One (as also Muslims confess) and if He is Love (as Christians believe), then His Love will necessarily be more unifying, His equality more equal, His connection stronger than any other kind of love. If God is to be called a substance, then God's Love should be understood as "substantial" or "essential" Love.[173]

---

lichen Möglichkeit war Raimundus Lullus überzeugt gewesen. Er war davon ausgegangen, daß ihm „rationes necessariae," d. h. stringente Gründe zur Vefügung stünden. Das Scheitern seiner umfangreichen Bemühungen hat ihm Unrecht gegeben, und Nikolaus ist ihm in diesem Punkt nicht gefolgt. Nicht die Rationalität des im Glauben Vorgegebenen, sondern dessen Rationabilität soll aufgewiesen werden. Ausgangsbasis cusanischer Trinitätsspekulation ist nicht die Vernunft, sondern der Glaube."

169. Cf. *CA* II, 7, 103:3–10. For caritas and amor, cf. *DI* III, 15.

170. Cf. *DVD* 17, 77:2–5: "Tu igitur es ipsa essentia perfectissima et simplicissima et naturalissima amoris. Hinc in te amore non est aliud amans at aliud amabile at aliud utriusque nexus, sed idem tu ipse, deus meus."

171. For a brief discussion of relationality, see the *WI*, 164–77.

172. Cf. *CA* II, 7, 104–5.

173. *CA* II, 7, 104:1–2: "amor perfectissimus ... cum sit substantialis, maxime unit." Cf. Hopkins's translation and *Nicholas of Cusa's De Pace Fidei*, 233 n. 31.

The concept of "substantial love" (*amor substantialis*) can be understood in two different ways. Either it will ultimately destroy substance metaphysics or else it substantiates the very category of relation itself. This ambiguity in interpretation may have to do with the fact that Nicholas was critical of medieval Aristotelianism, yet at the same time he was dependent on its terminology. Additionally, Nicholas's neo-Platonic inheritance was heavy with monistic allusions. Here I will not delve into the intricacies of the question as to what extent Aristotelian and neo-Platonic thought can be reconciled with each other. Within the framework of my study, I limit myself to Nicholas's case and try to find out in what way he thought of love.[174]

Fortunately, there are sufficient indicators in Nicholas's thought that favor a relational interpretation. For instance, a tension between the two main sources of Nicholas's inspiration can be observed in the first book of the *CC*, where both neo-Platonic metaphysics and Christian praxis play an important role.[175] Nevertheless, the hierarchy of being and of the Christian Church is presented there as a hierarchy of *giving*, i.e., a hierarchy of relation.[176] In the *CC*, neo-Platonic language and construction are at the service of articulating Christian faith and placing it into a cosmic perspective.[177] Turning to Nicholas's first philosophical-theological work, the *DI*, a similar observation can be made. Furthermore, there is a fundamental continuity between the *DI* and the *CA* in this respect. As I mentioned at several points of this investigation, the *CA* is a work of Christian apologetics.

The rather obvious reason for interpreting Nicholas more as a Christian than as a Neo-platonist is that the proper context of his thought, namely, the very praxis of medieval Christianity has to be taken seriously. This observation should be stressed because no present-day reader of the Cusanian oeuvre is living in the medieval cosmos or in the medieval Church and society. Hence, Christian life as a practice is not the evident horizon of our contemporary understanding.

---

174. This interpretative difficulty is naturally connected to a core problem of neo-Platonic thought, namely, to the question of how far this tradition is able to acknowledge Otherness and allow for Difference.

175. *CC* I, 2 and 3–5.

176. Since giving is a special sort of being in relation.

177. Cf. Weiler, "Nicholas of Kues on Harmony," 77–90 and also Bakos, "Recovering Nicholas's Early Ontology."

I suggest that Nicholas's relation to Aristotelian thought can be understood in a similar way. Earlier, I briefly discussed another manuductive work, the NA and summarized Nicholas's criticism of Aristotle on two points.[178] Of these two the first one, which is more important for now, shows that in Nicholas's opinion Aristotle remained at a rational level of inquiry (*rationalis venandi modus*) and therefore the Philosopher was not able to have an intellectual insight into the first principle of reality. He was mistaken because he was looking for the invisible within the visible realm and it is no wonder that he could not find what he sought. I think that such a strong anti-Aristotelian criticism makes reasonable the notion of God as *"substantial"* Love should be rather interpreted from Nicholas's own concern than from the perspective of a strictly Aristotelian science.

Much the same can be said concerning other concepts of Nicholas's Trinitarian discourse. Nicholas thought that not only are unity and equality prior respectively to plurality and inequality, but connection also precedes any division. An Aristotelian reader will be inclined to think connection or relation as linking two or more already existing substances (or their accidents). Yet, this supposition stands in contrast with the text of the CA that makes clear that without a kind of love nothing could exist and subsist.[179] For Cusanus, the very concept of being already implies some kind of harmony. Beings share both unity and equality. They are already connected in some sense. This is true before all plurality, inequality, and division. For Nicholas, connection cannot be thought of as posterior or additional to being.[180]

From a speculative point of view one can say that division and connection are a pair of mutually interdependent concepts, as the one always presupposes the other. From a merely logical perspective there is no way to settle the issue of priority between these two concepts. At first sight it seems that everyday experience cannot be a trustworthy guide in this question. Humans encounter both connected *and* separate or divided things in this world. The neo-Platonic emphasis on the One and the idea of the Good as well as the central Christian doctrine of the Trinity can all be interpreted as pointers towards a relational interpretation of reality. It can be added that division is usually recognized where

178. See my third chapter.
179. Cf. the earlier discussion of fecundity.
180. Cf. Biechler and Bond, "Introduction," ix–xlviii.

a former unity or equality has been breached.[181] Thus, it is reasonable to argue that connection is more fundamental than division. Since no being can be completely isolated from and unrelated to the rest of reality, even isolation presupposes at least the possibility of a relation with another. Therefore, viewing reality from a relational perspective is at least as much rational as taking division for a starting point.[182] Naturally, Nicholas of Cusa thought that anyone who prefers division to connection, inequality to equality, and plurality to oneness, is fundamentally mistaken. It can even be said that Nicholas could reasonably hope that Muslims would be able to share this relational perspective. His hope was justified by his recognition of their monotheism and by his knowledge of some Arabic philosophers.

The metaphysical priority of unity, equality, and connection also entails their respective eternity. Since they are prior to everything and they form the necessary structure of every being, they must be eternal. However, there cannot exist three eternals or eternities. Otherwise the very principle of unity would be offended. The three aspects must be of the same eternity: they must build a unity: they must be equal(ly eternal) and connected (with each other) in a fundamental unity. In this way, the three aspects of love form a unique unity in God.[183] Nicholas thus concludes that God is fundamentally triune Love.

Those terms of Cusanian theology that refer to the inner moments of the inner-Trinitarian love process are taken from the human language of the experience of love. These terms denote generating or bearing a child (*generans*), being born as a child (*genitus*), and their mutual connection (*nexus*). The names of the first two Persons of the Holy Trinity come from family life (*pater et filius*).[184] This suggests that in spite of the

---

181. Cf. *CA* II, 7, 105:5–6: "divisio vero cadit a conexione."

182. It is no accident that this is a weak argument establishing only the rationality of Nicholas's view.

183. *CA* II, 7, 106:1–5: "Patet igitur quomodo in essentia divini amoris unitas amoris, aequalitas amoris et nexus amoris non sunt tres amores, quia unus amor non est aliud ab alio, licet unitas amoris generantis non sit aequalitas amoris geniti aut nexus amoris utriusque ab ipsis procedens."

184. As for the question why to prefer the father–son relationship to other kinds of family bonds, cf. Nicholas's comment in *DVD* 18, 83:4–5: "Nexu enim filiationis non cognoscimus strictiorem." Hopkins adds the following note (355 n. 85): "This statement reflects the values of Nicholas's day. But it is also a consequence of his orthodox doctrine of the Trinity." For a discussion of God in terms of Love, see also *DVD* 17–18.

fact that the language of Divine Sonship is repellent to Muslims, it may still have positive potentials for an inter-religious dialogue.

The Language of Otherness

The next chapter of the *CA* declares the Holy Trinity to the readership of the book.[185] Interestingly, God is referred to as being positively beyond the language of Sameness (*idem*) and Otherness. Namely, God as the Not-other (*li non-aliud*) is prior to the first division of *idem* and *aliud*.[186] This statement squares well with the Cusanian negative theology according to which God is beyond normal human language. However, even if Nicholas's highly speculative language is accepted, a practical question arises concerning those who do not understand this language: How can one speak to those simple Muslims who would have difficulties in comprehending that the three Persons of the Trinity are one in essence *and* yet these three divine Persons are not simply identical with each other (*idem in essentia et non inter se idem*)? It is for these simple Arabs that chapter nine of book two of the *CA* offers a new symbol of the Trinity.

At this point, the difficulty of the concept of Not-other should first be recognized. Indeed, it can be argued that the recognition of this conceptual difficulty is a necessary condition for any genuine "understanding" of the Divine Mystery. The previous investigation of Nicholas's works has shown two things. On the one hand, no positive concept can be properly applied to God. On the other hand, mere negation will silence any form of positive religion. Since no concept—falling short of His Infinity—can properly function as God's name, therefore, the point of any theological discourse cannot be to deliver a precise description or definition of God. Absolutely objective descriptions or strict definitions of the Divine are not only impossible, but the very expectation of rational theology is dangerous. Namely, it is dangerous to the extent that it suggests that God can be properly cognized from a definite,

---

185. See *CA*, II, 8, 107–8 with the title "Declaratio sanctae trinitatis." Here "declaratio" means that Nicholas was trying to make a clear point. The term can be translated as manifestion, demonstration or explanation. Hagemann renders it as "Darlegung."

186. *CA* II, 107:2–4: "Nunc patet, quod, qui non attingunt li non aliud non esse idem et li non idem non esse aliud, non possunt capere unitatem, aequalitatem et nexum esse idem in essentia et non inter se idem." The concept of God as Not–other is prefigured in *DVD* 60–61.

limited, human perspective. Turning to the concept of the Not-other, one can say that this divine name is a name among the many possible and ultimately inadequate names of God, and at the same time it is no name at all. The concept of the Trinitarian God in the form of Not-other can avoid both the dangers of affirmative and negative theology. This "name" shows itself as conceptually difficult and precisely through manifesting this conceptual difficulty it does not conceal the Divine Mystery. The *CA* only evokes this concept, but it was at least present in Nicholas's mind, while he was working on his apologetic treatise. Later he further developed the same concept of God as Not-other in the *NA* and it can reasonably be argued that the metaphysical speculation of the *NA* not only profited from Nicholas's study of Dionysius, but was equally inspired by the Koranic anti-Trinitarian polemic he had been trying to cope with in his *CA*.[187] In this connection, verses 91–92 from *Surah* 23 are worth of quoting in full:

> Never has God begotten a son, nor is there any other god besides Him. Were this otherwise, each god would govern his own creation, each holding himself above the other. Exalted be God above their falsehood! He knows alike the unknown and the manifest. Exalted be He above the gods they serve beside Him!

I suppose that the full concept of Not-other was developed at least partly from Nicholas's efforts of trying to meet the challenge of this Muslim understanding of God. It is clear that Muhammad and Nicholas both wanted to secure God's transcendence in a radical way, albeit in different contexts: while the rhetoric of the Koranic verses was directed against the remainders of polytheism among Arabic tribes, the Cusanian conceptual effort fitted the enterprise of mystical theology. As far as Nicholas's Christian apology is concerned, the *CA* clearly states that anyone who does not accept the Trinity and the conceptual difficulty inherent therein will not have a perfect concept of the most perfect God. Any other possible name will necessarily say less of God and can declare His Mystery only in a less obvious way.[188]

---

187. Cf. *CA* I, 9, 49:5.10, 51:1–3.14–16, 52:1–2; and 11, 59:9–11 where the expression "alius deus" is employed. *CA* I, 11, 57:10–11 explicitly states that "filius ... dei est idem deus cum patre et non alius."

188. *CA* II, 8, 108:1–2: "Palam est illos, qui haec non capiunt, non habere conceptum perfectiorem de deo perfectissimo, sed sibi fingere deum quendam ..."

A Distant Symbol

However, for the sake of those who cannot have such a perfect concept of God, the next chapter offers another manuductive example in order that they, too, could be led to the Mystery of the Trinity.[189] Previously, Father, Son, and Holy Spirit were referred to as having or being the same vitalizing power. The manuductive example of chapter nine of book two is devised to make this claim more concrete with the help of a new symbol. The first sentences of this passage deserve to be quoted in full:

> With regard to these matters we must have recourse to a symbolism (*aenigma*), until such time as we have a well-versed understanding (*intellectum excertitatum*): I saw a large body of water (*aqua magna*) with shore all around it. It was without any inflow (*sine alterius aquae influxum*), or springing up, of any other water; and it remained always of the same quantity. On its circumference it had fruitful trees and crops and meadows; and the farmers (*rustici*) who lived nearby could not sufficiently praise the body of water, than which they thought there to be none better (*nulla melior*).[190]

This is a well-chosen example. First, it has many biblical allusions. Secondly, it can be directly related both to several Koranic passages and general views of ancient cosmogony.[191] The marvelous water makes the spectator wonder and he or she can only find the reason (*ratio*) for this mysterious phenomenon from an intellectual or speculative perspective.[192] Within the body of water three distinct moments can

---

189. CA II, 9, 109–10. Note the title "Aenigma licet remotum benedictae trinitatis." The first lines of the chapter show that the new similitude has a relative value and is only helpful as a *manuductio*.

190. CA II, 9, 109:1–7: "Oportet in istis ad aenigma recurri, quousque habeamus intellectum excertitatum: Vidi aquam magnam inter rotundas ripas sine alterius aquae influxu et semper effluxu eiusdem quantitatis habentem in circuitu fecundas arbores, segetes et prata, et rustici prope habitantes non sufficiebant laudare aquam, qua nullam putabunt dari meliorem."

191. Hagemann refers to Ezek 47:1–12; Ps 36:9b–10; John 4:14; and to *Surahs* 7:57; 22:5; 21:30; 24:45; 25:48–49.54; 32;8; 77:20; 86:6 respectively. He also reminds the reader that "[D]ie kosmogenetische Funktion des Wassers ist bereits aus der antiken Welterklärung bekannt; seit jeher galt das Wasser als Symbol der Lebenskraft." Nicholas of Cusa was aware of the Koran's employment of this water imagery. Cf. CA II, 9, 110:5–6.

192. CA II, 9, 109:21–22: "Nec haec vidi nisi intellectualiter considerans fontem de se generare fluvium."

be identified in the source, the stream, and the standstill (*fons, fluvius, stagnum*).[193] From an intellectual viewpoint the spectator will be able to identify successively these three aspects of the miraculous water with unity, equality, and connection. In this way, this wondrous mystery can be grasped in human thought—at least to some extent. Once the example of the miraculous water is well understood, one can dispense with it and ascend unto Eternity and comprehend Eternity better.[194] If perishable water can give so much life without drying itself up, then it is justified to call God "water" (i.e., *life giving source*) metaphorically (*transsumptive*), since every being receives life and existence from God. On this point the Bible and the Koran apparently agree.

Concluding the *Manuductiones*?

After the explicitly manuductive discussion of the *CA*, chapter eleven draws a surprising conclusion from the aforesaid by making the claim that Arabs must confess the Trinity.[195] The claim signals a change in Nicholas's manuductive strategy. Henceforth, Nicholas is only defending Christian claims, but he would insist that without accepting them Muslims will contradict the Koran.[196] From chapter eleven of book two of the *CA* rule 2 takes up the leading role. The internal contradiction recognized in the Koran is approached from an explicitly Christian Trinitarian perspective that has been established and secured in the earlier manuductive discussions. Nicholas was conscious of the circumstance that in a Christian-Moslem dialogue besides the doctrine of Trinity "not a few deviations of the Koran from the Gospel remain to

---

193. Hopkins translates "stagnum" with "pond." The translation "standstill" is inspired by Hagemann's German rendering as "Stillstand." Cf. p. 88 n. 4 of his translation.

194. *CA* II, 9, 110:2–5: "Conclusi igitur: Quoniam, si ad aeternitatem dimisso aenigmate ascendero, ipsam verioro modo comperio trinam et unam quam hanc visibilem aquam, et facilius superius dicta de generatione et processione aeterna indubia fide credidi."

195. *CA* II, 11, 112-4, has the title "Necesse est Arabes fateri trinitatem." For the moment, I leave the grammatical *manuductio* of *CA* II, 10, 111 aside, although I will briefly return to it at the end of this chapter.

196. Ibid., 112:2–4: "Quod autem Arabes oporteat hanc trinitatem, in divinis fateri patet, nam nisi fateantur, cum credant Alkoranum esse librum veritatis, convincuntur deo dare participem."

be clarified."[197] Hence, the remaining chapters of the second book of the *CA* are written to clarify and defend other important points of Christian doctrine, while the third book carries the same polemic further by not only protecting Christian claims, but also attacking Muhammad's person and the Koran.[198]

In sum, the remaining chapters of book two and the whole of book three are undoubtedly more polemical in tone than the earlier manuductive passages.[199] In the course of this polemic, an attempt is made to demonstrate the truth of Christian doctrine from the text of the Koran. This polemic is consistent with Nicholas's intent and with the method of pious interpretation. However, both because of their more polemic character and more narrow focus on special points of Christian doctrines, these discussions will concern my study only indirectly. Therefore, in my conclusion, I will briefly come back to the question concerning these doctrinal points. At this point of my investigation, I am going to inspect only one more particular passage of the *CA*. This section not only demonstrates the more polemical tone of the *CA*, but also provides me the possibility to reconsider Nicholas's exegetical strategy, the so-called "pious interpretation" and compare it with his approach in the *PF* and his letter to John of Segovia.

On Avicenna's Example of Devout Interpretation

The passage in question is made up by chapters eighteen and nineteen of book two of the *CA*. While chapter eighteen recaptures the earlier discussions of the Koranic Paradise, chapter nineteen places it into a more polemical perspective. As the beginning of chapter eighteen acknowledges, Nicholas has always perceived as much difference between the Muslim and Christian description of Paradise as between sensible and intellectual things, or between visible and invisible, in other words between temporal and eternal things.[200] He even generalized this ob-

197. CA II, 12, 115:2–3: "Restant non parvae discordantiae Alkorani ab evangelio elucidandae."

198. Cf. the table of contents.

199. The first book of the *CA* already displays polemical features (e.g., *CA* I, 9, 52–53).

200. Cf. Isa 64:3; Matt 22:30; Luke 20; 1 Cor 2:9; 2 Cor 4:18.:35; and *Surahs* 15:43; 39:71; 47:15; 55:25.72; 56:15–22.28–36, 67:6; 89:22.23. See also the discussion of the *DP* in my third chapter.

servation and applied it to the Koran and the Gospel in their entirety.²⁰¹ However, in continuity with his approach of the *PF* and his letter, the *CA* refers to certain people who excuse Muhammad by pointing out that the Prophet's sensual language was a concession to the uneducated Arabs (*rudes Arabes*).²⁰² Accordingly, Nicholas thought that Muhammad introduced many similitudes into the Koran while consciously leaving their explanation to the wise.²⁰³ In this way, Nicholas took seriously the special characteristic of the Koran as a religious discourse. He recognized the obvious, namely, that the Koranic texts have the characteristics of "preaching."²⁰⁴ That is the reason why the Koran employed similitudes. The important point is that in the last analysis (*finaliter*), there will be no real contradiction between the Koran and the Gospel with respect to the spiritual-intellectual nature of celestial happiness. The entire issue ultimately turns out to be a question of likeness.²⁰⁵ In this manner, Nicholas did not have to deny that Muhammad made use of a sensual language while he could still interpret the Koranic texts in a positive way.

All these points are more or less familiar from the similar discussions of the *PF* and the letter to John of Segovia. The *CA* states these points more clearly, but in one important point, its discussion differs from the earlier works. Here, Avicenna's approach to the Koran is recalled, but this time it is put to a more polemical use than before. The emphasis is on Avicenna's statement according to which the Koran does not describe a wholly intellectual happiness and the wise (*sapientes*) have a better description of this happiness.²⁰⁶ In Nicholas's opinion, this is not to deny that the Koran nevertheless—and less explicitly—does sug-

201. *CA* II, 18, 150:1–4.

202. Cf. *Surahs* 52:20; 56:22; 55:70.72.74; 37:48 The idea of "bestial copulation" in Paradise is not coming from the Koran but from Richard of Montcroce. Cf. *Surah* 52:24, 76:19; 56:17.

203. *CA* II, 18, 150:10–11: "plures similitudines introduxit, quas tamen non exposuit, sed sapientibus illas notas reliquit..."

204. *CA* II, 18, 151:1 uses the term "praedicare."

205. Nicholas also read in the *Doctrina Mahumeti* that properly speaking no likeness can be made of the future age. Cf. *CA* II, 18, 151:19–20.

206. *CA* II, 18, 153:1–4. In his marginal note to Avicenna's text, Nicholas wrote of the "sapientes theologi." His friend, Denys the Carthusian, also mentioned in his work Avicenna, Algazel, and "Arabes philosophi" referring to them as to those who see happiness "in contemplatione." Cf. Hagemann's samples from Denys's and Nicholas's remarks in his bilingual edition (*CA* III, 100 n. 220).

gest a less corporal heavenly beatitude. This is so, because Muhammad's mission was to teach the Arab idolaters and lead them to the cult of the One God.[207] This argument sounds familiar, but the *CA* makes explicit use of it for defending Christianity: it points out that since Christians are neither Arabs nor idolaters, they do not deserve persecution at Muslims' hands. Chapter nineteen also shows that Nicholas's polemics would not stop at this point.[208] There, the text recapitulates the necessity of employing likeness and some biblical and Koranic arguments for preferring an intellectual heaven, as well as attacking more explicitly the sensual imagery of the Koran.

It was already shown that Nicholas was taken aback by the apparent discrepancy between Islam and Christianity. He realized that Muslims share many points with Christianity, while the Koran's explicitly carnal language scandalized him.[209] He thought that the followers of that book were excused because of their pious interpretation.[210] However, he reached the conclusion that it was quite impossible to attribute the Koran to God. Nicholas was even wondering how the wise, chaste, and virtuous Arabs, Moors, Egyptians, Persians, Africans, and Turks could accept Muhammad as a prophet. Since the *CA* is concerned with a Christian reading of the Koranic message and not with a general argument-sketch for an inter-religious dialogue, there Nicholas's strategy changed. This change is reflected in the fact that the arguments of chapter nineteen of book two display an explicit *ad hominem* quality and the (real or alleged) faults of Muhammad's character and conduct are consciously exhausted.[211]

It is not necessary to go into further details of this anti-Islamic polemic. The reader is thus spared from marshalling medieval commonplaces. Nor is it necessary to analyze other passages where a less

207. Cf. *CA* I, 7, 44:1–8 and III, 17, 223:11–13.

208. *CA* II, 19, 154–8 with the title "Invectio contra Alkoranum."

209. These shared points concern the virginhood of Mary, John the Baptist, the prohibition of sexual intercourse in mosques and temples, the obligatory washing after intercourse (before praying), God's love for purity, and the final *visio Dei* in Paradise. Cf. *Surahs* 3:47, 19:20, 21:91, 66:12, 4:155, 3:39; 2:187; 5:6, 4:43; and 98:7–8; 9:72.

210. *CA* II, 19, 154:8–9: "intra me admittebam posse illa pia sequacium libri interpretatione excusari."

211. Nicholas realised that similar charges of immoral—especially sexual—conduct could be levelled against some holy men of the Old Testament. He pointed out that at least these were not sanctioned by all the prophets and lawgivers.

charitable use is made of what Nicholas perceived as the internal contradictions and inconsistencies of the Koran. Instead, the ultimate reason for Nicholas's theory of double authorship must be identified. This theory of double-authorship was a fundamentally religious (Christian) explanation for the difficulties posed by the Koran.[212] Nicholas came to the conviction that the Koran was not fully determined by Muhammad's own intent—no matter however abominable and diabolical this intent may have been. Nicholas believed that in the composition of the Koran Divine Providence was also at work. The theory of double authorship offers a solution to the riddle of the dirty ambiguities of the Koran. The same theory also became the underlying principle that determined Nicholas's enterprise of pious interpretation. According to his conviction, even amidst the moral turpitude, the Koran could make sense to a Christian reader. As he confesses, Nicholas believed that the "lux evangelica" lies hidden in the Koran—even behind its most appalling passages. The "theory" of double intent justified both his more sympathetic and more combative moves. However, Nicholas's Christian commitment and his anti-Islamic polemic does not entail that he was merely reading back his own prejudices into the Koran. It is true that a more neutral or a-religious standpoint was hardly available for him, but as Hopkins also points out, Nicholas tried to acknowledge as much from the Koran as he could while still remaining a medieval Christian. Most importantly, in the course of the *CA*, Nicholas gave special attention to the question of Trinity. The *CA* phrases this Trinitarian concern in terms of giving glory to God. In the last section of this chapter, this crucial topic of Christian-Muslim dialogue must be reconsidered.

On Giving Glory to the Triune God

In Nicholas of Cusa's eyes the ultimate question was whether the entire Koran tends towards the glory of God.[213] According to the very text of the Koran human beings should give glory to God and those who

---

212. *CA* II, 19, 158:4–8: "Tamen omnipotens deus inter omnia illa spurca et vana et sapientibus etiam Arabum abominabilia talia etiam inseri voluit, in quibus evangelicus splendor sic lateret occultatus, quod sapientibus diligenti studio quaesitus se ipsum manifestaret." Cf. *CA* III, 17, 223.

213. Cf. *CA* I, 8, 48:2–4.

endanger God's unity are detracting from His glory.[214] The basic question for Nicholas was: who can give God His glory in due measure and manner—the Muslims or the Christians?[215] In their polemics Muslims repeatedly accused Christians of positing and adoring a plurality of gods (*pluralitas deorum*). It was clear enough to Nicholas that the Koran will not allow (the worship of) "another God."[216] On the other hand, it can safely be said that most Christians do not actually believe in three Gods. Nicholas realized that Christians and Moslems agree that such a second God implies a contradiction and could not be God.[217] Nicholas insisted that in fact, Christians do not worship Christ as "alius deus."[218] He also argued that consequently, they are not to be seen as polytheists and should not be called unbelievers (*increduli*) by the Muslims.[219]

Traditionally, Christian theology discussed the problem of the Trinity with the help of such terms as communion (*societas*), participation (*participatio*), and sonship (*filiatio*).[220] As both the *PF* and the *CA* testify, Nicholas of Cusa recognized that to the extent these terms detract from God's glory, they are incorrect. Generally speaking, every kind of Trinitarian terminology is incorrect, if it implies a plurality in God. Nicholas had already hinted at this point in the *DI* by quoting the Augustinian dictum: "as soon as you start counting the Trinity, you leave the truth."[221] However, inasmuch as a Trinitarian terminology does not detract from God's glory, it can be accepted as correct. Giving glory to God means affirming all His perfections.[222] If *societas*, *participatio*, and

214. Ibid., 48:4–5. Cf. *Surahs* 2:116; 4:171–2; 6:100; 9:30–33; 10:68; 16:57; 17:40–44.111; 18:4; 19:88–91; 21:11; 23:91; 36:22; 37:149–66; 43:16; 52:39; 112:1–4.

215. Originally, what Muhammad attacked was not so much the doctrine of the Trinity, but the cult of pagan Arabic deities and he employed the term "participant" (Arabic "sharik") in his polemics. Later, Muslims viewed Christians as believing in "participation" ("shrik"). Cf. Goddard, *A History*, 26–28. For the following discussion, see especially *CA* I, 9, 49–53.

216. Cf. *Surah* 21:91. Hagemann notes that the Latin translations of this Koranic text is confusing.

217. *CA* I, 9, 49:17–19.

218. Hagemann's translation is expressive and clearly emphasises plurality: "ein zweiter Gott" (a second god). Cf. *PF* XI, 34:1–3.

219. *CA* I, 9, 49:3–10.

220. Hagemann mindfully renders "societas" with "Genossenschaft."

221. *DI* I, 19, 57:10–11: "Dum incipis numerare trinitatem, exis veritatem." Cf. footnote 222 in my third chapter.

222. Cf. *CA* I, 9, 49:10–19.

filiatio were to be excluded from God's being as perfections, that is to say not in the sense of imperfections or defects lessening God's glory, then the full perfection of the Divine Being would not be not affirmed.[223] Nicholas clearly thought that there is a positive sense according to which these terms must be affirmed of God as perfections.

It is still questionable whether the concept of "perfection"—especially when applied to God—has the same meaning for Muslims and Christians. As far as the former are concerned, they clearly refuse to accept such terms as community, participation, and sonship. One easily identifiable feature common to these is that they are all relational terms. They imply some kind of relationship and cannot be properly understood apart from a relation. Thus, for instance, the concept of sonship refers to the son's ontological relationship to his father. Without such a relationship to another—i.e., to the father—no being could properly be called a son. The son is therefore a son in virtue of his sonship, that is to say, through his relation to the father.

Within the framework of the present study, I cannot properly discuss the relational dimension of Nicholas's thought. At least its general function must be indicated. The role of the Trinitarian doctrine in Nicholas's thought is, namely, to capture and hint at the Divine Mystery as Father, Son, and Holy Spirit. These Divine Persons are solely distinguished from each other according to their different relationships with one another. In the *CA*, driven by his intellectual desire to rediscover and recover the same Trinity from the Koran, Nicholas boldly states that even the Arabs' interpretation could allow for divine sonship, provided that the usage of this concept does not imply a plurality of gods. It is clear that with this gesture he was re-interpreting the Koran for the Arabs.[224] My previous analysis of the manuductive passages of the *CA* has shown that these passages were directed at making the Muslims see that their own holy text can be read from a Christian perspective. In this way the Koran can lead them to accept Truth in Christ and in the Trinitarian God.

---

223. Cf. ibid., 49:15–16: "nec manet deus creator deus, quando non habet omnem gloriam et maior in gloria esse posset. Ideo nulla ratione hoc dici potest."

224. Hagemann calls this thought bold ("tollkühn") and well thought-out but far-fetched ("spitzfindig"). He notes that Nicholas's idea stands in a radical contradiction with the explicit teaching of the Koran. See his bilingual edition (*CA* I, 121 n. 179).

As already stated, the concept of "sonship"—so problematic for the Arabs—designates a relation.[225] When tackling the problem of Trinity and countering the Muslims' attacks, Nicholas was being tossed between two extremes. Within the framework of Aristotelian science, the category of relation had the least density of being. Because perfection always refers to a substance's perfection in terms of the fulfillment of its struggle for self-realization and independence, relation could hardly be called perfection in itself. On the other hand, Christian faith in the Trinity concerns a thoroughly relational reality as the principle one and the most perfect origin of all beings.[226] Nicholas admitted that if by calling God Father, one, as it were, elevates himself or herself to a (quasi-)divine status, then that person is mistaken. If by calling God Father, this appellation makes one forget his or her own finite, created being, then the usage of the term father cannot be justified.[227] Strictly speaking, no human can ever be called a "son" of God, since humans as finite creatures do not share the same essence with God: "[H]erefrom it seems that the Koran objects to presumptuousness (praesumptio) and the manner of speaking."[228] Thereby, Nicholas explicitly identified the Koranic criticism of the language of sonship with an objection directed against human *superbia*. Admittedly, the quoted sentence terminates with the phrase "as if sonship meant consubstantiality" and it is obvious that this terminology is alien to the Koran.[229] Yet Nicholas not only employed traditional Trinitarian terminology, but with the help of his different *manuductiones*, he also tried very hard to elucidate the Christian dogma from a more universal perspective. In the CA, he was looking for symbols that could intimate the Mystery of the Trinity to

225. It is not accidental that Nicholas refers to the fact that in the biblical prayer tradition God is called Father. Cf. *CA* I, 9, 51:3–6.

226. My analysis of the category of relation is inspired by Jos Decorte. Cf. especially Decorte, "Relation and Substance."

227. Note that an appellative *is* a relational term.

228. *CA* I, 9, 51:12–13: "Videtur ex hoc ipsum arguere praesumptionem et modum dicendi..."

229. Hagemann observes that the notion of "consubstantialitas" is completely alien to the Koran. In his view Nicholas tries to read into the Koran something that is simply not there. (Cf. *CA* I, 121 n. 181.) Hagemann is right to point out that strictly speaking the Koran cannot deny human consubstantiality with God, since this concept is foreign to its discourse. However, Nicholas of Cusa is also right in identifying Muhammad's intent as directed against human presumption. The quotation of *Surah* 5:18 in *CA* I, 9, 51:8–12 makes this latter point sufficiently clear.

Muslims. Nevertheless, the fact remains that the Koran does explicitly deny Christ's divine sonship thereby plainly contradicting the Gospels. It is small wonder that for Nicholas, the Koran cannot possibly be right on this issue.[230]

As we have seen, Nicholas wanted to settle the disagreement between Muslims and Christians with the help of the criteria of glory. As he himself wrote, "Jesus came only to give glory to God His Father: He did not in any way seek his own glory."[231] This statement squares well with Nicholas's negative judgment on Muhammad's vainglory. Even more significantly, Jesus Christ was important, because He revealed the mystery of God's relationality. Speaking in more traditional terms of Trinitarian theology, Christ revealed God as the Father and Himself as the Son. Yet, this would not entail any plurality within the Divine Being. Indeed, a plurality of gods would only contradict Divine Infinity and detract from God's glory. The reader of the earlier Cusanian treatises can remember that plurality and number are concepts devised for denoting finite and limited creatures and thus *a fortiori* inapplicable to the Infinite.[232]

Nicholas, for his part, was clearly convinced that the Trinitarian God is "greater," has more "being" or "perfection," and He is at once more mysterious and fascinating than the language of Divine Simplicity and Oneness alone could indicate. To employ traditional language, the Mystery of the Trinitarian God is like a Father-Son relationship and God is a Trinity because of His internal relations. Being a person entails being related to others and no human can become a person without being in relation with others. Moreover, no human being can even come to exist as a person without any relation to others. Among themselves humans are constituted in a relational manner.[233] Moreover, being a creature involves a fundamental relatedness that is constitutive to the human being. Nicholas clearly thought that these points and most importantly the last one could be recognizable and accepted both by

---

230. Cf. *CA* I, 9, 52:6–20 and *Surahs* 3:45; 4:159; 5:116–120; 23:50; 42:51; 43:61.

231. *CA* I, 9, 53:20–21: "Non enim venit Jesus nisi ut daret gloriam deo patri suo et suam nequaquam quaesivit."

232. Cf. the discussion in my third chapter.

233. On the necessity of love for the existence of the world, cf. the earlier discussion of the present chapter.

Christians and Muslims.[234] The manuductive examples of intellectual creativity and of the productive bond of loving reveal their full meaning within such a relational setting. This fundamental relational reality forms the basis for Nicholas's *manuductiones*.[235]

In the course of the *CA*, Nicholas made use of different concepts, examples, and symbols in order to accentuate different aspects of a reality that in his perception was constitutive to human beings. That is the reason why he kept on saying that God Himself cannot lack a reality so fundamental to human beings. If this is true, then the *CA* and other Cusanian works do not simply repeat a Trinitarian rhetoric, but they are pointing towards the ultimate dimension of all reality.[236] The Mystery of the Trinitarian Community of Divine Persons is clearly the most important issue of the *CA*. This Mystery and the fascination therewith are present in every human being in the form of human relationships and intellectual desires. This circumstance makes one understand the reason why rule 4—phrased in terms of giving glory—governs all other rules of pious interpretation and why the same rule also determines the goal of the Trinitarian *manuductiones*. The same fact also explains the Cusanian preference for Christianity over against Islam and why in spite of his Christian faith Nicholas could still reasonably hope that the Muslim is able to come to share this Trinitarian insight.

---

234. Namely, the Bible and the Koran agree that no one can exist without being related to the Creator.

235. Cf. *CA* II, 10, 111:1–16, where a *manuductio* is offered based on the grammatical notion of person.

236. Cf. *CA* II, 5, 100:1–6; 7, 103:7–8; 104:3–4; 10, 111:8–9.

6

Towards a Conclusion

Neither this world nor any writings can cause him any difficulty; for he is being transformed.[1]

—Nicholas of Cusa

The result proves the excellence of the means. The clarity of the object proves that the lens we saw it through is good.[2]

—C. S. Lewis

Manuductio ad Trinitatem

THE FORGOING DISCUSSION HAS DEMONSTRATED THAT NICHOLAS of Cusa's approach to Islam can be safely termed as a *manuductio ad Trinitatem* in the sense of a *manuductio ad mysterium*. The formal aspect of this Trinitarian manuductive project must be especially emphasized. As Jos Decorte maintained, a *manuductio* is based on and starts from lived faith as a formal attitude or formal conduct.[3] It is not primarily or exclusively the content of this faith what matters—in the sense of its objective truth claims—but the way such a faith functions is of equal importance. Seen from a formal perspective, this faith prescribes a particular conduct, a human practice or a concrete form of life lived out in Christian humility and charity. It is in this way that this faith enables the

---

1. Cf. *Epistola auctoris ad dominum Iulianum cardinalem*, in *DI* III, 264:14–17: "omnia cedunt et nihil ingerere possunt difficultatis quaecumque scripturae necque hic mundus, quoniam . . . hic transformatur."
2. Lewis, *An Experiment*, 31.
3. For the following analysis cf. Decorte, "Ter inleiding," esp. 32–40.

believer to show a genuine concern for the Other. At the same time, the same believer humbly acknowledges his or her own limitations.[4]

The Cusanian manuductive project can be criticized by pointing out that the insistence on Trinitarian doctrine comes ultimately from a Christian religious–theological bias. It is true that Nicholas—together with most medieval intellectuals—was attached to the Christian doctrine and way of life, but it is equally true that he made a more philosophical point concerning Trinity. The doctrine of Trinity was important for him both theologically *and* philosophically as it ruled his worship but also determined his thought. Nicholas's insistence on the doctrine of Trinity is also a pointer towards the relational Mystery of the Divine Being. Jos Decorte's writes thus:

> The point of the doctrine of the Trinity is this: *it makes one especially see that the Divine cannot be conceived*. That is the reason why this doctrine is the most adequate description: because it shows that what representational thought tries to think with its representations and concepts can neither be represented nor conceived. The doctrine of the Trinity shows the Divine Mystery as it is. Namely, through showing the unimaginability of the unimaginable and the inconceivability of the inconceivable, Trinity shows that which is unimaginable as unimaginable and that which cannot be thought as unthinkable. That is the reason why Nicholas keeps on hammering on the doctrine of Trinity.[5]

My analysis showed that this point does not only hold true for the *PF* but also for Nicholas's other works. Nicholas of Cusa realized that the concept of Trinity is only a human image of the Mystery and his never-ending appreciation for mystical theology went hand in hand with the

---

4. Cf. ibid., especially 9–7 and 32–42.

5. Decorte, "Ter inleiding," 37. Since this passage is crucial for my approach I also quote the Dutch original: "Wat de triniteitsleer doet is dit: *bij uitstek laten zien dat het goddelijke niet te denken is*. Daarom is deze leer de meest adequate beschrijving: omdat ze toont dat wat het voorstellende denken in zijn voorstellingen en begrippen probeert te denken, voorstelbaar noch denkbaar is; omdat ze het goddelijke mysterie toont zoals het is, d.w.z. omdat ze het onvoorstelbare als onvoorstelbaar, het ondenkbare als ondenkbaar toont, door de onvoorstelbaarheid van het onvoorstelbare en de ondenkbaarheid van hat ondenkbare te tonen. Daarom blijft Nicolaas telkens weer op die triniteitsleer hameren" (emphasis from the author).

On the same page, Jos Decorte also emphasises the importance of another point to Nicholas, namely, that the doctrine of the Trinity transcends the opposition between monotheism and polytheism.

omnipresence of a manuductive concern. This feature of his thought sharply contrasts Nicholas with more modern thinkers. That is to say, Nicholas of Cusa was neither a fideist nor relativist. He certainly would not give up his faith and turn to despair. As a Christian thinker and a *manuductor*, he thought that the Trinitarian discourse functions as the best *manuductio* possible: not because it would "represent" perfectly the Mystery, but because it makes the Christian believer best conscious of this Mystery. In this sense, Trinitarian language has an evocative function.[6] The faithful acceptance of the Trinity is also related to the central Cusanian ideal of *docta ignorantia*. Precisely because the doctrine of the Trinity shows that God cannot be reduced to any finite category of human thought, it can teach the believer learned ignorance. The same learned ignorance will also prompt the believer to search for ever new categories for spelling out the Divine Mystery. This was the ultimate philosophical motive behind Nicholas's urge to elucidate the mystery of the Trinity with the help of different images in his *CA*.[7]

However, even if my analysis is accepted, a further problem arises. The special strength of this Decortian analysis is that it does justice to the practical dimension of religious commitment in terms of *fides qua*. Yet, this in itself will not solve the question of *fides quae*. That is to say, the question concerning the importance of specific points or contents of Christian doctrine is still open. My analysis so far only touched upon this issue, but I did not discuss all the doctrinal points in detail. Nevertheless the three works so crucial for Nicholas's dialogue with Islam do treat such specific points in more or less detail. Generally speaking, the *PF* makes the importance of doctrinal points more relative, while the *CA* defends them more vigorously.[8] It seems that both in the polemic context of the *CA* and also in the more irenic approach of the *PF*, Nicholas did attach some importance to these positive dimensions of religiosity.[9] To a man like Nicholas of Cusa, these specific contents of faith have cer-

---

6. Cf. Bond, "Introduction," 48–55.

7. Jos Decorte noted in a lecture that the division of the *CA* into three books can be seen as a Trinitarian reference. Nicholas's other main work, the *DI* is also divided in the same way.

8. The account in the letter to Segovia is understandably very limited in its scope.

9. In contrast to Ramón, Nicholas did not think that all positive elements of religion can be reduced to a rational explanation. See my second chapter and also Decorte, "Ter inleiding," 42.

tainly more importance than being simply pious pieces of an otherwise brainlessly preserved religious tradition.

As a possible answer to this problem of *fides quae*, I suggest that all the specific religious positivities have to be read and understood from the "essence" of Christianity, that is to say from the doctrine of the Trinity and not vice versa. Understood form a medieval perspective, saying that Trinity is the "essence" of Christianity means at least two things. First, Trinity makes the Christian religion and its doctrine understandable as its basic principle. Secondly, Christian worship and life aim at the Trinity. Thereby Trinity gives the form–giving *principium* of Christianity defining both its origin and its teleology.[10] This is not to deny that the "essence" of Christian faith has any content. Indeed, it did not happen by accident that Nicholas of Cusa never got tired of reminding his readership of the fact that no definition or concept can ever communicate the fullness of the Divine Being. The doctrine of Trinity captures well something absolutely essential concerning Christian faith, but Nicholas always emphasizes that the proper content of this doctrine is Infinity. Therefore, its content is infinitely rich. Because humans can have no direct access to this Infinity, only symbols and metaphors can help one further towards the Divine. Hence, if one can speak of any "content" of this "essence" of Christian doctrine, it should be referred to as the relational reality of Divine Love, Self–Giving Agape, a gratuitous caring for the Other, Fecundity, Fertility, and Forgiveness. Precisely because of its infinite richness, the content of this reality can be never fully conceptualized; yet, it will remain the most important and most worthy subject of any human thought whatsoever. Limited propositions, human conjectures, and even different religions themselves will necessarily capture only some aspects from this Mystery. It is not surprising that Nicholas of Cusa made recourse to this Mystery, when he felt that precisely this Mystery was theologically misunderstood by Islam and debased in the continuous bloodshed of wars.

Nothing what have been said so far amounts to a denial of Nicholas's shortcomings, his lack of information, and his uncritically accepted negative opinions with respect to the Koran and its origins. Nor can the more polemic tone of the *CA* be always justified. On several points of this polemics Nicholas was undoubtedly carried away by his own religious zeal. Yet, within the given historical context he was doing

---

10. Cf. the discussion of essence in terms of teleology in my *Prolegomena*.

what he as a Christian and a theologian really had to do. What is more, he was doing this even better than other fellow Christian theologians of his own time. He was not just charitable, but was acting out *caritas*; not just troubled, but taking the trouble himself and carrying the burden of the historical confrontation with Islam in what seemed to him an intellectually responsible way.[11]

Earlier, it has been pointed out that for Nicholas—as for many medievals—*caritas* was the essential form-giving aspect of faith. This intrinsic relation between *fides* and *caritas* entails that without attending to *caritas*, Christian faith would be formless and pointless: such a faith would forsake its own proper teleology and would be simply vain (*vana, ad frustra*). Nicholas saw intellectual activity also from this perspective.[12] In this respect, it is worth recalling Nicholas's letter to Cardinal Cesarini.[13] There, Nicholas speaks of faith in terms of a basis (*fundamentum*) and connects text reading with (spiritual) life. The fact that reading formed a paradigm for any serious intellectual activity during the Middle-Ages indicates the importance of this reference. The letter, namely, asserts that a person who has made a certain progress on the way of (Christian) faith would not be troubled anymore by the reading of any kind of book whatsoever (*quaecumque scripturae*). Because of his or her many meditations and the growth of faith, such a person will be able to read anything without any spiritual harm. It seems plausible that this general Cusanian conviction became operative in the *CA*. Namely, through the project of pious interpretation, Nicholas wanted to show—at least to himself—that the Koran's reading should not be necessarily dangerous to a Christian, but a Christian thinker would be able to profit even from such a confused and devilish book. As the natural connection between intellectual activity, virtuous life, and love basically determined Nicholas's entire thought, it is possible and reasonable to see in his *manuductiones* and in the project of pious interpretation an act of Christian charity.[14] Placing the Cusanian intellectual enterprise into such context of a spiritual-intellectual journey means nothing else

---

11. See Decorte, "Ter inleiding," 42 and the analysis of *fides* and *tolerantia* ibid. 9–17.

12. See e.g., the discussion of the *DI* or the *DP* in my third chapter.

13. The letter accompanies the *DI*, see there III, 263–4. For Nicholas's treatment of faith see *DI* III, 9. On *love*, see also *C* II, 17.

14. Cf. Decorte, "Ter inleiding," 39–40.

than reading it consciously from a medieval perspective. Therefore the question as how Nicholas's intellectual responsibility can be understood today can be only answered by stepping back to the starting point of my study, to the form of medieval knowledge.

Between Vanity and Pride

It has been pointed out that the point of knowledge for medievals was not so much to know as much as possible, but rather to know *how* to employ this knowledge or *how* to live with it. This competence for *knowing-how* was referred to as *wisdom* (*sapientia*). It was also explained how this wisdom can be understood as wisely avoiding the respective extremes of "the vain curiosity of the world" (*vana curiositas mundi*) and "intellectual arrogance" or "pride" (*superbia*). Further, on several points I emphasized that for the medieval mind human rationality can only rest in its proper end, i.e., in seeing the invisible within the visible. The question of intellectual responsibility when addressed to a medieval intellectual project can be rephrased accordingly. Namely, a thinker and his respective enterprise can be interrogated in the following way: Does he manage to avoid those extremes? Is his way a wise way? In his procedure does he prove to be wise?

In other words, taking up the medieval perspective for a better understanding of Nicholas of Cusa would mean comparing his enterprise to the achievements of his fellow medievals. In the course of the present study I already introduced material for such comparisons. Now, it is time to revisit these data and to 'sift' the results.

The Defender and the Negotiator

John of Torquemada

When one compares Nicholas's approach to Islam with that of John of Torquemada, Nicholas proves to be a better guide to the invisible. Nicholas did not spare the Moslems from sharp criticism, but he was not only defending Christian claims. He was also trying to show that these claims would make sense and have some plausibility even when seen from another human perspective. John of Torquemada, from his own part, made almost no effort to acknowledge positive aspects of the

Other's (the Moslem) perspective. In the light of Nicholas's *manuductiones ad Trinitatem*, Torquemada's approach appears as inferior.

There remains the question whether in his anti-Islamic polemic, the Cardinal of Saint Sixtus committed the sin of vain curiosity or exhibited intellectual arrogance. John's detailed argument chopping and his speculations verging on absurdities indicate that his efforts were in vain. However, it does not seem reasonable to think that curiosity made him wonder, for instance, on the amount of dross produced in the Moslem Paradise. Apparently, his interest in the Koran and in Moslem doctrine did not go very far. It was sufficient for him to contrast the Koran with the Bible and to argue that the Bible was true while the Koran was wrong. Earlier I argued that John's approach can be seen as a form of totalitarian reason. This can be expressed in medieval language by identifying his approach as an instance of *superbia*.

JOHN OF SEGOVIA

John of Segovia's enterprise is clearly more pleasing to the modern mind. One can find his meticulous attention to details and his huge project of translation especially attractive and stimulating. Even today John's conviction according to which public debates are useful for clarifying both truth and falsity rings true with wisdom. The whole Segovian project for a peaceful rapprochement with Islam does not only sound benevolent, but also sufficiently realistic to be taken seriously by anyone seriously interested in a dialogue with different cultures and religions.[15]

On the other hand, Segovia's confidence in rational discussion and his self-assurance as a good disputant makes him vulnerable to criticism. I indicated earlier that Nicholas of Cusa himself may have had his own reservations concerning John's approach. A long time before receiving his friend's letter, Nicholas left the conciliar party, and at least one reason for his departure was that he became tired with and perhaps even desperate because of the never-ending discussions at Basle. Nicholas must have realized that such discussions can deteriorate and

---

15. Cf. Hagemann, *Der Kur'an*, 184: "Eine wesentliche Voraussetzung des Gespräches ist die beiderseitige Kenntnis von innen.... Das ist jedoch nur möglich, wenn die durch eine lange Tradition mächtig angewachsenen emotionale Barriren auf beide Seiten überwunden werden. Erst dann werden sich Wege und Möglichkeiten gegenseitigen Verstehens auftun." This remark points towards Segovia's project of gradual peaceful rapprochement, without, however, mentioning his name.

a (papalist) minority can become terrorized by a (conciliar) majority. He also saw the dangerous consequence that (papal) authority can be thrown up and thus whole social structures become ruptured. In contrast, John of Segovia remained a convinced conciliar up to his last days. It is true that finally John made peace with the church. Yet, with respect to the conciliar procedure and the ideal of rational discussion, hardly any critical awareness is observable from his part.[16]

It is probably more important that both Nicholas and John can have realized the futility of making more and more subtle distinctions in order to *deduce* the logical and ontological truth of a Trinitarian God. If one is thinking of the Divine Mystery, one cannot pride himself to find have *the* rational explanation for every detail. In this respect, Nicholas's *formal conduct* in the praxis of *docta ignorantia* seems better suited to avoid the dangers of intellectual arrogance than the type of rationality displayed by his friend Segovia. John's *praesumptio* in the form of an excessive confidence in his own rational abilities makes his approach to a form of *superbia*, while the continuous refinement of his distinctions and deductions of the Trinitarian Mystery make it appear as an instance of vain curiosity.

All this is not to deny either Torquemada's or Segovia's qualities, or the latter's unique knowledge of Islam. My aim is not simply either to debunk or to exalt any medieval thinker. To identify Torquedama's approach as totalitarian or arrogant is not to deny that he stated and contrasted Christian convictions with those of Islam with clarity. Similarly, to point out the dangers of rational debates in Segovia's approach is not to lessen the importance of his unique data and information with respect to Islam. I do not claim to be able to form an absolute judgment concerning any medieval form of thought; I offer only a relative evaluation.[17] My aim is first of all to identify the limitations of some rational enterprises as they can be seen from a medieval perspective.

---

16. On the awareness of the limits of human rationality from John's part cf. Haubst, "Die Wege der christologische manuductio," 129 (passage quoted in footnote 85 of my first chapter).

17. This is in line with the Cusanian conviction according to which truth is always seen form a particular perspective.

The Modest and the Fanatical

Fortunately, the comparison between Thomas Aquinas and Ramón Lull has been in fact prepared by their fellow medieval, Jean Gerson. In his anti-Lullist criticism, the Chancellor of the Sorbonne pointed out two problematic aspects of Ramón's thought. He identified one in the strange, unusual, and even fantastic character of the Art. The other problem was that Ramón tried to find necessary arguments for those religious truths that—both in Gerson's and Aquinas's opinion—lie beyond the possibility of proving or disproving.

Ramón Lull

These two mistakes of Ramón's approach can be connected with each other in the following way. If one thinks, as Ramón did, that he or she can devise a universal scientific Art applicable to all areas of reality, then that person can be tempted to go further. If he or she is a believer, as Ramón was, that person may think that the Art can be put in the service of his faith. For instance, one may think that one can rationally explain and even prove the doctrine of the Trinity. This step is a logical mistake, but at least a reasonable mistake. It is not difficult to see that the same mistake made appear Ramón's project as a result of vain intellectual pretensions. In this way, while his project displayed the characteristics of vain curiosity it was basically determined by a mistaken conviction of the possibilities of his own rational inventory. Ramón's approach can be clearly seen as an instance of *superbia*.

Thomas Aquinas

In contrast, Thomas Aquinas's approach to theology in general was a more modest one. This circumstance points towards Thomas's humble *sapientia* in his approach of Islam. Yet, the wise caution in itself does not make his approach better over against Ramón's in every respect. Ramón was not only interested in, but he was also knowledgeable about Islam, while Thomas was neither seriously interested nor well informed. In his own time and also in many times to come, Ramón's knowledge of Islam was indeed unique. Thomas, on the other hand, was sound in his theology and clever in his philosophy. From the perspective of an inter-religious dialogue, his points made in the *ScG* and *RF* are worth of a serious consideration, because both of these works offer a balanced and prudent approach to the Moslem arguments leveled against Christianity. However, neither of these works was devised with the intention that Moslems should share the Christian perspective on the invisible Divine Mystery.

The Manuductor

The previous observation when taken together with the other results of my investigation suggests that seen from a medieval perspective, Nicholas of Cusa's approach towards Islam should be judged positively to the extent that it succeeds to show the invisible within the visible. I already identified the special strength of Nicholas's approach in his manuductive concern. If the aim of every kind of knowledge was the *visio Dei* in the Middle-Ages, then the importance of Nicholas's manuductive concern can be hardly underestimated to a his intellectual project. Nicholas himself was able to transcend all the former medieval approaches towards Islam, while he was also able to learn from them precisely as a *manuductor*. Earlier, I indicated in relation to the *PF* that this dialogue should not be primarily read as a rational-technical argument against Moslems (or followers of other religions for that matter). If the Trinitarian manuductive project determines Nicholas's entire thought, then my observation can be generalized: if the general form of Nicholas's thought was *manuductive*, then it is not surprising that his approach towards Islam also took on the same basic form.

The goal of such a manuductive approach is not offering arguments from a neutral point of view. Neither it is guaranteed that the *manuductiones* will convince the (religious) Other. This approach has, indeed, some necessary conditions: it presupposes that the Other has some trust, takes the hand offered, follows it and, most importantly of all, he or she is ready to learn not to reduce the Mystery of Being to any particular form of limited human thought. While the insistence on this last point can be seen as Nicholas of Cusa's special strength, any attempt to attain a peaceful and open atmosphere of mutual trust can profit from John of Segovia's approach of a gradual rapprochement.

A Medieval Contribution to Our Contemporary Perspective

It is one thing to read a medieval thinker from a medieval perspective and yet another to ask what the same thinker can contribute to today's thought and problems. These two enterprises are connected, but different. In the previous sections I have tackled the first of these two questions and now, I will turn to the second one. This will also give me the opportunity to answer those questions concerning Nicholas of Cusa I set out to investigate in my third chapter. This move will also shed light on an important advantage of the interpretative framework of my study.

To begin with the latter question, I must point out that my framework helps the modern reader to take up the medieval perspective. My approach, by turning the table as it were, also immediately shows what is wrong with contemporary approaches either to Nicholas or to Islam and to the question of religious plurality. If knowledge necessarily shares both the dimension of *knowing-how* and *knowing-that*, then both of these aspects should be taken seriously. The problem of religious "knowledge" or *fides quae* must not be reduced to a set of propositions connected through a quasi-scientific theological theory, but the particular form of religious *knowing-how* or *fides qua* has to be also taken seriously. The observation that religion is in the first place a form of human practice also suggests the importance of the same dimension.[18] Finally, the symbolic structure of religious knowing indicates that only one who is ready to look beyond the positive data can come to a genuine understanding of any religion.

This has an important consequence for academic research. One has to realize, namely, that to the extent that one concentrates exclusively on the positive data, one runs the risk of losing sight of the invisible referent behind. This is not to deny that on contemporary academic grounds Nicholas will necessarily loose battle against (post-)modern scholars. For instance, it is all too likely that even one single scholar of Islamic studies from today's academic world has more knowledge of Arabic in his fingertip than poor Nicholas of Cusa or any other medieval intellectual had in all of their works. Yet, it is also very likely that few modern scholars would dare to ask the question what may lie behind the texts.

---

18. Concerning this point see also the third part of my study.

This is naturally not to say that the modern caution over against the symbolic dimension of the surveyed material is not understandable. The point I would like to stress is rather that this reluctance is not always reasonable; moreover it can be dangerous when employed as a general principle for interpretation.[19] If the symbolic dimension of medieval texts is systematically exluded from the practice of the inquiry, then this circumstance alone makes the researcher prone to misunderstand the investigated material and renders him or her incapable of seeing what is not immediately visible on the surface.

What I have said so far in no way amounts to a denial of the importance of modern scholarship. Instead, it should be read as a suggestion for a change of focus. Although (post-)modern scholarship delivers important data and details, it could be supplemented with the proper medieval way of knowing-how. If one is ready to follow this knowing-how, it will help him to place Nicholas into his own proper context. Thereby, he or she will be able to understand and appreciate Nicholas better as a medieval thinker. Furthermore, the same interpretative step can help one to see what is at stake in religion. Particularly, without acknowledging the symbolic structure as fundamental to religion and other basic human experiences (the ethical, the aesthetical, and the relationships of love and friendship), these issues can hardly be treated with any fairness.[20] Any serious dialogue on religion and ethics is bound up intrinsically with the same problem.

Earlier, I put forward two basic questions concerning Nicholas's approach to Islam and now it is appropriate to formulate a clear answer to each:

1. The real strength of Nicholas of Cusa's thought in general, but also of his approach to the questions of religious plurality and Islam in particular has to be judged from the perspective of medieval rationality itself. Such an evaluation does not only make one better appreciate Nicholas as a medieval thinker, but it can also open up useful perspective of his thought.

2. One such fundamental perspective is coming from Nicholas's mystical, neo-Platonic theology. The rediscovery of a symbolic

---

19. The question whether a particular researcher explicitly acknowledges this principle or it is only tacitly implied in his or her work, has no bearing on my argument.

20. Cf. *RA*, 11–13.

understanding of religion will make one sensitive to the question what is really at stake in any religious conflict and in any dialogue concerning basic human values.

In the history of Cusanus-studies, this is not the first time that the medieval character of Nicholas's thought receives special emphasis. Scholars making similar moves often react to an exceedingly modern reading of the Cusanian corpus, one that is eager to assimilate the Cardinal from Cusa to whatever strain of modern philosophy its author prefers. Perhaps, some would argue that philosophical distortions of this kind are rather the rule than exceptions, since one is always tempted to misunderstand a thinker from a distant past. If this is true, then one should become all the more careful in his or her reading. One should try to broaden, modify, and occasionally even change his or her own (modern) perspective. One necessary condition for such a change of one's own perspective is correct information. However, correct information in itself is not enough, if it is not implemented by a practical knowing-how. No amount of new data will make someone to change his mind, if he or she is not ready to effect such a change and has not learned how "go about" this change.

C. S. Lewis, a careful and well-informed reader of medieval texts, once confessed that "it would seem to me a waste of the past if we were content to see in the literature of every bygone age only the reflexion of our own faces."[21] It is worth remembering that Lewis himself tried very hard to do justice to his medieval reading through continuous efforts not to reduce medieval texts to twenty century tastes and standards. His warning does not only concern literary documents. What Lewis thought concerning literature is true of other texts as well. Similar dangers are present to the philosopher's modern mind when he or she encounters philosophical or theological texts from the Middle-Ages and similar intellectual efforts can save him or her from falling prey to the temptations of a more philosophical misunderstanding.[22] This strongly suggests that there is no way for a modern appreciation of any medieval

---

21. Lewis, "De audendis Poetis," 4.

22. Although it is not essential to the above argument, it is worth of noting that C. S. Lewis was not only a medievalist and literary scholar, but also an experienced reader of theological and philosophical texts. See, e.g., Lewis, *Discarded Image*.

figure except by diligent work and constant alertness against one's own modern prejudices.

Ultimately, that is the reason why Nicholas of Cusa only as a medieval thinker can be of any help to a reader from our age. If Nicholas of Cusa is expected to make a contribution to a proper understanding of the problem of religions today, it should not be surprising, that what he can do is something typically medieval.[23] This general observation squares well with the emphasis on the *manuductive* character of Nicholas's approach. If the modern reader is ready to learn how a symbolically structured vision works and he or she also wants to perceive the invisible within and beyond the visible, then, to such a reader, the medieval Nicholas of Cusa will prove a trustworthy guide.

It is a historical fact that Nicholas's voice was hardly even heard in his own life-time. It is also a fact that his voice never reached the Other of Islam. In the contemporary world, where the question of religious plurality is as acute as it has ever been, one can only hope that this voice will receive the kind of attention it deserves.

---

23. On the connection between religion and medieval culture, see the *Prolegomena* and the third part of my study.

Part Three

Questioning the Prolegomena

Resurrecting Wisdom or a Return to the Middle-Ages?

> There are more ways than one of reading old books. . . . what we find inside will always depend a great deal on what we have brought in with us. . . . untrained eyes or bad instrument produce both errors; they create phantasmal objects as well as miss real ones.[1]
>
> —C. S. Lewis

Wisdom Reconsidered

ON THE PREVIOUS PAGES AN ATTEMPT HAS BEEN MADE TO EMPLOY and to test an interpretative framework inspired by Jos Decorte's work for understanding medieval thought. I tried to show to my reader the advantages of such an approach in relation with Nicholas of Cusa's thought and particularly for his dialogue with Islam. To express it with a metaphor already applied in the *Prolegomena*, I ventured to try on medieval glasses and see what they could show. Thus my inquiry involved a change of perspectives—from a modern point of view to a more medieval one. In effect, my study can be read as an attempt at resurrecting the driving force of much ancient and medieval thought, i.e., wisdom or *sapientia*. However, crossing cultural boundaries in itself will not effect such a resurrection without proper mediations. An archaic form of wisdom cannot be revived within a different—(post-)modern—context without further considerations. Contrasting medieval wisdom with (post-)modern thought is only helpful when it is also shown how our intellectual enterprises are related to, and especially how they can profit from medieval forms of rationality. Therefore, I have to shed more light on medieval wisdom and its possible relationship with modern forms of thought.

---

1. Lewis, "De audendis Poetis," 1 and 4.

As far as the study of medieval thought is concerned, the contemporary academic world offers other, more traditional approaches to this subject.[2] The question must be addressed how these approaches can be evaluated from the point of view of the interpretative framework of my inquiry. Since a complete survey and evaluation of the whole field of *Mediavistik* would require another study, the next section can only offer a preliminary discussion. Thus I will limit myself to a comparison between my methodology and three further approaches to medieval philosophy, that is to say at least the neo-Thomistic, the analytic, and the more historically minded approaches will be considered briefly. By way of a comparison, the special strength of my approach will be borne out better. Thereafter, I will reflect on some possible criticism.

Medieval Wisdom and Modern Scholarship

Neo-Thomism or more generally neo-Scholasticism consciously followed a cultural agenda of Christian apologetics. In this way it opposed what it took modern philosophy to be. In contrast, the analytic way of approaching medieval philosophical texts does not have the same cultural scope. It can be regarded as a reaction against the excesses of neo-Scholastic aspirations. For the most part, the analytic approach claims to avoid ideological battles and tries to focus on the philosophical problems of medieval texts. It identifies and examines these problems by using the standards of modern analytic philosophy. Finally, the contemporary intellectual historian has yet another methodology. He or she recognizes the limits both of the neo-Scholastic and of the analytic approach. From his or her own part, the intellectual historian especially emphasizes the importance of the historical context for understanding a philosophical debate or a particular position.

All the aforementioned approaches towards medieval thought have their own strengths and limitations. Somewhat paradoxically, both the strength *and* the weakness of the neo-Scholastics lay in the same thing, namely, in their quest for a "Christian philosophy." This noble quest was equally motivated by their genuine appreciation of Christian faith and by the rejection of what they took modern philosophy and culture to be. This is not to deny that these scholars accomplished wonderful work

---

2. My comparison draws on Rosemann, "Introduction. A Change of Paradigm," 1–17, without, however, following his exposition in all details.

matching modern academic standards. Indeed, for their editions of texts every reader of medieval philosophy should be grateful. However, in their quest for an alternative to philosophical positivism, the neo-Scholastics proved to be very much children of their own age: they were as much determined by a modern, scientific world-view as the enemy they set out to fight. Although in discovering the "philosophia perennis," they were trying to find an alternative to modern philosophy, in fact, they only reconstructed their own version of Thomist thought in order to fight—for the most part—rather desperate cultural battles. It is small wonder that, generally speaking, their approach has lost its attraction today. Even though neo-Thomist thought has not yet completely disappeared from the academic world, its traditional form became rather obsolete and isolated.[3]

Analytic philosophy, on the other hand, have had from the beginning the advantages of a more limited and modest philosophical enterprise. The analytic philosopher needs not to be bothered with a vain attempt at resurrecting medieval thought. He or she can be content with analyzing medieval texts with the all the technical finesse of modern logic and semantic analysis. The more modest scope of this approach, in fact, prescribes both the methods and the aims of this philosophical enterprise. However, precisely this well-defined and modest character can make the analytic philosopher blind to other, less apparent dimensions of medieval thought. In this way, the strength *and* the weakness of the analytic approach are also connected with each other. When, namely, the analytic philosopher identifies philosophical problems in a medieval text by applying the standards of modern analytic philosophy, the special historical character of past discussions can easily escape his or her attention. Furthermore, it is something of a truism that even apart from the problem of the correct interpretation of medieval thought, within the contemporary academic context the analytic way of handling philosophical problems is only one possibility among others. At least it seems unlikely that analytic philosophy alone could exhaust the philosophical meaning of medieval texts or any other philosophical text for that matter.

---

3. Cf. Rosemann, "Introduction. A Change of Paradigm," 4: "there is no point in flogging a dead horse. For Neoscholasticism is dead; mainly, I think, because it lost the institutional support of the Catholic Church after the Second Vatican council."

As far as my methodology is concerned, it is not difficult to see how it could function as a corrective for both of these former approaches. I write *corrective*, because there is nothing in my approach that would discredit the methodology of the analytic one. The practitioner of my approach is able to profit from the conceptual analysis of analytic philosophy. However, he or she is also in a position to recognize and transcend the self-imposed limits of analytic philosophy. Admittedly, my approach has some affinity with the neo-Scholastic enterprise, but it is also significantly different. Both of these approaches towards medieval thought reveal an appreciation for its religious inspiration and content, but the researcher focusing on the formal aspect can avoid more easily the danger of interpreting medieval thought according to the standards set by modern science. Thus he or she is less liable to come up with a rationalistic interpretation of medieval texts.[4]

I have already referred to those contemporary philosophical attempts that try to understand religious faith or religious "knowledge" in terms of a certain human practice.[5] The distinction between form and content, practical and theoretical dimension makes clear that while my methodology aims at a recovery of medieval wisdom, I do not deny modern achievements. There is no reason for discarding the "content" or the data of much modern knowledge. Rather, I acknowledge this dimension, and at the same time I evoke another way of looking at the same data. Hence, my approach seems to have the same scope of inquiry as more traditional neo-Scholasticism, but its own relationship with modernity is clearer, and its cultural inspirations are more humble. Note that this last feature is not completely extrinsic to my approach, because a researcher who has recognized the limitations of his or her project from the outset will be less likely to become entangled in desperate cultural battles for resurrecting a civilization long lost and gone.

Thus, my approach is less apologetical than neo-Scholasticism without being merely analytical. It lies closest to the more historically interested research. Indeed, it seems that much of contemporary research into medieval thought displays a similar humility. One is not interested in crude generalizations. Sweeping statements are to be wisely avoided. Caution is called forth against vain attempts to actual-

---

4. Naturally enough the danger of a theological rationalism can be also more easily avoided in this approach.

5. See my sixth chapter.

ize hastily and unwittingly medieval thought. However, if a researcher follows my methodology, he or she will not only share this humility with historical research, but must also reflect on the existential importance of medieval knowledge.[6] In order to shed light on this practical importance of knowledge, the researcher can make use of a medieval evaluative scheme for this reflection.[7] Besides this existential-practical orientation of medieval thought, its essentially symbolic-religious and teleological character are also emphasized. In focusing on these dimensions of medieval thought, the researcher is not only more attentive to historical reality but also realizes that the same issues are still with us—even if nowadays they usually remain silent in academic discussions.

This is an important point, because in spite of the huge cultural differences, medievals and we (post)moderns still inhabit the same human world. Sometimes, when we try to understand our world, we are confronted with the same basic problems. This does not entail that we will always and necessarily share the same answers, but nevertheless it is possible that moderns can learn something from medieval questions and from the ways medievals answered those questions. Particularly, the questions concerning the existential-practical importance or the aim of knowledge for human life are still meaningful today. Nor has the symbolic dimension of human life been completely silenced.[8] An important advantage of approaching medieval thought with Jos Decorte's inspiration is that this approach teaches a specific sensitivity to these dimensions. Its special strength should be seen in its practical, *formal* focus.

The Limits of Wisdom

In the *Prolegomena*, the meaning of this formal dimension of knowing was interpreted with the help of a distinction between form and content of knowing. The same distinction can be also expressed with Gilbert

---

6. In this sense my approach to medieval texts can be called "hermeneutical" in contrast to more positivist and less existential readings of historical documents.

7. As I showed in the *Prolegomena*, knowledge considered from a medieval perspective cannot be mere knowledge but must necessarily have an importance for one's life.

8. Cf. Dupré, "Negative Theology," 101–2: "The loss of perspectiveness for religious symbols, however, does not mean that the sense of the symbolic has disappeared althogether. The opposite is the case. I doubt whether any previous age has seen a more powerful explosion of symbolic creativity as we witness today."

Ryle's words: "[L]earning *how* or improving in ability is not like learning *that* or acquiring information."⁹ Ryle's analysis reaffirms the distinction between the form and the content of knowledge. He emphasizes that

> Misunderstanding is a by-product of knowing *how*.... Mistakes are exercises of competences.... Misinterpretations are not always due to the inexpertness or carelessness of the spectator; they are due sometimes to the carelessness and sometimes to the cunning of agent or speaker. Sometimes, again, both are exercising all due skill and care ...¹⁰

Ryle is an important twentieth-century philosopher, because he recognizes the difference between the two dimensions of knowing so crucial for my study. He warns the reader that: "the ability to appreciate a performance does not involve the same degree of competence as the ability to execute it."¹¹ This entails that following my approach, the researcher will be able to take up a better position for appreciating medieval thought, but this in itself does not necessarily mean that he or she will also able to think in a similar—medieval—way when confronted with his or her own problems. Note, however, that the same general criticism can be leveled against any kind of intellectual competence. Learning to like and appreciate something is only the first step, but it is a necessary step.¹² Those who have ever learned a competence know that this is true. As Ryle writes:

> Of course, to execute an operation intelligently is not exactly the same thing as to follow its execution intelligently. The agent is originating, the spectator is only contemplating. But the rules which the agent observes and the criteria which he applies are one with those which govern the spectator's applause and jeers. The commentator on Plato's philosophy need not possess much philosophic originality, but if he cannot, as too many commentators cannot, appreciate the force, the drift or motive of a philosophical argument, his comments will be worthless. If he can appreciate them, then he knows how to do part of what Plato knew how to do.¹³

---

9. Ryle, *Concept of Mind*, 58.
10. Ibid.
11. Ibid., 55.
12. It is very unlikely that anyone will ever achieve any excellence in any field, if he or she is not able to appreciate the performances of others in the same field.
13. Ryle, *Concept of Mind*, 53–54.

In other words, "[T]he author is leading and the spectator is following, but their path is the same."[14] This statement squares well with a manuductive reading of such Cusanian works as the *DI*, the *DVD*, the *PF* or the *CA*, thus Ryle's observation is applicable to the present study itself. It suggests that if a researcher is both ready and able to learn from other, alternative approaches towards medieval thought, this should be regarded as an advantage for his own approach. More fundamentally, Ryle's special emphasis on the practical character of understanding in terms of a skill or competence confirms my claim that information in itself is not sufficient. Ryle is pointing again towards the *formal* character of knowing. In this way his analysis helps me to identify the special strength of my chosen methodology.

This is not to say that medieval thought cannot be understood by focusing more on its theoretical dimensions and it is evident that I cannot completely dispense with theory. Understanding medieval thought as a form of theorizing is possible and intellectual methodology does not necessarily fail. Naturally enough, theorizing has its own advantages, but it does have its own limitations too. Consequently, an approach focusing exclusively on theory can make sense of medieval thought—but only to some extent. Note again that the same general truth also holds for every other approach.

Returning to the concrete execution of my approach in relation with Nicholas of Cusa, it seems obvious to the reader of Jos Decorte's work that a Cusanian inspiration influenced and to a considerable extent even determined Decorte's own approach to medieval thought. If this is true, then the fact that an approach inspired by Decorte is applicable to Nicholas's enterprise is far from being a world-shaking discovery. The least I was able to show that applicability through a systematic examination of concrete features of Nicholas of Cusa's thought. Thereby the approach in question has been both tested *and* justified. This is important because, the Cusanian influence in itself does not entail the success of the Decortian approach—not even in relation to Nicholas and much less to other medieval thinkers.

Furthermore, the references in my *Prolegomena* and the examination of other medieval thinkers have shown that the same *sapiential* understanding has roots elsewhere. In this respect, a further inquiry into Jean Gerson's work seems to be especially promising—not the

---

14. Ibid., 54.

least for the question of terminology.¹⁵ John of Segovia's and John of Torquemada's respective cases seem to be quite clear, partly because of Nicholas's (for the most part silent) criticism of and self-distanciation from these two thinkers. Although Nicholas generally avoided mentioning Ramón Lull, the comparison of their respective epistemologies shows well the latter's shortcomings—even if Gerson's criticism is not taken into consideration.

Interestingly, it is Thomas Aquinas who does not completely fit the proposed *sapiential* scheme. Although some ambiguities can be recognized with relation to the other examined figures, it is not difficult to identify their epistemological-moral shortcomings. The fact that on the whole neither *superbia* nor *vana curiositas* characterize Thomas's thought signals that his case is different, yet his position does not need to trouble a *sapiential* evaluation. One can simply say that on the scale of medieval *sapientia*, Nicholas scored better than Thomas, but this does not necessarily means that the latter was unwise.¹⁶ This suggests that more research is desirable both for determining Thomas's position from the point of view of *sapientia* and for highlighting both the origins and the applicability of a *sapiential* evaluation. A more thorough examination of Thomas and other medieval intellectuals can only deepen this *sapiential* understanding of the Middle-Ages and will offer interesting contributions for testing the limits of a Decortian approach.

On Empathy and Sympathy

When considering the strength of my methodology, one has to realize that this approach presupposes the researcher's ability to effect a certain imaginative transfer in order to appreciate a form of medieval thought as genuinely medieval. Although this imaginative transfer must be differentiated both from empathy and moral sympathy, it can result in both. Most probably, one would progress in the following way: first imagination, then developing empathy, and finally coming to a certain

---

15. See my second chapter.

16. In his *ScG* Thomas himself tried to do the task of the wise. On the other hand, recent research established that in many respects his thought cannot be regarded as typical of the Middle Ages. Although e.g., Thomas's *ST* being a handbook for students offers good summaries on different issues of medieval theology, Thomas's own thought was already preparing Modernity.

sympathy for the object of one's research. Note that this is only a possible line of development and does not imply a necessary movement.

However, strictly speaking, neither empathy nor sympathy forms a necessarily starting point for understanding the Middle-Ages. Academic objectivity must come first. On the other hand, it is difficult to see how one can appreciate a thinker from a distant past without using his or her own imagination. As it was pointed out earlier, a more neutral, restricted, and theoretically oriented research can already achieve something, i.e. theoretical understanding. It would be absurd to deny the theoretical dimension of knowledge and exclude this dimension while approaching medieval texts. It is also clear that with empathy and sympathy one can go further. Neither of these necessarily endangers a claim on objectivity and a critical stance, although they certainly need a check from understanding. Clearly, the theoretical dimension of knowing will have an important role in such a critique.

The importance of this reflection on theory and empathy/sympathy can be also understood from the following consideration. When a person is confronted with something as complex and strange as medieval culture, it is very likely that he or she will have an emotional-moral stance towards this phenomenon. In and by itself, such a spontaneous reaction can be either positive or negative. This feeling can either stay or go away, but its presence indicates that in a sense there is no absolutely neutral starting point for an inquiry into medieval thought. The modern tendency for denying this emotional reaction in itself offers no guarantee for objectivity. Naturally, this holds true both for a more welcoming or a more repudiating attitude.[17] Leaving simply one's own reaction out of consideration will not solve the problem of interpretation and the very fact that such human emotions are often mixed already indicates the complexity of the situation.

On Nostalgia and Religious Ideology

There is probably a more serious objection against my appreciation of medieval thought as I put it forward in the present study. If the previous point about the complexity of emotional reactions is granted, still a rather complex emotion can be said to be operative throughout my

17. For instance, claiming that antipathy is ultimately justified and sympathy is bad faith, does not help one any further.

methodology. It can be argued that the driving force of this approach is a craving for a past long lost. In this way, my search for resurrecting wisdom could be unmasked as a fanciful form of *nostalgia*. The complexity of such an emotional reaction will not save me, because it is possible to describe *nostalgia*—at least for the most part—as an irrational desire. Since the medieval world is for ever gone, its wisdom can never be resurrected. Therefore, any attempt to effect such a resurrection will be necessarily useless and vain.

Here, I have no intention to analyze the notion of *nostalgia*. Nor do I want to argue against those who are not interested in anything that strikes them as strange and alien to (post-)modern tastes and standards.[18] Instead, I would like to make explicit one important reason for such an uncomplicated refusal of non-modern forms of knowing. This reason is to be sought beyond doubt in the sharp contrast between the fundamentally religious character of medieval culture and the essentially secular character of our own world. As it was said in the *Prolegomena*, neither the reality of this cultural fact nor its importance for the interpretation of medieval thought can be denied. This cultural difference makes also understandable that some of our contemporaries would certainly be hostile to any appreciation of a fundamentally religious mode of thinking—may it be put forward by any kind of methodology whatsoever. It is seems clear to me that such a hostile attitude is at least partly motivated by a fear from any form of religious ideology. There was a real danger of ideological deployment of religion during the Middle-Ages and the same danger is still with us today. Indeed the same danger is present in any form of thought—be it (post-)modern or medieval. I will come back to the question of ideology later. Here, I only want to emphasize that nothing what has been said so far amounts to denying the fact that within medieval culture, religion could or did work as a form of ideology. My approach at least makes clear that religion did and can do much more than that.[19]

---

18. Cf. Lewis, "De audendis Poetis," 3–4: "I have lived nearly sixty years with myself and my own century and am not so enamoured of either as to desire no glimpse of a world beyond them." The context of this remark is, naturally, literary and not directly philosophical.

19. Foucault already pointed out that the fact that science worked (also) as ideology does not entail that science's claim on truth can be denied.

On (Post-)Modernity

Another important characteristic of my approach is its self-conscious humility or reflexive character. As I have shown, by taking up the medieval perspective, a researcher will be able to learn also from non-medieval thinkers. It was also demonstrated that he or she can also both criticize others and at the same time remain humbly conscious of the limitations of his or her own approach. First, I will first briefly show how one can evaluate more modern forms of though with the help of a critical medieval perspective and in the next section I will address the question of humility.

As far as modern thought is concerned its self-assurance is often criticized by so-called post-modern intellectuals. Although technically speaking Friedrich Nietzsche (1844–1900) himself was not a post-modern, nevertheless he can be rightly considered as a fore-runner and even ur-father of this movement. His hermeneutics of the will-to-power (*Wille zur Macht*) as the ultimate interpretative key to all reality and all form of human discourse was explicitly directed against the presumptions of modern philosophy. In a similar way, post-modern thinkers consciously react to the arrogance of modern rationality. Viewing it from a medieval perspective, it is possible to recognize and to some extent appreciate this criticism. From such a point of view, modernity with its claim on absolute, neutral, objective, and scientific truth displays the excessive intellectual pretensions of *superbia*.

However, the Decortian approach does not only identify the shortcomings of modernity in the loss of a symbolic vision, but it also helps one to form a critical judgment on post-modernity itself. Post-modern thought, thus seen, appears similar to modern thought, because in both of them human rationality misses its proper end. Both modern and post-modern thought display an inability for recognizing the fundamental role of engagement for reason.[20] From a medieval perspective, both forms of human rationality appear as vain (*ad frustra*). However, when post-modern thought is compared with modern thinking, it is more appropriate to identify the former one as an instance of *vana curiositas mundi*.[21] Modern and post-modern thought appear to be mirror

---

20. Cf. the discussion of the *Prolegomena*.

21. If post-modernity is rightly understood as a conscious reaction against the arrogance and pretensions of modern rationality, this excludes the possibility of *superbia*.

images of each other: they mutually reflect the extreme criticism of the other one's extreme claims.

A Middle-Course with Hard Work: A Philosophy of Final Human Rationality

The previous discussion indicates that a *sapiential* thinking should not only be able to point out these extremes, but it should offer more than the criticized forms of thought. Its own standards prescribe that only if this approach reveals itself as a middle-position between the two extremes, can it be a viable alternative. If it cannot avoid the respective extremes of modern and post-modern thought, then its criticism will turn against itself.

For the most part, both modernity and post-modernity seem to presuppose a distinction, i.e., the sharp contrast between the theoretical and the practical dimensions of knowledge, which was alien to pre-modern thought. The parallel (post-)modern inability to relate these two dimensions of human life to each other is also significant. While the label 'practical' suggests engagement the label 'theoretical' implies non-engagement or neutrality. Once this distinction has been made and realized—as sharply as since modernity—it cannot be simply denied. Nevertheless, the question of integrating these two dimensions remains open. My foregoing discussion suggests that if the (post-)modern thinker wants to come to terms with this problem, he or she could learn something helpful from the message of pre-modern voices. Once, the ancient-medieval meaning of "theory" included both a critical stance and a consciousness of engagement. Without attacking or destroying (post-)modern knowledge, a Decortian approach to medieval thought can help to recapture a positive dimension of the pre-modern attitude.

This is an important point, because, realistically speaking, while theory is different from practice, it only acquires its full meaning within or in relation to the practice. Once they lost contact with the practical context, different forms of modern thought—just to name two: Hegelian philosophy or Marxism—have run the danger of becoming an *ideology*. The same holds true not only for (post-)modern enterprises, but also

---

The post-modern reaction is reasonable and well-motivated, but in becoming excessive, it makes the opposite mistake than modernity.

for any kind of theorizing whatsoever. Alasdair MacIntyre's following reminder is worth of a quote:

> Just as the propositions of scientific theorizing are not to be either understood or evaluated in abstraction from their relationships to the practices of scientific enquiry within which they are proposed, revised, and accepted or rejected, so it is too with other bodies of propositions. Detach any type of theorizing from the practical contexts in which it is legitimately at home, whether scientific, theological or political, and let it become a free-floating body of thought and it will be all too apt to be transformed into an ideology.[22]

In other words, the very inability of integrating theory with practice carries in itself the danger of an ideological deployment. This danger is not specifically related to religious ways of thinking. Furthermore, MacIntyre realizes the fundamental importance of engagement for any kind of theory:

> [M]etaphysics [is] a commitment that can never be fully justified. . . . human thought, human rationality always tends to be too abstract, and not to allow for the independence of those structures which man in society has created. There is an unpredictability here which is not to be overcome by more human cleverness but only by a greater humility, by a greater recognition of the limitation of human thought and action.[23]

MacIntyre's attitude is very close to the spirit of my study.[24] Both attitudes point towards the limitations of human thought and both call for a recognition of these limitations. Thereby, both refer to the virtue of humility.

Humility means both accepting one's own limitations *and* at the same time believing in something beyond these limitations. For the medieval man, humility had to do with acknowledging and accepting one's own place: as a creature a human person is not the Creator, nevertheless

---

22. MacIntyre, *Marxism*, xxix.
23. MacIntyre as quoted in McMylor, *Alasdair MacIntyre*, 16.
24. Cf. McMylor, *Alasdair MacIntyre*, 17: "MacIntyre's Christian humanism and its sense of finitude, expressed as the Christian virtue of humility, provides a sure defence against the dangers of a totalitarian Stalinist Marxism and a valuable inoculation against the later anti-humanist (and strongly atheistic) structuralist Marxism. . . . MacIntyre is rare among philosophers, at least as a professional group, in formally recognising the socially located particularity and self-interest of intellectuals and theorists."

as a creature he or she is created unto God's Image. Interestingly, the same conviction that denied that humans are the ultimate source of meaning of all reality did not deny the existence of an ultimate meaning. That is to say medieval rationality reinforced both the existence *and* the transcendent character of this meaning. In this respect, modernity and post-modernity seem to realize respectively only one part of the truth. While the latter attacks the pretentiousness of a universal rational discourse, the former insist on the inherent rational character of reality. What both of these forms of thought miss is the courage of a humble acceptance of a fundamentally transcendent meaning.

A Final Biblical Note on Wisdom

If the reader of my study wants a final word on my Decortian appreciation of a medieval thought, the following *sapiential* text seems to be a fitting summary:

> Who is among you wise and understanding? Let him show his good works by a good life in the humility that comes from wisdom. But if you have bitter jealousy and selfish ambition in your hearts, do not boast and be false to the truth. . . . the wisdom from above is first of all pure, then peaceable, gentle, compliant, full of mercy and good fruits, without inconstancy or insincerity. And the fruit of righteousness is sown in peace for those who cultivate peace.[25]

This text strongly suggest that true justice, even justice shown towards the philosophical opponent or to the religious Other can only be a result of hard work. But the metaphor of harvest also reminds us that we can never be certain of the result. The harvest of justice—as any kind of harvest—is not something ready-made and given from the outset. Its fruit can be only attained through a ripening process that starts with the modesty of wisdom. Only by maintaining this modesty, with a continuous openness to reasoning, and sincerely practiced mercy will this ripening process give practical proof of wisdom. Wisdom in the making? Rather living wisdom—animated by the recognition and acceptance of its own finality.

---

25. Jas 3:13–14, 17–18.

Epilogue

You enrapture me, in order that I may transcend myself.[1]

—Nicholas of Cusa

The man who is contended to be only himself, and therefore less than a self, is in prison. My own eyes are not enough for me, I will see through those of others.... I transcend myself; and am never more myself than when I do.[2]

—C. S. Lewis

IN SUCH TIMES AS OURS, IN TIMES OF DESPERATE LOSSES, DESTRUCTION and desolation prophets are needed to show us the way. In the course of my study, we have been honoring the memories of some such prophets. We have been listening to their voices, carefully examined their words and deeds and explored their perspectives. No matter how great or laborious these efforts have been, it should be still borne in mind, that my study is not meant as an easy summary either of Professor Jos Decorte's contribution to philosophy or that of Nicholas of Cusa's thought. Much less can I offer a comprehensive picture of such other great thinkers as Thomas of Aquinas, Ramón Lull, Jean Gerson, John of Segovia or John of Torquemada. Perhaps, any attempt to summaries these thinkers could be just vain curiosity or else it can easily produce an instance of intellectual pride. I believe that in the case of Jos Decorte and Nicholas of Cusa, such an attempt would be most probably both arrogant and curious.

Yet, I cherish the sincere hope that at its best my study itself can be read as a *manuductio*. While it is undoubtedly an academic effort to make sense of—and thereby also to actualize—some mediaeval approaches towards Islam, the *way* it functions is equally important. I wish myself a reader who has at least some trust, who will take the hand

---

1. *DVD* 25, 113:10–11: "Rapis me, ut sim supra me ipsum."
2. Lewis, *An Experiment*, 141–42.

offered, will follow and—most important of all—who will be ready to learn not to reduce the Mystery of Being to any limited category of finite human thought. Needless to say taking up the role of a *manuductor* cannot be a pretext for deflecting and thereby avoiding criticism. Rather, the contrary must be true: only after the reader has faithfully followed the way as it is shown on the previous pages, will he or she be in a position to critically evaluate my manuductive enterprise. My reader will decide whether the initial trust was deserved and whether it served him or her well—whether this way has effectively led him or her closer to wisdom and made him or her see the visible in and beyond the invisible.

Evidently both Jos Decorte and Nicholas of Cusa hold a very special place within my study and the reason for my preference for these thinkers can be gathered from the previous pages. An epilogue usually offers the additional possibility of explaining such a preference in a more personal and less academic manner. As I believe that such a testimony may be beneficiary and revealing I will take up the opportunity and confess that these two men are important to me personally. I find that both of them had something in common, something that is very unique indeed: in their intellectual inquiries they avoided both vanity and pride.

Admittedly, Nicholas of Cusa sometimes showed signs of intellectual arrogance and intolerance. To form a balanced and correct judgment on him as a person is far from being an easy task. As Donald F. Duclow's writes

> [H]is philosophical and theological writings set high standards for self-criticism, tolerance, dialogue, and the Christian life that few—in the fifteenth century or today—could easily live up to. So we should be surprised not that he failed to live up to these standards, but rather that he sometimes ... fell so far short of them. For better or worse, his long and entangled career illustrates the difficulties of thinking and living well in the fifteenth century.[3]

Nonetheless, successful as Nicholas was, a son of a Moselle merchant—at last made a cardinal—he came to value the simple layman whom he saw in a better position to attain true wisdom than the scholastic intellectual. Nicholas understood all too well that all human

---

3. Duclow, "Life and Work," 50.

knowledge is conjectural and thus no one has the right to boast. Yet, he did not give up either inquiry or hope—not even in the face of the fateful confrontation with Islam. In Jos Decorte's case, however, his complete lack of self-interest and the utter simplicity of his manners were manifest to everyone. Probably it was not a coincidence that he liked Nicholas so much. Both men humbly desired wisdom and perhaps had an air of wise humility.

I may be mistaken, but as far as I can see, these are not fashionable intellectual virtues nowadays. So much the worse for us. The need to realize their values seems to be imminent. Humility and wisdom belong together. One cannot have the one without the other. These virtues teach us to accept our human condition and shine forth in our everyday dimness as lights of hope. Most important of all: they shine the brighter the deeper the darkness closing in around us.

To me, this also means that ultimately my study will end on a hopeful note. This is not to forget the past failures or to deny the present tragedies, since it is all too obvious that the Other is not always reached and well understood. As Nicholas of Cusa himself pointed out several times, there are things hidden even to the wise. One can add that the wise too, do make mistakes and those wise masters who would deserve it do not necessarily receive due attention. Sometimes, true masters are brutally taken away from the disciple and only time can heal the wounds of the loss.

Yet, after the completion of this study, I cannot despair anymore, since my study has been just as much—or probably even more—of a *manuductio* to its writer as it is meant to become a *manuductio* to its reader. Moreover, it could not even become a *manuductio*—and thus neither a successful study—to the latter without being a humble experience of work to the former. The writing of my study has been indeed an academic experience—mediated by several institutions and assisted by the kindness of many different persons.

I believe that it is possible that such a work can become a kind of symbolic experience. When speaking about a symbolic experience I am especially thinking of something similar to the one described by Jos Decorte's in his last article. Such an experience can both teach humility and give hope. Therefore, it is perhaps only appropriate, that my study should be ended with Jos Decorte's own words:

In this sort of experience man looks intently towards the horizon to make out roughly the outlines of the House—being aware that this can never be wholly done, in truth, it may never be accomplished fully. While being aware of his finality, he certainly avoids the foolishness of pride and the nonsense of vanity and finds thus true wisdom: that of humility.[4]

---

4. See Decorte, "Middeleeuwse," 567. The English translation of the Flemish text was made with the kind assistance of Dr. Guy Guldenstop from the Insitute of Philosophy at the Catholic University of Leuven.

It may be of some interest to the reader that the same passage also recurs in *RA*, 218. There, it is immediately followed with a citation from de Saint-Exupéry's *Le petit prince* that I reproduce here in English:

"Goodbye," said the fox. "And now here is my secret, a very simple secret: It is only with the heart that one can see rightly; what is essential is invisible to the eye."

"What is essential is invisible to the eye," said the Little Prince in order to remember it well.

Appendix

A Note on Tolerance in the Middle-Ages and in Modernity[1]

CLASSICAL LATIN "TOLERATIO" MEANT A BEARING, SUPPORTING OR *enduring*, e.g., enduring pains.[2] The late Latin "tolerator" could designate *one who endures*.[3] "Tolerare" meant *to bear, support,* or *sustain*.[4] Generally speaking, medieval "tolerantia" was a rather pejorative term.[5]

In Modernity, the meaning of this word underwent a radical change, indeed so radical that in contemporary English it only perserved the negative or neutral meaning in medical language where a patient capable of bearing the action of a drug—inured by habit to considerable doses of poisonous drugs without suffering injury—is described as "tolerant," while everyday usage keeps the meaning of being able to resist or endure (e.g., the severties of a climate).[6] The word "tolerant" describes in the first place someone disposed to tolerate or forbearing

---

1. See Decorte, "Ter inleiding," 9–17. Occurrences of phrases and words in classical or medieval works are located with the help of Lewis and Short, *A Latin Dictionary* and the other dictionaries referred to in my footnotes.

2. See "toleratio dolorum" in Cicero's *De Finibus* 2.29,94. Blaise, *Dictionnaire latine-français* gives "usufruit" and "entretien" as two classical meanings of "toleratio."

3. Cf. Augustinus *In Psalmo* 99,11.

4. It is a lengthened form of the root "tol," whence "tollo" and "tuli," kindred with Greek τλαω.
Latin synonyms are "fero," "patior," "sustineo," and "sino." Blaise gives "appuyer," "défendre," and "approuver" as meanings of classical "tolerare."

5. Cf. "muliebris tolerantia" in Salv. *Gub.* 7, 79, meaning "le fait de se laisser traiter comme un femme," i.e. sodomy in plain language; *Gub.* 7, 18, 30 (reference from Blaise).

6. Cf. Wyld, *Universal Dictionary*. This everyday meaning is only one among others.

or indulgent, especially towards opinions and lines of conduct that are not one's own.[7]

Modernity understands tolerance both as a personal virtue and a basic human value, which is also legally sanctioned. This modern understanding rings through, for instance in Locke's *Letters on Tolerance* and Joseph II's (1765-1790 Emperor of the Holy Roman Empire of the German Nation, 1780-1790 king of Hungary) *Decretum tolerantiale*.[8] Another absolute monarch of the Enlightenment period, Frederick II of Prussia (1740-1786) summed up well the modern attitude of toleration in his famous dictum that is related to the question of religion(s):

> All religions must be tolerated and the public administrator must watch out only that no one should cause the other any harm, because here every one must attain salvation according to his own fashion.[9]

Thus, today "tolerance" is seen as something postive and desirable. "Toleration" in this sense is the opposite of bigotry. It is an act of tolerating while its mental conterpart is a disposition to allow freedom of opinion and belief towards Others. The word also refers to a (legal) practice of allowing such freedom, especially in religious beliefs. The term *"tolerationalist"* denotes a person who advocates toleration—especially in religious issues.[10]

---

7. Cf. Wyld, *Universal Dictionary*.

8. "Türelmi Rendelet" in Hungarian. Cf. Bartal, *Glossarium*: "[Joseph] Edicto *Tolerantiali* protestantes Hungaros ab interitu vindicat."

Later, in the legal language of the nineteenth century "tollelare" (a version of "tolerare") meant to *bear with* or *put up with* (Hungarian "elviselni").

9. Quoted in Hagemann, *Christentum contra Islam*, 103: "Die Religionen Müssen alle Toleriret werden, und Mus der Fiscal nuhr das Auge darauf haben, das keine der andern abtrug Tuhe, den hier mus ein jeder nach Seiner Faßon Selich werden." The "public administrator" (German "Fiscal") was the representant of the prince at the courts of law in Germany. For the accurate interpretation of this sentence my gratitude is due to my late confrere Miksa Bánhegyi OSB (1928-2009), erstwhile librarian and my former teacher at the Archabbey of Pannonhalma.

See also Hagemann's treatment of Lessing's *Nathan der Weise*, ibid., 99-102. A key expression in the famous poem is "kind tolerating" (German "herzliche Verträglichkeit").

10. Cf. Wyld, *Universal Dictionary*.

Bibliography

Primary sources

Nicholas of Cusa

(Latin *Nicolaus Cusanus*, German *Nikolaus von Kues*, Dutch *Nicolaas van Cusa*)

———. *A Concise Introduction to the Philosophy of Nicholas of Cusa. Trialogus de Possest: On Actualized-possibility.* Translated by Jasper Hopkins. Minneapolis: Banning, 1978.

———. *Cribratio Alkorani: Sichtung des Korans.* Philosophische Bibliothek. Translated by Ludwig Hagemann and Reinhold Glei. Hamburg: Meiner, I–1989, II–1990, III–1993.

———. *De Concordantia Catholica. Liber Tertius.* Edited by Gerhard Kallen. Nicolai de Cusa Opera omnia Vol. XIV. Hamburg: Meiner, 1959.

———. *De coniecturis.* 3rd ed. Philosophische Bibliothek. Translated by Josef Koch and Winfried Happ. Hamburg: Meiner, 2002.

———. *De docta ignorantia. Liber primus.* 4th ed. Philosophische Bibliothek. Translated by Paul Wilpert and edited by Hans G. Senger. Hamburg: Meiner, 1994.

———. *De docta ignorantia. Liber secundus.* 3rd ed. Philosophische Bibliothek. Translated by Paul Wilpert and edited by Hans G. Senger. Hamburg: Meiner, 1999.

———. *De docta ignorantia. Liber tertius.* Philosophische Bibliothek. Translated by Hans G. Senger. Hamburg: Meiner, 1977.

———. *De Pace Fidei. Cum epistola ad Iohannem de Segobia.* Nicolai de Cusa Opera Omnia Vol. VII. Edited by Raymund Klibansky and Hildebrand Bascour. Leipzig: Meiner, 1970.

———. *De venatione sapientiae.* Philosophische Bibliothek. Translated by Paul Wilpert and Karl Bormann, edited by Raymund Klibansky and Hans G. Senger. Hamburg: Meiner, 2003.

———. *Dialogus De Abscondito Deo.* Edited by Paul Wilpert. Nicolai de Cusa Opera Omnia, Vol. IV, 3–10. Hamburg: Meiner, 1969.

———. "Epistola ad Iohannem de Segobia." In *De Pace Fidei. Cum epistola ad Iohannem de Segobia*, edited by Raymund Klibansky and Hildebrand Bascour, 91–102. Leipzig: Meiner, 1970.

———. *Godsdienstvrede.* Translated by Jos Lievens and Jos Decorte. Kapellen: Pelckmans, 2000.

———. *Het zien van God*. Translated by Inigo Bocken and Jos Decorte. Kapellen: Pelckmans, 1993.

———. *Nicholas of Cusa on God as Not-Other. A Translation and an Appraisal of De Li Non Aliud*. Translated by Jasper Hopkins. Minneapolis: University of Minnesota Press, 1979.

———. *Nicholas of Cusa on Interreligious Harmony: Text, Concordance and Translation of De Pace Fidei*. Edited and translated by James E. Biechler and H. Lawrence Bond. Text and Studies in Religion. Lewiston, NY: Mellen, 1990.

———. *Nicholas of Cusa on Learned Ignorance*. Translated by Jasper Hopkins. Minneapolis: Banning, 1981.

———. *Nicholas of Cusa's Debate with John Wenck. A Translation and an Appraisal of De Ignota Litteratura* and *Apologia Doctae Ignorantiae*. Translated by Jasper Hopkins. Minneapolis: Banning, 1981.

———. *Nicholas of Cusa's De Pace Fidei and Cribratio Alkorani*. Translated by Jasper Hopkins. Minneapolis: Banning, 1990.

———. *Nicholas of Cusa's Dialectical Mysticism. Text, Translation and Interpretative Study of De Visione Dei*. 2nd ed. Translated by Jasper Hopkins. Minneapolis: Banning, 1988.

———. *Selected Spiritual Writings*. Translated by H. Lawrence Bond. The Classics of Western Spirituality. New York: Paulist, 1997.

———. *The Catholic Concordance*. Edited and translated by Paul E. Sigmund. Cambridge: University Press, 1991.

———. "On the hidden God." In *A Miscellany on Nicholas of Cusa*, translated by Jasper Hopkins, 131–37. Minneapolis: Banning, 1994.

———. *Vom Nichtanderen*. 3rd ed. Philosophische Bibliothek. Translated by Paul Wilpert. Hamburg: Meiner, 1987.

Other Primary Literature

Alfaquí. "Carte del alfaquí de Segovia al maestro salamantino." In *Juan de Segovia y el problema islamica*, 273–77. Madrid, 1952.

Aquin, Thomas von. *Summe gegen die Heiden, Erstes Buch*. Translated end edited by Karl Albert et al. Darmstadt: Wissenschaftliche Buchgesellschaft, 1974–1996.

Aquino, Thomas de. "De Rationibus Fidei ad Cantorem Antiochenum." In *Sancti Thomae de Aquino Opera Omnia iussu Leonis XIII. P. M. edita. Tomus XL*. Rome: Sancta Sabina, 1969.

Avicenna Latinus. *Liber de Philosophia Prima sive Scientia Divina. V–X*. Edited and translated by Simone van Riet. Louvain: Peeters, 1980.

Llull, Ramón. "The Book of the Gentile and the Three Wise Men." In *Selected Works of Ramón Llull (1232–1316)*, vol. 1. Translated by Anthony Bonner, 105–304. Princeton: Princeton University Press, 1985.

Sancti Thomae de Aquino Summa Theologiae. 3rd ed. Torino: San Paolo 1999.

Segovia, Juan de. "Sumarios del opusculo 'De mittendo gladio.'" In Cabanelas, Rodriguez, D. *Juan de Segovia y el problema islamica*, 265–72. Madrid: Universidad de Madrid, 1952.

Segovia, Juan de. "Texto de la donacion." In *Biblioteca de Juan de Segovia*, edited by Benigno H. Montes, 73-115. Bibliotheca Theologica Hispana. Madrid: Instituto "Francisco Suarez," 1984.

Bible and Koran Editions

Bibilia Sacra juxta Vulgata. Paris: Letouzey & Ané, 1887.
Novum Testamentum Graece et Latine. 4th ed. Stuttgart: Privilegierte Württenbergische Bibelanstalt, 1912.
The Saint Joseph Edition of the New American Bible. New York: Catholic Book Publishing, 1992.
The Koran: The Bilingual Edition. Translated by Nessim J. Dawood. Penguin Classics. Harmondsworth, UK: Penguin, 1990.

Secondary literature

Auty, Robert et al. *Lexikon des Mittelalters*. München: Artemis / Lexma, 1977-1999.
Bakos, T. Gergely. "'Ki a bölcs közületek' A skolasztikus teológia határaitól a vallásközi párbeszédig." (*'Who is wise among you?' From the limits of scholastic theology to inter-religious dialogue*) Korunk 18/3 (2006) 14-22.
Bakos, Tibor. "Recovering Nicholas's Early Ontology: A reading of the 'De concordantia catholica.'" In *Nicolas de Cues: les méthodes d'une pensée*, edited by Jean-Michel Counet and Stéphane Mercier, 155-73. Louvain-la-Neuve: l'Institut d'Études Médiévales, 2005.
Bakos, Gergely. "The "doctor angelicus" on Islam. Reading Thomas Aquinas's *De Rationibus Fidei*." In *Reflecting Diversity. Historical and Thematical Perspectives in the Jewish and Christian Tradition*, edited by Losonczi Péter and Xeravits Géza, 63-86. Schnittpunkte—Intersections. Münster: LIT, 2007.
Bakos, Gergely Tibor. "The Mirror, the Painter and Infinity. Images and Concepts in the manuductive strategy of De visione Dei." In *Spiegel und Porträt. Zur Bedeutung zweier zentraler Bilder im Denken des Nicolas Cusanus*, edited by Inigo Bocken and Harald Schwaetzer, 231-46. Maastricht: Shaker, 2005.
Bartal, Antal. *Glossarium mediae et infimae latinitatis regni Hungariae*. Leipzig: Teubner, 1901.
Bäumer, Remigius. "Die Erforschung des Konziliarismus." In *Die Entwicklung des Konziliarismus*, 3-56. Darmstadt: Wisssentschaftliche Buchgesellschaft, 1976.

———. "Vorwort." In *Die Entwicklung des Konziliarismus: Werden und Nachwirken der konziliaren Idee*, vii-viii. Darmstadt: Wisssentschaftliche Buchgesellschaft, 1976.
Beierwaltes, Werner. *Der verborgene Gott. Cusanus und Dionysius*. Trier: Paulinus, 1997.

———. "Eriugena und Cusanus." In *Eriugena Redivivus. Zur Wirkungsgeschichte seines Denkens im Mittelalter und im Übergang zur Neuzeit*, edited by Werner Beierwaltes. 311-43. Heidelberg: Winter, 1987.
Biechler, James E. "A New Face Toward Islam: Nicholas of Cusa and John of Segovia." In *Nicholas of Cusa in Search of God and Wisdom: Essays in Honor of Morimichi*

Watanabe by the American Cusanus Society, edited by Gerald Christianson et al., 185–202. Studies in the History of Christian Thought 45. Leiden: Brill, 1991.

Biechler, James E., and H. Lawrence Bond. "Introduction." In *Nicholas of Cusa on Interreligious Harmony: Text, Concordance and Translation of De Pace Fidei*, edited and translated by James E. Biechler and H. Lawrence Bond, ix–xlviii. Lewinston, NY: Mellen, 1990.

Black, Anthony J. *Council and Commune: The Conciliar Movement and the Fifteenth-Century Heritage*. London: Burns & Oates, 1979.

———. *Monarchy and Community: Political Ideas in the Later Conciliar Controversy 1430–1450*. Cambridge: Cambridge University Press, 1970.

Blaise, Albert. *Dictionnaire latine-français des auteurs du moyen-age. Corpus christianorum. Continuatio Mediaeualis. Lexicon latinitatis medii aevii—praesertim ad res ecclesiasticas investigandas pertinens*. Turnhout: Brepols, 1975.

Blum, Paul Richard. "Nicholas of Cusa and Pythagorean Theology." In *Philosophy of Religion in the Renaissance*, 21–42. Surrey, UK: Ashgate, 2010.

———. *Philosophy of Religion in the Renaissance*. Surrey, UK: Ashgate, 2010.

Bocken, Inigo. "Toleranz und Wahrheit bei Nikolaus von Kues." *Philosophisches Jahrbuch* 105 (1998) 241–66.

Bocken, Inigo, and Jos Decorte. "Inleiding." In *Het zien van God*, translated by Inigo Bocken and Jos Decorte, 7–33. Kapellen: Pelckmans, 1993.

Bond, H. Lawrence. "Introduction." In Nicholas of Cusa, *Selected Spiritual Writings*, translated by H. Lawrence Bond, 1–84. New York: Paulist, 1997.

Bonner, Anthony. "Der neue Weg Ramon Lulls." In *Ramon Lull: Buch vom Heiden und den drei Weisen*, by Raimundo Panikkar, et al., 26–31. Freiburg: Herder, 1986.

———. "Introduction." In *Selected Works of Ramón Llull (1232–1316)*, translated by Anthony Bonner, 1:91–103. Princeton: Princeton University Press, 1985.

Borsche, Tilman. "Der Dialog—im Gegensatz zu anderen literarischen Formen der Philosophie—bei Nikolaus von Kues." In *Gespräche lesen: Philosophische Dialoge im Mittelalter*, edited by Klaus Jacobi, 407–33. Tübingen: Gunter Nan, 1999.

Burger, Christoph. *Aedificatio, Fructus, Utilitas: Johannes Gerson als Professor der Theologie und Kanzler der Universität Paris*. Tübingen: Mohr/Siebeck, 1986.

Burms, Arnold. "Disenchantment." *Ethical Perspectives* 1.3 (1994) 145–55.

Bredow. Gerda von. "Einleitung." In *Nicolai de Cusa Dialogus de ludo globi*, translated by Gerda von Bredow. Philosophische Bibliothek. Hamburg: Meiner, 2000.

Cabanelas, Rodriguez, D. "Apéndices." In *Juan de Segovia y el problema islamica*, 263–349. Madrid, 1952.

Cabanelas, Rodriguez, D. *Juan de Segovia y el problema islamica*. Madrid: Universidad de Madrid, 1952.

Cantarino, Vincente. "John of Torquemada's Crusade against Islam." In *Religionsgespräche im Mittelalter*, edited by Bernard Lewis and Friedrich Niewöhner, 237–50. Wiesbaden: Harrassowitz, 1992.

Chazan, Robert. "The Barcelona Disputation of 1263: Goals, Tactics, and Achievements." In *Religionsgespräche im Mittelalter*, edited by Bernard Lewis and Friedrich Niewöhner, 77–91. Wiesbaden: Harrassowitz, 1992.

Christianson, Gerald. *Cesarini: The Conciliar Cardinal: The Basel Years. 1431–1438*. Erzabtei Sankt Ottilien: EOS, 1979.

Churchill, John. "Rat and Mole's Epiphany of Pan: Wittgenstein on Seeing Aspects and Religious Belief." *Philosophical Investigations* 21.2 (1998) 152–72.

Colomer, Eusebio. *Nikolaus von Kues und Raimund Lull. Aus Handschriften der Kueser Bibliothek*. Berlin: de Gruyter, 1961.

———. "Raimund Lulls Stellung zu den Andersgläubigen: Zwischen Zwie—und Streitgespräch." In *Religionsgespräche im Mittelalter*, edited by Bernard Lewis and Friedrich Niewöhner, 216–36. Wiesbaden: Harrassowitz, 1992.

Decorte, Jos. "De fascinatie van het niet-objektiverende denken. Enkele beschouwingen over de mystieke theologie van Nicolaas van Cusa." In *Een inleiding in het denken van Anselmus van Canterbury, Thomas van Aquino, Meester Eckhart en Nicolaas van Cusa*, edited by Harry Berghs, 117–58. Leuven: Acco, 1995.

———. "De man van het millenium. Over lezen in een geloofs—en geloven in een leescultuur." In *Kijken naar de zon. Filosofische essays over de godsvraag. Opgedragen aan Jan Van der Veken*, edited by Luc Braeckmans and André Cloots, 359–96. Antwerp: Pelckmans, 1998.

———. *Eine kurze Geschichte der mittelalterlichen Philosophie*. Translated by Inigo Bocken and Matthias Laarman. Paderborn: Schöningh, 2006.

———. "Geschichte und Eschatologie. Vom Nutzen und Nachteil der Historie für das mittelalterliche Leben." In *Ende und Vollendung:Eschatologische Perspektiven im Mittelalter*, edited by Jan Aertsen and Martin Pickavé, 150–61. Berlin: de Guyter, 2002.

———. "Middeleeuwse en hedendaagse appreciatie van de liefdesmystiek." *Tijdschrift voor Filosofie* 63 (2001) 543–68.

———. *Raak me niet aan. Over middeleeuwse en postmiddeleeuwse transcendentiedenken*. Kapellen: Pelckmans, 2001.

———. "Relation and Substance in Henry of Ghent's Metaphysics." In *Henry of Ghent and the Transformation of Scholastic Thought: Studies in Memory of Jos Decorte*, edited by Guy Guldentops et al., 3–14. Leuven: Leuven University Press, 2003.

———. "Sapientia: Between Superbia and Vanitas". In *Meeting of the Minds. The Relations between Mediaeval and Classical Modern European Philosophy*, edited by Stephen F. Brown, 477–506. Turnhout: Brepols, 1998.

———. "Ter inleiding." *Nicolaas van Cusa: Godsdienstvrede*. Translated by Jos Lievens, 7–46. Kapellen: Pelckmans, 2000.

———. "Tolerance and Trinity." In *Conflict and Reconciliation: Perspectives on Nicholas of Cusa*, edited by Inigo Bocken, 107–18. Brill's Studies in Intellectual History 126. Leiden: Brill, 2004.

———. *Waanzin van het intellect. Twee modellen van de eeuwige strijd tusssen goed en kwaad*. Kapellen: Pelckmans, 1989.

———. *Waarheid als weg. Beknopte geschiedenis van de middeleeuwse wijsbegeerte*. Kapellen: Pelckmans, 1992.

Denzinger, Henricus, and Adolfus Schönmetzer. *Enchiridion symbolorum: Definitionum et Declarationum de rebus fidei et morum*. 32nd ed. Freiburg im Breisgau: Herder, 1963.

Domínguez, Fernando. "Der Religionsdialog bei Raimundus Lullus. Apologetische Prämissen und kontemplative Grundlage." In *Gespräche lesen: Philosophische Dialoge im Mittelalter*, edited by Jacobi Klaus, 263–90. Tübingen: Gunter Nan, 1999.

Duclow, Donald F. "Life and Work." In *Introducing Nicholas of Cusa: A Guide to a Renaissance Man*, edited by Christopher M. Bellito et al., 25–56. New York: Paulist, 2004.

Dupré, Louis. "Negative Theology and Religious Symbols." In *Religious Mystery and Rational Reflection: Excursions in the Phenomenology of Religion*, 92–103. Grand Rapids: Eerdmans, 1998.

———. "Spiritual Life in a Secular Age." In *Religious Mystery and Rational Reflection*, 131–43. Grand Rapids: Eerdmans, 1998.

———. "Truth in Religion and Truth of Religion." In *Religious Mystery and Rational Reflection*, 19–40. Grand Rapids: Eerdmans, 1998.

Endres, Rudolf. "Nicolaus Cusanus und das Kloster Tegernsee." In *Nicholas of Cusa. A Mediaeval Thinker for the Modern Age*, edited by Yamaki Kazuhiko, 134–44. London: Curzon, 2002.

Franzen, A. "Konziliarismus." In *Die Entwicklung des Konziliarismus*, edited by Bäumer R. Remigius, 75–81. Darmstadt: Wisssentschaftliche Buchgesellschaft, 1976.

Fromherz, Uta. *Johannes von Segovia als Geschichtsschreiber des Konzil von Basel*. Basel: von Helbing & Lichtenhahn, 1960.

Gauthier, René-Antoine, *Introduction: Saint Thomas d'Aquin, Somme contre les gentils*. Paris: Editions Universitaires, 1993.

Goddard, Hugh. *A History of Christian-Muslim Relations*. Islamic Surveys. Edinburgh: Edinburgh University Press, 2000.

Haubst, Rudolf. "Die Wege der christologische manuductio." In *Der Friede unter den Religionen nach Nikolaus von Kues*, edited by Rudolf Haubst, 164–82 (discussion: 182–91). Mainz: Matthias Grünewald, 1984.

———. "Johannes von Segovia im Gespräch mit Nikolaus von Kues und Jean Germain über die göttliche Dreieinigkeit und ihre Verkündigung vor den Mohammedanern." *Münchener Theologische Zeitschrift* 2 (1951) 115–29.

Hagemann, Ludwig. *Christentum contra Islam. Eine Geschichte gescheiterter Beziehungen*. Darmstadt: Primus, Wissenschaftliche Buchgesellschaft, 1999.

———. "Einleitung." In *Cribratio Alkorani: Sichtung des Korans*, translated by Ludwig Hagemann and Reinhold Glei, vii–xix. Hamburg: Meiner, 1989.

———. *Der Kur'an in Verständnis und Kritik bei Nikolaus von Kues. Ein Beitrag zur Erhellung islamisch–christlicher Geschichte*. Frankfurter theologische Studien. Frankfurt: Knecht, 1976.

Happ, Winfried. "Anmerkungen." In *De coniecturis*. 3rd ed. Translated by Josef Koch and Winfried Happ, 218–28. Hamburg: Meiner, 2002.

———. "Einführung des Herausgebers." In *De coniecturis*, 3rd ed., translated by Josef Koch and Winfried Happ, ix–xxi. Hamburg: Meiner, 2002.

Hillgarth, Jocelyn N. *Ramon Lull and Lullism in the Fourteenth Century France*. Oxford-Warburg Studies. Oxford: Clarendon, 1971.

Hoping, Helmut. *Weisheit als Wissen des Ursprungs. Philosophie und Theologie in der "Summa contra gentiles" des Thomas von Aquin*. Freiburg in Breisgau: Herder, 1997.

Hopkins, Jasper. "Introduction." In *Nicholas of Cusa's De Pace Fidei and Cribratio Alkorani*, 3–29. Minneapolis: Banning, 1990.

———. "Islam and the West: Ricoldo Montecroce and Nicholas of Cusa." In *A Miscellany on Nicholas of Cusa*, 57–97. Minneapolis: Banning, 1994.

———. "John of Torquemada's *Evidentes Rationes*." In *A Miscellany on Nicholas of Cusa*, 99–118. Minneapolis: Banning, 1994.

———. *A Miscellany on Nicholas of Cusa*. Minneapolis: Banning, 1994.

———. "The Role of *pia interpretatio* in Nicholas of Cusa's Hermeneutical Approach to the Koran." In *A Miscellany on Nicholas of Cusa*, 39–55. Minneapolis: Banning, 1994.

Hösle, Vittorio. "Einfürung." In *Raimundus Lullus. Die neue Logik / Logica nova*, edited by Charles Lohr, ix–lxxxii. Hamburg: Meiner, 1985.

Hoye, William, J. "Die Vereinigung mit dem gänzlich Unerkannten nach Bonaventura, Nikolaus von Kues und Thomas Aquin." In *Die Dionysius-Rezeption im Mittelalter*, edited by Georgi B. Kapriev and Andreas Speer, 477–544. Recherches de Philosophie Médiévale. Turnhout: Brepols, 2000.

Huijgen, Moniqe, and Marja Verburg. *Van Dale Basiswoordenboek van de Nederlandse taal, tweede herziene druk—in de nieuwe spelling*. Utrecht: Van Dale Lexicographie, 1996.

Inwood, Michael. *A Hegel Dictionary*. Oxford: Blackwell, 1992.

Izbicki, Thomas M. *Protector of the Faith: Cardinal Johannes Turrecremata and His Defense of the Institutional Church*. Washington, DC: Catholic University of America Press, 1981.

Jacobi, Klaus "Einleitung." In *Gespräche lesen: Philosophische Dialoge im Mittelalter*, edited by Klaus Jacobi, 9–22. Tübingen: Gunter Nan, 1999.

Jedin, Hubert. "Bischöfliches Konzil oder Kirchenparlament?" In *Die Entwicklung des Konziliarismus*, edited by Remigius Bäumer, 198–228. Darmstadt: Wisssentschaftliche Buchgesellschaft, 1976.

Kerr, Fergus. *After Aquinas: Versions of Thomism*. Malden, MA: Blackwell, 2002.

Klibansky, Raimund, and Hildebrand Bascour. "Adnotationes." In *De Pace Fidei. Cum epistola ad Iohannem de Segobia*, edited by Raymund Klibansky and Hildebrand Bascour, 65–90. Leipzig: Meiner, 1970.

Klibansky, Raimund, and Hildebrand Bascour. "Praefatio." In *De Pace Fidei. Cum epistola ad Iohannem de Segobia*, edited by Raymund Klibansky and Hildebrand Bascour, ix–liii. Leipzig: Meiner, 1970.

Koyré, Alexandre. *From the Closed World to the Infinite Universe*. Baltimore: Johns Hopkins University Press, 1968 (1957).

Kolakowski, Leszek. Religion. *If there is no God . . . On God, the Devil, Sin and Other Worries of the so-called Philosophy of Religion*. Glasgow: Fontana, 1982.

Kremer, Klaus. "Die Hinführung (manuductio) von Polytheisten zum Einen, von Juden und Muslimen zum Dreieinen Gott." In *Der Friede unter der Religionen nach Nikolaus von Kues*, edited by Rudolf Haubst, 126–59 (discussion on 159–63). Mainz: Grünewald, 1984.

Kritzek, James. *Peter the Venerable and Islam*. Princeton Oriental Studies. Princeton: Princeton University Press, 1964.

Küng, H., and J. van Ess. *Christentum und Weltreligionen. Islam*. Munich: Piper, 1994.

Lewis, Charlton T., and Charles Short. *A Latin Dictionary*. Oxford: Clarendon, impression 1998 (1879).

Lewis, Clive Staples. "De audendis Poetis." In *Studies in Mediaeval and Renaissance Literature*, 1–17. Cambridge: Cambridge University Press, 2000 (1966).

———. *The Discarded Image: An Introduction to Mediaeval and Renaissance Literature*. Cambridge: University Press, reprint 1964.

———. *An Experiment in Criticism*. Cambridge: Cambridge University Press, 1961.

———. "Imagination and Thought in the Middle Ages." In *Studies in Mediaeval and Renaissance Literature*, 41–63. Cambridge: Cambridge University Press, 1966.

Lohr, Charles H. "Ramon Lull und der Dialog zwischen den Religionen." In *Ramon Lull: Buch vom Heiden und den drei Weisen*, by Raimundo Panikkar et al., 20–25. Freiburg: Herder, 1986.

———. "Ramón Lull und Nikolaus von Kues. Zu einem Strukturvergleich ihres Denkens." *Theologie und Philosophie* 56 (1981) 218–31.

MacIntyre, Alasdair. *Marxism and Christianity*. Eastbourne: Duckworth, 1995.

Madre, Alois. *Die theologische Polemik gegen Raimundus Lullus. Eine Untersuchung zu den Elenchi auctorum de Raimundo male sententium*. Freiburg im Breisgau, 1962. Printed in Münster, 1973.

McGrade, Arthur S. *The Cambridge Companion to Medieval Philosophy*. Cambridge: Cambridge University Press, 2003.

McNeill, John T. *Die Bedeutung des Konziliarismus*. In *Die Entwicklung des Konziliarismus*, edited by Remigius Bäumer, 82–100. Darmstadt: Wisssentschaftliche Buchgesellschaft, 1976.

McMylor, Peter. *Alasdair MacIntyre: Critic of Modernity*. London: Routledge, 1994.

Meuthen, Erich. "Der Fall von Konstantinopel und der lateinische Westen." In *Der Friede unter der Religionen nach Nikolaus von Kues*, edited by Rudolf Haubst, 35–60. Mainz: Grünewald, 1984.

———. *Nikolaus von Kues 1401–1464. Skizze einer Biographie*. 3rd ed. Münster: Aschendorf, 1976.

Moritz, Arne. "Das Sehen des Papstes und das Sehen Gottes. Zur Konstruktion und Aufhebung des epistemologischen Perspektivismus durch Nikolaus von Kues in *De coniecturis* und *De visionione Dei*." In *Spiegel und Porträt. Zur Bedeutung zweier zentraler Bilder im Denken des Nicolas Cusanus*, edited by Inigo Bocken and Harald Schwaetzer, 147–58. Maastricht: Shaker, 2005.

Moyaert, Paul. *De mateloosheid van het christendom. Over naastenliefde, betekenisincarnatie en mystike liefde*. Nijmegen: Sun, 1998.

Nederman, Cary J., and Kate L. Forhan. *Medieval Political Theory: A Reader. The Quest for the Body Politic, 1100–1400*. London: Routledge, 1993.

Oberman, Heiko A. *Contra vanam curiositatem. Ein Kapitel der Theologie zwischen Seelenwinkel und Weltall*. Zürich: Theologischer Verlag, 1974.

Pindl-Büchel, Theodor. "Einleitung." In *Die Exzerpte des Nikolaus von Kues aus dem Liber Contem-plationis Ramon Lull's*, 5–88. Frankfurt: Lang, 1992.

———. "The Relationship Between the Epistemologies of Ramon Lull and Nicholas of Cusa." *American Catholic Philosophical Quarterly* 64 (1990) 73–87.

Polanyi, Michael. *The Tacit Dimension*. Garden City, NY: Doubleday, 1967.

Radó, Polikarp. *Enchiridion liturgicum complectens theologiae sacramentalis et dogmata et leges iuxta novum codicem rubricarum*. 2 vols. 2nd ed. Rome: Herder, 1966.

Rosemann, Philip W. "Introduction: A Change of Paradigm." In *Understanding Scholastic Thought with Foucault*, 1–17. Hampshire: Macmillan, 1999.

———. *Understanding Scholastic Thought with Foucault*. New Middle Ages. Basingstoke, UK: Macmillan, 1999.

Ryle, Gilbert. *The Concept of Mind*. Middlesex: Harmondsworth, 1970.

Senger, Hans G. "Anmerkungen." In *De docta ignorantia. Liber tertius*. Translated by Hans G. Senger, 102–59. Hamburg: Meiner, 1977.

———. "Die Präfererenz für Ps-Dionysius bei Nikolaus Cusanus und seinem italienischem Umfeld." In *Die Dionysius-Rezeption im Mittelalter*, Georgi Kapriev B. and Andreas Speer, 505–39. Turnhout: Brepols 2000.
Sigmund, Paul, E. "Introduction." In Nicholas of Cusa, *The Catholic Concordance*. Cambridge: Cambridge University Press, 1991.
Steel, Carlos. "Beyond the Principle of Contradiction? Proclus' „Parmenides" and the Origin of Negative Theology." In *Festschrift für Jan Aertsen*, edited by Martin Pickavé, 581–99. Berlin: de Guyter, 2003.
Southern, Richard W. *Western Views of Islam in the Middle Ages*. Cambridge: Harvard Univeristy Press, 1962.
Taylor, Charles. "Gadamer on Human Sciences." In *The Cambridge Companion to Gadamer*, edited by Robert J. Dostal, 126–42. Cambridge: Cambridge University Press, 2002.
Tolkien, John Ronald Reuel. "Ofermod." In *Tree and Leaf. Including the poem Mythopoiea. The Homecoming of Beorhtnoth Beorhthelm's Son*, 143–50. London: HarperCollins, 2001.
Turner, Denys. *The Darkness of God. Negativity in Christian Mysticism*. Cambridge: Cambridge University Press, 1995.
Van Herck, Walter. *Religie en metafoor. Over het relativisme van het figuurlijke*. Leuven: Peeters, 1999.
Vansteenberghe, Edmond. "Un traité inconnu de Gerson 'Sur la doctrine de Raymond Lulle.'" *Revue des Sciences Religieuses* 16 (1936) 440–65.
Vooght, Dom Paul de. "Der Konzilarismus auf dem Konzil von Konstanz." In *Die Entwicklung des Konziliarismus*, edited by Remigius Bäumer, 177–97. Darmstadt: Wisssentschaftliche Buchgesellschaft, 1976.
Watanabe, Morichimi. "Nicholas of Cusa and the Idea of Tolerance." In *Concord and Reform. Nicholas of Cusa and Legal and Political Thought in the Fifteenth Century*, 217–26. Aldershot, UK: Ashgate, 2001.
———. "The Lawyer in an Age of Political and Religious Confusion: Some Fifteenth-Century Conciliarists." *Concord and Reform*, 3–13. Aldershot, UK: Ashgate, 2001.
Watts, Pauline M. "Talking to Spiritual Others: Ramon Lull, Nicholas of Cusa, Diego Valadés." In *Nicholas of Cusa, in Search of God and Wisdom. Essays in Honor of Morimichi Watanabe by the American Cusanus Society*, edited by Gerald Christianson and Thomas M. Izbicki, 203–18. Studies in the History of Christian Thought 45. Leiden: Brill, 1991.
Weiler, Anton G. "Nicholas of Cusa on Harmony, Concordance, Consensuns and Acceptance as Categories of Reform in the Church in *De concordantia catholica*." In *Conflict and Reconciliation: Perspectives on Nicholas of Cusa*, edited by Inigo Bocken, 77–90. Brill's Studies in Intellectual History 126. Leiden: Brill, 2004.
Wilpert, Paul. "Anmerkungen zum Text." In *Vom Nichtanderen*, translated by Paul Wilpert, 99–206. Hamburg: Meiner, 1987.
———. "Anmerkungen zur Einführung." In *Vom Nichtanderen*, translated by Paul Wilpert, 96–98. Hamburg: Meiner, 1987.
———. "Einführung." In *Vom Nichtanderen*, translated by Paul Wilpert, v–xxviii. Hamburg: Meiner, 1987.
———. "Vorwort de Herausgebers." In *De docta ignorantia. Liber primus*. Translated by Paul Wilpert and edited by Hans G. Senger, viii–xiii. Hamburg: Meiner, 1994.

Wyld, Henry C. *The Universal Dictionary of the English Language*. London: Routledge & Kegan, 1952.

www.ingramcontent.com/pod-product-compliance
Lightning Source LLC
Chambersburg PA
CBHW071151300426
44113CB00009B/1165